THE COLLECTED WRITINGS OF AL-ʿALLĀMA AL-ḤILLĪ
VOLUME II

EDITOR-IN-CHIEF
Wahid M. Amin

GENERAL EDITORS
Robert Gleave
Laura Hassan
Andreas Lammer

ASSOCIATE EDITORS
Jari Kaukua
Sayeh Meisami
Matthew Melvin-Koushki
Sajjad Rizvi
Abdulaziz Sachedina
Meryem Sebti
Tony Street
Robert Wisnovsky

The Collected Writings Of al-ʿAllāma al-Ḥillī

The Collected Writings of al-ʿAllāma al-Ḥillī is the first comprehensive attempt to translate the key works of a single scholar of the post-classical period of Islam. This collection provides translations of some of the major works composed by the fourteenth century Shīʿī-Imāmī scholar al-Ḥasan ibn Yūsuf ibn al-Muṭahhar al-Ḥillī (d. 726/1325), better known as al-ʿAllāma al-Ḥillī, in a range of disciplines including logic, law, legal theory, philosophy and theology. The texts are accompanied by extensive annotations and scholarly commentary which serve to showcase the breadth of al-Ḥillī's knowledge and expertise, as well as to illuminate the rich intellectual heritage of the Islamic middle ages.

منهاج الكرامة في معرفة الإمامة

المؤلّف

الحسن بن يوسف بن المطّهر الحلّي

المعروف بـ

العلاّمة الحلّي

THE COLLECTED WRITINGS OF AL-ALLAMA AL-HILLI
مجموعة مصنفات العلامة الحلي

The Way of Nobility
Knowledge of the Imam

Minhāj al-karāma fī maʿrifat al-Imāma

by

AL-ḤASAN IBN YŪSUF IBN AL-MUṬAHHAR AL-ḤILLĪ
(d. 726/1325)

also known as

AL-ʿALLĀMA AL-ḤILLĪ

A parallel English-Arabic text translated, introduced and annotated by

SAIYAD NIZAMUDDIN AHMAD

AMI PRESS

AMI Press
60 Weoley Park Road
Selly Oak
Birmingham
B29 6RB

A catalogue record for this book is available from the British Library

ISBN 978-1-8384996-6-2

Table of Contents

Epigraph ix
Preface xi
Introduction xiii

I ~ DELINEATING THE VARIOUS POSITIONS TAKEN ON THIS QUESTION 6

II ~ WHY THE IMĀMĪ POSITION MUST BE FOLLOWED 16

III ~ ON THE PROOFS ESTABLISHING THE IMĀMA OF THE COMMANDER OF THE FAITHFUL ʿALĪ B. ABĪ ṬĀLIB AFTER THE MESSENGER OF ALLAH 156

The First Way: Rational Proofs 158
The Second Way: Qurʾānic Evidence 168
The Third Way: Evidence From the Sunna Related From the Prophet 228
The Fourth Way: Evidence For His Imāma Based On His States 244

IV ~ ON THE IMĀMA OF THE REMAINING TWELVE IMAMS 274

V ~ THOSE WHO WERE PUT FORWARD DO NOT QUALIFY AS IMAMS 278

VI ~ INVALIDATING THEIR PROOFS FOR THE IMĀMA OF ABŪ BAKR 288

Bibliography 301
Index of Names 310
Index of Places 315
Index of Book Titles 316
Index of Battles and Treaties 317

EPIGRAPH

وَكُلَّ شَيْءٍ أَحْصَيْنَاهُ فِي إِمَامٍ مُبِينٍ (سورة يس ٣٦/١٢)

And We have enumerated all things in a manifest *imām.*

Qur'ān 36:12

قَالَ أَسَدُ اللهِ الغَالِبُ الإِمَامُ عَلِيُّ بْنِ أَبِي طَالِبٍ عَلَيهِ السَّلاَمُ:

لَا يُقَاسُ بِآلِ مُحَمَّدٍ صَلَّى اللهُ عليهِ وآلِهِ وَسَلَّمَ مِنْ هٰذِهِ الأُمَّةِ أَحَدٌ، وَلَا يُسَوَّى بِهِمْ مَنْ جَرَتْ عَلَيْهِمْ نِعْمَتُهُمْ، هُمْ أَسَاسُ الدِّينِ وَعِمَادُ اليَقِينِ؛

نهج البلاغة (خطبة ٢، ص ٤٢)

The Ever-Victorious Lion of Allah, the Imam ʿAlī b. Abī Ṭālib ﷺ said:

No one from this Umma may be compared with the Household of Muḥammad ﷺ nor can anyone who is a beneficiary of their blessings ever be held equal to them for they are the very foundation of religion as such and the very pillars of direct spiritual vision.

Nahj al-Balāgha (*The Peak of Eloquence,* Khuṭba 2, p. 42)

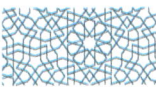

PREFACE

Among the most celebrated works in defence of the Shīʿī belief in the *imāma* is that which was authored by the extraordinary polymath Jamāl al-Dīn Abū Manṣūr al-Ḥasan b. Sadīd al-Dīn Yūsuf b. Zayn al-Dīn b. al-Muṭahhar al-Ḥillī, known to posterity by the honorific title of *al-ʿAllāma*, 'the extraordinarily erudite.' He was born on a Friday evening, 29 Ramaḍān 648/1250 to a family of scholars in the Iraqi town of al-Ḥilla. His father Sadīd al-Dīn was a man of prodigious learning as was his maternal uncle Najm al-Dīn, known as al-Muḥaqqiq al-Ḥillī. ʿAllāma received a distinguished education from his father and uncle as well as their contemporaries, which included some of the most distinguished figures in Shīʿī intellectual history, such as the two Sayyid brothers Jamāl al-Dīn b. Ṭāwūs and Raḍī al-Dīn b. Ṭāwūs, Kamāl al-Dīn Mītham al-Baḥrānī (author of a famous commentary on the *Nahj al-Balāgha*), and last but not least Naṣīr al-Dīn al-Ṭūsī who is easily one of the most widely-learned and accomplished scholars in the history of Islam. ʿAllāma authored hundreds of works in the areas of law, theology, logic, philosophy, and *ḥadīth* sciences. He died in his hometown of Ḥilla on a Saturday, the 21st of Muḥarram, 726/1325.

His most influential work in defence of the *imāmā* is his *Minhāj al-karāma fī maʿrifat al-imāma* (*The Way of Nobility: Knowledge of the Imam*). It is a concise summary of key arguments in favour of the Imamate of ʿAlī b. Abī Ṭālib and his descendants, peace be upon them. He also presents a summary of arguments for the fundamental doctrines that are logically prior to this, namely *tawḥīd* (Divine unity) and *nubuwwa* (prophethood) and related teachings, especially *ʿiṣma* (the protection from error which characterises prophets and Imams). He also marshals detailed evidence from Sunnī historical and *ḥadīth* sources to establish the lack of qualifications for leadership of the Muslim community by those persons whom the majority of Muslims followed, that is to say, the first three so-called 'rightly guided caliphs' (*al-khulafāʾ al-rāshidūn*).

There is a fascinating story behind how this work came to be written. Apparently, the Mongol ruler Öljeitü (also known as Muḥammad Khudābanda) after having first been a Buddhist, then a Christian, and then a Sunnī Muslim remained spiritually unsatisfied. When he learned of another 'version' of Islam he summoned ʿAllāma, who then proceeded to answer all of his questions as well as those of the Sunnī scholars of his court resulting in Öljeitü adopting the Shīʿa faith. Öljeitü subsequently ordered that the names of the Twelve Imams be mentioned in the sermon (*khuṭba*) of the Friday prayer in all the mosques in his sultanate and also erected a beautiful prayer-niche (*miḥrāb*) bearing the names of all Twelve Imams in ornate stucco in the Grand Mosque of Isfahan, which survives to this day. ʿAllāma compiled these arguments in the *Minhāj al-karāma* for Öljeitü. Subsequently, ʿAllāma was also inducted into the retinue of the Mongol ruler and travelled with him wherever he went instructing him and members of the court in a kind of 'mobile-academy' known as *al-madrasat al-sayyāra*.

The *Minhāj al-karāma* came to be very widely known. In fact, it caused such a stir in Sunnī circles that ʿAllāma's contemporary the Mamluk era scholar Ibn Taymiyya authored a 'refutation' entitled *Minhāj al-sunnat al-nabawiyya* which continues to be popular among Wahabi and Salafi scholars today. In the *Minhāj al-karāma*, ʿAllāma goes beyond the work of earlier scholars in arguing for the *imāma*, including the works of his teachers Sayyid Jamāl al-Dīn b. Ṭāwūs, Sayyid Raḍī al-Dīn b. Ṭāwūs, and Naṣīr al-Dīn al-Ṭūsī. He also streamlines many of the arguments in other works of which the most important is probably *al-Shāfī fī l-imāma* by al-Sharīf al-Murtaḍā (d. 436/1044).

Until now this seminal text remained unavailable to the English-speaking world. It is a convenient handbook that presents the case for the *imāma* without being long-winded or overly concise. It can be read by anyone: a Shīʿī believer, a Sunnī Muslim wanting to learn the Shīʿī 'side of the story,' or even a non-Muslim who is curious about the religion. It is with such an audience in mind that this translation is being presented to the public.

Saiyad Nizamuddin Ahmad
26 Jumādā al-Thāniya 1443
10 Bahman 1400
30 January 2022
Plano, Texas, USA

INTRODUCTION

The glorious message of Muḥammad as transmitted by his progeny, the *ahl al-bayt*, remains, despite the passage of nearly fifteen centuries, little understood. Often designated by the term 'Shīʿa Islam' or 'Shīʿism,' this message continues to suffer benign neglect or malignant distortion. The Arabic term *shīʿa* simply means a group of people who are supporters, or partisans of a particular cause or person.[1] Indeed, it is in this sense that it is used in the Qurʾān.[2] For example, the *Banū Isrāʾīl* (Children of Israel/Jacob) are referred to as Mūsā's 'people', his *shīʿa*.

> And when he [i.e. Mūsā] reached his full strength and attained maturity, We gave him judgment and knowledge. Thus do we reward the virtuous. He entered the city when its people were unaware and came upon two men fighting with one another—one from his own people (*min shīʿatihi*) and the other from his enemies. The one from his own people (*min shīʿatihi*) cried out for help against the one from his enemies. So he struck him a blow with his fist, killing him. He said, 'This is Shayṭān's doing. He is truly an outright and misleading enemy.'[3]

Similarly, Ibrāhīm is characterized as being from the 'party' of Nūḥ (*wa-inna min shīʿatihi la-Ibrāhīm*), that is to say, of the same 'spiritual persuasion' so to speak.[4] However, the first extra-Qurʾānic usage of the term was during the first inter-Muslim war (known as the Fitna) as *shīʿat ʿAlī*, i.e. 'the partisans of ʿAlī' in contradistinction to *shīʿat ʿUthmān*, 'the partisans of the murdered pseudo-caliph ʿUthmān' who were led by none other than his own kinsman Muʿāwiya b. Abī Sufyān. Terms such as 'party' and 'partisan,' however, when used as equivalents for *shīʿa*, create the unfortunate impression that the supporters of ʿAlī were akin to a modern political party. Many Sunnī Muslims as well as a significant number of non-Muslim orientalists characterise Shīʿism as the outgrowth of what was merely a 'political dispute' between the grandson of the Prophet Muḥammad, Ḥusayn b. ʿAlī b. Abī Ṭālib, and Yazīd b. Muʿāwiya. In other words, it was a mere power

1 al-Ḥusayn b. Muḥammad al-Rāghib al-Iṣfahānī (d. 502/1108), *al-Mufradāt fī gharīb al-Qurʾān*, edited by Muḥammad Saʿīd al-Kaylānī (Tehran: 1362 Sh).

2 Qurʾān 19:69, 28:15, 37:83, 15:10, 6:65, 6:159, 28:4, 30:32.

3 Qurʾān 28:14–15. All translations of the Qurʾān are our own.

4 See Jalāl al-Dīn al-Maḥallī (d. 863/1459) and Jalāl al-Dīn al-Suyūṭī (d. 911/1505), *Tafsīr al-Jalālayn* (Cairo: Dār al-Qalam, 1385/1966), 413.

struggle between the two men and their supporters. Yet, nothing could be further from the truth. To read back into ancient Arabia modern notions of politics, which are regarded as separate from religion, is a grave mistake. Beyond any modern notions of the political, the dispute between Shīʿa and Sunnī lies at the very heart of what it means to be a Muslim. The polarisation which it embodies goes back to the earliest period of Islamic history during the final illness leading to the death of the Prophet of Islam.[5] Indeed, the very first 'theological' issue to confront the Muslim community was none other than that of the Imamate,[6] which is none other than the question of the succession to Muḥammad: *Who—if anyone—inherits the mantle of the Prophet?* Al-ʿAllāma al-Ḥillī's *The Way of Nobility: Knowledge of the Imam* is one of a vast number of polemical treatises that have been written in the rich history of the Islamic intellectual tradition in answer to this question. To truly understand this treatise, and indeed to understand what was and is at stake in the millennium-and-a-half long dispute between different factions within the Muslim community, one must examine the historical and linguistic background to the central doctrine at issue, namely the roots of authority in Arabia prior to and after Islam.

Shīʿī Islam is distinguished from Sunnī Islam by its doctrine of the Imamate (*imāma*), that is to say, by the comprehensive authority, both spiritual and temporal, of the divinely appointed guide (*imām*). It is around the central point of this divine guide that the Shīʿī faith revolves. This notion of the divinely appointed guide is conspicuously absent from Sunnī Islam and other non-Shīʿī factions. As already noted, to reduce this polarisation to mere politics is a gross oversimplification rooted in the modern world's (mis)understanding of what the term 'politics' (as well as 'religion') truly mean.

Modern people, both Muslim and non-Muslim, almost unanimously view 'religion' and 'politics' as distinct from one another. This is a notion of thoroughly modern Western pedigree and its prevalence in the modern world, even among non-Western peoples, is due to the hegemonic power of the West that even in this supposed 'post-colonial' and 'de-colonial' age continues to exercise control over the entire globe through its myriad transnational institutions and, most sinisterly, in its occupation of the mental

5 See Muḥammad b. ʿAbd al-Karīm al-Shahrastānī (d. 548/1153), *al-Milal wa-l-niḥal*, edited by Saʿīd al-Ghānimī (Beirut and Baghdad: Manshūrāt al-Jamal, 2013), 100–105. ʿAllāma also cites the same passage at the end of section 2 of *The Way of Nobility*.

6 See Abū l-Ḥasan al-Ashʿarī (d. 330/941), *Maqālāt al-islāmiyyīn*, edited by Muḥammad Muḥyī al-Dīn ʿAbd al-Ḥamīd (Beirut and Sidon: al-Maktabat al-ʿAṣriyya, 1411/1990), 1:39.

landscape as well. Thus, most people think in Western terms. The contemporary notion of two distinct and divergent realms designated as 'sacred' and 'secular' is an anomaly in history. Such a notion has never existed in any traditional society and ancient Arabia was no exception. To project modern Western notions of the political onto the ancient Arabian *weltanschauung* is an anachronism which dooms any further historical inquiry into the matter. Before examining the situation in ancient Arabia, let us first briefly examine the modern notions of 'the state' and 'the political'.

The *Oxford English Dictionary* (*OED*) under sense 28a of the term 'state,' defines the latter as, 'A particular form of polity or government. *the state*, the form of government and constitution established in a country; e.g. *the popular state*, democracy (cf. F. état *populaire*).'[7] As for the term 'polity,' it refers to the 'civil organisation (as a condition)'; 'civil order' as well as the 'mode of administering or managing public or private affairs [...]'[8] We further find the following under sense 29a of the term 'state,' namely, 'the body politic as organised for supreme civil rule and government (either generally and abstractly, or in a particular country); hence, the supreme civil power and government vested in a country or nation.'

Thus, the modern notion of the state includes a form of civil organisation constituted as a government institution. The latter is typically divided into separate but interdependent bodies whose functions are either established and maintained by custom or are explicitly set out in some kind of a formal written document often termed a 'constitution.' *We find none of this in ancient Arabia.* The authority of Prophet Muḥammad, to put it in contemporary terms, was both spiritual and temporal, religious and political; and such authority had its roots among the Arabs prior to Islam.

Ancient Arabian society was composed of both nomadic as well as sedentary groups. What both nomads and town-dwellers had in common was that they were both organised on the basis of tribal affiliation. Of all social bonds, it was loyalty to one's tribe which was paramount. This sentiment of tribal solidarity, known as *'aṣabiyya*, along with other aspects of tribal social structure are abundantly on display in pre-Islamic poetry, often our only source of knowledge for Arabian life before Islam. In odes hundreds of verses in length the ancient bards celebrated the noble deeds and warrior exploits of their ancestors. Fictitious or actual historical descent from an

7 *OED*, vol. 16, 554, col. 1.
8 Ibid., vol. 12, 35, col. 3 (bottom) – 36, col. 1.

ancient noble patriarch whose noble conduct was, in turn, upheld by his descendants was the determining factor of the social and moral standing of the tribe. Those who could not boast of their forebears in such fashion were of scant social standing and subject to contempt and derision. Such claims to nobility are termed *ḥasab* in Arabic and this word derives from the same root as *ḥisāb* meaning 'to enumerate' or 'count,' that is to say, in the sense of enumerating or re-counting the noble deeds of one's forebears. Another crucial term in this context is *sharaf*, which conveys the meanings of tribal 'dignity' or 'honour'. Additional to these is the notion conveyed by another Arabic term, *ʿirq*, which is the ability to trace qualities of morals and virtue backwards through the family tree since the word means the 'root' or 'origin of a man'. It is crucial, then, to note that *sharaf* and *ḥasab* were regarded as being *hereditary*, and were thus believed by the ancient Arabs to adhere to certain bloodlines. Virtues, then, were held to be propagated through a certain stock via a noble ancestor or ancestors. Such inherited nobility was held in the highest esteem, and nobility acquired by merely personal merit was of much less, if not little, account. Such a pedigree of noble ancestors with virtuous deeds and valorous exploits was deemed in numerous examples of pre-Islamic poetry to be akin to a mighty lofty structure.

By way of example, Labīd b. Rabīʿa (d. ca. 40/660) declaims in his celebrated *Muʿallaqa*:[9]

وَإِذَا الأَمَانَةُ قُسِّمَتْ فِي مَعْشَرٍ   أَوفَى بِأَوْفَرِ حَظِّنَا قَسَّامُهَا
فَبَنَا لَنَا بَيْتًا رفيعًا سَمْكُهُ   فَسَمَا إِلَيهِ كَهْلُهَا وَغُلَامُهَا

And when trustworthiness was portioned out amidst the assembly of men;
  the apportioner afforded us an abundant portion.
Thus did he raise for us a lofty, firm edifice (*baytan rafīʿan samkuhu*)
  to which young and old aspired to rise up to.

Elsewhere in the same ode Labīd uses two terms of great significance.[10]

9 See al-Zawzanī (d. 468/1093), *Sharḥ al-Muʿallaqāt al-sabʿ*, (Cairo: n.d.), 116; cf. al-Shinqīṭī (d. 1331/1913), *Sharḥ al-Muʿallaqāt al-ʿashar wa-akhbār shuʿarāʾihā* (Beirut: Dār al-Kitāb al-ʿArabī, 1405/1986), 81, our translation. Zawzanī has *wa* and *fa* at the head of the first and second verses; al-Shinqīṭī does not.

10 See al-Zawzanī, *Sharḥ al-Muʿallaqāt al-sabʿ*, 115; cf. al-Shinqīṭī, *Sharḥ al-Muʿallaqāt al-ʿashar wa-akhbār shuʿarāʾihā*, 80, our translation. In this case both editions have the same wording.

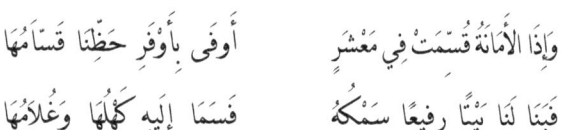

The first of these is *sunna*, which here means a pattern of nobility and virtuous behaviour established by Labīd's forefathers and which was upheld by descendants such as him. In Islam the term *sunna* came to mean the totality of the behaviours and habits of the Prophet Muḥammad. The second term is none other than *imām*:

من معشرٍ سنّت لهم آباؤهم   ولكلّ قومٍ سنّة وإمامها

[I come] from those for whom their forefathers established
a pattern of noble deeds;
and for every people there is [such] a pattern and its guide (*imām*).

Thus for pre-Islamic Arabs like Labīd, every tradition of noble deeds established as a pattern by one's forefathers had an *imām* who embodies this tradition, lives in accordance with this pattern, and is followed as exemplar of this *sunna*. Perhaps it can be argued, therefore, that in this verse of pre-Islamic poetry we have a precursor to the notion of *imām* which was further elaborated in the Qur'ān wherein the term *imām* occurs seven times in the singular and five time in the plural form *a'imma*.[11]

In Sūrat al-Isrā'[12] we read: *On the day we summon every people by their imām.* Here it is clear that what is meant is a leader. It is true that the term *imām* in some contexts carries the sense of a written document (*kitāb*); however, the latter is a metaphorical usage,[13] and, moreover cannot be

11 The term *imām* is further attested in ancient Arabic usage in Qatabanian as well as in Sabaean meaning 'to be at the head, lead' and related to the Classical Arabic verbs *i'tamma*, *ittaba'a*, and *aṭā'a*. See Stephen D. Ricks, *Lexicon of Inscriptional Qatabanian* (Rome: Editrice Pontificio Istituto Biblico, 1989), 𐩱𐩣𐩣 'MM, 11–12; 𐩫𐩧𐩨 KRB I, 86–87 and 'Ādil Muḥād Mas'ūd Mirīkh, *al-'Arabiyya al-qadīma wa-lahjātuhā: dirāsa muqārana bayn alfāẓ al-mu'jam al-saba'ī wa-alfāẓ lahjāt 'arabiyya qadīma: al-Gibbāliyya wa-l-Mihriyya* (Abu Dhabi: al-Majma' al-Thaqāfī, 1421/2000), 'MM, 151; cf. Martin R. Zammit, *A Comparative Lexical Study of Qur'ānic Arabic* (Leiden: E. J. Brill, 2002), *'mm* under the entry for ESA (Epigraphic South Arabian), 79. For an introduction to ESA see Maria Höfner, *Altsüdarabische Grammatik* (Leipzig: Otto Harrassowitz, 1942). Other examples from the ancient poets could be adduced, but, in the interests of brevity, have been left for another occasion.

12 Qur'ān 17:71.

13 See Abū l-Qāsim Mahmūd b. 'Umar b. Muḥammad al-Zamakhsharī (d. 538/1143), *Asās al-balāgha* (Beirut: Dār Ṣadir, 1399/1979), 21, col. b; cf. his *al-Kashshāf 'an ḥaqā'iq al-tanzīl wa-'uyūn al-aqāwīl fī wujūh al-ta'wīl* (Beirut: Dār al-Ma'rifa, n.d.), 2:369. There are two instances in the Qur'ān where there is no doubt from the context that *imām* clearly refers to a book, in this case the scripture revealed to Mūsā, in which both instances share the exact same wording: *Yet before it was the Book of Mūsā, a guide* (46:12 and 11:17). As for 36:12, *And We have enumerated all things in a manifest imām*, here there is no unanimity regarding its meaning.

justifiably invoked here as the verse continues: *then whomsoever is given his register (kitābahu) [of worldly deeds] in his right hand, such will read their register (kitābahum) and they will not be wronged so much as a shred.* The use of the term *imām* in the sense of 'leader' is also found in these verses, albeit in the plural form *a'imma*:

> *We made them imāms, guiding by Our command, and we revealed to them [the doing of] good works, establishing the prayer, and giving the zakāt, and Us [alone] did they worship.*[14]

> *And once they [i.e. the people of Mūsa] had been steadfast and had attained conviction in Our signs, We appointed imāms from amongst them to guide them by Our command.*[15]

> *And We wished to show favour to those who had been oppressed in the land and make them imāms and to make them inheritors...*[16]

There is also an instance when it occurs in the singular indefinite form, but is perhaps better translated into English as a plural and also does not necessarily exclusively convey the sense of leader, but of an example or model to be emulated and followed:

> *And those who say: 'Our Lord! Give to us joy in our spouses and descendants, and make of us imāms of those who are mindful of You.*[17]

The last part may be rendered as: *and make [of each] of us a worthy exemplar*

The *tafsīr* literature gives a range of meanings such as 'book,' referring to the Qur'ān, for example, or the Guarded Tablet (*al-lawḥ al-maḥfūẓ*), or to 'Alī. See, by way of example, al-Sayyid 'Abdullāh Shubbar (d. 1242/1826), *Tafsīr al-Qur'an al-karīm* (Beirut: al-A'lamī, 1415/1995), 382 and al-'Allāma al-Sayyid Muḥammad Ḥusayn al-Ṭabāṭabā'ī (d. 1402/1981), *Tafsīr al-Mīzān* (Qom: n. d.), 18:70. Finally, in another place the term *imām* means a 'road,' 'path,' or 'way', referring to the ruins of both the People of Lūṭ, i.e. the Biblical Sodom and Gomorrah and the *Aṣḥab al-Ayka* (*'The People of the Thicket'*), i.e. the inhabitants of Madyan/Midian whom Allah destroyed due to their wickedness: *Indeed the People of the Thicket were also wicked. So we took vengeance on them as well. They are both beside a well-beaten track* (*wa innahumā la-bi-imāmin mubīn*) (15:79).

14 Qur'ān 21:73. This is a reference to Isḥāq (Isaac) and Ya'qūb (Jacob/Israel).

15 Qur'ān 32:24.

16 Qur'ān 5:28.

17 Qur'ān 25:74.

of those who are mindful of You. These are all instances of the term *imām* used in reference to the righteous. We also find the term used for wicked leaders as well, as in the verse '*then fight the imāms of unbelief* (*a'immat al-kufr*) [...]'[18] and in the verse '*We made them imāms summoning to the Fire*'.[19]

In the above-mentioned contexts we therefore see then that Qur'ān uses the term *imām* in the sense of a leader (whether righteous or wicked) as well as of a righteous person whose pattern of behaviour is worthy of emulation. The most emphatic usage of the term in the sense of righteous leader, however, occurs when Allah Himself declares Ibrāhīm to be the *imām* of all human beings, and by implication his righteous descendants as well.

> *And once His Lord had tried Ibrāhīm with certain commandments, and he had fulfilled them, He said, 'I am making you the imām of humankind.' He asked: 'And from among my descendants* [*as well*]*?' He said: 'My covenant does not embrace transgressors.'* [20]

This last example is seen by Shī'a Muslims to extend to the Prophet Muḥammad and his progeny as they are all genealogically in the line of Ibrāhīm via his son Ismā'īl. We will return to this theme of the Qur'ān speaking of the special favour conferred upon select descendants of prophets below.

In addition to being divided into tribes, the ancient Arabs were also differentiated by geography. Among the north and central Arabian tribes, the Quraysh was the most dominant tribal confederation since its clans controlled the city of Mecca and administered the pilgrimage. Most of the northern and central Arabian tribes were nomadic. In southern Arabia there was a sedentary society practicing rain-based irrigation and agriculture. In north and central Arabia, despite the notions of *ḥasab*, *sharaf*, and *'irq* the concept of tribal authority and leadership was often based on seniority in age and perceived ability to lead. North Arabian tribes also boasted of their courage and victories in battle but did not typically ritually thank their deities for such favours. In contrast, the south Arabian tribes always made votive offerings to their gods for such blessings. They also had a system of sacred kingship in which there was an hereditary succession based on inherited sanctity. It is extremely important to note that the Medinan tribes of Aws and Khazraj were of south Arabian,

18 Qur'ān 9:12.
19 Qur'ān 28:41.
20 Qur'ān 2:124.

specifically Yemenite, origin. Thus, they naturally understood Islam to be a religio-spiritual teaching as well as a political movement. The northern Arabs, on the other hand, saw it as a socio-political movement rooted in a religion taught by the Prophet Muḥammad. This despite the fact that each tribe had a specific idol erected on a sacred stone altar (*naṣab/naṣb*) which was designated as the lord of its specific temple or 'house' (*rabb al-bayt*). Such temple sanctuaries (sing. *ḥaram*) were under certain tribal clans who acted as guardians of these sanctuaries. These guardian clans were seen to have a sanctity which was hereditary in the same fashion as the sacred kingship of the southern Arabs. However, for the northern Arabs such clans formed a kind of tribal spiritual aristocracy and did not exercise leadership over the whole tribe. The Kaʿba was such a temple, but it was the Temple, or House of Allah (*bayt Allāh*) and all the tribes of Arabia recognised its association with Ibrāhīm and his line through Ismāʿīl. The tribal clan to which the Prophet Muḥammad belonged, namely the Banū Hāshim, held the guardianship of the Kaʿba and were its *ahl al-bayt*. The privilege and honour of providing the pilgrims to Mecca with food and water had belonged to the Banū Hāshim since the days of ʿAbd Manāf, the great-great-great-grandfather of the Prophet Muḥammad.

In light of the above, is it at all surprising that the Prophet Muḥammad should appoint ʿAlī to be his successor given the ancient Arabian notions of inherited ancestral nobility, guardianship of a divine temple sanctuary and hereditary sanctity of the guardians, and the belief that these qualities are personified in an exemplary figure designated by the term *imām*? Indeed, we find the very same pattern elaborated in the Qurʾān when Allah speaks of the special favour conferred upon select descendants of the prophets, such as Ibrāhīm and his line, as already noted above.[21] The word used in that example for the descendants of Ibrāhīm is *dhurriyya*, which could also be translated as 'direct descendants', 'progeny' or 'offspring.' It occurs 32 times in the Qurʾān[22] and always in the context of a prophet's supplication to Allah that his *dhurriyya* remain righteous or that their work of guiding people should be perpetuated in their *dhurriyya*, i.e., in their progeny. Moreover, the Qurʾān continually exhorts all believers to uphold and respect the ties of blood-kinship. Kindness to relatives and materially supporting those of them in need is a paramount religious obligation.[23] In the case of the prophets mentioned in the Qurʾān,

21 Qurʾān 2:124.

22 See the Qurʾān concordance of Muḥammad Fuʾād ʿAbd al-Bāqī, *al-Muʿjam al-mufahras li-alfāẓ al-qurʾān al-karīm* (Cairo: Dār al-Ḥadīth, 1407/1988).

23 Qurʾān 2:83, 2:177, 2:215, 4:7–8, 4:36, 16:90, 17:26.

generally speaking, their families are shown as providing vital assistance to them in their missions. After the death of a prophet, his descendants become his spiritual and material heirs. Thus, Sulaymān inherits (*waritha*) from Dāwūd.[24] Zakariyya beseeches Allah to favour him with a successor (*walī*) who will 'inherit from me' (*yarithunī*) and from the House of Ya'qūb (Āl Ya'qūb). These families are singled out for divine favour. Thus, the prophets of the Banū Isrā'īl (the Children of Israel/Jacob) are all one family, all the way from Ādam, to Nūḥ, until 'Īsā: '*Verily Allah chose Ādam and Nūḥ and the Āl of Ibrāhīm and the Āl of 'Imrān above all the worlds, dhurriyya of one another.*'[25] Another important term is used in this verse (and the one referred to previously), namely *āl*, which means one's nearest relations by descent from the same father or ancestor, or one's family or kinsmen. It is used in the Qur'ān 26 times[26] to refer to 'the descendants of prophets or those who succeeded them in guidance and special favour from Allah.'[27] Indeed, this chain of prophets receives and successively inherits not only the revealed scripture (*al-kitāb*), but the power to judge and rule as well. Thus,

> And We bestowed upon him Isḥāq and Ya'qūb; each of them We guided. And Nūḥ did We guide aforetime. And among his *dhurriyya* Dāwūd, and Sulaymān, and Ayyūb, and Yūsuf, and Mūsā, and Hārūn [did We guide]: for thus, do We reward the excellent in virtue (*muḥsinīn*). Zakariyya, and Yaḥyā, and 'Īsā, and Ilyās, each one [of them] was of the righteous. And Ismā'īl, and Ilyās, and Yūnus, and Lūṭ each one of them did We favour over all the worlds. And from among their forefathers, and their *dhurriyya*, and their brethren—We chose them and guided them to a straight path. Such is the guidance of Allah. He guides to it whomsoever He wills from among His servants. And were they to associate partners [with Him] the acts which they used to perform will be of no avail to them. It is upon them that We conferred the Book, and judgment-rule (*ḥukm*), and prophethood. But if they disbelieve therein, then We shall indeed entrust it to a people who will never disbelieve therein.[28]

It is abundantly clear that the Qur'ān affirms a special status for select

24 Qur'ān 27:16.

25 Qur'ān 3:33–34; also see 19:58, 35:32, 53:40.

26 'Abd al-Bāqī, *al-Mu'jam al-mufahras li-alfāẓ al-qur'ān al-karīm*.

27 S. H. M. Jafri, *The Origins and Early Development of Shī'a Islam* (Beirut: Librairie du Liban, 1979), 15.

28 Qur'ān 6:84–89. Recall that Isḥāq and Ya'qūb were described as *imāms* in 21:73.

descendants of past prophets. This immediately raises the question that if this was the case with past prophets, then does not such a principle also apply to the Prophet Muḥammad and his family? Indeed, Wilferd Madelung makes this very point:

> The eminent position of the families and the descendants of the past prophets and the parallelism often observed between the history of the former prophets in the Qurʾān and that of Muḥammad must raise expectations of a distinguished place reserved for his family.[29]

S. H. M. Jafri also argues in the same vein:

> The total number of verses that mention special favour requested for and granted to the families of the various prophets by God runs to well over a hundred in the Qurʾān. From this we may draw two conclusions. If one accepts the axiom that the Qurʾān was revealed in terms understandable in the cultural atmosphere of seventh-century Arabia, then it is obvious that the idea of the sanctity of a prophet's family was a commonly accepted principle at that time. Even more important is the fact that the Qurʾān's constant repetition of this idea must have left the impression among some of the Muslims that Muḥammad's family had a religious prerogative over others.[30]

Al-ʿAllāma al-Ḥillī devotes a large portion of *The Way of Nobility* to arguments based on quotations from the Qurʾān. In the third section of his treatise, after a brief presentation of arguments based entirely on reason without recourse to scripture, he introduces another series of arguments which takes up the rest of the section and consists of forty demonstrations all based on the Qurʾān. However, these arguments are not based on the verses we have examined above, but on yet other verses which ʿAllāma argues were revealed in connection with ʿAlī or ʿAlī and his family. The most famous example of the latter is known as *āyat al-taṭhīr* (The Verse of Purification): '*Truly Allah only wishes to remove all impurity from you, O People of the House, and to purify you exceedingly*',[31] which ʿAllāma quotes in Demonstration 5. A number of *ḥadīth* from Sunnī sources are then cited as evidence to establish that this verse of the Qurʾān was revealed regarding ʿAlī, Fāṭima, Ḥasan, and

29 Wilferd Madelung, *The Succession to Muḥammad. A Study of the Early Caliphate* (Cambridge: Cambridge University Press, 1997), 12.

30 Jafri, *The Origins and Early Development of Shīʿa Islam*, 16.

31 Qurʾān 33:33.

Ḥusayn along with the Prophet Muḥammad. An example of a verse relating to ʿAlī alone is used in Demonstration 1: ʿ*Your guardian can only be Allah; and His Messenger and the faithful who establish the prayer and give zakāt while bowing down.*ʾ[32] Here too, ʿAllāma cites a number of Sunnī *ḥadīth*s to establish that this was revealed in reference to ʿAlī giving his ring to a beggar who entered the Prophet's Mosque while he was bowing in prayer. This is the approach employed in all forty of the demonstrations, namely a verse from the Qurʾān is cited and then it is argued, on the basis of *ḥadīth*s recorded in Sunnī compilations, that this verse applies to ʿAlī.

Indeed, quite a few works by Sunnī scholars have been written over the centuries that argue that numerous verses of the Qurʾān were, in fact, revealed regarding ʿAlī. This genre of works may be considered a subset of the larger genre of *manāqib* literature, that is to say, works devoted to recording the noble qualities and deeds of the Prophet's Companions. *Manāqib* works devoted to ʿAlī often contain a great deal of Qurʾānic material as well and so there is some overlap here. Works of the *manāqib* genre devoted to ʿAlī far exceed in number any works devoted to other figures. ʿAllāma makes full use of both these types of sources.

In the case of works devoted to the merits of ʿAlī in the light of the Qurʾān, two are of particular interest. The first of these is a work by al-Ḥāfiẓ Abū Nuʿaym Aḥmad b. ʿAbdullāh al-Iṣfahānī, generally known as Abū Nuʿaym al-Iṣfahānī (d. 430/1038), or as al-Ḥāfiẓ Abū Nuʿaym. ʿAllāma cites him by name without mentioning which work of this prolific author he has in mind. In the case of the merits of ʿAlī there can only be two possibilities, either his *Ḥilyat al-awliyāʾ wa-ṭabaqāt al-aṣfiyā* (*The Adornment of the Saints and the Ranks of the Pure*)[33] or his *Kitāb Mā nuzila min al-Qurʾān fī ʿAlī ʿalayhi l-salām* (*The Book of what was sent down in the Qurʾān about ʿAlī upon whom be peace*). It is a most unfortunate fact that the latter has not survived to our times completely intact and only exists in fragments quoted in other works. We are, however, fortunate to have a reconstruction of this work due to the indefatigable researches of Muḥammad Bāqir al-Maḥmūdī.[34] In our translation, all such instances have been appropriately glossed with the exact citation.

32 Qurʾān 5:55.

33 al-Ḥāfiẓ Abū Nuʿaym Aḥmad b. ʿAbdullāh al-Iṣfahānī, *Ḥilyat al-awliyāʾ wa-ṭabaqāt al-aṣfiyā* (Cairo: Maktabat al-Khānjī, 1351/1932).

34 al-Ḥāfiẓ Abū Nuʿaym Aḥmad b. ʿAbdullāh al-Iṣfahānī, *al-Nūr al-mushtaʿal min Kitāb Mā nuzila min al-qurʾān fī ʿAlī ʿalayhī l-salām*, edited by Muḥammad Bāqir al-Maḥmūdī (Qom: Wizārat al-Irshād al-Islāmī, 1406/1986).

The second is an extremely significant full-length commentary (*tafsīr*) on the entire Qurʾān by Abū Isḥāq Aḥmad b. Muḥammad b. Ibrāhīm al-Thaʿlabī (d. 427/1035) entitled *al-Kashf wa-l-bayān ʿan tafsīr al-Qurʾān* (*Unveiling and Exposition: A Commentary on the Qurʾān*).[35] It is easily the richest source of *manāqib* material on the Prophet and his family ever to have been written by a Sunnī Muslim. This work remains in manuscript form and has yet to be published in a proper critical edition. A number of manuscripts survive, however, two in particular taken together constitute the most significant manuscript witnesses of this crucial work. These are the Maḥmūdiyya manuscript housed in the Maḥmūdiyya collection of the Public Library of Medina (Maktabat al-Madīnat al-Munawwara al-ʿĀmma), which is incomplete, and the Veliyüddin Efendi manuscript housed in the Veliyüddin collection of the Bayezid Kütüphanesi in Istanbul. The latter, although it is rather late, having been copied in 1186/1772, is complete and seems to be based on a very old copy.[36] Regarding the edition prepared by the contemporary Shīʿī scholar Abū Muḥammad ʿAlī b. ʿĀshūr, it is wholly inadequate[37]; as noted by Walid Saleh, 'the value of the edition is gravely compromised by its failure to use any of the manuscripts'[38] which he describes in his study. In our translation, we have always cited from these two manuscripts, albeit in some cases we have had to rely exclusively on the Veliyüddin Efendi manuscript since the Maḥmūdiyya manuscript is incomplete.[39]

As for *manāqib* works the most important of those utilised by ʿAllāma is probably the *Faḍāʾil al-ṣaḥāba* (*The Merits of the Companions*) by Aḥmad b. Ḥanbal (d. 241/855).[40] ʿAllāma does not cite it explicitly, but just states that a particular *ḥadīth* was transmitted by Aḥmad b. Ḥanbal. This leaves open the possibility that ʿAllāma may be alluding either to it or to Ibn Ḥanbal's

35 For a detailed study of this work and its author see Walid A. Saleh, *The Formation of the Classical Tafsīr Tradition. The Qurʾān Commentary of al-Thaʿlabī* (d. 427/1035) (Leiden: E. J. Brill, 2004).

36 We have listed the manuscript numbers in the bibliography, but for a detailed description of these and other manuscripts of Thaʿlabī's *tafsīr* see Saleh, *The Formation of the Classical Tafsīr Tradition*, 231–244.

37 Published Beirut: Dār Iḥyāʾ al-Turāth al-ʿArabī, 2002.

38 Saleh, *The Formation of the Classical Tafsīr Tradition*, 229.

39 We have often also cited another work, which ʿAllāma did not use but which is now considered a standard reference work, namely the *Shawāhid al-tanzīl li-qawāʿid al-tafḍīl*, 3 vols., edited by Muḥammad Bāqir al-Maḥmūdī (Qom?: Majmaʿ Iḥyāʾ al-Turāth al-Islāmī, 1427/2006) by the Sunnī Ḥanafī scholar ʿUbaydullāh b. ʿAbdullāh b. Aḥmad, known as al-Ḥāfiẓ al-Ḥaskānī (fl. 5th/11th cen.).

40 Aḥmad b. Ḥanbal, *Faḍāʾil al-ṣaḥāba*, edited by Waṣīyullāh b. Muḥammad ʿAbbās (Mecca Jāmiʿat Umm al-Qurā, 1403/1983).

Musnad[41] and thus the researcher must check both of these works. In this case as well, all such instances have been appropriately glossed with the exact citation in the footnotes to our translation.

Besides Ibn Ḥanbal's *Faḍā'īl*, ʿAllāma relies heavily on two other *manāqib* works, namely that of al-Muwaffaq b. Aḥmad b. Muḥammad al-Makkī al-Khawārizmī, also known as Akhṭab Khawārizm (d. 568/1172). His work is simply entitled *al-Manāqib*[42] but is mostly referred to as *Manāqib al-Khawārizmī* to distinguish it from other works in this genre such as *Manāqib Ibn al-Maghāzilī* by Abū l-Ḥasan ʿAlī b. Muḥammad al-Jallābī, known as Ibn al-Maghāzilī (d. 483/1090), whose proper title is actually *Manāqib Ahl al-Bayt*,[43] which is the second work which ʿAllāma heavily relies on.

ʿAllāma also cites traditions from some of the main Sunnī collections, namely those of Bukhārī (d. 256/870), Muslim (d. 261/874), Abū Dāwūd (d. 275/888), Tirmidhī (d. 279/892), Ibn Māja (d. 273/886), the *Muwaṭṭa'* of Mālik (d179/795), as well as the *Musnad* of Aḥmad b. Ḥanbal (d. 241/855).

In two instances (demonstrations 17 and 18), ʿAllāma cites another Sunnī *ḥadīth* collection of interest. This is the collection known as *al-Jamʿ bayna l-ṣiḥāḥ al-sitta* (*The Ḥadīths found in All Six of the Rigorously Authenticated Books*). It was compiled by an Andalusian *ḥadīth* scholar from Saragossa named Abū l-Ḥasan Razīn b. Muʿāwiya b. ʿAmmār al-ʿAbdarī, or Razīn b. Muʿāwiya for short, which is how ʿAllāma refers to him. He died in 524/1129 or 535/1140. To the best of my knowledge this work remains in manuscript. However, it is known that after the five well-known Sunnī collections, rather than Ibn Māja as the sixth, he relied on the *Muwaṭṭa'* of Mālik instead. Thus, it is also known by the title *Kitāb al-Tajrīd fī l-jamʿ bayna l-Muwaṭṭa' wa-l-ṣiḥāḥ al-khamsa*. Another title is *Tajrīd al-ṣiḥaḥ al-sitta fī l-ḥadīth*. A copy of this work existed in the library of Raḍī al-Dīn Ibn Ṭāwūs (d. 644/1266).[44]

Finally, ʿAllāma cites from another work in demonstration 19, which does not seem to have survived. This is a summary by Abū Nuʿaym al-Iṣfahānī of *al-Istīʿāb fī maʿrifat al-aṣḥāb* (*The Comprehensive Register of the Compan-*

41 Aḥmad b. Ḥanbal, *al-Musnad* (Vaduz, Lichtenstein: Thesaurus Islamicus Foundation, 2006).

42 al-Muwaffaq b. Aḥmad b. Muḥammad al-Makkī al-Khawārizmī, *al-Manāqib* (Qom: al-Nashr al-Islāmī, 1421/2000).

43 Abū l-Ḥasan ʿAlī b. Muḥammad al-Jallābī, known as Ibn al-Maghāzilī, *Manāqib Ahl al-Bayt*, edited by Muḥammad Kāẓim al-Maḥmūdī (Tehran: Markaz al-Taḥqīqāt wa-l-Dirāsāt al-tābiʿ li-l-Majmaʿ al-ʿIlmī li-l-Taqrīb bayna l-Madhāhib al-Islāmiyya, 1427/2006).

44 See Etan Kohlberg, *A Medieval Muslim Scholar at Work. Ibn Ṭāwūs and his Library* (Leiden: E. J. Brill, 1992), 201.

ions) by Ibn ʿAbd al-Barr (d. 463/1071).[45] Apparently it was known as *Kitāb Mukhtaṣar al-Istīʿāb* and was extant at the time ʿAllāma wrote *The Way of Nobility*. This work also existed in the library of Ibn Ṭāwūs (664/1266).[46]

Clearly, even in the section devoted to arguments derived from the Qurʾān, *ḥadīth*s and historical reports (*akhbār*) from Sunnī sources play the central role. It is worth mentioning the most important of these which are often cited more than once in *The Way of Nobility*. They refer to pivotal events in the life of ʿAlī that single him out as being uniquely qualified to be the spiritual and temporal successor of the Prophet. Six events stand out in particular and all of them are mentioned by ʿAllāma, sometimes more than once. The most important of these is the event of Ghadīr Khumm.

The Ḥadīth of Ghadīr Khumm is also known as Ḥadīth al-Walāya and ʿAllāma refers to this *ḥadīth* many times. It refers to the incident after the Farwell Pilgrimage when the Prophet halted at an oasis known as Ghadīr Khumm[47] and made the famous announcement that 'Whomsoever's master I am, ʿAlī is his master.' This *ḥadīth* has been very widely transmitted; indeed, entire studies have been devoted to the transmission history of this *ḥadīth* in its various versions. Among the most significant and oldest of these specialised works is the *Kitāb al-wilāya* (*The Book of Nearmostness*) by Abū l-ʿAbbās Aḥmad b. Muḥammad b. Saʿīd who is known as Ibn ʿUqda al-Kūfī (d. 322/934). Although his work is lost it has been reconstructed from quotations in other surviving works by ʿAbd al-Razzāq Muḥammad Ḥusayn Ḥirz al-Dīn and it was published in Qom in 1421 AH. This reconstructed work contains narrations by 98 different companions of the Prophet. An eminent Sunnī contemporary of Ibn ʿUqda, namely the jurist, Qurʾān commentator, and historian Abū Jaʿfar Muḥammad b. Jarīr al-Ṭabarī (d. 310/921), also devoted a work entitled *Kitāb al-Ghadīr* (*The Book of Ghadīr*) to the large number of narrations of this *ḥadīth* which has subsequently been lost. However, there are references to it in works contemporaneous with him, for example in the Ismāʿīlī Shīʿī scholar Qāḍī Abū Ḥanīfa al-Nuʿmān b. Muḥammad al-Tamīmī al-Maghribī's

45 Abū ʿUmar Yūsuf b. ʿAbdullāh b. ʿAbd al-Barr al-Qurṭubī, *al-Istīʿāb fī maʿrifat al-aṣḥāb* (Beirut: al-Maktabat al-ʿAṣriyya, 1431/2010) and *al-Istīʿāb fī maʿrifat al-aṣḥāb*, edited by ʿAbd al-Ghanī Muḥammad ʿAlī Mistū (Beirut: 1431/2010).

46 See Kohlberg, *A Medieval Muslim Scholar at Work*, 279–280.

47 It is located about 164 km to the North of Mecca, or about 450 km to the South of Medina, and is 26 km to the East of the modern settlement of Rābigh toward the South-East which would put it at about 8 km to the East of the present mosque of the *mīqāt* of al-Juḥfa. The coordinates of this location are 22 degrees, 42 minutes, 18 seconds North; by 39 degrees, 8 minutes, 50 seconds East.

(d. 363/873) *Sharḥ al-akhbār fī faḍā'il al-a'immat al-aṭhār* (*Commentary on the Traditions regarding the Superiority of the Infallible Imams*).[48] Numerous scholars subsequently devoted their efforts over the centuries to the study of the transmission history of this *ḥadīth*. Notable later works include *'Abaqāt al-anwār* by Mīr Ḥāmid Ḥusayn Lakhnawī (1306/1888)[49] and *Kitāb al-ghadīr fī l-kitāb wa-l-sunna wa-l-adab* by 'Abd al-Ḥusayn Aḥmad al-Amīnī al-Najafī (d. 1390/1971).[50] This designation by the Prophet Muḥammad of 'Alī as his successor was prefigured in another event from the earliest days of his mission in Mecca and is known as *da'wat dhī l-'ashīra* (inviting the closest relatives of Muḥammad to Islam).

The verse *Warn the nearest of your kinfolk*[51] was revealed at the every beginning of the Prophet's mission, about three years after his first revelation. Fulfilling this command, he gathered the men of the Banū 'Abd al-Muṭṭalib and called them to Islam. In the course of explaining to them his mission and to further his cause, he appealed to them for their support and assistance, only to be met with ridicule. In the end it was only 'Alī who pledged to him his unwavering support despite his being a mere lad.[52]

After the Hijra (migration) to Medina the Prophet instituted a mutual brotherhood pact (*mu'ākhāt*) between those who had migrated (the *muhājirūn*) and the residents of Medina (the *anṣār*). He took 'Alī to be his brother. In fact, the Prophet had adopted him as brother before the Hijra and acted as his guardian during the famine of Mecca as well.[53]

'Alī was appointed the standard bearer during the siege of the Fortress of Khaybar and it was he alone who succeeded in ripping open its massive door thereby enabling the fortress to be stormed. [54]

48 Qāḍī Abū Ḥanīfa al-Nu'mān b. Muḥammad al-Tamīmī al-Maghribī, *Sharḥ al-akhbār fī faḍā'il al-a'immat al-aṭhār*, 3 vols., edited by Muḥammad Ḥusayn al-Ḥusaynī al-Jālālī (Qom: 1409), 1:130–133.

49 Original copies of this multivolume lithographed work are very rare. I saw an original in the private library of His Royal Highness the Raja of Maḥmūdābād about a decade ago. I also saw an Iranian reprint from the time of the last Shah in the Princeton University library in 1993.

50 'Abd al-Ḥusayn Aḥmad al-Amīnī al-Najafī, *Kitāb al-ghadīr fī l-kitāb wa-l-sunna wa-l-adab* (Beirut: 1414/1994).

51 Qur'ān 26:214.

52 al-Ḥāfiẓ al-Ḥaskānī, *Shawāhid al-tanzīl li-qawa'id al-tafḍīl,* edited by Muḥammad Bāqir al-Maḥmūdī (Qom: Majma' Iḥyā' al-Thaqāfa al-Islāmiyya, 1427/2006), 1:630–636..

53 Abū Muḥammad 'Abd al-Malik b. Hishām (d. 218/833), *al-Sīrat al-nabawiyya*, edited by Muṣtafā al-Saqā, Ibrāhīm al-Abyārī and 'Abd al-Ḥāfiẓ Shalabī (Cairo: n. d.) 2:504–505.

54 Ibn Hishām, *al-Sīrat al-nabawiyya*, 2:334–335; Abu Ja'far Muḥammad b. Jarīr al-Ṭabarī (d. 310/921), *Ta'rīkh al-rusul wa-l-mulūk* (Cairo: n. d.), 3:12–13 = *Ta'rīkh al-rusul wa-l-mulūk* (Leiden), 1:1579–1581; 'Izz al-Dīn Abū l-Ḥasan 'Alī b. Muḥammad, known as Ibn al-Athīr (d. 630/1233), *al-Kāmil fī*

In the year 9/630–31, the ninth *sūra* of the Qur'ān, known as *Sūrat al-Barā'a* or *Sūrat al-Tawba* was revealed, and the Prophet was commanded to convey it to the idolators of Mecca. He had already sent Abū Bakr to lead the pilgrimage caravan to Mecca. When he was asked if he would send the *sūra* to him to be communicated to the Meccans, he said: 'No, I will not send it but with a man from amongst the people of my family (*rajul min ahl baytī*).' He then summoned 'Alī and sent him forth on his own camel to convey the *sūra* to the Meccans on his behalf.[55]

Finally, there is the Ḥadīth al-Manzila ('The Ḥadīth of the Hārūnic/Aaronic Station').[56] During the Tabūk campaign, the Prophet Muḥammad appointed 'Alī to be his deputy over Medina while he would be away. It was on the occasion of his departure that he announced to 'Alī: 'Do you not then accept that your status in relation to me is as the station of Hārūn in relation to Mūsā, except that there shall be no prophet after me?' It would not be out of place here to examine this *ḥadīth* in some detail as we are of the opinion that its deeper significance has yet to be truly appreciated. The Prophet Muḥammad is clearly identifying the station, status, and rank of 'Alī with the station, status, and rank of the Prophet Hārūn, but at the same time he is very careful to point out that there will be no other prophet coming after him. Thus, it behoves us to ask just what this special status entails. Here looking into the nature of the status of Hārūn in relation to Mūsā as given in the Tawrāt (Torah תורה) is very instructive. Thus, we find in Book of Exodus, 28:1

וְאַתָּה הַקְרֵב אֵלֶיךָ אֶת־אַהֲרֹן אָחִיךָ וְאֶת־בָּנָיו אִתּוֹ מִתּוֹךְ בְּנֵי יִשְׂרָאֵל לְכַהֲנוֹ־לִי
אַהֲרֹן נָדָב וַאֲבִיהוּא אֶלְעָזָר וְאִיתָמָר בְּנֵי אַהֲרֹן׃

> And bring thou near unto thee Aaron thy brother, and his sons with him, from among the children of Israel, that they may minister unto Me in the priests office (even) Aaron, Nadab and Abihu, Eleazar and Ithmar, the sons of Aaron.[57]

l-tārīkh, edited by Khalīl Ma'mūn Shīhā (Beirut: 1422/2002), 2:200–201; and al-Tirmidhī, *al-Sunan*, 2:9451, *ḥadīth* 4090.

55 al-Ḥāfiẓ al-Ḥaskānī, *Shawāhid al-tanzīl li qawa'id al-tafḍīl*, 1:359–380..

56 It is very widely reported. See for example the following eminent classical Sunnī traditionists: Aḥmad b. Ḥanbal, *al-Musnad*, 1:386, *ḥadīth* 1566 and 1:367, *ḥadīth* 1481; Muslim b. al-Ḥajjāj, *al-Jāmi' al-ṣaḥīḥ*, 2:1030, *ḥadīths* 6370, 6372, 6373 and 2:1031, *ḥadīth* 6374; Ibn Mājah, *al-Sunan*, 21, *ḥadīths* 121, 122 and 22, *ḥadīth* 126; al-Tirmidhī, *al-Sunan*, 2:951, *ḥadīth* 4090 and 2:952, *ḥadīths* 4095, 4096

57 *The Pentateuch and Rashi's Commentary. A Linear Translation into English* by Rabbi Abraham Ben Isaiah and Rabbi Benjamin Sharfman in collaboration with Dr Harry M. Orlinsky and Rabbi Morris Charner (Brooklyn, New York: S. S. & R. Publishing Co., 1950), 2:338.

The Biblical Hebrew term in question above is *kohēn* (pl. *kohanīm* כהנים). According to the *Encyclopaedia Judaica*: '...Aaron undoubtedly held an outstanding position of leadership, as may be determined by the fact that Allah often addresses Moses and Aaron *jointly* [emphasis added] (Ex. 9:8–10; 12:1,43; Lev. 11:1; 13:1; 14:33; 15:1, etc.)'[58] Also, 'Aaron and his sons were appointed priests [*kohanīm*] and consecrated to that office by Moses himself (Ex. 28–29 [1st verse quoted above], Lev. 8–9).[59] Moreover, the most authoritative lexicon of Biblical Hebrew defines *kohēn* (כהן) as 'divine-seer, priest-king.'[60] The *International Standard Bible Encyclopaedia* glosses this term as follows: 'Priest, ... prince, minister [in the sense of vizier]... Nature of Priestly Office: 1. Implies Divine Choice. 2. Implies Representation. 3. Implies Offering Sacrifice. 4. Implies Intercession.'[61] Thus, all of the foregoing establishes that Aaron, as well as the line of Aaron, embody the station of the *kohēn* who is a divine-seer, priest-king, prince, and vizier. It is also interesting to note that the Qur'ān refers to Hārūn many times as the *wazīr* (vizier) of Mūsā. Finally, it is remarkably interesting to note that Saadia Gaon (Sa'd al-Fayyūmī), the 9/10th century Jewish rabbinical authority of Baghdad was the first Jewish authority to translate the Torah into Arabic. He rendered the passage cited above as follows:[62]

وَأَنْتَ أَيضًا ، فَقَدِّمْ إِلَيكَ آهْرُونَ أَخَاكَ وَبَنِيهِ مَعَهُ، مِنْ بَينَ بَنِي يِسْرَئِيلَ لِيُؤُمُّوا لِي، آهْرُونُ، نَدَابَ وأَبِيهُو، إِلْعَازَارَ وإِتْمَارَ بَنِيهِ

58 *Encylopaedia Judaica* (Jerusalem: Encyclopaedia Judaica, 1972), vol. 2, col. 5.

59 Ibid.

60 See Francis Brown, C. A. Driver, and Charles A Briggs, *A Hebrew and English Lexicon of the Old Testament with an Appendix containing the Biblical Aramaic based on the Lexicon of William Gesenius as translated by Edward Robinson* (Oxford: Clarendon Press, 1951), 462–464.

61 See *The International Standard Bible Encyclopaedia* edited by James Orr MA DD (Grand Rapids, Michigan: Wm. B. Erdmans Publishing Co., 1946), 4:2439; cf. Georg Benedict Winer, *Biblisches Realwörterbuch* (Leipzig: Carl Hienrich, 1847), 2:269–74.

62 The Judae-Arabic text (Arabic written in Hebrew script) appears in *Ḥamishah Ḥamushei Torah ʿim perūsh Rashī: 'Unqelōs, Saʿadyāh Gaōn, 'Even ʿĒzrā'*, 5 vols. (Jerusalem: Derekh Khadmonim, 1989-90), 2:509, left margin, lines 3–6. This interpretation is also supported by the Aramaic Targum of Onkelos (which appears on the same page of the text just cited on the same page, opposite marign) as well as the Syriac Peshīṭṭā version. For a version transcribed into Arabic script see *al-Tawrāt: al-Tafsīr al-aṣlī min Maʿālī al-Ḥākhām Saʿdiyā Ghā'ūn b. Yūsuf al-Fayyūmī*, transcribed into Arabic script by Rabbi Yomtov Chaim Ben Yakov Daknish Hacohen (Jerusalem: Project Saadia Gaon, 2015), 198. This interpretation is also supported by both the Greek text of the Septuagint as well as the Latin Vulgate as well which read, respectively: καὶ σὺ προσαγάγου πρὸς σεαυτὸν τόν τε Ααρων τὸν ἀδελφόν σου καὶ τοὺς υἱοὺς αὐτοῦ ἐκ τῶν υἱῶν Ισραηλ ἱερατεύειν μοι, Ααρων καὶ Ναδαβ καὶ Αβιουδ καὶ Ελεαζαρ καὶ Ιθαμαρ υἱοὺς Ααρων; and Applica quoque ad te Aaron fratrem tuum cum filiis suis de medio filiorum Israel, ut sacerdotio fungantur mihi: Aaron, Nadab, et Abiu, Eleazar, et Ithamar.

He translates the portion reading *li-ya'ummū lī* as *that they might be imāms of mine*. The fact he used the verbal form from which the term *imām* derives is highly significant. To the best of our knowledge, this striking fact has never before been noticed and enables a far better and deeper understanding of the Ḥadīth of the Hārūnic/Aaronic Station. Even without this added insight from the Mosaic tradition, these *ḥadīth* and historical reports make a compelling case for ʿAlī being the true successor of Muḥammad.

Madelung writes:

> In the Qurʾān the descendants and close kin of the prophets are their heirs also in respect of kinship (*mulk*), rule (*ḥukm*), wisdom (*ḥikma*), the book and the imamate.[63]

The status and qualifications of ʿAlī make him alone among the Companions of the Prophet to be uniquely qualified to succeed him. As noted by S. H. M. Jafri:[64]

> Neither Banū Taym b. Murra, the clan of Abū Bakr, nor Banū ʿAdī b. Kaʿb, the people of ʿUmar, had ever been regarded with esteem on any grounds, thus those who laid stress on the religious principle could not accept them as candidates for succession to Muḥammad. The candidate could only come from the Banū Hāshim, and amongst them the figure of ʿAlī was by far the most prominent. He too was the great-grandson of Hāshim and the grandson of ʿAbd al-Muṭṭalib. He was the son of Abū Ṭālib, Muḥammad's uncle, who had given the Prophet the care and love of the father Muḥammad had lost before birth. ʿAlī was the nearest and closest associate of Muḥammad, for the Prophet had acted as his guardian during the famine of Mecca, and he had subsequently adopted him as a brother both before the Hijra and again in Medina. He was the first male to embrace Islam, Khadījā being the first woman. He was also the husband of Fāṭima, the Prophet's only surviving daughter, and by her fathered two of the Prophet's grandsons, Al-Ḥasan and Al-Ḥusayn, both of whom Muḥammad loved dearly.

ʿAllāma is not the first to set out such arguments. The most noteworthy treatise on the Imamate prior to his is *al-Shāfī fī l-imāma* by al-Sharīf al-Murtaḍā (d. 436/1045) which was written in response to a work by his teacher

63 Madelung, *The Succession to Muḥammad*, 17.

64 S. H. M. Jafri, *The Origins and Early Development of Shīʿa Islam* (Beirut: Librairie du Liban, 1979), 16–17.

al-Qāḍī ʿAbd al-Jabbār al-Hamadhānī.[65] This is a very complex work that is intended for scholars. ʿAllāma's *The Way of Nobility* in contrast is accessible to any educated reader. In this regard it is similar to an earlier work by Raḍī al-Din Ibn Ṭāwūs, the *Kitāb al-Ṭarāʾif*. The latter is much larger than *The Way of Nobility* and is written in the form of a running exchange of questions-and-answers by a fictional narrator named ʿAbd al-Maḥmūd who is a new convert to Islam who seeks to know which school (*madhhab*) to follow. In the end, as a result of many of the same arguments that ʿAllāma also employs, he becomes a Shīʿī. ʿAllāma also resorted to many of the same arguments used by his teacher Naṣīr al-Dīn al-Ṭūsī in the latter's *Tajrīd al-iʿtiqād* (*Abstracta Theologica*) upon which he wrote a commentary entitled *Kashf al-murād*.

***

The Arabic text of this dual-language edition is that of the critical edition established by ʿAbd al-Raḥīm Mubārak and published by Muʾassasat ʿĀshūrāʾ li-l-Taḥqīqāt wa-l-Buḥūth al-Islāmiyya in Qom. No publication date is given; however the end of the editor's introduction bears the date 1419/1998–1999. Mubārak relied on three manuscripts:[66]

1. *MS Mashhad, Library of the Āstān-e Quds-e Rażawī 13754.*
Dated colophon: end of Jumādā al-Thāniya, 974/1566.
Copyist: Muḥammad Bāqir b. Ḥajjī Muḥammad al-Sharīf.

Notes: The latter was in turn copied from an older MS copied by Muḥammad b. ʿAlī b. Ḥasan al-Jabāʿī (?) who claims to have used a copy in the handwriting of the author. The latter copyist tells us that he completed his work on the 12th of Ramaḍān but does not mention in which year.

2. *MS Qom, Library of Āyatullāh Marʿashī, in Majmūʿa 29.*
Dated colophon: 5 Rabīʿ al-Awwal 941/1534.
Copyist: Masʿūd b. Jārullāh al-Muṭallabī.

65 Edited by al-Sayyid ʿAbd al-Zahrāʾ al-Ḥusaynī al-Khaṭīb, 4 vols in 2 (Tehran: Muʾassasat al-Ṣādiq, 1426/2005). The work by Qāḍī ʿAbd al-Jabbār was in the form of a large commentary on the Qurʾān defending the principles of the Muʿtazilī school to which he adhered. The section on *imāma* was the 20th and final volume of the work.

66 See pages 3–4 of the introduction to his critical edition.

3. MS Qom, Library of Āyatullāh Marʿashī, in Majmūʿa 2523.
Dated colophon: end of Jumādā al-Thāniya, 951/1544
Copyist: Not mentioned.

I have tried as much as possible to avoid being literal in order to produce a flowing, readable English text without distorting the meaning of the original. It is up to each reader to judge if I have been successful. All translations from the Qur'ān are by us.

I owe a double debt of gratitude to Wahid M. Amin of the Al-Mahdi Institute and AMI Press for not only inviting me to translate this work for The Collected Writings of al-ʿAllāma al-Ḥillī series but for also devoting untold hours to editing the typescript. I am grateful to my friends Aftab Ahmed, Sibtain Abidi, and Sajjad Rizvi for their encouragement and support. I would also like to thank Aftab for his corrections to an early draft of the translation.

This work was completed under conditions of extreme personal hardship and would have been impossible were it not for the undying devotion and love of my wife Hajra Saleem and our children Zainab, Zahra, Husayn and Hadi. I will always be grateful to them.

Finally, I must record a debt of eternal gratitude to my teachers Āyatullāh al-Sayyid Muḥammad Ḥusayn al-Ḥusaynī al-Jalālī and Ḥujjat al-Islām wa-l-Muslimīn Mawlānā al-Sayyid Tilmīdh al-Ḥasanayn al-Raḍawī for sharing their knowledge with me. Both of them died, a few months apart, while this work was still in progress. I humbly dedicate this work to their memory and request the readers of this translation to remember them with *al-Fātiḥa*.

The Way of Nobility: Knowledge of the Imam

منهـــاج الكرامـة في معرفة الإمـامة

In the Name of Allah,
the Infinitely Compassionate, the Ever-Merciful.

Praise is due to Allah, the Non-Originated, the One, the Generous, the Noble. He Who is sanctified by His perfection over having any partner, opposite, or one who can resist Him. He Who through the necessity of His Existence transcends having any progenitoress, partner, progeny, or progenitor. I praise Him with the praise of one who truly acknowledges His blessings, not of one who doubts or denies. I give thanks to Him for His unceasing, ever-increasing blessings; a thanks which neither the one who genuflects or prostrates is capable of offering. Benedictions upon the Master of every ascetic, and the most noble of worshippers — Muḥammad the Chosen One, and upon his Noble and Glorious Family; a benediction abiding through the ages in perpetuity.

To proceed: this is a noble treatise and a subtle discourse devoted to the most important of issues among the doctrines of the faith (*dīn*) as well as the most sublime question that has confronted Muslims, namely the question of *imāma*; true knowledge of which enables one to attain the rank of nobility, for it is one of the pillars of belief (*īmān*) by which abiding in paradise is merited and deliverance from the wrath of the Infinitely Compassionate is attained. Indeed, the Messenger of Allah ﷺ has said: *Whomsoever dies not knowing the Imam of his age dies the death of the days of pre-Islamic ignorance.*[1] I have

1 This saying, attributed to the Prophet, is widely quoted in polemical works. However, we have yet to come across it with this exact wording even in the Shīʿa *ḥadīth* collections. Thus, in *al-Kāfī* 1: 376–77 we find 4 *ḥadīth*s in a chapter entitled *mān māta wa-laysa lahu imāmun*

بِسْمِ اللَّهِ الرَّحْمَنِ الرَّحِيمِ

الحمد لله القديم الواحد الكريم الماجد المقدس بكماله عن الشريك والضدّ والمعاند، المتنزّه بوجوب وجوده عن الوالدة والصاحبة والولد والوالد؛ أحمده حمد معترف بآلائه غير شاكٍ ولا جاحد، وأشكره على إنعامه المتضاعف المتزايد، شكراً يعجز عنه الراكع والساجد، والصلاة على سيّد كلّ زاهد وأشرف كلّ عابد، محمّد المصطفى وعترته الأكارم والأماجد، صلاة تدوم بدوام الأعصار والأوابد.

أمّا بعد، فهذه رسالة شريفة ومقالة لطيفة اشتملت على أهمّ المطالب في أحكام الدين وأشرف مسائل المسلمين، وهي مسألة الإمامة التي يحصل بسبب إدراكها نيل درجة الكرامة، وهي أحد أركان الإيمان المستحقّ بسببه الخلود في الجنان والتخلّص من غضب الرحمن؛ فقد قال رسول الله ﷺ من مات ولم يعرف إمام زمانه مات ميتة جاهليّة، خدمت بها خزانة السلطان الأعظم مالك رقاب الأمم ملك ملوك طوائف العرب والعجم موليّ النعم ومسدي الخير والكرم شاهنشاه المعظم غياث الحقّ والملّة والدين

composed it in service to the Mightiest Sultan, Sovereign over the Necks of all Nations, King of the Kings of the throngs of Arabs and Persians, Master of Favours, Bestower of Goodness and Generosity, the Exalted King of Kings, the Succour of Truth, the Nation and the Faith (*dīn*), Uljāytū[2] Khudābanda Muḥammad [reigned 704–716/1304–1316] — may Allah perpetuate his sultanate, make firm the foundations of his dominion, fortify its pillars, extend to him His aid and blessings, and help him with the generosity of His support prolonging his dynasty until the day of judgment. I have summarised herein the essence of the proofs and have pointed to the key issues without being long-winded or overly concise. I have entitled the work *The Way of Nobility: Knowledge of the Imam.*

min a'immati'l-hudā… (Whomsoever dies without having an *imām* from amongst the *imāms* of guidance…) of these the first three *ḥadīth*s are close in wording to the version cited by 'Allāma. These three versions are given below.
Ḥadīth 1: *mān māta wa laysa 'alayhi imāmun fa-mītatuhu mītatun jāhiliyyatun* (Whomsoever dies without having an *imām* over him dies the death of the days of pre-Islamic ignorance).
Ḥadīth 2: *mān māta wa laysa lahu imāmun fa-mītatuhu mītatun jāhiliyyatun* (Whomsoever dies without having an *imām,* his death is the death of the days of pre-Islamic ignorance).
Ḥadīth 3: *mān māta lā ya'rifu imāmahu māta mītatan jāhilliyatan* (Whomsoever dies without knowing his *imām,* dies the death of the days of pre-Islamic ignorance).
The same applies to the Sunnī *ḥadīth* collections where one finds something close to this but not exactly the same as the version cited by 'Allāma in two sources, namely Muslim b. al-Ḥajjāj, *al-Ṣaḥīḥ,* 2: 816: 4899 (cf. Jamāl al-Dīn al-Mizzī, *Tuḥfat al-ashrāf,* 7664) and Aḥmad b. Ḥanbal, *al-Musnad,* 3: 96: 22–23/7: 3727: 17150. The version in *Ṣaḥīḥ Muslim* has *man khala'a yadan min ṭā'atin laqiyallāhu yawma al-qiyāma lā ḥujjata lahu wa man māta wa laysa fī 'unuqihī bay'atun māta mītatan jāhiliyyātan* (Whomsoever repudiates his oath of allegiance by withdrawing from obedience, shall meet Allah on the Day of Resurrection without any excuse and whomsoever dies without having made the oath of allegiance will die death of the days of pre-Islamic ignorance). In what must be regarded as one of the supreme ironies of history is that the version in Aḥmad b. Ḥanbal's *Musnad,* which matches 'Allāma's citation the most closely, is related by none other than Mu'āwiya b. Abī Sufyān: *man mātā bi-ghayri imāmin māta mītatan jāhiliyyatan* (Whomsoever dies without an *imām,* dies the death of the days of pre-Islamic ignorance).

2 A Mongolian name generally Romanised as Öljeitü. 'Allāma has given the elements of his name in a non-standard order. His full form name with genealogy back to Chinggis (Chingēz/Chingīz) Khān (d. 624/1227) is: Ghiyāth al-Dīn Muḥammad Khudābanda Öljeitü b. Arghun b. Abaqa b. Hülegü (Hulākū) b. Toluy b. Chinggis. See Clifford Edmund Bosworth, *The New Islamic Dynasties. A Chronological and Genealogical Manual* (New York: Columbia University Press, 1996), 250–251, 246–247, and 243–245.

أولجايتوخدابنده محمّد خلّد الله سلطانه وثبّت قواعد ملكه وشيّد أركانه وأمدّه بعنايته وألطافه وأيده بجميل إسعافه وقرن دولته بالدوام إلى يوم القيامة؛ قد لخّصت فيها خلاصة الدلائل وأشرت إلى رؤوس المسائل من غير تطويل مملّ ولا إيجاز مخلّ، وسمّيتها منهاج الكرامة في معرفة الامامة. والله الموفّق للصواب وإليه المرجع والمآب.

ورتّبتها على فصول:

Section 1:
Delineating the Various Positions taken on this Question

الفصل الأوّل
في نقل المذاهب في هذه المسألة

The Imāmīs have taken the position that Allah is the Perfectly Just and All-Wise. He neither commits evil nor relinquishes a duty, and that His acts, indeed, only occur for a sound end and a wisdom; and further that He does not commit oppression or perversity. He is Ever-Merciful and Infinitely Kind to His servants. He only does what is most salutary and most beneficial for them. He has imposed duties upon them whilst conferring upon them free-will but not compelling them and promised them reward as well as punishment as conveyed to them by His infallible prophets and messengers such that neither error, nor forgetfulness, nor sin are committed by them. Were that not so, their statements could not have been trusted, thus eliminating the benefit of dispatching them [to mankind in the first place].

Then, upon the death of any messenger, He made *imāma* to follow upon messengership and thus he appointed infallible guardians (*awliyā' maʿṣūmīn*) to safeguard people from their errors, faults, and mistakes by following their commands, and it is thereby that Allah ﷻ has not left the world bereft of His gentle kindness (*luṭf*) and compassion.

Moreover [the Imāmīs hold] that when He ﷻ sent His Messenger Muḥammad ﷺ (d. 11/632), he, the Prophet, conveyed the message and explicitly designated ʿAlī b. Abī Ṭālib (d. 40/661) as the successor after him, then his son al-Ḥasan al-Zakī (d. 49/669), then designated al-Ḥusayn al-Shahīd (d. 61/680), then designated ʿAlī b. al-Ḥusayn Zayn al-ʿĀbidīn (d. 95/713), then designated Muḥammad b. ʿAlī al-Bāqir (d. 114/733), then designated Jaʿfar b. Muḥammad al-Ṣādiq (d. 148/765), then designated Mūsā b. Jaʿfar al-Kāẓim (d. 183/799), then designated ʿAlī b. Mūsā al-Riḍā (d. 203/818), then designated Muḥammad b. ʿAlī al-Jawād (d. 220/835), then designated ʿAlī b. Muḥammad al-Hādī (d. 254/868), then designated al-Ḥasan b. ʿAlī al-ʿAskarī (d. 260/874), then designated the Scion, the Proof, Muḥammad b. al-Ḥasan (b. 256/869)[1] — peace be upon them all; and that he, the Prophet ﷺ, did not die without explicitly appointing the Imam.

1 The Twelfth Imam is believed to still be alive to this day, albeit in a state of occultation (*ghayba*) which, it is held, began in 260/874. This date commences what is known as the "Lesser Occultation" (*al-ghaybat al-ṣughrā*) and continued until 329/941. During the Lesser Occultation the Twelfth Imam maintained contact with his followers through a succession of four intermediaries or *safīrs*:
1. ʿUthmān b. Saʿīd al-ʿUmarī. Despite his importance no one gives a precise death date for him. Modern historians have tried to provide plausible dates. Among these is 256/879, but it seems that the general consensus is that he died sometime between 260/874 and 267/880.
2. Abū Jaʿfar Muḥammad b. ʿUthmān b. Saʿīd al-ʿUmarī (d. 305/917).
3. Abū l-Qāsim al-Ḥusayn b. Rawḥ b. Abī Baḥr al-Nawbakhtī (d. 326/938).
4. Abū l-Ḥasan ʿAlī b. Muḥammad al-Sammarī (d. 329/941). With his death began what is known as the "Greater Occultation" (*al-ghaybat al-kubrā*) which, it is held, will continue until the Twelfth Imam merges near the end of time.

ذهبت الإماميّة إلى أنّ الله تعالى عدل حكيم لا يفعل قبيحاً ولا يخلّ بواجب، وأنّ أفعاله إنّما تقع لغرض صحيح وحكمة، وأنّه لا يفعل الظلم ولا العبث، وأنّه رحيم رؤوف بالعباد، يفعل بهم ما هو الأصلح لهم والأنفع، وأنّه تعالى كلّفهم تخييراً لا إجباراً، ووعدهم بالثواب وتوعّدهم بالعقاب على لسان أنبيائه ورسله المعصومين، بحيث لا يجوز عليهم الخطاء ولا النسيان ولا المعاصي وإلّا لم يبق وثوق بأقوالهم فتنتفي فائدة البعثة.

ثمّ أردف الرسالة بعد موت الرسول بالإمامة، فنصب أولياء معصومين ليأمن النّاس من غلطهم وسهوهم وخطائهم، فينقادون إلى أوامرهم لئلاّ يخلي الله تعالى العالم من لطفه ورحمته.

وأنّه تعالى لمّا بعث رسوله محمداً ﷺ قام بنقل الرسالة ونصّ على أنّ الخليفة بعده عليّ بن أبي طالب، ثمّ من بعده ولده الحسن الزكيّ، ثمّ على الحسين الشهيد، ثمّ على علي بن الحسين زين العابدين، ثمّ على محمّد بن عليّ الباقر، ثمّ على جعفر بن محمّد الصادق، ثمّ على موسى بن جعفر الكاظم، ثمّ على عليّ بن موسى الرضا، ثم على محمّد بن علي الجواد، ثمّ على عليّ بن محمد الهادي، ثم على الحسن بن عليّ العسكريّ، ثمّ على الخلف الحجّة محمّد بن الحسن، وأن النبي ﷺ لم يمت إلا عن وصية بالإمامة.

The Sunnīs have taken a diametrically opposite position to all of the foregoing. Thus, they have upheld neither justice nor wisdom in His acts — may He be exalted. They allow for Him to commit evil as well as relinquish an incumbent duty, and hold that He does not act for an end, indeed, all of His acts have no particular end and no particular wisdom at all.

He may commit oppression or perversity. He may do what is *not* best for His servants, in fact He may even do what is, in truth, detrimental for them because, in such a case, sinful acts, varieties of unbelief, oppression, and all kinds of wickedness in the world ultimately trace back to Him — may Allah be far exalted above such a thing!

[They further hold] that one who is obedient is not necessarily deserving of reward; and the sinner of punishment; rather someone who has been obedient for his whole life and spared no effort in fulfilling His commands — such as the Prophet ﷺ — may be punished, and that someone who has sinned for his whole life having committed every sort of evil deed — such as the Pharaoh [who opposed Moses] and Iblīs — may be rewarded. [They further hold] that the prophets are not infallible, rather they may fall prey to errors, backsliding, lying, immorality, lying, forgetfulness, and so on.

وذهب أهل السنة إلى خلاف ذلك كلّه، فلم يثبتوا العدل والحكمة في أفعاله تعالى وجوّزوا عليه فعل القبيح والإخلال بالواجب، وأنه تعالى لا يفعل لغرضٍ بل كل أفعاله لا لغرضٍ من الأغراض ولا لحكمةٍ البتة.

وأنه تعالى يفعل الظلم والعبث وأنه لا يفعل ما هو الأصلح للعباد، بل ما هو الفساد في الحقيقة؛ لأنّ فعل المعاصي وأنواع الكفر والظلم وجميع أنواع الفساد الواقعة في العالم مستندة إليه، تعالى الله عن ذلك.

وأنّ المطيع لا يستحق ثواباً والعاصي لا يستحقّ عقاباً، بل قد يعذب المطيع طول عمره المبالغ في امتثال أوامره تعالى كالنبي ﷺ ويثيب العاصي طول عمره بأنواع المعاصي وأبلغها كإبليس وفرعون. وأنّ الأنبياء غير معصومين بل قد يقع منهم الخطاء والزلل والفسوق والكذب والسهو وغير ذلك.

And [they further hold] that the Prophet ﷺ did not explicitly appoint an Imam for them, that he died without making an explicit directive, and that the Imam after the Messenger of Allah ﷺ was Abū Bakr b. Abī Quḥāfa[2] because allegiance had been given to him by ʿUmar b. al-Khaṭṭāb with the consent of four others, namely Abū ʿUbayda (d. 18/639),[3] Sālim the bondsman (*mawlā*) of Abū Ḥudhayfa,[4] Usayd b. Ḥuḍayr (d. 28/648),[5] and Bashīr b. Saʿ[ī]d (d. 13/634).[6] And then [they hold] that the [next Imam] was ʿUmar b. al-Khaṭṭāb[7] having been explicitly designated by Abū Bakr, and then ʿUthmān b. ʿAffān[8] by virtue of ʿUmar having appointed six persons, of which he was one, to choose among themselves, and then ʿAlī b. Abī Ṭālib to whom the masses pledged their allegiance.[9] After that they [meaning the Sunnīs] differed among themselves. Some held that the Imam after him was his son al-Ḥasan, whilst some held that it was Muʿāwiya b. Abī Sufyān.[10]

2 Abū Bakr ruled from the death of the Prophet in 11/632 until he died of natural causes in 13/634. See Bosworth, Dynasties, 1.

3 This is his patronym. His actual name is ʿĀmir b. ʿAbdullāh b. al-Jarrāḥ. He is best known however as Abū ʿUbayda al-Jarrāḥ. See Jamāl al-Dīn Abū l-Ḥajjāj Yusuf al-Mizzī (d. 742/1342), *Tahdhīb al-kamāl fī asmāʾ al-rijāl*, edited by Bashshār ʿAwwād Maʿrūf (Beirut: Muʾassasat al-Risālā, 1422/2002), 14:52–57, entry 3084.

4 The Abū Ḥudhayfa in question is Abū Ḥudhayfa b. ʿUtba b. Rabīʿa al-Qurashī who died in 12/633. The sources indicate that his name was either Hāshim, Hishām, Hushaym, or Mahsham. Sālim was his bondsman (*mawlā*). The sources I consulted do not give a death date for Sālim. See ʿIzz al-Dīn Abū l-Ḥasan ʿAlī b. Muḥammad al-Jazarī, known as Ibn al-Athīr (d. 630/1232), *Usd al-ghāba fī maʿrifat al-ṣaḥāba*, edited by Khalīl Maʾmūn Shaykhā (Beirut: Dār al-Maʿrifa, 1428/2007), 4:416–417; Abū ʿUmar Yūsuf b. ʿAbdullāh b. ʿAbd al-Barr (d. 463/1071), *al-Istīʿāb fī maʿrifat al-aṣḥāb* (Beirut: al-Maktabat al-ʿAṣriyya, 1431/2010), 3:9, entry 2879.

5 See al-Mizzī, *Tahdhīb*, 3:246–254, entry 517.

6 See al-Mizzī, *Tahdhīb*, 4:166–167, entry 718.

7 ʿUmar b. al-Khaṭṭāb ruled from 13/634 until he was assassinated in 23/644. See Bosworth, *Dynasties*, 1.

8 ʿUthmān ruled from 23/644 until he was assassinated in 35/656. See Bosworth, *Dynasties*, 1.

9 ʿAlī ruled from 35/656 until he was assassinated in 40/661.See Bosworth, *Dynasties*, 1.

10 Muʿāwiya b. Abī Sufyān's reign was between 41–60/661–680. See Bosworth, *Dynasties*, 3.

وأنّ النبي لم ينص على إمام بينهم وأنه مات عن غير وصيّةٍ، وأنّ الإمام بعد رسول الله ﷺ أبو بكر بن أبي قحافة، لمبايعة عمر بن الخطّاب له برضا أربعة – أبي عبيدة وسالم مولى حذيفة وأسيد بن حضير وبشير بن سعيد؛ ثم من بعده عمر بن الخطّاب بنصّ أبي بكر عليه، ثم عثمان بن عفّان بنصّ عمر على ستة هو أحدهم فاختاره بعضهم، ثم علي بن أبي طالب عليه السلام لمبايعة الخلق له.

Then they regarded the Imāma to go over to the Umayyads[11] until al-Saffāḥ of the Abbasids emerged, and so they held the Imama went over to him, only to move to his brother al-Manṣūr, Finally, they regarded the Imama to continue amongst the Abbasids until al-Must'aṣim, i.e. until the 40th to rule.[12]

11 The Umayyad dynasty began with the reign of Mu'āwiya in 41/661. He was followed by 13 successors the last of whom was Abū 'Abd al-Malik Marwan II b. Muḥammad al-Ja'dī al-Ḥimār who ascended the throne in 127/744. His reign was brought to an end by the Abbasid revolution in 132/750. See Bosworth, *Dynasties*, 3.

12 The Abbasid dynasty began in 132/750 with the reign of Abū l-'Abbās 'Abdullāh b. Muḥammad, known as al-Saffāḥ who was indeed succeeded by his brother Abū Ja'far 'Abdullāh b. Muḥammad, known as al-Manṣūr who ruled from 136/754 to 158/775. His was followed by forty other reigns (not persons because al-Muqtadir ruled three different times and al-Qāhir twice) ending with that of al-Musta'ṣim with the Mongol sack of Baghdad in 656/1258 led by Hülegü, grandson of Chinggis Khan. This is when the Abbasid dynasty is traditionally considered to have come to an end. However, Abū l-'Abbās Aḥmad b. al-Ḥasan, known as al-Ḥākim I held on in Aleppo, Ḥarrān, and northern Syria for about a year, i.e. 659–660/1261 then moving to Cairo where the re-located dynasty held on until the Ottoman conquest of Egypt in 923/1517. See Bosworth, *Dynasties*, 6–7. It is also important to take note of the fact that 'Allāma's teacher Naṣīr al-Dīn al-Ṭūsī (d. 672/1274) closely witnessed these events as he was an adviser to Hülegü. Moreover, as already noted above, this very treatise was penned by 'Allāma for none other than Öljeitü, a direct descendent of Hülegü.

ثمّ اختلفوا فقال بعضهم أنّ الإمام بعده ابنه الحسن، وبعضهم قال أنّه معاوية بن أبي سفيان، ثمّ ساقوا الإمامة في بني أميّة إلى أن ظهر السفّاح من بني العباس، فساقوا الإمامة إليه؛ ثمّ انتقلت الإمامة منه إلى أخيه المنصور، ثمّ ساقوا الإمامة في بني العباس إلى المعتصم ﴿إلى أربعين﴾.

Section 2:
Why the Imāmī Position Must be Followed*

* The full title of the section is "That the Imāmī position must be the one adhered to for whereas the crisis resulting from the death of the Prophet ﷺ afflicted the entirety of the Muslims so much so that people differed thereafter and the opinions proliferated as a result of their varying whims." For the sake of brevity, however, we have chosen to use an abbreviated title.

الفصل الثّاني
في أنّ مذهب الإماميّة واجب الاتّباع

There were persons who sought rule for themselves without any right to it and most people gave their allegiance to them seeking this world. Such was the case with ʿUmar b. Saʿd who preferred the rulership of Rayy — although it lasted only a short time — by taking part in the killing of Ḥusayn ﷺ even though he knew that doing this would lead him to the Fire and he admitted as much in a poem in which he said:

Really — by Allah I swear — I don't know, and in this I am truthful.
I ponder my predicament: two monumental choices.
Should I forswear the rule over Rayy whilst Rayy is my dream?
Or should I become soiled with the murder of Ḥusayn?
In murdering him lies the Fire — escape from which there is none,
but in Rayy lies the coolness of mine eye.

Others had doubts about the matter, but saw that the ones who had sought this world had been given allegiance, so they too followed along and gave allegiance to him not so much as even bothering to examine the matter and thus did the truth remain concealed from them. By allowing a right to be conferred on one who does not deserve it, such persons deserve to be reprimanded by Allah since they neglected to even investigate the question.

Others simply followed along due to their lack of critical insight (*quṣūr faṭanatihi*). They simply saw that a great number had given allegiance and they aped them. They were deluded into thinking that the majority must be right having been heedless of what the Exalted said: [...] *but how few are they!*[1]; [...] *but very few of My servants are truly grateful.*[2] Yet, others sought rule for themselves having the right to it, but only the very few followed them: those who had turned their faces away from this world and its allurements, those who in obeying Allah could not be swayed by the anathema of those who hurl abuses, rather they remained true to Allah ﷻ and carried out what he commanded by following him who deserved to be given precedence.

Now, given that this calamity did befall upon the Muslims, it is incumbent upon each individual to look deeply into exactly where the truth lies, and to be even-handed, in order that the truth may be revealed and the one who deserved it is not wronged, for Allah ﷻ has said: *Behold! The curse of Allah is upon the wrongdoers*[3].

1 Qur'ān 38:24.
2 Qur'ān 34:13.
3 Qur'ān 11:18.

لأنّه لمّا عمّت البليّة على كافّة المسلمين بموت النبى ﷺ واختلف الناس بعده وتعدّدت آراؤهم بحسب تعدّد أهوائهم فبعضهم طلب الأمر لنفسه بغير حقّ، وبايعه أكثر الناس طلباً للدنيا، كما اختار عمر بن سعد ملك الري أياماً يسيرة لما خيّر بينه وبين قتل الحسين مع علمه بأنّ في قتله النار وإخباره بذلك في شعره حيث قال:

فوالله ما أدري وإني لصادق أفكّر في أمري على خطرين

أأترك ملك الري والري منيتي أم اصبح مأثوماً بقتل حسين

وفي قتله النار التي ليس دونها حجاب ولي في الري قرة عين

وبعضهم اشتبه الأمر عليه ورأى طالب الدنيا مبايعاً له، فقلده وبايعه وقصّر في نظره فخفي عليه الحقّ، واستحقّ المؤاخذة من الله تعالى بإعطاء الحقّ لغير مستحقّه، بسبب إهمال النظر. وبعضهم قلّد لقصور فطنته ورأى الجمّ الغفير فبايعهم، وتوهّم أن الكثرة تستلزم الصواب وغفل عن قوله تعالى ﴿وقليلٌ مّا هم﴾ ﴿وقليلٌ من عباديَ الشّكور﴾. وبعضهم طلب الأمر لنفسه بحقّ وتابعه الأقلّون الّذين أعرضوا عن الدنيا وزينتها، ولم تأخذهم في الله تعالى لومة لائم؛ بل أخلص لله تعالى واتّبع ما أمر به من طاعة من يستحق التقديم.

وحيث حصلت للمسلمين هذه البليّة وجب على كلّ واحد النظر في الحقّ واعتماد الإنصاف وأن يقرّ الحق مقرّه ولا يظلم مستحقّه، فقد قال الله تعالى ﴿الا لعنة الله على الظالمين﴾.

There is indeed no doubt that the position of the Imāmīs necessarily must be adopted. This is true for a number of reasons (*wujūh*).

The First [Reason]

Once we investigate the different positions we will find that the most true, the most correct, the most pure of admixtures of falsity, as well as the most exalted in affirming the perfection of Allah, His messengers (*rusul*), and his legatees (*awṣiyāʾ*), is the one which is the most excellent in the foundations of belief (*uṣūl al-dīn*) as well as in matters of sacred law (*furūʿ al-dīn*), namely the Imāmī position. This is because the Imāmīs believe that it is Allah ﷻ alone Who is exclusively characterised by beginning-less duration (*al-azal-iyya*) and pre-eternity (*al-qidam*), that all that is other than Him (*kullu mā siwāhu*) is originated (*muḥdath*) for He is Unique.

[The Imāmīs further believe] that He is neither a body, nor is He found anywhere in space, for were it so He would have been originated. On the contrary, they uphold His transcendence above resemblance to all created things and that He is able to do all that is capable of being done.

[The Imāmīs further believe] that He is the Perfectly Just and All-Wise. He neither wrongs anyone nor commits evil for were it so this would entail Him being ignorant and in need — may He be far exalted above such things! He rewards the obedient, otherwise He would be an oppressor. He either forgives the sinner or punishes him for his wrong-doing without oppressing him in any way.

[The Imāmīs further believe] that His acts are wise and carried out with a purpose and a rationale, otherwise He would be perverse for He has said: *We did not create the heavens and the earth and everything between them in jest.*[4] [The Imāmīs further believe] that He sent forth prophets for the guidance of the whole world.

[The Imāmīs further believe] that He can neither be seen, nor perceived by any of the physical senses due to His having said: *Vision encompasses Him not, rather it is He Who encompasses vision.*[5] [The Imāmīs further believe] that He is not directionally localised.

4 Qurʾān 44:38.

5 Qurʾān 6:103.

وإنّما كان مذهب الإماميّة واجب الاتباع لوجوهٍ:

الأوّل:

لمّا نظرنا في المذاهب وجدنا أحقّها وأصدقها وأخلصها عن شوائب الباطل وأعظمها تنزيهًا لله تعالى ولرسله ولأوصيائه أحسنـ(ها في) المسائل الأصولية والفروعيّة مذهب الإماميّة. لأنهم اعتقدوا أنّ الله تعالى هوالمخصوص بالأزليّة والقدم، وأن كلّ ما سواه محدّث لأنه واحد .

وأنه ليس بجسم ولا في مكان وإلّا لكان مُحدثاً؛ بل نزّهوه عن مشابهة المخلوقات، وأنّه تعالى قادر على جميع المقدورات.

وأنّه عدل حكيم لا يظلم أحداً ولا يفعل القبيح، وإلّا لزم الجهل والحاجة تعالى الله عنها؛ ويثيب المطيع لئلا يكون ظالماً، ويعفو عن العاصي أو يعذّبه بجرمه من غير ظلم له. وأنّ أفعاله محكمة واقعة لغرض ومصلحة، وإلّا لكان عابثاً، وقد قال: ﴿وما خلقنا السّماوات والأرض وما بينهما لاعبين﴾، وأنّه أرسل الأنبياء لإرشاد العالم.

وأنه تعالى غير مرئيّ ولا مدرك بشيء من الحواسّ لقوله تعالى: ﴿لا تدركه الأبصار﴾، وأنه ليس في جهة.

[The Imāmīs further believe] that His commandments, prohibitions and communications are originated due to the impossibility of commanding, forbidding and communicating with the non-existent. And that the prophets are safeguarded from falling prey to error, forgetfulness, as well as sins — both minor and major — from the beginning of their lives until the end, were this not to so, one could not[6] rely on what they conveyed and thus the purpose of their being sent could not be realised and, moreover, people would be repulsed by them. And that the Imams — like the prophets — are also safeguarded from all of that for the same reasons.

And because [the Shīʿa] took their legal rulings from the Infallible Imams which were transmitted to them from their grandfather, the Messenger of Allah ﷺ, who received them from Allah conveyed as revelation via Jibraʾīl ﷺ, all of it transmitted by reliable persons, generation-by-generation, in each case stretching all the way back to one of the Infallibles. And they did not give any credence to mere opinion (*raʾy*), or deriving rulings based on personal expertise (*ijtihād*), and they forbade juridical analogy (*qiyās*)[7] as well as juristic preference (*istiḥsān*).[8]

As for the rest of the Muslims, they have adopted all sorts of other positions. Some, namely the Ashʿarīs, said that there is a plurality of eternal [realities] alongside Allah ﷻ and these are none other than the meanings which they affirm to exist in the external world, such as power, knowledge, and the like. In this fashion did they render Him needy in that His being knowledgeable requires the affirmation of a meaning — namely knowledge — and His being powerful requires affirmation of a meaning — namely power — and the like. They did not conceive Him to be essentially powerful, nor essentially knowledgeable, nor essentially Ever-Merciful, nor essentially perceiving, rather, in each case they affirm a meaning which He is in need of for each attribute. Thus, they have rendered Him indigent and incomplete in His Essence and only perfected through other than Him — may Allah be far exalted above such a thing!

6 Reading *lam yabqā wuthūqun* instead of *yabqā wuthūqun*.

7 This is the fourth key source of law in Sunnī jurisprudence after the Qurʾān, the Sunna, and Juristic consensus (*ijmāʿ*). For an in-depth treatment of *qiyās* in English see Mohammad Hashim Kamali, *Principles of Islamic Jurisprudence*, rev. Edn. (Cambridge, UK: Islamic Texts Society, 1991), 197–228.

8 For an in-depth treatment of *istiḥsān* in English see Kamali, *Principles*, 245–266. I have followed Kamali (p. 246) in translating this term as "juristic preference".

وأنّ أمره ونهيه وإخباره حادث لاستحالة أمر المعدوم ونهيه وإخباره، وأن الأنبياء معصومون عن الخطاء والسهو والمعصية صغيرها وكبيرها من أوّل العمر إلى آخره، وإلّا يبق وثوق بما يبلّغونه فانتفت فائدة البعثة؛ ولزم التفسير عنهم، وأنّ الأئمّة معصومون كالأنبياء في ذلك لما تقدّم.

و(لأن الشيعة) أخذوا أحكامهم الفروعيّة عن الأئمة المعصومين الناقلين عن جدّهم رسول الله ﷺ، الآخذ ذلك من الله تعالى بوحي جبرئيل إليه، يتناقلون ذلك عن الثقات خلفاً عن سلف إلى أن تتّصل الرواية بأحد المعصومين؛ ولم يلتفتوا إلى القول بالرأي والاجتهاد وحرّموا الأخذ بالقياس والاستحسان.

أمّا باقي المسلمين، فقد ذهبوا كلّ مذهب: فقال بعضهم وهم جماعة الأشاعرة أنّ القدماء كثيرون مع الله تعالى، وهي المعاني التي يثبتونها موجودة في الخارج كالقدرة والعلم وغير ذلك؛ فجعلوه تعالى مفتقراً في كونه عالماً إلى ثبوت معنى هو العلم، وفي كونه قادرًا إلى ثبوت معنىً هو القدرة، وغير ذلك؛ ولم يجعلوه قادراً لذاته ولا عالماً لذاته ولا رحيماً لذاته ولا مدركاً لذاته بل لمعانٍ قديمة يفتقر في هذه الصفات إليها فجعلوه محتاجاً ناقصاً في ذاته كاملاً بغيره تعالى الله عن ذلك علواً كبيراً.

Even their own scholar Fakhr al-Dīn al-Rāzī[9] objected to them and pointed out that the Christians became disbelievers by saying that the eternals were three, yet the Ashʿarīs affirmed nine eternals. The anthropomorphist Ḥashwiyya sect claimed that Allah ﷻ is a body having length, width, and depth and that He may even shake someone's hand and that the sincere believers will embrace Him in this world.

It is said that al-Kaʿbī (d. 319/931)[10] related from one of them that he claimed it was possible to see Him in this world and that He can visit them and they Him. It is said that Dāwūd al-Ẓāhirī[11] said: "Forget about the beard and private parts and ask me instead about anything else apart from these," and affirmed that the object of his worship had a body of flesh and blood with limbs and body parts: liver, foot, tongue, two eyes and two ears. It is said that he claimed He was hollow from the top to His chest and otherwise solid with short curly hair. They even went so far as to say He lost His eyesight and the angels restored it and that He wept over Noah's flood until His eyes swelled. They claim that there is an empty space of four finger-widths in all directions around the Divine Throne.

Some of them held that He descends every Thursday night in the form of a beardless youth mounted upon a donkey. It is even said that one of their number from Baghdad set up a trough on his roof which every Thursday he used to fill with grain and straw just in case Allah happened to alight on that very roof mounted on His donkey so that the donkey could busy itself with eating while the Lord called out: "Are there any who wish to repent! Are there any who wish to seek forgiveness!" — may Allah be far exalted above such vile doctrines!

9 An extremely influential Sunnī Qur'ān commentator and theologian of the Ashʿarī school. He died in 606/1209.

10 The person in question was a prominent Muʿtazilī theologian best known simply as al-Kaʿbī, as here, or as Abū l-Qāsim al-Balkhī. His actual name was ʿAbdullāh b. Aḥmad b. Maḥmūd. On him see the in-depth study of Racha El Omari, *The Theology of Abū l-Qāsim al-Balkhī/al-Kaʿbī (d. 319/931)* (Leiden: E. J. Brill, 2016).

11 Dāwūd b. ʿAlī b. Khalaf al-Iṣfahānī (d. 270/884), founder of the literalist Ẓāhirī school. On him and the school he founded see the classic study of Ignaz Goldziher, *The Ẓāhirīs: Their Doctrine and their History. A Contribution to the History of Islamic Theology*, translated and edited by Wolfgang Behn (Leiden: E. J. Brill, 2008).

واعترض شيخهم فخر الدين الرازي عليهم بأن قال: إنّ النصارى كفروا لأنّهم قالوا أنّ القدماء ثلاثة، والأشاعرة أثبتوا قدماء تسعة، وقال جماعة الحشويّة والمشبّهة أن الله تعالى جسم له طول وعرض وعمق، وأنّه يجوز عليه المصافحة، وأنّ المخلصين من المسلمين يعانقونه في الدّنيا.

وحكى الكعبي عن بعضهم أنّه كان يجوّز رؤيته في الدنيا، وأن يزورهم ويزورونه. وحكي عن داود الظاهريّ أنّه قال: أعفوني عن اللحية والفرج واسألوني عمّا وراء ذلك؛ وقال أنّ معبوده جسمٌ ولحمٌ ودمٌ وله جوارح وأعضاء وكبد ورجل ولسان وعينين وأذنين؛ وحكي أنه قال: هو مجوّف من أعلاء إلى صدره، مصمت ما سوى ذلك، وله شعر قطط (حتى قالوا: اشتكت) عيناه فعادته الملائكة، وبكى على طوفان نوح حتى رمدت عيناه، وأنّه يفضل من العرش عنه من كلّ جانب أربع أصابع.

وذهب بعضهم إلى أنّه تعالى ينزل في كلّ ليلة جمعة على شكل أمرد حسن الوجه راكباً على حمار، حتى أنّ بعضهم ببغداد وضع على سطح داره معلفاً، يضع كل ليلة جمعة فيه شعيراً وتبناً لتجويز أن ينزل الله تعالى على حماره على ذلك السطح فيشتغل الحمار بالأكل، ويشتغل الرّب بالنداء هل من تائب هل من مستغفر تعالى الله عن مثل هذه العقائد الرديّة في حق الله تعالى.

It is said that one of the ascetics of the Ḥashwiyya sect who had renounced the world happened one day to come across an oil-presser who was accompanied by a beardless youth of beautiful form with short curly hair — that is to say he was of the fashion that they imagine their Lord to be. The shaykh persisted in looking in his direction repeatedly and kept on staring at him. The oil-presser presumed something was a stir with him so he visited him that night and told him: "Old man! I noticed you staring at this boy, so I have brought him to you. If you have some intention about him, that is your business." At this he became furious and said: "I only kept looking at him because it is my belief that Allah ﷻ descends every night in the form of this boy. So, I thought that He was Allah." The oil-presser said: "This lowly profession of oil-pressing is much nobler than whatever nonsense asceticism you are mixed up in."

The Karrāmiyya[12] claimed that Allah is directionally located above. They did not realise that whatever exists in a particular direction is originated and in need of being directionally situated.

Some of them took the position that Allah is not capable of doing anything similar to what a human being can do, and others that He cannot do anything exactly the same as a human being can do. Most of them held that Allah commits evil and that all sorts of sins, unbelief, all varieties of wickedness happen by Allah's foreordainment and decrees and that a person has no agency in any of that and that Allah does not have any end in view behind His Acts, that He does not act at all in the best interests of His servants, that He wills sins on the part of the unbelievers and does not wish them to be obedient. This entails a number of repugnant conclusions.

[1] One of them is that this would render Allah more oppressive than any oppressor because He punishes the unbeliever for his unbelief which He already decreed for him and did not create in him the capacity to believe. Just as it would be oppressive to punish him for the colour of his skin, or his being tall or short — since he has no control over that — it would be oppressive of Him to punish him for sins which He made him do.

12 A peculiar sect founded by the scholar Abū ʿAbdullāh Muḥammad b. Karrām (d. 255/869). For a detailed treatment of his life as well as an in depth look at the sect's doctrines and influence see the entry "Karrāmiyya" by Aron Zysow in *Encyclopaedia Iranica*, edited by Ehsan Yarshater (London and Boston: Routledge and Kegan Paul, 1982–in progress), 15:590–601.

وحكي عن بعض المنقطعين التاركين (الدنيا) من شيوخ الحشوية أنه اجتاز عليه في بعض الأيام نقاط ومعه أمرد حسن الصورة قطط الشعر على الصفات التي يصفون ربّهم بها؛ فألحّ الشيخ في النظر إليه وكرّره وأكثر تصويبه إليه، فتوهّم فيه النّفاط، فجاء إليه ليلاً وقال: أيها الشيخ رأيتك تلح بالنظر إلى هذا الغلام وقد أتيت به إليك، فإن كان لك فيه نية فانت الحاكم فحرد عليه، وقال: إنما كرّرت النظر إليه لأنّ مذهبي أنّ الله تعالى ينزل على صورة هذا الغلام فتوهّمت أنّه الله؛ فقال له النفّاط: ما أنا عليه من النفاطة أجود مما أنت عليه من الزهد مع هذه المقالة.

وقالت الكرامية أنّ الله تعالى في جهة فوق، ولم يعلموا أنّ كل ما هو في جهة فهو محدث ومحتاج إلى تلك الجهة.

وذهب آخرون إلى أنّ الله تعالى لا يقدر على مثل مقدور العبد وآخرون إلى أنّه لا يقدر على عين مقدور العبد، وذهب الأكثر منهم إلى أنّ الله تعالى يفعل القبائح وأنّ جميع أنواع المعاصي والكفر وأنواع الفساد واقعة بقضاء الله تعالى وقدره، وأنّ العبد لا تأثير له في ذلك؛ وأنّه لا غرض لله تعالى في أفعاله ولا يفعل لمصلحة العباد شيئاً، وأنّه تعالى يريد المعاصي من الكافر ولا يريد منه الطاعة؛ وهذا يسلتزم أشياء شنيعة:

منها أن يكون الله تعالى أظلم من كلّ ظالم؛ لأنّه يعاقب الكافر على كفره وهو قدّره عليه ولم يخلق فيه قدرة على الإيمان؛ فكما أنّه يلزم الظلم لو عذّبه على لونه وطوله وقصره لأنّه لا قدرة له فيها، كذا يكون ظالماً لو عذّبه على المعصية الّتي فعلها فيه.

[2] Another is that it utterly dumbfounds any of the Prophets and nullifies their arguments, for if a prophet were to say, "Believe in me and accept my teaching," he could reply by saying, "Say to the One Who sent you to create such faith or the effective capacity for it in me in order that I may be able to believe and accept your teaching, otherwise how can He impose belief on me when I have no capacity for it [in the first place], rather He created in me disbelief and I am unable to oppose Allah ﷻ." Thus, would any prophet be silenced and unable to respond.

[3] Another is that it would mean that Allah could punish the Master of the Messengers for his obedience and reward Iblīs for his defiance, because He does not have any end in view behind His Acts. Thus, a person who is obedient should be deemed an idiot because he diligently works and strives to perform acts of worship, and spends of his wealth toward the construction of mosques and caravansaries and alms for the needy without any benefit accruing to him since He may punish him for all of that; and were he instead to do whatever he takes pleasure in and desires amongst the varieties of transgression, He may reward him for it. Adopting such a doctrine can only lead to the destruction of the world and the disruption of the Sacred Law of Muḥammad.

[4] Another is that it entails the impossibility of anyone believing any of the prophets ﷺ, since because that rests upon two premises. The first of these is that Allah ﷻ brings about miracles at the hand of a prophet for the purpose of him being believed. The second is that whatever Allah affirms is true, but neither of these two premises can hold due to their doctrine that it is impossible for Him to have any end in view in His acts which entails that it is impossible for Him to cause a miracle with the end of a prophet being believed. Moreover, if it is possible for Him to affirm a liar this would mean that it is therefore impossible to adduce any evidence for the truthfulness of any prophet or follow any part of any of the religions.

[5] Another is that one could not then describe Allah as All-Forgiving, Ever-Merciful, All-Forbearing, or All-Pardoning since these qualities can only be affirmed if Allah nullifies the punishment that is justly deserved by wrongdoers,[13] but one deserves to be punished only when the sin committed emanates from the servant rather than from Allah.

13 'Allāma's point here is that the qualities of forgiveness and mercy, etc., can only be truly affirmed of God if and only if (a) there are wrongdoers who deserve to be punished because of *their* actions, and (b) if He subsequently nullifies their justly deserved punishments.

ومنها إفحام الأنبياء وانقطاع حجّتهم؛ لأن النبي ﷺ إذا قال للكافر «آمن بي وصدّقني» يقول له «قل للذي بعثك يخلق فيّ الإيمان أو القدرة المؤثّرة فيه حتّى أتمكّن من الإيمان فأومن، وإلّا فكيف تكلّفني الإيمان ولا قدرة لي عليه، بل خلق فيّ الكفر وأنا لا أتمكّن من مقاهرة الله تعالى» فينقطع النبيّ ولا يتمكّن من جوابه.

ومنها تجويز أن يعذب الله تعالى سيّد المرسلين على طاعته ويثيب إبليس على معصيته، لأنه يفعل (الأشياء) لا لغرض، فيكون فاعل الطاعة سفيها؛ لأنه يتعجّل بالتعب من الاجتهاد في العبادة، وإخراج ماله في عمارة المساجد والرّبط والصدقات من غير نفع يحصل له؛ لأنه قد يعاقبه على ذلك. ولو فعل عوض ذلك ما يلتذّ به ويشتهيه من أنواع المعاصي قد يثيبه، فاختيار الأول يكون سفهًا عند كلّ عاقل؛ والمصير إلى هذا المذهب يؤدّي إلى خراب العالم واضطراب أمر الشريعة المحمّديّة.

ومنها أنّه يلزم أن لا يتمكّن أحد من تصديق أحدٍ من الأنبياء عليهم السلام؛ لأن التوصّل إلى ذلك والدليل عليه إنّما يتم بمقدّمتين: إحداهما أنّ الله تعالى فعل المعجز على يد النبي لأجل التصديق، والثانية أنّ كل ما صدّقه الله تعالى فهو صادق، وكلتا المقدّمتين لا تتم على قولهم؛ لأنّه إذا استحال أن يفعل لغرض استحال أن يظهر المعجز لأجل التصديق، وإذا كان فاعلاً للقبيح ولأنواع الإضلال والمعاصي والكذب وغير ذلك جاز أن يصدّق الكذاب فلا يصحّ الاستدلال على صدق أحد من الأنبياء ولا التديّن بشيء من الشرائع والأديان.

ومنها أنّه لا يصح أن يوصف الله تعالى بأنّه غفورٌ رحيمٌ حليمٌ عفوٌ لأنّ الوصف بهذه إنّما يثبت لوكان الله تعالى مسقطاً للعقاب في حقّ الفسّاق بحيث إذا أسقطه عنهم كان غفوراً عفواً رحيماً؛ وإنما يستحقّ العقاب لو كان العصيان من العبد لا من الله تعالى.

[6] Another is that it entails the imposition of responsibility upon one who has no power to discharge it, since it amounts to Him demanding faith from the non-believer whilst he lacks the capacity thereof, which — by the verdict of reason — is reprehensible as well as having been forbidden by revelation: *Allah does not burden anyone with more than he is able to bear.*[14]

[7] Another is that it entails that all of our voluntary acts that come about in accordance with our goals and intentions — such as our turning this way and that, and our use of hands and feet in the activities we need to perform — become involuntary actions such as the beating of the heart or our being pushed off a cliff by someone. Yet, experience compels us to concede that there is a difference between the two, for every rational person acknowledges that we possess the capacity to perform voluntary acts, but we do not possess the capacity to levitate.

Abū l-Ḥudhayl al-ʿAllāf said: "The donkey of Bishr is more intelligent than Bishr, but if I were to bring him before a low hurdle and hit him so that he leaps over the hurdle he would do so, whereas if I brought him in front of a high hurdle he would not try to jump over it. This is because he knows the difference between what he is capable of jumping over and what he is incapable of jumping over, whereas Bishr cannot differentiate between what he has the capacity for and what he does not."

[8] Another is that it entails there being no difference to us between a person who has been kind to us for his whole life and someone who has mistreated us to the *n*-th degree for his whole life, as well as meaning that we have no basis to thank the first person and condemn the second because, in both cases, the action in question originates from Allah.

14 Qurʾān 2:286.

ومنها أنّه يلزم منه تكليف ما لا يطاق؛ لأنّه يكلف الكافر بالإيمان (ولا قدرة له عليه، وهوقبيح عقلاً والسمع قد منع منه، فقال): ﴿لا يكلف الله نفساً إلّا وسعها﴾ .

ومنها أنّه يلزم منه أن يكون أفعالنا الاختياريّة الواقعة بحسب قصودنا ودواعينا مثل حركتنا يمنة ويسرة وحركة البطش باليد والرجل في الصنائع المطلوبة لنا كالأفعال الاضطرارية مثل حركة النبض وحركة الواقع من شاهق بإيقاع غيره؛ لكنّ الضرورة قاضية بالفرق بينها . أنّ كل عاقل يحكم بأنّا قادرون على الحركات الاختيارية وغير قادرين على الحركة إلى السماء .

قال أبوالهذيل العلاّف: «حمار بشر أعقل من بشر، لأنّ حمار بشر لو أتيت به إلى جدول صغير وضربته للعبور فإنّه يطفره، ولو أتيت به إلى جدول كبير لم يطفره، لأنّه فرق بين ما يقدر على طفره ومالا يقدر عليه؛ وبشر لا يفرّق بين المقدور له وغير المقدور»

ومنها أنّه يلزم أن لا يبقى عندنا فرق بين من أحسن إلينا غاية الإحسان طول عمره وبين من أساء إلينا غاية الإساءة طول عمره، ولم يحسن منّا شكر الأولّ وذمّ الثاني؛ لأنّ الفعلين صادران من الله تعالى عندهم .

[9] Amongst these are the logical possibilities mentioned by Our Master and Leader Mūsā b. Ja'far al-Kāẓim when he was queried by a very young Abū Ḥanīfa, "Whence cometh transgression?" to which al-Kāẓim replied: "Transgression logically either originates from the servant, or from his Lord, or from both. The claim that it originates from Allah, is refuted by the fact that He is far more just and fair than to wrong His servant by punishing him for something that he did not do. The claim that it originates from both is refuted by the fact that it would entail the servant being a partner of Allah. He that is strong is more worthy of being just toward his weak servant. Thus, if we claim that it originates from the servant alone, then the matter devolves upon him, and it is toward him that praise or blame is directed, and thus is he more deserving of reward or punishment, and merits Heaven or Hell," whereupon Abū Ḥanīfa recited: *Descendants one of another.*[15]

[10] Another is that it would mean that an unbeliever would be deemed obedient by virtue of his unbelief since he had done none other than what Allah had wanted, for Allah had wanted unbelief from him and thus did he act and did not believe since this is not what Allah liked for him. Therefore, he was obedient since he carried out what Allah wanted and did not carry out what Allah disliked for him.

[11] Another is that it implies the imputation of idiocy to Allah in as much as He demands faith from the unbeliever while not wanting it and demands that he refrain from transgression while wanting it. Every rational person deems anyone who demands what he does not want and forbids what he wants to be an idiot — may Allah be far exalted above such a thing!

[12] Another is that it would mean that the impossibility of being content with the decree of Allah and his foreordainment. This is because to be content with unbelief is, by unanimous consensus, forbidden. Whereas to be content with the decree of Allah and his foreordainment is obligatory, thus we must be content with it [i.e. unbelief], however it is not permitted to be content with unbelief.

[13] Another is that it would imply that we must seek refuge from Allah with the Devil and moreover results in the repudiation of His statement: *seek then refuge with Allah from the accursed Satan* [Qur'ān 16:98]. This is because they have in effect absolved the Devil and the unbeliever of transgression and instead attributed it to Allah thereby rendering Him more harmful to them then the Devil — may Allah be far exalted above such a thing!

15 Qur'ān 3:34.

ومنها التقسيم الذي ذكره مولانا وسيّدنا موسى بن جعفر الكاظم عليه السلام وقد سأله أبو حنيفة وهو صبي، فقال: المعصية ممن؟ فقال الكاظم عليه السلام: «المعصية إمّا من العبد أو من ربّه أو منها، فإن كانت من الله تعالى فهو أعدل وأنصف من أن يظلم عبده ويأخذه بما لم يفعله؛ وإن كانت المعصية منهما فهو شريكه، والقويّ أولى بإنصاف عبده الضعيف؛ وإن كانت المعصية من العبد وحده فعليه وقع الأمر وإليه توجّه المدح والذم، وهوأحقّ بالثواب والعقاب، وجبت له الجنة أو النار». فقال أبو حنيفة «ذرّية بعضها من بعض».

ومنها أنّه يلزم أن يكون الكافر مطيعاً بكفره لأنّه قد فعل ما هو مراد الله تعالى؛ لأنّه أراد منه الكفر وقد فعله، ولم يفعل الأيمان الذي كرهه الله تعالى منه، فيكون قد أطاعه لأنّه فعل مراده ولم يفعل ما كرهه.

ومنها أنه يلزم نسبة السفه إلى الله تعالى لأنّه أمر الكافر بالإيمان ولا يريده منه، وينهاه عن المعصية وقد أرادها، وكل عاقل ينسب من يأمر بما لا يريد وينهى عما يريد إلى السفه، تعالى الله عن ذلك.

ومنها أنه يلزم عدم الرضا بقضاء الله تعالى وقدره لأنّ الرضا بالكفر حرام بالإجماع، والرضا بقضاء الله تعالى وقدره واجب؛ فلوكان الكفر بقضاء الله تعالى وقدره وجب علينا الرضا به، لكن لا يجوز الرضا بالكفر.

ومنها أنّه يلزم أن نستعيذ بإبليس من الله تعالى، ولا يحسن قوله تعالى ﴿فاستعذ بالله من الشّيطان الرّجيم﴾؛ لأنهم نزّهوا ابليس والكافر من المعاصي وأضافوها إلى الله تعالى، فيكون على المكلّفين شراً من ابليس عليهم، تعالى الله عن ذلك.

[14] Another is that it would mean that no reliance could be placed upon the promises and threats of Allah. This is because if they attribute to Him the possibility of lying concerning matters in the world, then He could have lied about all that He has informed us, and thus the very purpose of sending prophets would be repudiated. Indeed, it would be entirely possible for Him to have sent liars. Therefore, there would not remain any means for us to distinguish the true prophets from the false.

[15] Another is that it would entail the nullification of all legal punishments and restrictions against transgressions. For if adultery and fornication were indeed in accordance with the will of Allah, and if indeed theft issued from Allah, and if His will is efficacious, then it is not right for the Sultan to punish people for these things for that would mean that he would be keeping people from fulfilling the will of Allah and forcing them to do what He does not like; for we would all acknowledge that if one of us were to prevent another person from doing the will of Allah and forcing him to do what He does not like, it would be reprehensible. This would also mean that Allah simultaneously wills two contradictories since He would have willed transgression while wishing at the same time to prevent it.

[16] Another is that it this leads to a conflict between reason and revelation. As for reason, we have already seen an example of this above when we noted that it is a necessary truth that we are justified in ascribing voluntary acts to ourselves, for if we decide to turn to the right we do not end up turning to the left and vice versa, and to doubt the truth of this is the height of sophistry.

As for revelation, the Qur'ān is replete with instances of the acts of humans being ascribed to them, such as:

... and of Ibrāhīm, who to his trust was true;[16]
... woe then unto all who disbelieve;[17]
Enter Paradise by virtue of what you used to do;[18]
... this day each soul shall be requited for what it has earned;[19]
... this day you shall be requited for all that you ever did;[20]
... so that every soul may be rewarded for that which it strove for;[21]

16 Qur'ān 53:37.
17 Qur'ān 19:37/51:60.
18 Qur'ān 16:32.
19 Qur'ān 40:17.
20 Qur'ān 45:28.
21 Qur'ān 20:15.

ومنها أنّه لا يبقى وثوق بوعد الله تعالى ووعيده لأنّهم إذا جوّزوا استناد الكذب في العالم إليه جاز أن يكذب في إخباراته كلّها، فتنتفي فائدة بعثة الأنبياء؛ بل وجاز منه إرسال الكذّابين، فلا يبقى لنا طريق إلى تميّز الصادق من الأنبياء والكاذب.

ومنها أنّه يلزم منه تعطيل الحدود والزواجر عن المعاصي؛ فإنّ الزنا إذا كان واقعاً بإرادة الله تعالى والسرقة إذا صدرت من الله تعالى وإرادته هي المؤثّرة لم يجز للسلطان المؤاخذة عليها؛ لأنّه يصدّ السارق عن مراد الله تعالى ويبعثه على ما يكرهه الله تعالى، ولوصدّ الواحد منّا غيره عن مراده وحمله على ما يكرهه استحقّ منه اللوم. ويلزم أن يكون الله مريداً للنقيضين لأن المعصية مرادة الله تعالى والزجر عنها مراد له أيضا.

ومنها أنّه يلزم منه مخالفة المعقول والمنقول. أمّا المعقول فلما تقدّم من العلم الضروري بإسناد أفعالنا الاختياريّة إلينا ووقوعها بحسب إرادتنا؛ فإذا أردنا الحركة يمنة لم يقع يسرة، وبالعكس. والشكّ في ذلك عين السفسطة.

وأمّا المنقول فالقرآن مملوء من إسناده أفعال البشر إليهم، كقوله تعالى

﴿وإبراهيم الذي وفّى﴾

﴿فويل للّذين كفروا﴾

﴿ادخلوا الجنّة بما كنتم تعملون﴾

﴿واليوم تجزى كلّ نفس بما كسبت﴾

﴿اليوم تجزون ماكنتم تعملون﴾

﴿لتجزى كلّ نفس بما تسعى﴾

... can you expect to be rewarded for anything other than whatever you used to do;[22]

... whoever shall come with a good deed will receive tenfold the like thereof, while whoever shall ... come with an evil deed will be requited with no more than the like thereof;[23]

... so that He may grant them their reward in full;[24]

... in its favour shall be whatever good it does, and against it whatever evil it does;[25]

... because of the wickedness committed by the Jews we denied them certain good things;[26]

... every man is bound by what he has earned;[27]

... anyone who does evil shall be punished for it;[28]

I had no power over you at all, except that I called you and you responded to me;[29]

Indeed, Allah does not wrong anyone by so much as the smallest speck;[30]

... and never does Allah do the least wrong to his creatures;[31]

... we did not wrong them, rather they wronged themselves;[32]

... they will not be wronged by as much as a hair's breadth;[33]

... and Allah does not will injustice for any of His slaves.[34]

Can there be any greater injustice than to punish another person for something that he did not do, but rather was done by the one punishing him?

An adversary would respond that: [1] It is impossible for someone with the capacity to act to prefer one act over another without some preponderating factor as the basis for choosing to do the act in question, in which case it *must* be performed and thereby negates any capacity to act. [2] This implies that man is partner with Allah. [3] This is also supported by His statement *when it is Allah who created both you and what you do.*[35]

22 Qur'ān 27:90.
23 Qur'ān 6:160.
24 Qur'ān 35:30.
25 Qur'ān 2:286.
26 Qur'ān 4:160.
27 Qur'ān 52:21.
28 Qur'ān 4:123.
29 Qur'ān 14:22.
30 Qur'ān 4:40.
31 Qur'ān 41:46.
32 Qur'ān 16:118.
33 Qur'ān 4:49/17:71.
34 Qur'ān 40:31.
35 Qur'ān 37:96.

﴿هل تجزون إلّا ما كنتم تعملون﴾

﴿من جاء بالحسنة فله عشر أمثالها ومن جاء بالسّيّئة فلا يجزى إلّا مثلها﴾

﴿ليوفيهم أجورهم﴾

﴿لها ما كسبت وعليها ما اكتسبت﴾

﴿فبظلم من الّذين هادوا حرّمنا عليهم طيّبات﴾

﴿كلّ أمريء بما كسب رهين﴾

﴿من يعمل سوءا يجز به﴾

﴿وما كان لي عليكم من سلطان إلّا أن دعوتكم فاستجبتم لي﴾

﴿إنّ الله لا يظلم مثقال ذرّة﴾

﴿وما ربّك بظلاّم للعبيد﴾

﴿وما ظلمناهم ولكن كانوا أنفسهم يظلمون﴾

﴿ولا يظلمون فتيلا﴾

﴿وما الله يريد ظلماً للعباد﴾

وأيّ ظلم أعظم من تعذيب الغير على فعل لم يصدر منه بل ممّن يعذّبه؟

قال الخصم: القادر يمتنع أن يرجّح مقدوره من غير مرجّح، ومع المرجّح يجب الفعل فلا قدرة؛ ولأنّه يلزم أن يكون الانسان شريكاً لله تعالى، ولقوله تعالى ﴿والله خلقكم وما تعملون﴾.

In reply to the first point, Allah has the power to act. Now, if this capacity to act were in need of some preponderating factor, and moreover, if this preponderating factor necessitated the bringing about of the effect of the action, then this would mean that Allah was bound rather than free, and this is unbelief.

In reply to the second point, how is there here any associating of partners with Allah? Allah has the power to overcome him and to make him cease to exist. By way of analogy, if a Sultan appoints someone as a governor over some lands and he loots its inhabitants, oppresses them and causes them distress, the Sultan can execute him or avenge his wrongdoings and return whatever he looted, and this does not make him a partner of the Sultan.

In reply to the third, the fact is that the verse is referring to the idols that people used to make and then worship, and thus He is denouncing this by saying *Do you worship what you yourselves have carved, when it is Allah who created both you and what you do?*[36]

The Ashʿarīs upheld the view that Allah ﷻ can be seen by the human eye despite the fact that He cannot be bound by directionality and despite the fact that He has said *Vision cannot encompass Him* [Qurʾān 6:103]. They denied the necessary truth that whatever is visually perceptible must be opposite to the eye or what amounts to being opposite to it.[37] In this they went against all rational persons and claimed that it was possible for there to be mountains of many hues towering before us from the ground all the way up to the sky which we cannot see, as well as tremendous sounds which we cannot hear, formidably equipped attacking armies such that our bodies touch their bodies yet we cannot perceive them or their movements nor hear their terrifying voices, and that we can perceive the tiniest speck in one corner of the earth while we are in another despite the tremendous distance between us and it. All of this is the height of sophistry.

36 Qurʾān 37:95–96.

37 That is, it must be in some line of sight of the eye somewhere in the field of vision.

والجواب عن الأوّل: المعارضة بالله تعالى، فإنّه تعالى قادر؛ فإن افتقرت القدرة إلى المرجّح وكان المرجّح موجباً للأثر لزم أن يكون الله تعالى موجباً لا مختاراً، فيلزم الكفر.

وعن الثاني: أيّ شركة هنا ؟ ! والله تعالى هو القادر على قهر العبد وإعدامه، ومثال هذا أنّ السلطان إذا ولّى شخصاً بعض البلاد فنهب وظلم وقهر فإنّ السلطان يتمكّن من قتله والانتقام منه واستعادة ما أخذه، وليس يكون شريكاً للسلطان.

وعن الثالث: أنّه إشارة إلى الأصنام التي كانوا ينحتونها ويعبدونها، فأنكر عليهم وقال ﴿أتعبدون ما تنحتون والله خلقكم وما تعملون﴾.

وذهبت الأشاعرة إلى أنّ الله تعالى مرئيّ بالعين، مع أنّه مجرّد عن الجهات؛ وقد قال تعالى ﴿لا تدركه الأبصار﴾؛ وخالفوا الضرورة في أنّ المدرك بالعين يكون مقابلاً أو في حكمه؛ وخالفوا جميع العقلاء في ذلك وذهبوا إلى تجويز أن يكون بين أيدينا جبال شاهقة من الأرض إلى السماء مختلفة الألوان لا نشاهدها، وأصوات هائلة لا نسمعها، وعساكر مختلفة متحاربة بأنواع الأسلحة، بحيث يماسّ أجسامنا أجسامهم، لا نشاهد صورهم ولا حركاتهم، ولا نسمع أصواتهم الهائلة، وأن نشاهد جسماً أصغر الأجسام كالذرّة في المشرق ونحن في المغرب مع كثرة الحائل بيننا وبينها؛ وهذا عين السفسطة.

They also upheld the view that Allah has been issuing commandments and prohibitions since pre-eternity when no created thing existed, saying such things as: *O Prophet! Fear Allah,*[38] *O you who believe!*[39] *Fear Allah, O humankind! Fear your Lord.*[40] Were a person to sit in his house with no slaves present and then call out, "O Sālim! Get up," "O Ghānim! Eat," "O Najāḥ! Enter." It would be said to him: "Whom are you calling?" And were he to say, "I am calling out to slaves whom I will purchase after twenty years," all rational people would call him an idiot and a buffoon. How is it then that they ascribe such things to Allah in pre-eternity?

Everyone but the Imāmī and Ismāʿīlī Shīʿīs consider the prophets and Imams to be fallible. They believe that it is possible for Allah to send people who lie, forget, commit errors, and steal. What reliance then can the Sunnīs (*ʿāmma*) place on their teachings? How can they then submit to their authority? How can it be obligatory to obey them when the command could be wrong? They also did not limit the Imams to a specific number, rather anyone of Quraysh who is able to gain followers who pledge loyalty to him becomes, according to them, an Imam whom all must follow so long as his inner state is concealed even if he be concealing the height of sinfulness, unbelief, and hypocrisy.

All of them also upheld the doctrines of juridical analogy (*qiyās*) and reliance upon autonomous legal judgement and thus introduced into the religion of Allah what had no part in it. They thereby distorted the injunctions of the Sacred Law and innovated four schools of law that never existed in the time of the Prophet ﷺ nor in the time of the Companions. They even rejected the statements of the Companions in which they explicitly spoke against juridical analogy saying that the first one to resort to analogy was the Devil.

38 Qurʾān 33:1.

39 Qurʾān 2:278.

40 Qurʾān 4:1.

وذهبوا إلى أنّه تعالى أمر وناه في الأزل ولا مخلوق عنده قائلاً ﴿يا أيها النّبي اتّق الله﴾، ﴿يا أيها الّذين آمنوا اتّقوا الله﴾، ﴿يا أيها النّاس اتّقوا ربّكم﴾ . ولو جلس شخص في منزله ولا غلام عنده فقال: يا سالم قم، يا غانم كل، يا نجاح ادخل، قيل لمن تنادي؟ فيقول لعبيد أشتريه بعد عشرين سنة، نسبه كلّ عاقل إلى السفه والحمق؛ فكيف يحسن منهم أن ينسبوا الله تعالى إليه في الأزل.

وذهب جميع من عدا الإماميّة والإسماعيلية إلى أنّ الأنبياء والأئمة غير معصومين، فجوّزوا بعثه من يجوز عليه الكذب والسهو والخطاء والسرقة؛ فأيّ وثوق يبقى للعامّة في أقاويلهم؟ وكيف يحصل الانقياد إليهم؟ وكيف يجب اتباعهم مع تجويز أن يكون ما يأمرون به خطاء؟ ولم يجعلوا الأئمة محصورين في عدد معيّن، بل كل من تابع قرشيّاً انعقدت إمامته عندهم، ووجبت طاعته على جميع الخلق إذا كان مستور الحال، وإن كان على غاية من الفسوق والكفر والنفاق.

وذهب الجميع منهم إلى القول بالقياس والأخذ بالرأي، فأدخلوا في دين الله ما ليس منه، وحرّفوا أحكام الشريعة وأحدثوا مذاهب أربعة لم تكن في زمن النبي ﷺ ولا في زمن صحابته؛ وأهملوا أقاويل الصحابة مع أنّهم نصوا على ترك القياس، وقالوا: أوّل من قاس إبليس.

As a result they took a number of odious positions, such as the permissibility of the girl born of fornication; the nullification of any punishment for someone who marries his mother, or sister, or daughter despite him knowing that they were forbidden to him by relation and on the basis of concluding a contract which he knows to be invalid; as well as the nullification of any punishment for one who wraps a cloth around his penis and fornicates with his mother or daughter; as well as the nullification of any punishment for the homosexual despite the fact that this is even more obscene and depraved than fornication. Also, maintaining the paternity of a man in the west for the offspring of a woman in the east, that is to say if a father were to give his daughter in marriage to a man in the west whilst she was absent residing in the east and were the father then to remain night-and-day with the man in the west until six months had passed and his daughter were to give birth in the east, the offspring would be held to be that of the man even though he remains with her father in the west at a distance taking years to traverse; indeed even if the Sultan were to imprison him from the moment the marriage contract was concluded and placed him under constant guard for fifty years only then to be released and returned to the town of the girl and seeing a vast number of her children and her children's children and so on for many branches, all of them would belong to the man who never ever went near this woman or any other woman.

They also deemed fermented date juice (*nabīdh*) to be licit even though it is classified as wine due to it being an intoxicant. They also permitted prayer whilst clad in dog leather as well as upon dried faeces.

Once, while in the presence of a king and some jurists of the Ḥanafī school of Law, a jurist described the prayer of a Ḥanafī man who entered a house which had been usurped from the rightful owner, performed his ablution with fermented date juice, raised both his hands to commence the prayer while pronouncing the expression *Allāhu Akbar* (Allah is great) but in Persian (i.e. *khudā buzurg ast*) without making any intention to pray, then he recited the 64th verse of Sūrat al-Raḥmān: *mudahāmmatān* (two green leaves) and no other part of the Qur'ān and that too in Persian (i.e. *dō barg-e sabz*) then he swiftly bowed down his head without a single moment's pause, prostrated on the ground in the same fashion, and barely raised his head up again only to prostrate once more and then stood up and did all of that a second time and then farted out loud. At this the king, having been a Ḥanafī, immediately renounced this school of law.

وذهبوا بسبب ذلك إلى أمور شنيعة كإباحة البنت المخلوقة من الزنا، وسقوط الحدّ عمن نكح أمّه وأخته وبنته مع علمه بالتحريم والنسب بواسطة عقد يعقده وهو يعلم بطلانه، وعمّن لفّ على ذكره خرقة وزنا بأمّه أوبنته، وعن اللائط مع أنّه أفحش من الزنا وأقبح؛ وإلحاق نسب المشرقيّة بالمغربيّ، فإذا زوّج الرجل ابنته وهي في المشرق برجل هو وإيّاه في المغرب، ولم يفترقا ليلا ونهاراً حتّى مضت مدّه ستّة أشهر، فولدت البنت في المشرق، التحق نسب الولد بالرجل، وهو وأبوها في المغرب مع أنّه لا يمكنه الوصول إليها إلّا بعد سنين متعدّدة؛ بل لو حبسه السلطان من حين العقد وقيّده وجعل عليه حفظة مدّه خمسين سنة ثم وصل إلى بلد المرأة فرأى جماعة كثيرة من أولادها وأولاد أولادهم إلى عدّة بطون التحقوا كلّهم بالرجل الذي لم يقرب هذه المرأة ولا غيرها أبتّة.

وإباحة النبيذ مع مشاركته للخمر في الإسكار، والوضوء والصلاة في جلد الكلب، وعلى العذرة اليابسة.

وحكى بعض الفقهاء لبعض الملوك وعنده بعض فقهاء الحنفيّة صفة صلاة الحنفيّ، فدخل داراً مغصوبة وتوضّأ بالنبيذ وكبّر بالفارسية من غير نيّة وقرأ ﴿مدهامّتان﴾ لا غير بالفارسيّة، ثم طأطأ رأسه من غير طمأنينة وسجد كذلك، ورفع رأسه بقدر حد السيف، ثم سجد وقام ففعل كذلك ثانية ثم أحدث، فتبرّأ الملك وكان حنفيّا من هذا المذهب؛

They permitted usurpation as long as the usurper changed the nature of the thing usurped, so if, they argued, a thief were to get inside someone's property and find there a mule, millstone, and some grain, and then if the thief were to grind the grain of the owner of the property with the millstone using the mule he would become the owner of the flour. Even if the owner were to arrive and try to rest it from him, he would be the wrongdoer and the thief would be deemed the wronged party. And if they were to fight with one another and the owner to be killed, he would be deemed the wrongdoer, and if the thief were to die he would be deemed a martyr.

They deemed it an obligation to carry out the punishment (of stoning to death) on an adulterer if he denied the veracity of witnesses, and they nullified it if he confirmed their testimony. Thus, they nullified the punishment despite both witnesses and acknowledgement of guilt. This opens the door toward the nullification of the punishments imposed by Allah ﷻ for anyone accused by witnesses of adultery could simply confirm their testimony and the punishment would be dropped. They also permitted the eating of dog meat, frivolous amusements, such as chess, gatherings of song, and other matters which a short work like this cannot go into.[41]

41 For further discussion of these matters see, for example, al-Faḍl b. Shādhān al-Azdī al-Naysabūrī (d. 260/ 873), *al-Iḍāḥ*, edited by al-Sayyid Jalāl al-Dīn al-Ḥusaynī al-Urmawī (Tehran: Tehran University Press, 1351Sh).

وأباحوا المغصوب لو غيّر الغاصب الصفة، فقالوا لو أنّ سارقا دخل بدار شخص له فيه دوابّ ورحىّ وطعام فطحن السارق طعام صاحب الدار بدوابّه وأرحيته ملك الطحين بذلك؛ فلو جاء المالك ونازعه كان المالك ظالماً والسارق مظلوماً، فلو تقاتلا فإن قتل المالك كان ظالماً وإن قتل السارق كان شهيداً .

وأوجبوا الحدّ على الزاني إذا كذّب الشهود، (وأسقطوه إذا صدّقهم) فأسقط الحدّ مع اجتماع الإقرار والبيّنة، وهذا ذريعة إلى إسقاط حدود الله تعالى؛ فإنّ كل من شهد عليه بالزنا يصدّق الشهود ويسقط عنه الحدّ . وإباحة الكلب وإباحة الملاهي كالشطرنج والغناء وغير ذلك من المسائل التي لا يحتملها هذا المختصر.

The Second Reason

Namely that which is exemplified in the observation made by our Shaykh, the Great Master, Khwāja Naṣīr al-Dīn Muḥammad b. al-Ḥasan al-Ṭūsī [d. 672/1274], may Allah sanctify his spirit, when we asked him about the various doctrinal schools. He said: "We have plumbed their depths alongside the words of the Messenger of Allah ﷺ: 'My community shall split into seventy-two sects, only one of which shall be saved and the rest shall be in the Fire,'[42] and we found the saved sect to be none other than that of the Imāmīs for theirs is distinct from all of the doctrinal schools and all of the doctrinal schools share the same foundational principles."

42 This is known as *ḥadīth al-iftirāq* ("The Ḥadīth of the Schism"). See Tirmidhī, *al-Sunan*, 2:673 nr. 2852, 2853; Abū l-Qāsim Sulayman b. Aḥmad al-Ṭabarānī (d. 360/970), *al-Mu'jam al-Kabīr*, edited by Sa'd b. 'Abdullāh al-Ḥumayyid and Khālid b. 'Abd al-Raḥmān al-Juraysī (Beirut?: n. d.), 14:53 nr. 14646; al-Ḥākim al-Naysābūrī, *al-Mustadrak 'alā al-ṣaḥīḥayn*, edited by Muṣṭafā 'Abd al-Qādir 'Aṭā (Beirut: Dār al-Kutub al-'Ilmiyya, n.d.) 1:217 nr. 441–1 and 1:219 nr. 445; Jamāl al-Dīn al-Mizzī, *Tuḥfat al-ashrāf*, 8864, 15082.

الوجه الثاني في الدلالة على وجوب اتباع مذهب الإماميّة

ما قاله شيخنا الإمام الأعظم خواجه نصير الملّه والدين محمّد بن الحسن الطوسي قدّس الله روحه، وقد سألته عن المذاهب فقال: بحثنا عنها وعن قول رسول الله ﷺ: «ستفترق أمّتي على ثلاث وسبعين فرقة، فرقة منها ناجية والباقي في النار» فوجدنا الفرقة الناجية (هي فرقة) الإماميّة؛ لأنهم باينوا جميع المذاهب، وجميع المذاهب قد اشتركت في أصول العقائد .

The Third Reason

The Imāmīs are certain of themselves and their Imams attaining salvation. They are firm in this while also being certain of the opposite for others. The Sunnīs do not regard this to be certain for themselves or for others. Thus, it is better to follow the former. This is because if, for example, we imagine two people who set out from Baghdad for Kufa but following different routes and then a third person sets out who encounters one of them and asks him where he is headed. The person tells him Kufa, and then he asks if the route he is following will get him there safe and sound and whether the route followed by the other traveller is the same, only to be told by the first traveller that he has no idea at all. Then, when the third man asks the same question to the second traveller and he says that he is sure that his route will get him to Kufa safe and sound whereas the route taken by the other traveller will not get him to Kufa nor is it a secure route, then if the third man were to end up following the first all reasonable people would regard him as an idiot, whereas if he were to follow the second he would be acting in accordance with certainty.

الوجه الثالث

إنّ الإماميّة جازمون بحصول النجاة لهم ولأئمتّهم قاطعون على ذلك وبحصول ضدّها لغيرهم، وأهل السنّة لا يجزمون بذلك لا لهم ولا لغيرهم فيكون اتّباع أولئك أولى لأنّا لو فرضنا مثلاً خروج شخصين من بغداد يريدان الكوفة، فوجدا طريقين سلك كلّ منها طريقاً فخرج ثالث يطلب الكوفة فسأل أحدهما «إلى أين يريد ؟» فقال «إلى الكوفة» فقال له «هذا طريقك يوصلك إليها ؟ وهل طريقك أمن أم مخوف ؟ وهل طريق صاحبك يؤديه إلى الكوفة؟ وهل هو آمن أم مخوف؟» فقال: «لا أعلم شيئاً من ذلك»، ثمّ سأل صاحبه عن ذلك فقال «أعلم أنّ طريقي يوصلني إلى الكوفة، وأنّه آمن، وأعلم أنّ طريق صاحبي لا يؤديه إلى الكوفة وليس بآمن؛» فإن الثالث إنْ تابع الأوّل عدّه العقلاء سفيهًا، وإنْ تابع الثاني نُسب إلى الأخذ بالجزم.

The Fourth Reason

The Imāmīs took their school of thought from their infallible Imams who are well known for their nobility, knowledge, asceticism, scrupulous piety, being constantly immersed in acts of worship, supplication, recitation of the Qurʾān, and being constant in all of this from childhood until the end of their lives. It is from them that people acquired learning. It was regarding them that the Sūrat al-Insān[43] was revealed as were the verse of purification,[44] the verse that made loving them an obligation,[45] as well as the verse of the imprecation,[46] not to mention others. ʿAlī used to perform 1000 units of prayer every day and night and regularly recited the Qurʾān despite the severity of his trials in combat and *jihād*. The first of the Imams is ʿAlī b. Abī Ṭālib. He was the best of creation after the Messenger of Allah. Allah called him the "soul" (*nafs*) of the Messenger of Allah when he said *and our souls and your souls*.[47] The Messenger of Allah took him as a brother and gave his daughter in marriage to him. His excellence is obvious. Numerous miracles took place at his hand so much so that some even claimed lordship for him so he executed them. Others such as the Nuṣayrīs and the Ghālīs also said such things and came to the same end.

His two sons were the maternal grandsons of the Messenger of Allah, the two princes of the youths of paradise. They are both Imams by the explicit designation of the Prophet. They were both the most ascetic people of the day and the most knowledgeable among them. They fought in the way of Allah until they were killed. Ḥasan used to wear wool under his magnificent garments without anyone realising it. One day the Prophet sat with Ḥusayn on his right thigh and his son Ibrāhīm on the left. Jibrīl descended and said: "Allah will not allow you to have them both, so choose which of them you prefer." He thought, "If Ḥusayn dies then I along with ʿAlī and Fāṭima shall weep over him, whereas if it is Ibrāhīm who dies it is only I who shall weep over him." So he chose the death of Ibrāhīm who passed away three days later. Thereafter whenever Ḥusayn came to him he would kiss him and say: "Welcome to the one for whom I offered up by my son Ibrāhīm."

---

43   The 76th chapter of the Qurʾān
44   Qurʾān 33:33.
45   Qurʾān 42:23.
46   Qurʾān 3:61.
47   Qurʾān 3:61.

الوجه الرابع

إنّ الإماميّة أخذوا مذهبهم عن الأئمّة المعصومين المشهورين بالفضل والعلم والزهد والورع والاشتغال في كلّ وقت بالعبادة والدعاء وتلاوة القرآن والمداومة على ذلك من زمن الطفوليّة إلى آخر العمر. ومنهم تعلّم الناس العلوم ونزل في حقّهم هل أتى وآية الطهارة وإيجاب المودّة لهم وآية الابتهال وغير ذلك؛ وكان علي يصلّي في كلّ يوم وليلة ألف ركعة ويتلو القرآن مع شدّة ابتلائه بالحروب والجهاد؛ فأوّلهم عليّ بن أبي طالب عليه السلام، كان أفضل الخلق بعد رسول الله صلى الله عليه وآله، وجعله الله تعالى نفس رسول الله؛ حيث قال: ﴿وأنفسنا وأنفسكم﴾. وأخاه الرسول صلى الله عليه وآله وزوّجه ابنته، وفضله لا يحصى؛ وظهرت عنه معجزات كثيرة حتّى ادّعى قوم فيه الربوبيّة وقتلهم، صار إلى مقالتهم آخرون إلى هذه الغاية، كالنصيرية والغلاة.

وكان ولداه سبطا رسول الله صلى الله عليه وآله سيّدا شباب أهل الجنّة إمامين بنصّ النبي صلى الله عليه وآله وكانا أزهد الناس وأعلمهم في زمانهم، وجاهدا في سبيل الله حتّى قتلا؛ ولبس الحسن الصوف تحت ثيابه الفاخرة من غير أن يشعر أحداً بذلك. وأخذ النبي صلى الله عليه وآله يومًا الحسين على فخذه الأيمن، وولده إبراهيم على فخذه الأيسر، فنزل عليه جبرئيل وقال «إنّ الله لم يكن ليجمع لك بينهما، فاختر من شئت منها؛»، فقال صلى الله عليه وآله «إذا مات الحسين بكيت عليه أنا وعليّ وفاطمة، وإذا مات إبراهيم بكيت أنا عليه؛» فاختار موت إبراهيم فمات بعد ثلاثة أيام، فكان إذا جاء الحسين بعد ذلك يقبّله ويقول «أهلا ومرحباً بمن فديته بابني إبراهيم».

ʿAlī b. al-Ḥusayn Zayn al-ʿĀbidīn used to fast during the day and stand in worship at night. He would recite the Mighty Book [i.e., the Qurʾān] and perform 1000 units of prayer every day and night. After every two units of prayer he would recite the supplications which are transmitted by him and his forefathers, upon whom be peace. Then he would let go of the text [from which he was reciting] in sorrow and cry out, "Who am I to attempt to worship like ʿAlī?" He used to weep a great deal, so much so that his tears caused his cheeks to become marked. He used to prostrate so much that he became known as the calloused one [due to the callouses that formed on his forehead from prostration]. The Messenger of Allah ﷺ had named him the Prince of the Worshippers (*sayyid al-ʿābidīn*).

When Hishām b. ʿAbd al-Malik went on the pilgrimage to Mecca, he was unable to reach the black stone due to the crowd, but when Zayn al-ʿĀbidīn arrived all the people stopped where they were and gave way until he reached the black stone where none remained but him alone. Hishām asked: "Who is this!?" [The poet] al-Farazdaq [who was present] recited these lines:[48]

None other than the one whose very footsteps are known
  by the Plain of Mecca, he is!
The Kaʿba itself recognizes him as does the sacred precinct
  and that which bounds it.

None other than the son of the best of all of Allah's servants, he is!
  None other than the most pious, most pristine, most pure person, he is!

Almost reaching out to take hold of him, for it knows his hand
  is the cornerstone of the Kaʿba whenever he approaches it.

Whenever the tribes of Quraysh see him someone will always exclaim:
  Nobility itself finds its origin in his noble traits.

Were the people of rectitude to be counted, he would be their Imam,
  or be it asked: "Who is the best of Allah's creation?"
    It would be said: "Him."

48 We have translated this ode as it appears in the text. However, this version does not match up with the published versions of the *Dīwān al-Farazdaq* currently in circulation. See, for example, *Dīwān al-Farazdaq*, edited by Karam al-Bustānī (Beirut: Dār Bayrūt, 1404/1984), 178–181 and *Dīwān al-Farazdaq*, edited by ʿAlī Fāʿūr (Beirut: Dār al-Kutub al-ʿIlmiyya, 1407/1987), 511–514.

وكان عليّ بن الحسين زين العابدين عليه السلام يصوم نهاره ويقوم ليله، ويتلو الكتّاب العزيز ويصلّي كل يوم وليلة ألف ركعة، ويدعو بعد كلّ ركعتين بالأدعية المنقولة عنه وعن آبائه عليهم السلام، ثمّ يرمي الصحيفة كالمتضجّر، ويقول: .أنّى لي بعبادة علي ! وكان يبكي كثيراً حتّى أخذت الدموع من لحم خدّيه، وسجد حتى سمّي ذا الثفنات، وسمّاه رسول الله صلى الله عليه وآله سيّد العابدين.

وكان قد حجّ هشام بن عبد الملك فاجتهد أن يستلم الحجر فلم يمكنه من الزحام؛ فجاء زين العابدين فوقف الناس له وتنحّوا عن الحجر حتّى استلمه، ولم يبق عند الحجر سواه؛ فقال هشام: من هذا ؟ فقال الفرزدق الشاعر:

هذا الذي تعرف البطحاء وطأته	والبيت يعرفه والحل والحرم
هذا ابن خير عبد الله كلّهم	هذا التقي التقي الطاهر العلم
يكاد يمسكه عرفان راحته	ركن الحطيم إذا ما جاء يستلم
إذا رأته قريش قال قائلها	إلى مكارم هذا ينتهي الكرم
إن عد أهل التقى كانوا أئمتهم	أو قيل من خير خلق الله؟ قيل هم

None other than Fāṭima's child he is, if you know him not!
 With his Grandfather was sealed the line of Allah's prophets!

His eyes lowered in humility, theirs lowered in awe of him.
 Yet, whenever spoken to he is always smiling.

The light of guidance bursts forth from the dawn of
 his beaming countenance,
 like the Sun dispelling the gloom with its luminosity.

Cleaving from the Messenger of Allah his origin bursts forth.
 Made good are the elements of his temperament,
 his disposition, and his habits.

Allah honoured him eternally and ennobled him.
 Thus, did the Pen inscribe it in His Celestial Tablet.

Such it is for a company of souls; love of whom is religion itself,
 and hatred of whom
 is nothing but unbelief and being close to them is a refuge and safeguard.

None among the generous can arrive at the far-reaches of their utmost rank,
 nor can any people come close to them no matter how honourable.

They are the abundant rain of succour whenever any calamity strikes,
 and the lions of hardship and adversity are enflamed.

Hardship diminishes not their open-handed giving,
 whether they are in abundance or scarcity, they do the same.

Never did he utter the word "No," save in uttering the testimony of faith.[49]
 Were it not for the testimony of faith, his "No" would have been a "Yes."

In loving them evil is repulsed and calamity is averted
 and benevolence and blessings are brought to perfection.

49 An allusion to the *shahāda* or Muslim testimony of faith, namely *lā ilāha illa Llāh* (*There is no deity but Allah*).

هـذا ابن فاطمة إن كنت جاهله   بجده أنبياء الله قد ختموا
يغضي حياء ويغضي من مهابته   فـمـا يكلّم إلا حين يبتسم
ينشق نور الهدى عن صبح غرته   كالشمس تنجاب عن إشراقها الظلم
مشتقة من رسـول الله تبعته   طابت عناصره والخيم والشيم
الله شـــرّفه قدماً وفضّله   جرى بذاك له في لوحه القلم
من معشر حبّهم دين وبغضهم   كر وتربهم ملجاً ومعتصم
لا يستطيع جواد بند غايتهم   ولا يدانم قوم وإن كرموا
هـم الغيوث إذا ما أزمة أزمت   والأشد أشد الشرّي والرأي محتدم
لاينقص المسر بشطا من أكفهم   بيان ذلك إن أثروا وإن عدموا
ما قال: لا، قد إلا في تشهده   لولا التشهد كانت لاؤه نعم
يستدفع السوة والبلوى بحبهم   ويسترق به الإحسان والنّعم

First and foremost it is them, after Allah, who are commemorated
at every beginning; and it is with them that every speech is concluded.

He who recognizes Allah, recognizes the supremacy of this one,
for religion itself was conferred upon the nations through his House.

Your quip of "Who is this!?" impugns him not,
for the Arabs know well the one whom you deny, as all others.

This only angered Hishām and he ordered that al-Farazdaq be seized and imprisoned somewhere between Mecca and Medina. The Imam Zayn al-ʿĀbidīn sent him 1000 gold coins, but al-Farazdaq refused to accept it saying: "I only spoke these words out of fury for the sake of Allah and His Messenger. I cannot accept any reward for it." To this ʿAlī b. al-Ḥusayn replied: "We the Ahl al-Bayt are a family which does not take back what we have already given," and so al-Farazdaq accepted it.

There were people in Medina who received their sustenance by night yet none knew whence it came. When Our Master the Imam Zayn al-ʿĀbidīn ﷺ passed away, it stopped coming and thus did they realise that it was from him.

His son Muḥammad al-Bāqir ﷺ was the foremost of men in asceticism and worship. The intensity of prostration had rent the skin of his forehead. He was the most learned person of his time. The Messenger of Allah ﷺ had named him "al-Bāqir." [The Companion] Jābir b. ʿAbdullāh al-Anṣārī came to him once when he was a child learning in the mosque school [*kuttāb*] and he said to him: "Your grandfather the Messenger of Allah ﷺ sends you greetings of peace." He said to him" "And upon my grandfather greetings of peace." It was asked of Jābir, "How can this be?" and he said, "Once I was sitting with the Messenger of Allah ﷺ and Ḥusayn was in his lap playing with him, when he said to me, 'O Jābir! He shall have a child whose name shall be ʿAlī. On the day of judgement a caller shall call out, 'Let the Prince of the Worshippers come forward!' and his son shall come forward. After him, there shall be born a child whose name will be Muḥammad al-Bāqir. He shall split knowledge wide open. Should you live to meet him then convey to him my greeting of peace.'" This was narrated from him by Abū Ḥanīfa as well as others.[50]

50 See Etan Kohlberg, "An Unusual Shīʿī isnād," *Israel Oriental Studies* 5 (1975):142–149 which is included as article VIII in his anthology *Belief and Law in Imāmī Shīʿism* (Aldershot: Variorum Reprints, 1991).

مــــقدم بعد ذكـر الله ذكرهم | في كل برّ، ومختوم به الكلم
مـن يعرف الله يعرف أولويّة ذا | الدين من بيت هـذا نالة الأمم
وليس قولك: من هـذا، بضائره | العرب تعرف من أنكرت والعجم

فغضب هشام وأمر بحبس الفرزدق بين مكّة والمدينة، فبعث إليه الإمام زين العابدين بألف دينار، فردّها وقال: «إنّما قلت هذا غضباً لله ولرسوله، فما أخذ عليه أجراً؛» فقال علي بن الحسين (عليه السلام): «نحن أهل بيت لا يعود إلينا ماخرج منّا؛» فقبلها الفرزدق.

وكان بالمدينة قوم يأتيهم رزقهم ليلاً ولا يعرفون ممّن هو، فلمّا مات مولانا الإمام زين العابدين (عليه السلام) انقطع ذلك عنهم، وعرفوا به أنّه كان منه.

وكان ابنه محمّد الباقر (عليه السلام) أعظم الناس زهداً وعبادة، بقر السجود جبهته، وكان أعلم أهل وقته ؛ سمّاه رسول الله ﷺ الباقر. وجاء جابر بن عبد الله الأنصاري إليه وهو صغير في الكتّاب، فقال له: «جدّك رسول الله ﷺ يسلّم عليك»، فقال: «وعلى جدّي السلام». فقيل لجابر: كيف هذا؟ قال: «كنت جالساً عند رسول الله ﷺ، والحسين في حجره وهو يلاعبه، فقال: «يا جابر! يولد له مولود اسمه عليّ، إذا كان يوم القيامة نادى مناد: ليقم سيّد العابدين! فيقوم ولده، ثم يولد له مولود اسمه محمّد الباقر، إنّه يبقر العلم بقراً، فإذا أدركته فأقرئه منّي السلام»؛ روى عنه أبو حنيفة وغيره.

His son was al-Ṣādiq. The most excellent of the people of his time and the most devoted of them to worship. Biographers have noted that he devoted himself to worship rather than the seeking of power. ʿUmar b. Abī l-Miqdām said: "Whenever I looked at Jaʿfar b. Muḥammad, I knew he was from the lineage of the prophets." It was through him that the law of the Imāmīs, the science of inner reality, and the true doctrine were disseminated. Never did he make a prognostication that did not come true, and it was thus that he became known as "The Truly Upright".

ʿAbdullāh b. al-Ḥasan gathered together the notables among the ʿAlids to offer the oath of fealty to his son. Al-Ṣādiq said to him, "This affair will not come to pass." That made him angry. To which he said, "It shall be for the one clad in the yellow tunic," by which he meant to allude to al-Manṣūr. When al-Manṣūr heard of this he rejoiced for he knew that it would come to pass and that the affair would reach him, but when he had to escape he used to say, "What of the word of their Ṣādiq?!" However, after that, the affair did alight upon him.

His son was Mūsā al-Kāẓim. He was known as "the righteous servant." He was the most devoted to worship among the people of his time. He would pass the night standing in worship and spend the day in fasting. He was known as "al-Kāẓim" because whenever someone would send him anything, he would always send him some money. His excellence has been acknowledged by both admirer and adversary.

The Ḥanbalī scholar Ibn al-Jawzī relates a story from Shaqīq al-Balkhī. He said: "I set out for the pilgrimage to Mecca in the year 149 AH. I reached al-Qādisiyya and lo and behold there was a young man beautiful of countenance, of deep complexion clad in a woollen garment draped in a cloak wearing leather shoes. He was seated away from the people. I thought to myself this young man must be one of the Sufis who wishes to exploit people, I swear by Allah I will certainly go to him and rebuke him. As soon as he saw me coming toward him, he said: 'O Shaqīq! *shun much suspicion for indeed some suspicion is itself a sin* [Qurʾān 49: 12].' I said to myself this is a righteous servant who has given expression to what was in my mind. I shall follow him and ask him to forgive me, but he disappeared from my sight."

"Once we reached Wāqiṣa, I found him at prayer, his limbs quaking and his tears flowing. I thought let me go up to him and apologise. He then concluded his prayer and said to me, 'O Shaqīq! *But I am Ever-Forgiving of anyone who repents and believes and does good, and afterward keeps to the right path.*' I thought he must be one of the saints known as the *abdāl*. He has divined my inner thoughts twice!"

وكان ابنه الصادق عليه السلام أفضل أهل زمانه وأعبدهم، قال علماء السيرة: انّه انشغل بالعبادة عن طلب الرياسة. قال عمرو بن أبي المقدام: «كنتُ إذا نظرت إلى جعفر بن محمّد علمت أنّه من سلالة النبيين». وهوالذي نشر منه فقه الإماميّة والمعارف الحقيقيّة والعقائد اليقينيّة، وكان لا يخبر بأمر إلا وقع، وبه سمّوه الصادق الأمين.

وكان عبد الله بن الحسن جمع أكابر العلويين للبيعة لولده فقال له الصادق عليه السلام: إنّ هذا الأمر لا يتم؟ فاغتاظ من ذلك، فقال إنّه لصاحب القباء الأصفر؛ وأشار بذلك إلى المنصور؛ فلمّا سمع المنصور بذلك فرح لعلمه بوقوع ما يخبر به، وعلم أنّ الأمر يصل إليه؛ ولمّا هرب كان يقول: أين قول صادقهم؟! وبعد ذلك انتهى الأمر إليه.

وكان ابنه موسى الكاظم عليه السلام يدعى بالعبد الصالح، كان أعبد أهل وقته، يقوم الليل ويصوم النهار؛ سمّي الكاظم لأنّه كان إذا بلغه عن أحد شيء بعث إليه بمال، ونقل فضله المخالف والمؤالف.

قال ابن الجوزي من الحنابلة عن شقيق البلخي، قال «خرجت حاجّاً في سنة تسع وأربعين ومائة، فنزلت القادسيّة فإذا شاب حسن الوجه شديد السمرة عليه ثوب صوف مشتمل بشملة، في رجليه نعلان، وقد جلس منفرداً عن الناس؛ فقلت في نفسي هذا الفتى من الصوفيّة يريد أن يكون كلاّ على الناس؛ والله لأمضينّ إليه وأوبّخه فدنوت منه، فلما رآني مقبلاً فقال: يا شقيق! اجتنبوا كثيراً من الظنّ إنّ بعض الظنّ إثم؟! فقلت في نفسي: هذا عبد صالح قد نطق على ما في خاطري، لألحقنه ولأسألنه أن يحللني، فغاب عن عيني.

فلمّا نزلنا (واقصة)، إذا به يصلّي وأعضاؤه تضطرب ودموعه تتحادر. فقلت: أمضي إليه وأعتذر؛ فأوجز في صلاته، ثم قال: يا شقيق، وإنّي لغفّار لمن تاب وأمن وعمل صالحاً ثم اهتدى؛ فقلت: هذا من الأبدال قد تكلّم على سرّي مرّتين.

"When we reached Zabāla, I found him standing over a well holding a water skin in his hand intending to draw some water. The water skin slipped out of his hand and fell into the well. He then turned heavenward and said: 'You are my Lord when I am thirsty for water and my sustenance when I desire food. My Master, I have no other water skin!' I swear by Allah that there and then the water level in the well rose and he was able to take hold of the water skin and fill it up. He also performed the ablution and then prayed four units. He then went toward a sand dune and began putting handfuls of sand into the water skin and drinking. I said: 'Feed me out of the abundance of what Allah has sustained you by and blessed you with.' He said: 'O Shaqīq! The blessings of Allah upon us, both the outwardly manifest and the inwardly hidden, never cease. Think better of your Lord!' He then passed me the water skin and I drank from it when lo and behold it became a sweetened barley beverage. I swear by Allah I have never drank anything more delicious or fragrant! I became satiated and satisfied. Thereafter I passed many a day without desiring food or drink. I did not see him again until we came to Mecca. I saw him there one night on the side of the Ka'ba with the rain gutter in the middle of the night. He was deeply immersed in prayer weeping and wailing. He remained in this condition until the night had passed. When the time for the morning prayer came, he remained seated in his place glorifying Allah. Then he stood up to offer the prayer. He then circled the Ka'ba seven times and went out. I followed him and saw that he had a large entourage, wealth, and servants in complete contrast to what I had seen of him during the journey. People were circling around him giving greetings and touching him in order to gain his blessing. I asked one of them who he was and was told, he is Mūsā b. Ja'far. I was amazed for such marvels could only be from such a Master." All of this was recorded by the Ḥanbalī scholar Ibn al-Jawzī.[51]

It was at his hand the Bishr al-Ḥāfī ("Bishr the Barefoot") repented. He was passing by his house in Baghdad when he heard the sounds of amusement, singing, and flutes coming from inside the dwelling. A slave girl came out to dispose of the kitchen refuse. As she threw it in the alleyway, he said to her, "Is the master of the house a free man or a slave?" She said to him, "A free man, of course!" He said, "You speak the truth, for had he been a slave he would have feared his Master!"

---

51 See Sibṭ Ibn al-Jawzī, *Tadhkirat khawāṣṣ al-umma fī khaṣā'is al-a'imma* edited by al-Sayyid Muḥammad Ṣādiq Baḥr al-'Ulūm (Tehran: Maktabat Nineveh al-Ḥadītha, n. d.), 348–349.

فلمّا نزلنا زبالة إذا به قائم على البئر وبيده ركوة يريد أن يستقي ماء، فسقطت الركوة في البئر، فرفع طرفه إلى السماء وقال. أنت ربّي اذا ظمئن إلى الماء، وقولي اذا اردت الطعام، يا سيدي ما لي سواها ! قال شقيق: فوالله لقد رأيت البئر قد ارتفع ماؤها، فأخذ الركوة وملأها وتوضّأ وصلّى أربع ركعات، ثمّ مال إلى كثيب رمل هناك، فجعل يقبض بيده ويطرحه في الركوة ويشرب. فقلت: أطعمني من فضل ما رزقك الله وأنعم الله عليك ! فقال: يا شقيق لم تزل نعم الله علينا ظاهرة وباطنة، فأحسن ظنّك بربّك؛ ثمّ ناولني الركوة فشربت منها فإذا سويق وسكر ما شربت – والله – ألذّ منه وأطيب ريحاً؛ فشبعت ورويت وأقمت أياماً لا أشتهي طعاماً ولاشراباً. ثم لم أره حتى دخل مكّة، فرأيته ليلة إلى جانب قبّة السراب نصف الليل يصلّي بخشوع وأنين وبكاء، فلم يزل كذلك حتّى ذهب الليل؛ فلما طلع الفجر جلس في مصلاّه يسبّح، ثم قام إلى صلاة الفجر وطاف بالبيت أسبوعاً، وخرج فتبعته؛ فإذا له حاشية وأموال وغلمان، وهو على خلاف ما رأيته في الطريق، ودار به الناس يسلّمون عليه ويتبرّكون به؛ فقلت لبعضهم: من هذا ؟ فقال: موسى بن جعفر؛ فقلت: قد عجبت أن تكون هذه العجائب إلّا لمثل هذا السيّد».

رواه الحنبلي.

وعلى يده عليه السلام تاب بشر الحافي لأنه اجتاز على داره ببغداد، فسمع الملاهي وأصوات الغناء والقصب تخرج من تلك الدار؛ فخرجت جارية وبيدها قامة البقل، فرمت بها في الدرب؛ فقال لها: يا جارية! صاحب هذه الدار حرّ أم عبد ؟ فقالت: بل حر فقال: صدّقت؛ لو كان عبداً خاف من مولاه ! فلمّا دخلت قال مولاها وهو على مائدة السكر: ما أبطأك علينا ؟ فقالت: حدّثني رجل بكذا وكذا، فخرج حافياً حتّى لقي مولانا الكاظم عليه السلام فتاب على يده.

When she went back inside, her master, who was at a table with intoxicants, asked her, "What took you so long?" When she told him that a man told me such-and such, he ran out barefoot until he caught up with Our Master al-Kāẓim ﷷ and repented at his hand.

His son was ʿAlī al-Riḍā ﷷ. He was the foremost ascetic and learned man of his time. Many scholars amongst the Sunnīs studied with him. Al-Ma'mūn designated him as his successor due to the perfection and excellence of his learning. He once admonished his brother Zayd thus, "O Zayd! How will you face the Messenger of Allah ﷺ when you have shed blood, frightened travellers, and taken hold of wealth unlawfully? The fools among the people of Kufa have tempted you. The Messenger of Allah ﷺ did say that "Fāṭima has guarded her honour, and so Allah has forbidden her descendants the Fire." I swear by Allah that they did not attain to that except by obedience to Allah. If you wish to attain by transgression against Allah what they attained by obedience to Him, then you must deem yourself more worthy of honour by Allah than them.

Al-Ma'mūn minted gold and silver coins bearing his name. He sent out instructions to the farthest reaches that allegiance should be sworn to him and that black [the colour of the official Abbasid attire] be replaced with green [the official colour of the Imams]. The renowned poet Abū Nuwās was asked why he did not compose verses in praise of al-Riḍā ﷷ. He replied in verse:

It was said to me: "You are the foremost of men without exception
in poetic expression and extempore recitation.

To you belong the gems of ornate speech:
pearls bursting forth in the hands of those who pluck them.

Why then did you leave off versifying the praises of the son of Mūsā
when so many good qualities are united in him?

I answered: "I cannot versify the praises of an Imam
whose forefather was served by Angel Jibrīl.

وكان ولده عليّ الرضا عليه السلام أزهد أهل زمانه وأعلمهم؛ وأخذ عنه فقهاء الجمهور كثيراً، وتولّا المأمون لعلمه بما هوعليه من الكمال والفضل؛ ووعظ يوماً أخاه زيداً فقال له يا زيد ما أنت قائل لرسول الله صلى الله عليه وآله إذا سكت الدماء وأخفت السبيل وأخذت المال من غير حلّه؟! غرّك حماء أهل الكوفه، وقد قال رسول الله صلى الله عليه وآله: إنّ فاطمة أحصنت فرجها فحرّم الله ذرّيتها على النار، والله ما نالوا ذلك إلّا بطاعة الله؛ فإن أردت أن تنال بمعصية الله ما تنالوه بطاعته، إنّك إذا لأكرم على الله منهم.

وضرب المأمون اسمه على الدراهم والدنانير، وكتب إلى الآفاق ببيعته وطرح السواد ولبس الخضرة.

وقيل لأبي نواس لم لا تمدح الرضا عليه السلام؟ فقال:

قيل لي أنت أفضل النّاس طرّاً	في المعاني وفي الكلام البديه
لك من جوهر الكلام بديع	يثمر الدر في يدي مجتنيه
فلما ذا تركت مدح ابن موسى	والخصال التي تجمّعن فيه
قلت لا أستطيع مدح إمامٍ	كان جبريل خادماً لأبيه

His son Muḥammad al-Jawād followed the path of his father in knowledge, piety, and generosity. When his father al-Riḍā passed away, al-Ma'mūn became enamoured of him because of his knowledge, religiosity, and abundant intelligence despite his young age. He wanted him to marry his daughter Umm al-Faḍl. He had given his daughter Umm Ḥabīb in marriage to his father al-Riḍā. That had infuriated the members of the Abbasid house who looked upon themselves as being better than him. They feared that rule would pass away from them and that he would follow him just as he had followed his father. His subordinates gathered and asked him to drop the idea, telling him that he was young and had no knowledge. He told them that he knew better and that if they were in doubt they could put him to the test. They set aside a great amount of wealth for Yaḥyā b. Aktham [the chief Qāḍī] if he could set a question which he would not be able to answer. They set a date and al-Ma'mūn summoned him and the Qāḍī [Yaḥyā b. Aktham] along with the Abbasid notables. "May I ask you a question?" said the Qāḍī. "Ask!" he replied. "What is your verdict regarding a person in the state of *iḥrām* who kills game?" "Did he kill it within the sacred precinct or outside of it? Was it done knowingly or unknowingly? Was it small game or large? Was the person free or slave? Young or old? Was the game fowl or another species?"

At this Yaḥyā b. Aktham was most astonished and visibly shocked and all those present realised this. Al-Ma'mūn said to his household, "Do you now understand what you had denied?" He then went up to the Imam and said, "Are you ready for marriage?" to which he said, "Yes" and then he said to him, "In that case, recite the marriage sermon on your own behalf." He did so and the marriage was concluded for 500 silver coins which was the amount of the dowry of his grandmother Fāṭima and so he married the daughter of al-Ma'mūn.

وكان ولده محمّد الجواد عليه السلام على منهاج أبيه في العلم والتقوى والجود. ولمّا مات أبوه الرضا عليه السلام شغف به المأمون لكثرة علمه ودينه ووفور عقله مع صغر سنّه؛ فأراد أن يزوجه ابنته أم الفضل، وكان قد زوّج أباه الرضا عليه السلام بابنته أم حبيب. فغلظ ذلك على العبّاسيين واستكبروه، وخافوا أن يخرج الأمر منهم وأن يتابعه كما تابع أباه؛ فاجتمع الأدنون منه وسألوه ترك ذلك، وقالوا إنّه صغير لا علم عنده؛ فقال: أنا اعرف به. فإن شئتم فامتحنوه فرضوا بذلك، وجعلوا ليحيى بن أكثم مالاً كثيراً على امتحانه في مسألة يعجزه فيها؛ فتواعدوا إلى يوم فأحضره المأمون وحضر القاضي وجماعة العبّاسيين. فقال القاضي: أسألك عن شيء؟ فقال عليه السلام له سل. فقال: ما تقول في محرم قتل صيداً؟ فقال له الإمام عليه السلام أقتله في حلّ أو حرم؟ عالماً كان أو جاهلاً؟ مبتدئاً بقتله أو عائداً؟ من صغار الصيد كان أو من كبارها؟ عبداً كان المحرم أو حرّاً؟ صغيراً كان أو كبيراً؟ من ذوات الطير كان الصيد أو من غيرها؟

فتحيّر يحيى بن أكثم وبان العجز في وجهه، حتّى عرف جماعة أهل المجلس أمره؛ فقال المأمون لأهل بيته: عرفتم الآن ما كنتم تنكرونه؟! ثمّ أقبل على الإمام فقال: أتخطب؟ فقال: نعم. فقال اخطب لنفسك خطبة النكاح، فخطب وعقد على خمسمائة درهم جياداً مهر جدّته فاطمة عليها السلام، ثم تزوّج بها.

His son was ʿAlī al-Hādī ﷺ. He was also known as "al-ʿAskarī" because al-Mutawakkil had him expelled from Medina to Baghdad and from there to Samarra where he resided at a place nearby called "al-ʿAskar." Ultimately, he moved to Samarra lived there for 20 years and nine months. Al-Mutawakkil had had him expelled because of his hatred for ʿAlī ﷺ. He had been told of the high status of ʿAlī in Medina and how the people were inclined toward him. He feared him and so he summoned Yaḥyā b. Harthama and ordered him to expel him. This caused a tumult among the people of Medina because they feared for his life, and because he had been kind to them and devoted to worship in the mosque. So Yaḥyā swore that no harm would come to him. He searched his house, but he found nothing but manuscripts of the Qurʾān, supplications, and scholarly texts. This made him hold him in awe and he took the responsibility of personally waiting on him. When they reached Baghdad he first went to see the governor, Ishāq b. Ibrāhīm al-Ṭāhirī who told him, "O Yaḥyā, this man is a descendent of the Messenger of Allah ﷺ, and al-Mutawakkil is as you know him to be. He will kill him at the slightest provocation and then you will have made an enemy of the Messenger of Allah ﷺ." Yaḥyā said to him, "By Allah, I only have the best expectation from him."

When he went to see al-Mutawakkil he told him of his excellent character, his asceticism, and his scrupulous piety. So al-Mutawakkil gave him a place of honour. Sometime later al-Mutwakkil fell ill. He made a vow that if he recovered he would give a large sum in charity. He then asked the legal scholars about this but found no answer among them. So he sent someone to ask ʿAlī al-Hādī. He told him: "Give in charity 83 silver coins." Al-Mutwakkil enquired about the reason. He told him, "Because of the saying of the Exalted *Indeed Allah granted you victory in many places.*[52] These places in all are this number because the Prophet participated in 27 expeditions and sent out 56 combat units.

52 Qurʾān 9:25.

وكان ولده عليّ الهادي عليه السلام ويقال له العسكريّ لأن المتوكّل أشخصه من المدينة إلى بغداد، ثم منها إلى سرّ من رأى، فأقام بموضع عندها يقال له العسكر؛ ثم انتقل إلى سرّ من رأى فأقام بها عشرين سنة وتسعة أشهر، وإنّما أشخصه المتوكّل لأنه كان يبغض عليّا عليه السلام فبلغه مقام عليّ بالمدينة وميّل الناس إليه، فخاف منه، فدعا يحيى بن هرثمة فأمره بإشخاصه؛ فضجّ أهل المدينة لذلك خوفاً عليه لأنّه كان محسناً إليهم ملازماً للعبادة في المسجد؛ فحلف لهم يحيى أنه لا مكروه عليه، ثمّ فتّش منزله فلم يجد فيه سوى مصاحف وأدعية وكتب العلم (فعظم في عينه) وتولّى خدمته بنفسه. فلمّا قدم بغداد بدأ بإسحاق بن ابراهيم الطاهري والى بغداد فقال له: يا يحيى، هذا الرجل قد ولده رسول الله صلى الله عليه وآله والمتوكّل من تعلم، فإن حرّضته عليه قتله، وكان رسول الله صلى الله عليه وآله خصمك. فقال له يحيى: والله ما وقعت منه إلّا على خير.

قال: فلمّا دخلت على المتوكّل أخبرته بحسن سيرته وزهده وورعه فأكرمه المتوكّل. ثمّ مرض المتوكّل فنذر إن عوفي تصدّق بدراهم كثيرة، فسأل الفقهاء عن ذلك فلم يجد عندهم جواباً؛ فبعث إلى عليّ الهادي عليه السلام يسأله، فقال: تصدّق بثلاثة وثمانين درهمًا؛ فسأله المتوكّل عن السبب فقال: لقوله تعالى: ﴿لقد نصركم الله في مواطن كثيرة﴾، وكانت المواطن هذه الجملة، فإنّ النبي صلى الله عليه وآله غزا سبعاً وعشرين غزاة وبعث ستا وخمسين سرية.

Al-Masʿūdī relates that someone told al-Mutawakkil that ʿAlī b. Muḥammad was stockpiling weapons in his house from his supporters among the people of Qom and that he was planning to seize the throne by force. So he sent out a detachment of Turkish soldiery who raided his house at night but found nothing. They found him in a closed room reciting the Qurʾān, covered in wool, seated upon on the sand and pebble floor, wholly focused on Allah. They seized him in this condition and went to al-Mutawakkil. He was brought before him when he was in a gathering in which alcohol was being consumed and the glass was in al-Mutawakkil's hand. He showed him great respect and had him seated next to him and presented the glass to him. He said: "By Allah! Alcohol has never ever entered my body, desist then!" So, he excused him and said, "Let me hear your voice." So he ﷺ recited: *How many were the gardens and springs they left behind...*[53]

He said: "Recite some poetry." To which he replied, "I have little poetry." He said: "You must do so." So he recited these lines:

They passed their nights on the summits of lofty peaks guarded by
mighty men, yet these summits availed them not;

for they were made low after having gloried in their strongholds,
and made their abodes in dry ditches into which they were lowered.

Someone called out, screaming, after their burial:
"Alas, where are your bracelets, and crowns, and magnificent garments?"

"Where are those faces, so joyous?"
"Now worn out and draped over with shrouds?"

The graves responded on their behalf when they were asked:
"Those faces now are where maggots fight it out."

"They spent an eternity in eating and drinking,"
"yet after such a prolonged feast, now it is they who are the eaten."

At this al-Mutwakkil wept so much that his beard became soaked with his tears.

53 Qurʾān 44:25.

قال المسعودي نمي إلى المتوكل بعليّ بن محمّد أنّ في منزله سلاحاً من شيعته من أهل قم وأنّه عازم على الملك؛ فبعث إليه جماعة من الأتراك فهجموا على داره ليلاً فلم يجدوا شيئاً، ووجدوه في بيت معلق عليه وهو يقرأ وعليه مدرعة من صوف، وهو جالس على الرمل والحصباء متوجّه إلى الله تعالى يتلو القرآن؛ فحمل على حاله تلك إلى المتوكّل، فأدخل عليه وهو في مجلس الشراب والكأس في يد المتوكّل؛ فأعظمه وأجلسه إلى جانبه وناوله الكأس، فقال: والله ما خامر لحمي ودمي قط فأعفني! فأعفاه.

وقال له: أسمعني صوتاً، فقال ﴿كم تركوا من جنات وعيون﴾ . . . الآيات؛ فقال: أنشدني شعراً، فقال: إني قليل الرواية للشعر، فقال: لابدّ من ذلك، فأنشده:

باتُوا على قُلَلِ الأجبال تحرُسُهُم … غُلْبُ الرِّجَال فما أغنتهم القُلَلُ
واستُنزِلُوا بعدَ عزٍّ مِن مَعَاقِلِهِم … وأُسكِنُوا حُفْراً يابئسَ ما نَزَلُوا
ناداهُم صارِخٌ من بعدِ دَفْنِهِم … أينَ الأساوِر والتِيجَانُ والحُلَلُ
أين الوجوه التي كانت منعّمةً … من دونها تُضرَبُ الأَستارُ والكُلَلُ
فأفصَحَ القَبرُ عنهم حين سائلَه … تلك الوجوه عليها الدُودُ يَقْتَتِلُ
قد طالما أَكَلُوا دهراً وقَد شَرِبُوا … فأَصْبَحُوا بعدَ طُولِ الأكل قد أُكِلُوا

فبكى المتوكّل حتى بلّت دموعه لحيته.

His son al-Ḥasan al-ʿAskarī ﷺ was a scholar, a noble person, an ascetic; the best of his age. The Sunnīs transmitted a great deal from him.

His son is Our Master the Imam Mahdī Muḥammad ﷺ. Ibn al-Jawzī relates through his chain of transmitters from Ibn ʿUmar who said, "The Messenger of Allah ﷺ said: 'There shall come forth at the end of time a man from my progeny whose name shall be as my name and his patronym shall be my patronym and who shall fill the world with justice just as it had been filled with oppression aforetime. That is none other than the Mahdī.'"[54]

These then are the infallible Imams who reached the peak of perfection. They never became involved in what other supposed Imams occupied themselves with by way of dominion, all sorts of sins, vanities, wine parties, and debauchery with even their own relations, as has all been widely reported by people.

The Imāmīs say, let Allah then be the Judge between us and them and He is the best of judges. Someone put it so well when he said:

If you wish to put yourself at ease regarding which way to follow
and to know how people have transmitted reports

Then discard the words of al-Shāfiʿī and Mālik
and Aḥmad and what has been related from Kaʿab al-Aḥbār

And give your loyalty to a people whose words and speech
are "It was conveyed to us by our Grandfather from Jibrīl
from the Creator."

I do not think that any well-educated person who has studied these schools of doctrine has ever chosen to follow anything but the Imāmī school inwardly even if outwardly desire for worldly gain compelled him to follow one of the other schools since they have established centres of learning and endowments in order to perpetuate the Abbasid propaganda and fortify their claim to the Imama among the populace.

54 See Sibṭ Ibn al-Jawzī, *Tadhkirat khawāṣṣ al-umma fī khaṣāʾis al-aʾimma*, edited by al-Sayyid Muḥammad Ṣādiq Baḥr al-ʿUlūm (Tehran: Maktabat Nineveh al-Ḥadītha, nd), 363–364.

وكان ولده الحسن العسكري عليه السلام عالماً فاضلاً زاهداً أفضل أهل زمانه، روت عنه العامّة كثيراً.

وولده مولانا الإمام المهديّ محمّد عليه السلام. روى ابن الجوزي بإسناده إلى ابن عمر قال: قال رسول الله صلى الله عليه وآله: «يخرج في آخر الزمان رجلٌ من ولدي إسمُهُ كإسمِي وكنيته كنيتي، يملأ الأرض عدلا كما ملئت جورًا»، فذلك هو المهديّ.

فهؤلاء الأئمّة المعصومون الذين بلغوا الغاية في الكمال، ولم يتّخذوا ما اتّخذ غيرهم من الأئمة المشتغلين بالملك وأنواع المعاصي والملاهي وشرب الخمور والفجور حتّى بأقاربهم على ما هو المتواتر من الناس.

قالت الإماميّة: فالله يحكم بيننا وبين هؤلاء وهو خير الحاكمين، وما أحسن قول بعض الناس:

إذا شئت أن ترضى لنفسك مذهباً ... وتعلم أن النّاس في نقل أخبار
فَدَعْ عنك قول الشافعي ومالكٍ ... وأحمدَ والمرويّ عن كعب أحبار
ووالِ أناساً قَولُهم وحَدِيثُهم ... روى جَدُّنا عن جبرئيلَ عن الباري

وما أظن أحداً من المحصّلين وقف على هذه المذاهب فاختار غير مذهب الإماميه باطناً، وإن كان في الظاهر يصير إلى غيره طلباً للدنيا، حيث وضعت لهم المدارس والربط والأوقاف حتّى تستمر لبني العبّاس الدعوة ويشيّدوا للعامّة اعتقاد إمامتهم.

I have come across many who inwardly profess the doctrine of the Imāmīs, but are prevented from making it public by their love of the world and desire for position. I came to know of one of the leading Ḥanbalī scholars who told me that he adhered to the Imāmī school. When I asked why then did he teach the Ḥanbalī school, he told me that there are no monthly stipends and provisions for income in your school. When one of the most prominent teachers of the Shāfiʿī school in our time died it came to be that he had instructed that one of the Shīʿī believers manage the affairs of his washing and shrouding, his burial in the shrine of al-Kāẓim ﷺ, and that he bear witness on his behalf that he had been an Imāmī.

وكثيراً ما رأينا من يدين في الباطن بمذهب الإماميّة، ويمنعه عن إظهاره حبّ الدنيا وطلب الرياسة؛ وقد رأيت بعض أئمّة الحنابلة يقول: إنّي على مذهب الإماميّة، فقلتُ له: لم تدرس على مذهب الحنابلة؟ فقال: ليس في مذهبكم البغلات والمشاهرات. وكان أكبر مدّرسي الشافعيّة في زماننا حيث توفيّ أوصى بأن يتولّى أمره في غسله وتجهيزه بعض المؤمنين، وأن يدفن في مشهد الكاظم عليه السلام وأشهد عليه أنّه على دين الإماميّة.

The Fifth Reason

The Imāmīs are zealous for nothing but the truth. Al-Ghazālī and al-Muzanī — both scholars of the Shāfiʿī school — mentioned that the correct practice was for graves to be level with the ground. However, since this was a practice taken up by the "Rāfiḍa," they abandoned the practice and advocated raising them up.

Al-Zamakhsharī — a scholar of the Ḥanafī school — mentioned in his commentary on the statement of the Exalted: *He it is who sends benedictions upon you as do His angels*[55] that on the basis of this verse it is permitted to send benedictions on any Muslim person, but because the "Rāfiḍa" practiced this regarding the names of their Imams, he forbade it.

The author of *The Guide* (*al-Hidāya*)[56] — who was a Ḥanafī — said that the proper practice according to Islamic law was to wear rings on the right hand. However, since this was a practice adhered to by the "Rāfiḍa," he changed this to wearing rings on the left hand. Such examples are many.

Who is it then that has changed the Sharīʿa, altered the rules which the Prophet ﷺ instituted, and chosen to go against what is correct; all out of obstinate opposition to a particular group? Is it permitted to follow them and adhere to what they uphold despite them having introduced practices which even they acknowledge as being innovations in religion when it was the Prophet ﷺ himself who said: "Every innovation in religion is misguidance, and every misguidance leads to the Fire," and also said: "Whomsoever introduces into this religion of ours that which has no part in it, it shall revert back to him." Yet, if they are prevented from introducing such innovations their souls become distraught and their hearts are troubled by it. This is what happened in the case with the mention of the names of the caliphs in their Friday sermons even though it is unanimously acknowledged that this was never done in the time of Prophet ﷺ, nor in the time of any of the Companions or the generation immediately after them, nor in the Umayyad period, nor in the early Abbasid period, rather it was something innovated by al-Manṣūr due to what happened between him the descendants of ʿAlī. So he said: "By Allah! No matter what I will surely exalt the Banū Taym [the tribe of Abū Bakr] and Banū ʿAdī [the tribe of ʿUmar] above them, and he mentioned the Companions in his Friday sermon and this innovation has continued down to our own time.

55 Qurʾān 33:56.

56 The *Hidāya* is a major work of Ḥanafī jurisprudence authored by Burhān al-Dīn al-Marghinānī (d. 593/1197).

الوجه الخامس

إن الإماميّة لم يذهبوا إلى التعصّب في غير الحقّ، فقد ذكر الغزالي والمتولي وكانا إمامين للشافعيّة أنّ تسطيح القبور هوالمشروع، لكن لمّا جعلته الرافضة شعاراً لهم عدلنا عنه إلى التسنيم.

وذكر الزمخشري وكان من أئمة الحنفيّة في تفسير قوله تعالى ﴿هو الّذي يصلّي عليكم وملائكته﴾ أنّه يجوز بمقتضى هذه الآية أن يصلّى على أحاد المسلمين لكن لمّا اتخذت الرافضة ذلك في أئمّتهم منعناه.

وقال مصنّف الهداية من الحنفيّة: المشروع التختّم في اليمين، لكن لمّا اتخذته الرافضة عادة جعلنا التختم في اليسار؛ وأمثال ذلك كثير.

فانظر إلى من يغيّر الشريعة ويبدّل الأحكام التي ورد بها النبي ﷺ ويذهب إلى ضدّ الصواب؛ معاندة لقوم معيّنين، هل يجوز اتّباعه والمصير إلى أقواله؟ مع أنّهم ابتدعوا أشياء اعترفوا بأنّها بدعة، وأنّ النبيّ ﷺ «قال كلّ بدعة ضلالة وكلّ ضلالة فإنّ مصيرها إلى النار؛» وقال ﷺ «من أدخل في ديننا ما ليس منه فهو ردّ عليه»، ولو ردّوا عنها كرهته نفوسهم ونفرت قلوبهم، كذكر الخلفاء في خطبتهم، مع أنّه بالإجماع لم يكن في زمن النبي ولا في زمن أحد من الصحابة والتابعين، ولا في زمن بني أميّة ولا في صدر ولاية العباسيّين، بل هو شيء أحدثه المنصور لمَا وقع بينه وبين العلويّة، فقال: والله لأرغمنّ أنفي وأنوفهم وأرفع عليهم بني تيم وعدي، وذكر الصحابة في خطبته، واستمرّت هذه البدعة إلى هذا الزمان.

There is also the example of wiping the feet with wet hands (rather than washing them) in the ritual ablution which Allah stipulated unequivocally in His Mighty Book: *O you who believe! When you stand up for the prayer, wash your faces and your hands up to the elbows, and wipe a part of your heads and your feet, up to the ankles.*[57] Ibn ʿAbbās explained: "Two pairs of limbs, one pair washed, the other pair wiped over." Yet, they changed this and made washing obligatory. There is also the example of the two *mutʿas*[58] which are both mentioned in the Qurʾān. Thus, He said regarding *mutʿat al-ḥajj*: *...then whoever enjoys from the ʿUmra to the Ḥajj should make a sacrifice according to their means.*[59] The Prophet regretted ﷺ losing this when he performed the conjuncted pilgrimage (*ḥajj al-qirān*), and said: "Had I realised what I now realise, I would not have offered the sacrifice [and completed the state of *iḥrām*].[60]

Regarding *mutʿat al-nisāʾ*, He said: *For the enjoyment you have had from them thereby, give them their dowries.*[61] This practice continued throughout the time of the Prophet ﷺ, as well as during the reign of Abū Bakr, and for part of the reign of ʿUmar until he ascended the *minbar* and announced: "The two *mutʿas* which were practiced in the period of the Prophet, I now hereby ban and will punish those who practice them."[62]

57 Qurʾān 5:6.

58 The two *mutʿas* is a reference to *nikāh al-mutʿa* (temporary marriage) or *mutʿat al-nisāʾ* (the *mutʿa* of women) and *ḥajj al-tamattuʿ* or *mutʿat al-ḥajj* (the form of the Hajj pilgrimage which includes within its rites the ʿUmra).

59 Qurʾān 2:196.

60 Abū ʿAbdullāh Muḥammad b. Ismāʿīl al-Bukhārī, *al-Jāmiʿ al-musnad al-ṣaḥīḥ al-mukhtaṣar* (henceforth *al-Ṣaḥīh*) (Vaduz, Lichtenstein: Thesaurus Islamicus Foundation, 2000), 3:1460, *ḥadīths* 7314, 7315; Abū Dāwūd Sulaymān b. al-Ashʿath b. Shaddād al-Azdī, *al-Sunan* (Vaduz, Lichtenstein: Thesaurus Islamicus Foundation, 2000), 1:306, *ḥadīth* 1791; Jamāl al-Dīn al-Mizzī, *Tuḥfat al-ashrāf*, entry 16559 and entry 2405.

61 Qurʾān 4:24.

62 See for example Abū l-Ḥusayn Muslim b. al-Hajjāj al-Naysābūrī, *al-Jāmiʿ al-ṣaḥīḥ* (henceforth *al-Ṣaḥīḥ*) (Vaduz, Lichtenstein: Thesaurus Islamicus Foundation, 2000), 1:571, *ḥadīths* 3482, 3483.

وكمسح الرجلين الذي نصّ عليه الله تعالى في كتابه العزيز، فقال ﴿فاغسلوا وجوهكم وأيديكم إلى المرافق وامسحوا برؤسكم وأرجلكم إلى الكعبين﴾، قال ابن عبّاس: عضوان مغسولان وعضوان ممسوحان؛ فغيّروه وأوجبوا الغسل؛ وكالمتعتين اللّتين ورد بها القرآن، فقال في متعة الحجّ: ﴿من تمتع بالعمرة إلى الحجّ فما أستيسر من الهدي﴾، وتأسّف النبي ﷺ على فواتها لمّا حجّ قارناً، وقال: لو استقبلت من أمري ما استدبرت لما سقت الهدي.

وقال في متعة النساء ﴿فما استمتعتم به منهنّ فاتوهنّ أجورهنّ﴾، واستمرّ فعلها مدّة زمان النبيّ ﷺ ومدّة خلافة أبي بكر وبعض خلافة عمر، إلى أن صعد المنبر وقال: متعتان كانتا على عهد رسول الله ﷺ أنا أنهى عنها وأعاقب عليها

Another example is that Abū Bakr prevented Fāṭima ﷺ from her inheritance.[63] She said to him: "O Ibn Abī Quḥāfa! So! Your father can have heirs, but my father cannot?!" Here he resorted to a report which only he transmits — and which he adores since he was eligible to receive alms — claiming the Prophet to have uttered: "We the assembly of the prophets have no heirs. Whatever we leave behind is alms." Yet, the Qurʾān contradicts that because Allah says: *Allah commands you regarding your children...*[64] and this command was not meant for everyone else in the *umma* while excluding the Prophet ﷺ, and He repudiates this narration of theirs when He says: *and Sulaymān inherited from Dāwūd.*[65] Allah also said about Zakariyya: *And indeed I fear for my heirs after me, and my wife is barren, bestow then upon me out of your munificence a successor who will be my heir as well as an heir of the House of Yaʿqūb.*[66]

When Fāṭima ﷺ mentioned that the Messenger of Allah ﷺ had granted her Fadak, he said to her: "Bring me anyone who can bear witness to the that!" So she came to him with Umm Ayman and she bore witness to that; to which he said: "She is a woman whose testimony cannot be accepted," despite the fact that all have related that the Messenger of Allah ﷺ had said regarding her, "Umm Ayman is of the people of Paradise."

63 An allusion to the Grove of Fadak. On Fadak and the Prophet's inheritance see J. Schleifer, "Fadak" in *Encyclopaedia of Islam*, First Edition, 3:35 and L. Veccia Vaglieri, "Fadak" in *Encyclopaedia of Islam*, New Edition, 725–727; al-Balādhurī, *Futūḥ al-buldān*, edited by M. J. de Goeje as *Liber Expungnationis Regionum* (Leiden: E. J. Brill, 1866), 23–29; also English trans. by Phillip K. Hitti, *The Origins of the Islamic State* (New York: Columbia University Press, 1916), 1:42–50; Muḥammad b. Jarīr al-Ṭabarī (d. 310/923), *Taʾrīkh al-rusul wa-l-mulūk*, edited by M. J. de Goeje *et al* (Leiden: 1879–1901), 1:1825 (= edited by Muḥammad Abū l-Faḍl Ibrāhīm [Cairo: Dār al-Maʿārif, 1960], 3:207–208); Muḥammad b. Saʿd (d. 230/845), *al-Ṭabaqāt*, edited by Eduard Sachau (Leiden: E. J. Brill, 1905–1940), vol. 2, pt. 2, 86; ʿUmar b. Shabba (d. 262/875), *Taʾrīkh al-Madīnat al-Munawwara*, edited by Fahīm Maḥmūd Shaltut (Beirut: Dār al-Turāth, 1410/1990), 192–202. See also Wilferd Madelung, *The Succession to Muḥammad. A Study of the Early Caliphate* (Cambridge: Cambridge University press, 1997), 360–363. The issue of Fadak is also important in the formation of the Islamic law of inheritance. In this regard see Ignaz Goldziher, *Muslim Studies*, translated and edited by S. M. Stern (Chicago: Aldine-Atherton, 1971), 2:102–103; Wilferd Madelung, "Shīʿī Attitudes to Women as reflected in Fiqh," in *Society and Sexes in Medieval Islam*, edited by A. Lutfi al-Sayyid-Marsot (Malibu, California: Undena Publications, 1979), 74–75; David S. Powers, *Studies in Qurʾān and Ḥadīth. The Formation of the Islamic Law of Inheritance* (Berkeley, California: University of California Press, 1986), 123–128.

64 Qurʾān 4:11.

65 Qurʾān 27:16.

66 Qurʾān 19:5-6.

ومنع أبو بكر فاطمة عليها السلام إرثها فقالت له: يابن أبي قحافة! أترث أباك ولا أرث أبي؟! والتجأ في ذلك إلى رواية انفرد بها - وكان هو الغريم لها لأنّ الصدقة تحلّ له - أنّ النبيّ ﷺ قال: نحن معاشر الأنبياء لا نورّث ما تركناه صدقة، على ما رووه عنه؛ والقرآن يخالف ذلك لأنّ الله تعالى قال ﴿يوصيكم الله في أولادكم﴾، ولم يجعل الله تعالى ذلك خاصّاً بالأمّة دونه ﷺ، وكذّب روايتهم فقال تعالى ﴿وورث سليمن داود﴾، وقال تعالى عن زكريّا ﴿وإنّي خفت الموالي من ورائي وكانت امرأتي عاقرا فهب لي من لّدنك وليا * يرثني ويرث من ءال يعقوب﴾.

ولما ذكرت فاطمة عليها السلام أنّ رسول الله ﷺ وهبها فدكاً قال لها: هات أسود أو أحمر يشهد لك بذلك! فجاءت بأمّ أيمن فشهدت لها بذلك فقال: امرأة لا يقبل قولها؛ وقد رووا جميعاً أنّ رسول الله ﷺ قال أمّ أيمن امرأة من أهل الجنّة؛

Then the Commander of the Faithful عليه السلام came and bore witness. To this he said: "This is your husband; he just wants it for himself. We cannot accept his testimony in your favour;" this despite the fact that all have narrated that the Messenger of Allah ﷺ said about him: "'Alī is with the truth and the truth is with 'Alī, going with him wherever he goes and will not leave him until the two reach me at the Heavenly Pool." This angered Fāṭima عليها السلام and she left swearing never to speak to him or to his friend [by which she meant 'Umar] until she was re-united with her father and complained to him. So, when she was on her deathbed, she directed 'Alī to bury her by night and not permit any of them to pray over her.

All have narrated that the Prophet ﷺ said: "O Fāṭima! Truly Allah is angered at that which you are angered at, and is satisfied with that which you are satisfied." All have also narrated that he ﷺ said: "Fāṭima is part-and-parcel of me, whomsoever harms her has harmed me, and whomsoever seeks to harm me seeks to harm Allah." Were this report [of Abū Bakr] to be true then it would not have been permissible for the Prophet ﷺ to have left behind a mule, his sword and his turban for the Commander of the Faithful عليه السلام, and when it was judged that these belonged to him, al-'Abbās would not have disputed the claim. Yet, he [i.e. Abū Bakr] would have the Ahl al-Bayt — whom Allah had declared in His Book to be purified of all filth — [in seeking the inheritance of Fadak] to commit a forbidden act, because alms are forbidden to them [and he claimed Fadak was alms].

After this the revenue from Bahrain arrived with Jābir b. 'Abdullāh al-Anṣārī. He told him that "The Prophet ﷺ said to me: 'When the revenue of Bahrain arrives, know that I have dispersed it to you' — thrice repeating this." He said: "Take it all then." And so Abū Bakr appropriated funds from the treasury of the Muslims with no clear evidence save this mere claim.

All of them have related that the Prophet ﷺ said concerning Abū Dharr: "Never has the earth carried nor has the sky covered one more true in speech than Abū Dharr," and yet they never referred to him by the title of *al-Ṣiddīq* (the eminently truthful), but applied this title to Abū Bakr even though nothing of the kind is related about him.

فجاء أمير المؤمنين فشهد لها فقال: هذا بعلك يجرّه إلى نفسه ولا نحكم بشهادته لك! وقد رووا جميعاً أنّ رسول الله ﷺ قال: عليّ مع الحقّ والحقّ مع علي يدور معه حيث دار، لن يفترقا حتّى يردا عليّ الحوض، فغضبت فاطمة عند ذلك وانصرفت وحلفت لا تكلّمه ولا صاحبه حتى تلقى أباها وتشكو إليه، فلمّا حضرتها الوفاة أوصت عليّاً أن يدفنها ليلاً ولا يدع أحداً منهم يصلّي عليها.

وقد رووا جميعاً أنّ النبي ﷺ قال: يا فاطمة، إنّ الله يغضب لغضبك ويرضى لرضاك. ورووا جميعاً أنّه قال: فاطمة بضعة منّي، من آذاها فقد آذاني، ومن آذاني فقد آذى الله. ولوكان هذا الخبر حقّاً لما جاز له ترك البغلة التي خلّفها النبي ﷺ وسيفه وعمامته عند أمير المؤمنين عليه السلام ولما حكم به له لمّا ادعاها العبّاس؛ ولكان أهل البيت الذين طهّرهم الله تعالى في كتابه عن الرجس مرتكبين ما لا يجوز، لأنّ الصدقة عليهم محرّمة.

بعد ذلك جاء إليه مال البحرين وعنده جابر بن عبد الله الأنصاري، فقال له: إنّ النبي ﷺ قال لي إذا أتى مال البحرين حثوت لك ثمّ حثوت لك ثلاثاً. فقال له: تقدّم فخذ بعدّتها؛ فأخذ من مال بيت المسلمين من غير بيّنة بل لمجرّد الدعوى.

وقد روت الجماعة كلّهم أنّ النبيّ ﷺ قال في حقّ أبي ذر ما أقلّت الغبراء ولا أظلّت الخضراء على ذي لهجة أصدق من أبي ذر ولم يسمّوه صدّيقاً، وسمّوا أبا بكر بذلك مع أنه لم يرو مثل ذلك في حقّه.

They also named him *Khalīfat Rasūl Allāh* (the Successor to the Messenger of Allah), even though the Messenger of Allah ﷺ never appointed him to be his successor in his lifetime nor even after his death, as recorded in their own sources. They never referred to the Commander of the Faithful ؑ as *Khalīfat Rasūl Allāh* even though he declared him to be his successor at numerous places, such as in Medina during the expedition to Tabūk when he said to him: "Truly, Medina cannot be set in order except by me or by you. Do you not then accept that your status in relation to me is as the station of Hārūn in relation to Mūsā, except that there shall be no prophet after me?"[67]

He appointed Usāma as commander of the troops which included Abū Bakr and ʿUmar, and he never relieved him of this command until he died, yet they never referred to him as a *khalīfa*. When Abū Bakr took over, Usāma became angered and said: "The Messenger of Allah ﷺ appointed me over you, so who then made you in charge of me?!" He and ʿUmar managed to persuade him, yet both referred to him as "the commander" throughout their lives.

They conferred the title of *al-Fārūq* ("The Separator") on ʿUmar but never referred to ʿAlī by the same despite the fact that Messenger of Allah ﷺ had said about him: "This is the *Fārūq* of my *umma*, he separates the true from the false." Ibn ʿUmar said: "We were only able to recognise who were hypocrites in the time of the Messenger of Allah ﷺ by their hatred for ʿAlī."

They have elevated the status of ʿĀʾisha above his other wives, even though he ﷺ used to remember Khadīja bint Khuwaylid a great deal. So ʿĀʾisha said to him: "You remember her a great deal, but Allah has given you better in place of her!" At this he said to her: "I swear by Allah that I have not been given anyone better than her! She believed in me when the people denied me. She was my refuge when the people drove me out. She made me happy with what she had. Allah blessed me with children borne by her and I was not blessed with children except from her."[68]

---

[67] This is known as the *Ḥadīth al-Manzila* ("The Ḥadīth of the Hārūnic/Aaronic Station"). See for example the following eminent classical Sunnī traditionists: Aḥmad b. Ḥanbal, *al-Musnad* (Vaduz, Lichtenstein: Thesaurus Islamicus Foundation, 2006), 1:386, *ḥadīth* 1566 and 1:367, *ḥadīth* 1481; Muslim b. al-Ḥajjāj, *al-Ṣaḥīḥ*, 2:1030, *ḥadīth*s 6370, 6372, 6373 and 2:1031, *ḥadīth* 6374; Abū ʿAbdullāh Muḥammad b. Yazīd Ibn Māja al-Qazwīnī al-Ribʿī, *al-Sunan* (Vaduz, Lichtenstein: Thesaurus Islamicus Foundation, 2006), 21 *ḥadīth*s 121, 122 and 22, *ḥadīth* 126; Abū ʿĪsā Muḥammad b. ʿĪsā b. Sawra al-Tirmidhī, *al-Jāmiʿ al-mukhtaṣar min al-sunan* (Vaduz, Lichtenstein: Thesaurus Islamicus Foundation, 2000), 2: 951, *ḥadīth* 4090 and 2:952, *ḥadīth*s 4095, 4096.

[68] See Aḥmad b. Ḥanbal, *al-Musnad*, 11:6003–6004, *ḥadīth* 25504.

وسمّوه خليفة رسول الله مع أنّ رسول الله ﷺ لم يستخلفه في حياته ولا بعد وفاته عندهم، ولم يسمّوا أمير المؤمنين عليه السلام خليفة رسول الله ﷺ مع أنّه استخلفه في عدّة مواطن، منها أنّه استخلفه على المدينة في غزاة تبوك وقال له: إنّ المدينة لا تصلح إلّا بي أو بك، أما ترضى أن تكون منّي بمنزلة هارون من موسى إلّا أنّه لا نبي بعدي؛ وأمّر أسامة على الجيش الذين فيهم أبو بكر وعمر، ومات ولم يعزله، ولم يسمّوه خليفةً. ولمّا تولّى أبو بكر غضب أسامة وقال: إنّ رسول الله ﷺ أمّرني عليك، فمن استخلفك عليّ؟! فمشى إليه هو وعمر حتّى استرضياه؛ وكانا يسمّيانه مدّة حياتهما أميراً.

وسمّوا عمر الفاروق ولم يسمّوا عليّاً عليه السلام بذلك مع أن رسول الله ﷺ قال فيه: هذا فاروق أمّتي يفرق بين الحقّ والباطل؛ وقال ابن عمر ما كنّا نعرف المنافقين على عهد رسول الله ﷺ إلّا ببغضهم عليّاً.

وعظّموا أمر عائشة على باقي نسوانه مع أنّه ﷺ كان يكثر من ذكر خديجة بنت خويلد، وقالت له عائشة: إنّك تكثر من ذكرها وقد أبدلك الله خيراً منها! فقال لها: والله ما بدّلت بها من هو خير منها؛ صدّقتني إذا كذّبني الناس وأوتني إذا طردني الناس وأسعدتني بما لها ورزقني الله الولد منها ولم أرزق من غيرها.

She [i.e., ʿĀʾisha] made public the secrets of the Messenger of Allah ﷺ. The Prophet ﷺ once said to her: "You will one day do battle against ʿAlī and it shall be you who is the transgressor."[69] She disobeyed the command of Allah in His statement: *And remain in your houses* [...][70] yet she ventured out amongst a great throng of people to do battle against ʿAlī who was innocent of any wrongdoing, for the Muslims had reached a consensus to kill ʿUthmān; and it was her who all the while had been pressing for his murder saying: "Kill the senile-old-hyena-looking-jew! Kill, Kill the senile-old-hyena-looking-jew!"[71] When news of his murder reached her she was overjoyed and asked, "Who has taken the *khilāfa*?" They said, "ʿAlī." She then resolved to fight him seeking vengeance for the blood of ʿUthmān.

Where was the sin of ʿAlī ؏ in any of that? And what was the justification of Ṭalḥa and Zubayr in following her in that? With what face shall they come before the Messenger of Allah ﷺ? Whereas if any one of us were to become chatty with the wife of another man and make her come out of her house and then travel with her, such a person would be regarded with the strongest disgust. How was it that tens of thousands of Muslims followed her and backed her in making war on the Commander of the Faithful ؏ yet none of them supported the daughter of the Messenger of Allah ﷺ when she sought her right from Abū Bakr and no one uttered even a single word? And they dubbed her *Umm al-Muʾminīn* (the Mother of the Believers) and referred to no one else in this way. And yet, despite his exalted station and his closeness to his father and his sister ʿĀʾisha "the Mother of the Believers," they never dubbed her brother, Muḥammad b. Abī Bakr, *Khāl al-Muʾminīn* (the Maternal Uncle of the Believers), but they did so in the case of Muʿāwiya b. Abī Sufyān ostensibly for the reason that his sister Umm Ḥabība Bint Abī Sufyān was one of the wives of the Prophet ﷺ. One would have thought the sister of Muḥammad b. Abī Bakr and his father to have been more exalted than the sister of Muʿāwiya and her father? This despite the fact that the Messenger of Allah ﷺ cursed Muʿāwiya — this fellow who was granted amnesty, the son of an accursed one granted amnesty — about whom he said: "If you see Muʿāwiya on my *minbar*, kill him!"

---

69 See al-Ḥākim al-Naysābūrī, *al-Mustadrak ʿalā al-Ṣaḥīḥayn*, 3:119. Two *ḥadīth*s here support the above account but do not match the wording.

70 Qurʾān 33:33. This command occurs in the original Arabic in the imperative feminine plural and was addressed to the wives of the Prophet.

71 The expression in Arabic here is *naʾthal*. It literally means a male hyena as well as a senile old man. Moreover, in that period there had been in Medina and old jew who was known by this epithet and also happened to resemble ʿUthmān b. ʿAffān. A man of the Banū Liḥyān employed this epithet to insult him. See Majd al-Dīn Muḥammad b. Yaʿqūb al-Fīrūzābādī, *al-Qāmūs al-muḥīṭ* (Beirut: Muʾassat al-Risāla 1407/1987), 1374.

وأذاعت سرّ رسول الله ﷺ وقال لها النبي ﷺ: إنّك تقاتلين عليّاً وأنت ظالمة؛ ثمّ إنّها خالفت أمر الله تعالى في قوله ﴿وقرن في بيوتكنّ﴾، وخرجت في ملأ من الناس تقاتل عليّا عليه السلام على غير ذنب لأنّ المسلمين أجمعوا على قتل عثمان، وكانت هي كلّ وقت تأمر بقتله؛ وتقول: اقتلوا نعثلاً قتل الله نعثلاً! فلمّا بلغها قتله فرحت بذلك، ثم سألت: من تولّى الخلافة؟ فقالوا: عليّ؛ فخرجت لقتاله على دم عثمان.

فأيّ ذنب كان لعلي عليه السلام على ذلك؟ وكيف استجاز طلحة والزبير مطاوعتها على ذلك؟ وبأيّ وجه يلقون رسول الله ﷺ؟ مع أنّ الواحد منّا لو تحدّث على امرأة غيره وأخرجها من منزله وسافر بها كان أشدّ الناس عداوة؛ وكيف أطاعها على ذلك عشرات الألوف من المسلمين وساعدوها على حرب أمير المؤمنين عليه السلام ولم ينصر أحدٌ منهم بنت رسول الله ﷺ لمّا طلبت حقّها من أبي بكر، ولا شخصٌ واحدٌ بكلمة واحدة. وسمّوها أمّ المؤمنين ولم يسمّوا غيرها بذلك. ولم يسمّوا أخاها محمّد بن أبي بكر مع عظم شأنه وقرب منزلته من أبيه ومن أخته عائشة أمّ المؤمنين خال المؤمنين (وسمّوا معاوية بن أبي سفيان خال المؤمنين) لأن أخته أم حبيبة بنت أبي سفيان بعض زوجات النّبي ﷺ، وأخت محمّد بن أبي بكر وأبوه أعظم من أخت معاوية ومن أبيها، مع أنّ رسول الله ﷺ لعن معاوية الطليق بن الطليق اللّعين وقال: إذا رأيتم معاوية على منبري فاقتلوه!

He was amongst those leading figures of that time about whom it was hoped that they would accept Islam (*al-mu'allafatu qulūbuhum*), but he made war on ʿAlī even though they believed him to be the fourth *khalīfa* and rightful Imam, but [if that is the case] then whoever makes war on the rightful Imam is a rebel and transgressor [and this is how Muʿāwiya should then be regarded]. The reason for this [i.e. their stance toward Muḥammad b. Abī Bakr] was Muḥammad b. Abī Bakr's devotion to ʿAlī ؑ, his disavowal of his father, and Muʿāwiya's hatred for ʿAlī and his making war on him.

They dubbed Muʿāwiya *Kātib al-waḥy* ("Scribe of the Revelation") even though he never transcribed a single word of divine writ; rather he transcribed correspondence for him. There were fourteen people who wrote down the revelation in the presence of the Prophet ﷺ of whom the foremost, the choicest, and the closest to him was none other than ʿAlī b. Abī Ṭālib ؑ; whereas Muʿāwiya remained an idolater for the entirety of the Prophet's ﷺ mission, rejecting the revelation and making light of the Sharīʿa. He was in Yemen on the day of the conquest of Mecca denouncing the Messenger of Allah ﷺ and wrote to his father Ṣakhr b. Ḥarb:

O Ṣakhr! In no way become a muslim and humiliate us
after those who were at Badr were taken from us —

My grandfather, my maternal uncle, and the third one:
the paternal uncle of my mother
— kinsfolk, and Ḥanẓala the most superior who had been given to us.

Death is better for us than the speech of liars.
Leave the son of Hind to be distinguished thus from ʿUzza.

وكان من المؤلّفة قلوبهم، وقاتل عليّاً وهو عندهم رابع الخلفاء إمام حقّ، وكلّ من حارب إمام حقّ فهو باغٍ ظالمٌ؛ وسبب ذلك محبّة محمد بن أبي بكر لعليّ عليه السلام ومفارقته (لأبيه، وبغض معاوية لعليّ) ومحاربته له.

وسمّوه كاتب الوحي ولم يكتب له كلمة واحدة من الوحي، بل كان يكتب له رسائل، وقد كان بين يدي النبيّ صلى الله عليه وآله أربعة عشر نفساً يكتبون الوحي، أوّلهم وأخصّهم به وأقربهم إليه عليّ بن أبي طالب، مع أنّ معاوية لم يزل مشركاً مدّة كون النبي صلى الله عليه وآله مبعوثاً يكذّب بالوحي ويهزأ بالشرع؛ وكان باليمن يوم الفتح يطعن على رسول الله صلى الله عليه وآله ويكتب إلى أبيه صخر بن حرب يعيّره بإسلامه، ويقول له: أصبوت إلى دين محمّد ؟! وكتب إليه:

يا صخر لا تُسلِمَنّ طوعاً فتفضحنا ... بعد الذين ببدرٍ أصبحوا فِرَقا
جدّي وخالي وعمّ الأمّ ثالثهم ... قوماً وحنظلةُ المُهدي لنا الأَرَقا
فالموت أهون من قول الوشاة لنا ... خلّى ابنُ هندٍ عن العُزّى كذا فَرَقا

The conquest of Mecca took place in the month of Ramaḍān, eight years after the Prophet's ﷺ arrival in Medina. At that time Muʿāwiya remained established in idolatry. He had fled from the Prophet ﷺ because he had said he should be killed on sight (*hadar damahu*). So he fled to Mecca and when he had no other refuge he was forced to go to the Prophet ﷺ and outwardly profess Islam. His becoming a Muslim preceded the death of the Prophet ﷺ by only five months. He threw himself at the mercy of al-ʿAbbās who interceded on his behalf with the Messenger of Allah ﷺ who then forgave him. Then he pleaded on his behalf to confer some distinction on him by adding him to the group of scribes. So, he relented and made him one of fourteen scribes. How much could he possibly have been tasked with transcribing in this [short] period — assuming he was even a scribe of the revelation — so how is it that he is given this distinction to the exclusion of others? Moreover, al-Zamakhsharī, who is a Ḥanafī scholar, relates in *Rabīʿ al-abrār* (*The Spring of the Righteous*) that four different men claimed to be his father.[72] It is also a fact that among the scribes of the revelation was one Ibn Abī Sarḥ, who had returned to idolatry, regarding whom was revealed: *and as for those whose hearts opens up to unbelief, upon them shall be the wrath of Allah and theirs shall be a painful doom.*[73]

ʿAbdullāh b. ʿUmar related that: "I went to the Prophet ﷺ and heard him saying, 'A man will come to you who will die on other than my *sunna*.' Then Muʿāwiya arrived."

One day the Prophet ﷺ stood up to deliver a sermon and Muʿāwiya took hold of the hand of his son Yazīd and walked out without listening to the sermon. Then the Prophet ﷺ said: "May Allah curse the one leading and the one led." What good could accrue to the *umma* from such a disrespectful one as Muʿāwiya?

He did his utmost in making war on ʿAlī ؓ, and killed a great many of the choicest Companions. He cursed ʿAlī from the *minbar* and this cursing went on for a period of 80 years [after him] until a stop was put to it by ʿUmar b. ʿAbd al-ʿAzīz. He had Ḥasan poisoned. His son Yazīd had Our Master Imam Ḥusayn killed. His grandfather broke the front tooth of the Prophet ﷺ and his mother ate the liver of Ḥamza, the uncle of the Messenger ﷺ.

---

72 al-Zamakhsharī, *Rabīʿ al-abrār*, edited by ʿAbd al-Amīr Munnā (Beirut: al-Aʿlamī, 1412/1192), 4:275–276.
73 Qurʾān 16:106.

والفتح كان في شهر رمضان لثمان سنين من قدوم النبي ﷺ المدينة، ومعاوية حينئذ مقيم على الشرك، هارب من النبيّ ﷺ لأنّه قد هدر دمه؛ فهرب إلى مكّة؛ فلّما لم يجد له مأوى صار إلى النّبي ﷺ مضطراً فأظهر الإسلام وكان إسلامه قبل موت النبىّ ﷺ بخمسة أشهر، وطرح نفسه على العبّاس، فسأل فيه رسول الله ﷺ فعفا عنه؛ ثم شفع إليه أن يشرّفه ويضيفه إلى جملة الكتّاب فأجابه وجعله واحداً من أربعة عشر. فكم كان يخصّه من الكتابة في هذه المدّة لو سلّمنا أنّه كان كاتب الوحي حتّى استحقّ أن يوصف بذلك دون غيره؛ مع أنّ الزمخشري من مشايخ الحنفيّة ذكر في ربيع الأبرار أنّه ادّعى بنوّته أربعة نفر على أنّ من جملة كتبة الوحي ابن أبي سرح، وارتدّ مشركاً، وفيه نزل ﴿ولكن من شرح بالكفر صدراً فعليهم غضب من الله ولهم عذاب عظيم﴾.

وقد روى عبد الله بن عمر قال: أتيت النبي ﷺ فسمعته يقول: يطلع عليكم رجل يموت على غير سنّتي! فطلع معاوية.

وقام النبي ﷺ يوماً يخطب فأخذ معاوية بيد ابنه يزيد وخرج ولم يسمع الخطبة، فقال النبي ﷺ: لعن الله القائد والمقود! وأيّ يوم يكون لهذه الأمّة من معاوية ذي الإساءة؟

وبالغ في محاربة عليّ عليه السلام وقتل جمعاً كثيراً من خيار الصحابة ولعنه على المنابر، واستمر سبّه مدّة ثمانين سنة إلى أن قطعه عمر بن عبد العزيز؛ وسّم الحسن؛ وقتل ابنه يزيد مولانا الإمام الحسين عليه السلام، وكسر جدّه ثنيّة النبي ﷺ، وأكلت أمّه كبد حمزة عم الرسول ﷺ.

They dubbed Khālid b. al-Walīd *Sayf Allāh* ("The Sword of Allah") out of aversion toward the Commander of the Faithful ﵇ who was most worthy of such a title, for it is he who killed with his sword the unbelievers, and by whose sacred combat the foundations of the faith were made firm. The Messenger of Allah ﷺ said of him: "ʿAlī is the sword of Allah and the arrow of Allah." ʿAlī proclaimed from the *minbar*: "I am the sword of Allah drawn against His enemies as well as His mercy for His friends."

Khālid remained an enemy of the Messenger of Allah, firm in his denial of him. It was because of him that Muslims took casualties at Uḥud, that the Prophet's ﷺ teeth were broken, and his uncle Ḥamza was martyred. After he outwardly professed Islam, the Prophet ﷺ sent him to the Banū Khuzayma to collect alms from them, but he betrayed him and went against his instructions and killed the Muslims. The Prophet ﷺ delivered an address in the midst of his Companions denouncing him, raising his hands toward the sky so that his armpits were visible proclaiming, "O Allah! I am innocent of whatever Khālid has done!" He then sent out the Commander of the Faithful ﵇ to set aright his transgression. He ordered him to work to conciliate them and regain their trust, which he did. Once the Prophet had died, Abū Bakr dispatched him to massacre the people of Yamāma. He killed 1200 of them despite them professing Islam. He killed Mālik b. Nuwayra[74] by horizontally slicing him into two and he also raped his wife.

They declared the Banū Ḥanīfa to be apostates simply for their refusal to send their *zakāt* to Abū Bakr because they did not recognise him as the Imam, and he declared their blood to be lawful as well as their wealth and womenfolk — and even ʿUmar opposed him in this. Thus, they declare those who did not pay *zakāt* to be apostates, yet somehow do not declare to be apostates those who deemed the blood of Muslims to be lawful and who fought the Commander of the Faithful ﵇, even though they are aware that the Messenger of Allah ﷺ said: "O ʿAlī! Your war is my war, and your peace is my peace."[75] It is a matter of consensus that whoever makes war on the Messenger of Allah is an unbeliever.

74 Mālik b. Nuwayra b. Jamra b. Shaddād b. ʿUbayd b. Thaʿlaba b. Yarbū. He was considered to be chieftain of the Banū Yarbūʿ during the lifetime of the Prophet Muḥammad. He was brother of the poet Mutammim b. Nuwayra as well as being a poet in his own right. He was known as a noble and brave warrior, but not much is known of his exploits. Rather, it is for the unfortunate circumstances of his death in 11 AH at the hands of Khālid b. al-Walīd that he is most well-known. See Landau-Tasseron, Ella, "Mālik b. Nuwayra", in *Encyclopaedia of Islam, Second Edition,* edited by P. Bearman, Th. Bianquis, C.E. Bosworth, E. van Donzel, W.P. Heinrichs. Consulted online on 07 November 2022 <http://dx.doi.org.uoelibrary.idm.oclc.org/10.1163/1573-3912_islam_COM_0650>

75 See al-Ḥākim al-Naysābūrī, *al-Mustadrak ʿalā al-Ṣaḥīḥayn*, 3:149; al-Tirmidhī, *al-Jāmiʿ al-mukhtaṣar min al-sunan*, 2:978, *ḥadīth* 4244.

وسمّوا خالد بن الوليد سيف الله عناداً لأمير المؤمنين الذي هو أحقّ بهذا الاسم حيث قتل بسيفه الكفّار وثبتت بواسطة جهاده قواعد الدين؛ وقال فيه رسول الله ﷺ: عليّ سيف الله وسهم الله. وقال علي على المنبر: أنا سيف الله على أعدائه، ورحمته لأوليائه.

وخالد لم يزل عدوّاً لرسول الله مكذّبًا له؛ وهو كان السبب في قتل المسلمين في يوم أحد وفي كسر رباعيّة النبيّ ﷺ، وفي قتل حمزة عمّه؛ ولمّا تظاهر بالإسلام بعثه النبيّ ﷺ إلى بني خزيمة ليأخذ منهم الصدقات فخانه وخالفه على أمره، وقتل المسلمين؛ فقام النبي ﷺ في أصحابه خطيباً بالإنكار عليه رافعاً يديه إلى السماء حتّى شوهد بياض إبطيه وهو يقول: اللهمّ إنّي أبرأ إليك ممّا صنع خالد، ثم أنفذ إليهم أمير المؤمنين لتلافي فارطته، وأمره أن يسترضي القوم ففعل. ولمّا قبض النبيّ وأنفذه أبو بكر لقتال أهل اليمامة قتل منهم ألفاً ومائتي نفس مع تظاهرهم بالإسلام، وقتل مالك بن نويرة صبرا وهو مسلم، وعرّس بامرأته.

وسمّوا بني حنيفة أهل الردّة؛ لأنّهم لم يحملوا الزكاة إلى أبي بكر لأنّهم لم يعتقدوا إمامته؛ واستحلّ دماءهم وأموالهم (ونساءهم) حتّى أنكر عمر عليه؛ فسمّوا مانع الزكاة مرتداً، ولم يسمّوا من استحلّ دماء المسلمين ومحاربة أمير المؤمنين مرتدّاً، مع أنهم سمعوا قول رسول الله ﷺ: يا عليّ حربك حربي، وسلمك سلمي، ومحارب رسول الله كافر بالإجماع.

It was so nicely put by someone when they said that, "More evil than Iblīs is one whose obedience did not surpass Iblīs' in the past, yet went along with him in the realm of transgression!" There is no doubt among the scholars that Iblīs was the best of worshipers among the angels and that he solely bore the divine throne for 6000 years. When Allah created Ādam and made him his vicegerent on earth, he ordered him to bow down to him, but he was arrogant and thus merited expulsion [from Paradise] and damnation. Now, consider Muʿāwiya who spent his days in associating partners with Allah in the worship of idols for quite a long time even after the coming forth of the Prophet ﷺ until he finally professed Islam. Then only to be too arrogant to obey Allah the Exalted in the appointment of the Commander of the Faithful ؏ as Imam. All followed him after ʿUthmān, and he sat in his place.[76] Thus, he was more evil than Iblīs. Some of them exceeded the bounds of fanaticism and professed the Imama of Yazīd b. Muʿāwiya even though he perpetrated such heinous crimes as the murder of Ḥusayn ؏, the looting of his possessions, taking prisoner his womenfolk and parading them through the land on camel back without saddles, with Our Master ʿAlī Zayn al-ʿĀbidīn in shackles. It was not enough for them to have killed Ḥusayn, but they had to crush his ribs and chest by trampling him underfoot on horseback and raised up the severed heads of the dead on lances. Yet, their scholars have narrated that on the day of the murder of Ḥusayn the skies rained down blood. This was mentioned by al-Rāfiʿī in *Sharḥ al-wajīz*.[77] Ibn Saʿd has narrated in *al-Ṭabaqāt* (*The Book of Generations*) that on the day of the death of Ḥusayn the sky turned so red

---

76   He means to say that after the murder of ʿUthmān, those who later became the "Sunnīs" all followed Muʿāwiya who then arrogated to himself the title of *khalīfa*, an office which, in the eyes of al-ʿAllāma al-Ḥillī and the Shīʿa generally, rightly belonged only to ʿAlī.

77   This would appear to be a reference to the commentary (*sharḥ*) by al-Rāfiʿī (d. 623/1226) on *al-Wajīz* which is an important manual of Shāfiʿī *fiqh* by al-Ghazālī (d. 505/1111). However, I could not find mention therein of the skies raining down blood on 10 Muḥarram 61, the day Ḥusayn was martyred. Yet, I did find mention in it of a solar eclipse occurring on that day with the skies so thoroughly darkening that the stars became visible. See Abū l-Qāsim ʿAbd al-Karīm b. Muḥammad al-Rāfiʿī, *al-ʿAzīz sharḥ al-Wajīz*, edited by ʿAlī Muḥammad Muʿawwaḍ and ʿĀdil Aḥmad ʿAbd al-Mawjūd (Beirut: Dār al-Kutub al-ʿIlmiyya, 1417/1997), 2:381–382. This report is ascribed by al-Rāfiʿī to al-Bayhaqī (d. 458/1065) who in turn is quoting Muḥammad b. ʿUmar al-Wāqidī (d. 207/823). However, no such eclipse could have occurred on 10 Muḥarram 61 AH in Karbala = 10 October 680 CE (or anywhere else on earth for that matter). See the table in A. Steinbrüchel, *Tafel der Sonnen- und Mondfinsternisse, der Neu- und Vollmonde von 1265 v. Chr. biis 2345 n. Chr., mit erläuterndem Text* (Zürich: Naturforschenden Gesellschaft in Zürich, 1937), and Bryant Tuckerman, *Planetary, Lunar, and Solar Positions, AD 2 to AD 1649 At Five-day and Ten-day Intervals* (Philadelphia: The American Philosophical Society, 1964), 358, as well as "Catalog of Solar Eclipses 601 CE to 700 CE," *NASA Eclipse Website* https://eclipse.gsfc.nasa.gov/SEcat5/SE0601-0700.html (permanent link).

وقد أحسن بعض العقلاء في قوله: شرّ من إبليس من لم يسبقه في سالف طاعته، وجرى معه في ميدان معصيته! ولاشكّ بين العلماء أنّ إبليس كان أعبد الملائكة وكان يحمل العرش وحده ستّة آلاف سنة. ولمّا خلق الله تعالى آدم وجعله خليفة في الأرض وأمره بالسجود فاستكبر فاستحقّ الطرد واللّعن، ومعاوية لم يزل في الإشراك وعبادة الأصنام إلى أن أسلم بعد ظهور النبي ﷺ بمدّة طويلة، ثمّ استكبر عن طاعة الله تعالى في نصب أمير المؤمنين عليه السلام إماماً وتابعه الكلّ بعد عثمان وجلس مكانه؛ فكان شرّاً من إبليس وتمادي البعض في التعصّب، حتّى اعتقد إمامة يزيد بن معاوية مع ما صدر عنه من الأفعال القبيحة من قتل الامام الحسين عليه السلام ونهب أمواله وسبي نسائه والدوران بهم في البلاد على الجال بغير قتب، ومولانا زين العابدين عليه السلام مغلول اليدين، ولم يقنعوا بقتله حتّى رضّوا أضلاعه وصدره بالخيول، وحملوا رؤوسهم على القنا، مع أنّ مشايخهم رووا أنّ يوم قتل الحسين قطرت السماء دماً؛ وقد ذكر ذلك الرافعي في شرح الوجيز

that it had never been seen like that before.⁷⁸ He also said that [on that day] no stone was turned but that fresh blood was found under it and that the skies rained down blood and the traces thereof remained on clothes until they became threadbare.⁷⁹

Al-Zuhrī said: "None of those who took part in killing Ḥusayn remained without meeting punishment in this world in a very short time, either by themselves being killed, or being struck blind, or losing their status or wealth." The Messenger of Allah ﷺ repeatedly admonished the Muslims regarding his two sons Ḥasan and Ḥusayn, saying that "They are my trust to you," and Allah revealed regarding them: *Say: I ask not of you any recompense for it, save that you love those close to me.*⁸⁰

There is a group who, while they do not uphold [i.e. Yazīd's] Imāma, nevertheless suspend judgment on his cursing; this despite the fact that they acknowledge him to be a transgressor who killed Ḥusayn and looted his womenfolk, and are aware of Allah having said: *Yes, indeed the curse of Allah is upon the transgressors.*⁸¹

Abū l-Faraj Ibn al-Jawzī, a Ḥanbalī scholar, said narrating via Ibn ʿAbbās, who said: "Allah the Exalted revealed to Muḥammad ﷺ: 'I took the lives of 70,000 when Yaḥyā b. Zakariyyā [John the Baptist] was martyred, and I shall take the lives of 70,000 and 70,000 more when the son of your daughter Fāṭima ؑ is martyred.'"

---

78   Muḥammad b. Saʿd's (d. 230/845) *Kitāb al-Ṭabaqāt* was first critically edited by Eduard Sachau *et al* and published by E. J. Brill, Leiden between 1904–1918. The latest edition was published at Beirut by Dār al-Kutub al-ʿIlmiyya in 1411/1991 in 8 volumes under the editorship of Muḥammad Qādir ʿAṭāʾ. However, none of these editions is complete and much material was not included that remains preserved in manuscripts which were not used in preparing these two editions. This includes the section on Imam Ḥusayn and his martyrdom. The latter was published separately, and it is from that edition that we cite, namely, *Tarjamat al-Imām al-Ḥusayn wa-maqtaluhu min al-qism ghayr al-maṭbūʿ min Kitāb al-Ṭabaqāt al-kabīr li-Ibn Saʿd*, edited by al-Sayyid ʿAbd al-ʿAzīz al-Ṭabāṭabāʾī (Beirut: Muʾassasat Āl al-Bayt ʿalayhim al-salām li-Iḥyāʾ al-Turāth, 1416/1995), 91. See also Muḥammad Zubayr Ṣiddīqī, *Ḥadīth Literature. Its Origin, Development and Special Features* (Cambridge: Islamic Texts Society, 1993), 136–137.
79   Ibid., 90.
80   Qurʾān 42:23.
81   Qurʾān 11:18.

وذكر ابن سعد في الطبقات أنّ الحمرة ظهرت في السماء يوم قتل الحسين ولم تُر قبل ذلك وقال أيضاً: ما رفع حجر في الدنيا إلّا وتحته الدم عبيط ولقد مطرت السماء مطراً بقي أثره في الثياب مدّة حتى تقطّعت.

قال الزهري: ما بقي أحد من قاتلي الحسين إلّا وعوقب في الدنيا، إمّا بالقتل أوالعمى أو سواد الوجه أو زوال الملك في مدّة يسيرة. وقد كان رسول الله ﷺ يكثر الوصيّة للمسلمين في ولديه الحسن والحسين ويقول لهم: هؤلاء وديعتي عندكم، وأنزل الله تعالى فيهم ﴿قل لا أسألكم عليه أجراً إلّا المودّة في القربى﴾.

وتوقف جماعة ممّن لا يقول بإمامته في لعنته مع أنّه عندهم ظالم بقتل الحسين ونهب حريمه، وقد قال الله تعالى ﴿ألا لعنة الله على الظّالمين﴾.

وقال أبو الفرج بن الجوزي من شيوخ الحنابلة عن ابن عبّاس قال: أوحى الله تعالى إلى محمّد ﷺ إني قتلت بيحيى بن زكريّا سبعين ألفاً، وإنّي قاتل بابن بنتك فاطمة سبعين ألفاً وسبعين ألفاً.

Suddī, who is one of their excellent scholars relates: "I visited Karbala and I had some items of food with me for commerce. I stayed with a man there and as we were sharing a meal, we began to talk about the murder of Ḥusayn ﷺ. I noted that there was not a single person who had taken part in the murder of Ḥusayn who did not thereafter die in the most horrible fashion. At this the man exclaimed, 'What a preposterous liar you are! I took part in shedding his blood and was among those who took part in his killing and yet nothing has happened to me!'" He then said: "No sooner did the night come to an end that I heard a scream. I asked: 'What is happening?' People told me that: 'The man had risen to adjust the oil lamp and burnt his finger, and then the flames engulfed his body and he went up in flames.'" Suddī then says, "I then saw him, and I swear by Allah, he looked as though he was a mass of charcoal."

Muhannā b. Yaḥyā asked Aḥmad b. Ḥanbal about Yazīd, so he said to him, "He is the one who did what he did." "And what exactly was that?" he asked. "He looted Medina," he answered. One day Ṣāliḥ, his son, asked him: "Some accuse us of loyalty to Yazīd." "My son, can anyone believing in Allah and the last day show loyalty to Yazīd?" "Why then do you not curse him?' he asked. "How can I not curse someone whom Allah has cursed in his book?" "And where did He curse him?" He said: "When He said *Would you then, if you were given power, wreak havoc in the land and sever the bonds of kinship? Such are they whom Allah has cursed so that He renders them deaf and makes blind their eyes.*"[82]

Is there any havoc greater than killing, looting Medina for three days, taking its people prisoner, murdering its prominent citizens among the Quraysh, Anṣār, and Muhājirīn — some 700 souls — as well as 10,000 ordinary people — slaves, free men, and women? People were so drowned in bloodshed that blood even reached the tomb of the Messenger of Allah ﷺ filling the garden and the mosque. He also fired upon the Kaʿba with catapults. He razed it and burned it to the ground.

82 Qur'ān 47:22–23.

وحكى السدّي وكان من فضلائهم قال: نزلت بكربلاء ومعي طعام للتجارة، فنزلنا على رجل فتعشّينا عنده وتذاكرنا قتل الحسين عليه السلام وقلنا: ما شرك أحد في قتل الحسين إلّا ومات أقبح موتة! فقال الرجل: ما أكذبكم! أنا شركت في دمه وكنت فيمن قتله فما أصابني شيء؛ قال: فما كان في آخر الليل إذا بالصياح قلنا: ما الخبر؟ قالوا: قام الرجل يصلح المصباح فاحترقت إصبعه ثمّ دب الحريق في جسده فاحترق؛ قال السدّي: فأنا والله رأيته كأنّه حممة.

وقد سأل مهنا بن يحيى أحمد بن حنبل عن يزيد فقال: هو الذي فعل ما فعل. قلت: وما فعل؟ قال نهب المدينة. وقال له صالح ولده يوماً: إنّ قوماً ينسبوننا إلى توالي يزيد، فقال: يابني؛ وهل يتوالى يزيد أحد يؤمن بالله واليوم الآخر؟ فقلت: لم لا تلعنه؟ فقال: وكيف لا ألعن من لعنه الله في كتابه؟ فقلت: وأين لعن يزيد؟ فقال: في قوله ﴿فهل عسيتم إن تولّيتم أن تفسدوا في الأرض وتقطّعوا أرحامكم أولئك الذين لعنهم الله فأصمّهم وأعمى أبصارهم﴾.

فهل يكون فساد أعظم من القتل ونهب المدينة ثلاثة أيام وسبي أهلها وقتل جمع من وجوه الناس فيها من قريش والأنصار والمهاجرين يبلغ عددهم سبعمائة، وقتل من لم يعرف من عبد أو حرّ أو امرأة عشرة الآف؟ وحاض الناس في الدماء حتّى وصلت الدماء إلى قبر رسول الله صلى الله عليه وآله وامتلأت الروضة والمسجد؛ ثم ضرب الكعبة بالمناجق وهدمها وأحرقها.

The Messenger of Allah ﷺ said: "The person who kills Ḥusayn shall be in a coffin of flame and shall bear the torment of half of the people of the world. His hands and feet will be bound by chains of flame turning over and over as he plummets to the deepest pit of Hell. He shall have a stench so abominable that the denizens of the Hellfire will seek refuge from it with their Lord. He shall abide therein tasting painful torment. As often as their skins become scorched, Allah shall replace them with fresh skins that they may taste the torment.[83] They will not be granted even a moment's respite and shall be made to drink from the scalding water pools of Hell." And he ﷺ also said: "The wrath of Allah the exalted as well as my own wrath intensified against the one who shed my blood and sought to harm me through my Family." Let the intelligent then ponder which of the two sides are more deserving of Allah's protection? Those who exalt Allah, and His angels, and his prophets, and His Imams; those who keep the Sharīʿa pure of base rulings or those who invalidate their [Friday] prayers by not invoking blessings upon the Imams and mention Imams other than them, or those who went against this this and did not believe in this?

83 This is a paraphrase of Qurʾān 4:56 which reads: *As often as their skins become scorched, We shall replace them with fresh skins that they may taste the torment.*

وقال رسول الله ﷺ إنّ قاتل الحسين في تابوت من نار، عليه نصف عذاب أهل الدنيا؛ وقد شدّت يداه ورجلاه بسلاسل من نار، منكّس في النار حتّى يقع في قعر جهنّم، له ريح يتعوذ أهل النار إلى ربّهم من شدّة نتن ريحه، وهو فيها خالد ذائق للعذاب الأليم؛ كلّما نضجت جلودهم بدّل الله لهم الجلود حتّى يذوقوا العذاب، لا يفتر عنهم ساعة ويسق من حميم جهنّم. الويل لهم من عذاب الله عزّ وجل.

وقال ﷺ : اشتدّ غضب الله تعالى وغضبي على من أهراق دمي وآذاني في عترتي. فلينظر العاقل أي الفريقين أحقّ بالأمن: الذي نزّه الله تعالى وملائكته وأنبياءه وأئمّته ونزّهوا الشرع عن المسائل الردّية ومن يبطل الصلاة بإهمال الصلاة على أئمّتهم ويذكر أئمّة غيرهم، أم الذي فعل ضدّ ذلك واعتقد خلافه؟

The Sixth Reason

When the Imāmīs noticed that the merits of the Commander of the Faithful ﷺ and his perfections are without number and have been related by both his friends as well as his adversaries, as well as having seen that the great multitude of the Muslims have recorded the many shameful acts of the other Companions and that not a single shameful act by ʿAlī ﷺ has come ever down to us, they obeyed his word and took him as their Imam; for he has been deemed as unblemished by both his friends as well as his adversaries and thus did they leave behind the others who were regarded as being Imams due to the reports of shameful acts which render their Imāma to be invalid.

Here we shall relate but a small portion of what is regarded by them as true and which they have recorded in their own works deemed reliable [by them] in order that it stand as a proof against them on the Day of Judgement.

An example of this is what was related by Abū l-Ḥasan al-Andalusī in *al-Jamʿ bayn al-Ṣiḥāḥ al-Sitta*[84] [*The Ḥadīths Common to the Six Authentic Collections*] — by which is meant Mālik's *Muwaṭṭā'* the two *Ṣaḥīḥ*s of Muslim and Bukhārī, *Sunan Abī Dāwūd*, *Ṣaḥīḥ al-Tirmidhī*, *Ṣaḥīḥ al-Nasā'ī* — on the authority of Umm Salama, wife of the Prophet ﷺ who said that the statement of Allah the Exalted *Truly Allah only wishes to remove all impurity from you, O People of the House, and to purify you exceedingly*[85] was revealed in her house and said: "I was sitting at the door, and I asked, 'O Messenger of Allah, am I not too from the *People of the House*?' He said: 'You are truly in a good position. You are one of the wives of the Messenger of Allah ﷺ.'"

She goes on to relate that: "The Messenger of Allah, ʿAlī, Fāṭima, Ḥasan, and Ḥusayn were inside the house and he had covered them with a cloak and said: 'O Allah! These are the People of my House, remove all impurity from them and purify them exceedingly.'"

84 It appears that this work either remains in manuscript and has not been published or has not survived to our time. However, the sources on which it was based are readily available and the event in question is recorded in Muslim b. al-Ḥajjāj, *al-Ṣaḥīḥ*, 2:1038, 6414; Abū Dāwūd, *al-Sunan*, 2:675, *ḥadīth* 4034; al-Tirmidhī, *al-Jāmiʿ*, 2:710, *ḥadīth* 3044; cf. Jamāl al-Dīn al-Mizzī, *Tuḥfat al-ashrāf*, entry 17858 not to mention many other sources, such as Muḥammad b. Saʿd, *Tarjamat al-Imām al-Ḥusayn*, edited by al-Sayyid ʿAbd al-ʿAzīz al-Ṭabāṭabā'ī (Beirut: Mu'assasat Āl al-Bayt ʿalayhim al-salām li Iḥyā' al-Turāth, 1416/1995), 22.

85 Qur'ān 33:33.

الوجه السادس

إنّ الإماميّة لمّا رأوا فضائل أمير المؤمنين عليه السلام وكمالاته لا تحصى قد رواها المخالف والمؤالف، ورأوا الجمهور قد نقلوا عن غيره من الصحابة مطاعن كثيرة ولم ينقلوا في علي عليه السلام طعناً البتّة، اتّبعوا قوله وجعلوه إماماً لهم حيث نزّهه المخالف والمؤالف، وتركوا غيره حيث روى فيه من يعتقد إمامته من المطاعن ما يطعن في إمامته؛ ونحن نذكر هنا شيئاً يسيراً ممّا هو صحيح عندهم ونقلوه في المعتمد من كتبهم ليكون حجّة عليهم يوم القيامة.

فمن ذلك ما رواه أبو الحسن الأندلسي في الجمع بين الصحاح الستة - موطّأ مالك، وصحيحي مسلم والبخاري، وسنن أبي داود، وصحيح الترمذي، وصحيح النسائي، عن أمّ سلمة زوج النبي أنّ قوله تعالى ﴿إنّما يريد الله ليذهب عنكم الرجس أهل البيت ويطهّركم تطهيرا﴾ أنزلت في بيتها وأنا جالسة عند الباب، فقلت: يا رسول الله، ألست من أهل البيت؟ فقال: إنّك على خير إنك من أزواج رسول الله صلى الله عليه وآله.

قالت: وفي البيت رسول الله وعليّ وفاطمة وحسن وحسين، فجلّلهم بكساء وقال: اللهمّ هؤلاء أهل بيتي فأذهب عنهم الرجس وطهّرهم تطهيراً.

The like thereof was related by Aḥmad b. Ḥanbal.[86] He also said regarding the statement of Allah: *when you consult the Messenger privately precede your private consultation by giving alms*[87] that ʿAlī b. Abī Ṭālib said: "No one but me acted upon this verse, and it is by me that Allah the Exalted eased the burden of the verse."

On the authority of Muḥammad b. Kaʿb al-Quraẓī who said: "Ṭalḥa b. Shayba of the Banū ʿAbd al-Dār, ʿAbbās b. ʿAbd al-Muṭṭalib were boasting in the presence of ʿAlī b. Abī Ṭālib ﷺ. Ṭalḥa b. Shayba said: 'I possess the keys of the Kaʿba, and if I wished I could spend the night inside!' ʿAbbās said: 'I am water bearer of the pilgrims. It is I who am tasked with its care and if I wish I could spend the night in the mosque!' ʿAlī said: 'Listen to what the two of you are saying! It is *I* who prayed in the direction of the Kaʿba for six months before any of the people and I am the man of *jihād*. And then Allah sent down the verse: *Would you deem the giving of water to pilgrims and looking after the Holy Precinct the same as believing in Allah, and the last day, and doing jihād in the Way of Allah? They are not equal in the sight of Allah and Allah does not guide the transgressing folk.*[88]

Another example is what was related by Aḥmad b. Ḥanbal,[89] on the authority of Anas b. Mālik who said: "We said to Salmān, 'Ask the Prophet about his will.' So Salmān said to him, 'O Messenger of Allah, who shall be your legatee?' 'O Salmān, who was the legatee of Mūsā?' 'It was Yūshaʿ b. Nūn.' 'My legatee who shall establish my religion and fulfil my promises is ʿAlī b. Abī Ṭālib.'"

86 See Aḥmad b. Ḥanbal, *al-Musnad*, 2:735, *ḥadīth* 3119 (Ibn ʿAbbās); 6:291, *ḥadīth* 13936 (Anas b. Mālik); 7:3758, *ḥadīth* (Wāthila b. al-Asqaʿ); 12:6397, *ḥadīth* (Umm Salama).

87 Qur'ān 58:12.

88 Qur'ān 9:19.

89 See Aḥmad b. Ḥanbal, *Faḍā'il al-Ṣaḥāba*, 2:615, *ḥadīth* 1052.

ونحوه ما رواه أحمد بن حنبل. وقال في قوله تعالى ﴿إذا ناجيتم الرّسول فقدّموا بين يدي نجواكم صدقة﴾ قال أمير المؤمنين عليّ بن أبي طالب عليه السلام: ما عمل بهذه الآية غيري، وبي خفّف الله تعالى أمر هذه الآية.

وعن محمد بن كعب القرظي، قال: افتخر طلحة بن شيبة من بني عبد الدار وعبّاس بن عبد المطلب وعليّ بن أبي طالب عليه السلام، فقال طلحة بن شيبة: معي مفتاح البيت ولو أشاء بتّ فيه! وقال العبّاس: أنا صاحب السقاية والقائم عليها، ولو أشاء بتّ في المسجد! وقال عليّ عليه السلام: ما أدري ماتقولان! لقد صلّيت إلى القبلة ستّة أشهر قبل الناس، وأنا صاحب الجهاد، فأنزل الله تعالى ﴿أجعلتم سقاية الحاجّ وعمارة المسجد الحرام كمن آمن بالله واليوم الآخرة جاهد في سبيل الله لا يستوون عند الله والله لايهدي القوم الظّالمين﴾.

ومنها ما رواه أحمد بن حنبل، عن أنس بن مالك قال: قلنا لسلمان: سل النبيّ عن وصيّه! فقال له سلمان: يا رسول الله، من وصيّك؟ فقال: يا سلمان، من كان وصي موسى؟ فقال: يوشع بن نون؛ قال: قال: وصيّي ووارثي يقضي ديني وينجز موعدي عليّ بن أبي طالب.

On the authority of Abū Maryam, on the authority of ʿAlī b. Abī Ṭālib ﷺ who said: "The Prophet ﷺ and I set out until we reached the Kaʿba. Then the Messenger of Allah ﷺ said to me: 'Sit.' Then he climbed up on my shoulders and I began to start to lift him up, but he sensed that I was straining and so he stepped down and the Prophet of Allah ﷺ himself sat down for me and said, 'Get on my shoulders.' I did so and he lifted me up. It seemed to me as though if I had so wished I could have reached above the heavens. I got up on top of the Kaʿba where there was a brass or copper idol. I began to jerk it left-and-right, forward-and-backward, until I was able to pry it loose. The Messenger of Allah told me: 'Throw it down.' So I threw it and it broke, shattering like a glass bottle. Then I climbed down and left along with the Messenger of Allah. We were rushing with one another to reach the cover of the houses [in the vicinity of the Kaʿba] since we were afraid someone might catch us."

On the authority of Maʿqal b. Yasār, that the Prophet ﷺ said to Fāṭima: "Would you not like me to get you married to the earliest person of my community to accept Islam, and the most abundant of them in knowledge, and the mightiest of them in forbearance?"

On the authority of Ibn Abī Laylā who said that the Messenger of Allah ﷺ said: "The supremely veracious are three: Ḥabīb al-Najjār, the believer among the Family of Yāsīn who said *O my people! Pay heed to the messengers!*;[90] Ḥazaqīl, the believer among the Family of Pharaoh who said *Will you all kill a man for saying 'Allah is my Lord?'*[91]; and ʿAlī b. Abī Ṭālib, who is the most excellent of all of them." It is transmitted from the Prophet that he said to ʿAlī: "You are from me, and I am from you."

On the authority of ʿAmr b. Maymūn who said, "ʿAlī has ten qualities which no one else has. The Prophet ﷺ said to him: 'I will send forth a man whom Allah will never disgrace and who loves Allah and His Messenger.' One and all longed to be that man. He [then] said, 'Where is ʿAlī?' They said, 'He is at the mill grinding grain.' He said, 'And none of you could do that?' He then came but his eyes were so swollen he could hardly see. So, he spit in his eyes and then shook the banner thrice before passing it to him alone. He later returned having taken Ṣafiyya Bint Ḥuyay prisoner." "Also, he sent out Abū Bakr with Sūrat al-Tawba,[92] only to later send ʿAlī behind him in order that he take it from him, saying that none can convey it but a man who is from me and I am from him."

90 Qur'ān 36:20.

91 Qur'ān 40:28.

92 The ninth Sūra of the Qur'ān.

وعن أبي مريم عن عليّ عليه السلام قال: انطلقت أنا والنبي صلى الله عليه وآله حتّى أتينا الكعبة، فقال لي رسول الله صلى الله عليه وآله: اجْلس! فصعد على منكبي فذهبت لأنهض به، فرأى منّي ضعفاً فنزل وجلس لي نبي الله صلى الله عليه وآله وقال: اصعد على منكبي، فصعدت على منكبيه، قال: فنهض بي قال: فإنّه تخيّل لي أني لو شئتُ لنلت أفق السماء حتّى صعدت على البيت، وعليه تمثال صفر أو نُحاس فجعلت أزاوله عن يمينه وعن شماله وبين يديه ومن خلفه، حتّى إذا استحكمت منه؛ قال لي رسول الله صلى الله عليه وآله: اقذف به! فقذفت به فتكسّر كما تتكسّر القوارير، ثم نزلت وانطلقت أنا ورسول الله نستبق حتّى توارينا بالبيوت خشية أن يلقانا أحد من الناس.

وعن معقل بن يسار، أنّ النبي صلى الله عليه وآله قال لفاطمة: ألا ترضين أنّي زوّجتك أقدم أمّتي سلماً وأكثرهم علماً وأعظمهم حلماً؟

عن ابن أبي ليلى، قال: قال رسول الله صلى الله عليه وآله: الصّديقون ثلاثة: حبيب النجّار مؤمن آل يس الذي قال ﴿يا قوم اتّبعوا المرسلين﴾، وحزبيل مؤمن آل فرعون الذي قال ﴿أتقتلون رجلا أن يقول ربّي الله﴾، وعليّ بن أبي طالب وهو أفضلهم. وعن رسول الله صلى الله عليه وآله أنه قال لعليّ: أنت مني وأنا منك.

وعن عمرو بن ميمون قال: لعليّ عشر خصال ليست لغيره، قال له النبي صلى الله عليه وآله لأبعثنّ رجلاً لا يخزيه الله أبداً، يحبّ الله ورسوله، فاستشرف لها من استشرف، قال: أين عليّ؟ قالوا: هو في الرحى يطحن؛ قال: وما كان أحدكم يطحن قال: فجاء وهو أرمد لا يكاد أن يبصر، قال: فنفث في عينيه ثمّ هزّ الراية ثلاثاً فأعطاها إيّاه، فجاء بصفيّة بنت حيي. قال: ثم بعث أبا بكر بسورة التوبة، فبعث علياً خلفه فأخذها منه، وقال: لا يذهب بها إلّا رجل هو منّي وأنا منه.

"Also, he said to his paternal cousins: 'Whom from amongst you will be my loyal supporter in this world and in the next?' 'Alī was seated in their midst. They all refused, but 'Alī said, 'I will be your loyal supporter in this world and in the next.' He left it at that and turned to one of them saying 'Whom from amongst you will be my loyal supporter in this world and in the next?' Again, they all refused, but 'Alī said, 'I will be your loyal supporter in this world and in the next.' To this he said, 'You are my loyal supporter in this world and in the next.'"

"Also, 'Alī was the first person to accept Islam among the people after Khadīja."

"Also, the Messenger of Allah ﷺ took his own garment and draped it over 'Alī, Fāṭima, Ḥasan, and Ḥusayn ؊ and recited, *Truly Allah only wishes to remove all impurity from you, O People of the House, and to purify you exceedingly.*"[93]

"Also, 'Alī took the place of the Messenger of Allah ﷺ donning his garments and sleeping in his place. The idolaters used to pelt him with stones."

"Also, the Prophet ﷺ went out to the troops being dispatched to Tabūk. 'Alī said to him, 'Should I not go with you?' He said, 'No.' At this 'Alī wept, so he said, 'Will you not be content with being in relation to me as was Hārūn to Mūsā — except that you are not a prophet. It is not right for me to leave unless you are the one who stands in my place.'"

"Also, the Messenger of Allah ﷺ said, 'You are my guardian over every believer after me.'"

"Also, he blocked the doors of everyone whose door opened into the mosque except the door of 'Alī. Thus, he used to enter the mosque in a state of the greater ritual impurity. This was the pathway he used and he had no other pathway."

"Also, he said, 'Whomsoever's master I am, 'Alī is his master.'"[94]

---

93 Qur'ān 33:33.
94 This is the Ḥadīth of Ghadīr Khumm or Ḥadīth al-Walāya. 'Allāma refers to this *ḥadīth* many times in the course of this book and it is known as the *ḥadīth* of Ghadīr Khumm. See Ibn 'Uqda al-Kūfī (d. 322/94), *Kitāb al-wilāya*, edited by 'Abd al-Razzāq Muḥammad Ḥusayn Ḥirz al-Dīn (Qom: 1421/2000), 155–255. On him see the monograph-length introduction to the aforementioned work, 9–152. This edition is a reconstruction based on surviving quotations in still extant primary sources of a work by Ibn 'Uqda containing all of the narrations of the *ḥadīth* of Ghadīr Khumm known to him. This reconstructed work contains narrations by 98 different companions of the Prophet. An eminent Sunnī contemporary of Ibn 'Uqda, namely the jurist, Qur'ān commentator, and historian Abū Ja'far Muḥammad b. Jarīr al-Ṭabarī (d. 310/921), also devoted a work entitled *Kitāb al-Ghadīr* to the large number of narrations of this *ḥadīth* which has subsequently been lost. However, there are references to it in works contemporaneous with him, for example see

وقال لبني عمّه: أيكم يواليني في الدنيا والآخرة؟ قال: وعليّ معهم جالس، فأبوا فقال عليّ: أنا أواليك في الدنيا والآخرة، قال: فتركه ثمّ أقبل على رجل منهم فقال: أيكم يواليني في الدنيا والآخرة؟ فأبوا، فقال عليّ: أنا أواليك في الدنيا والآخرة؛ فقال: أنت وليّي في الدنيا والآخرة.

قال: وكان علي أوّل من أسلم من الناس بعد خديجة.

قال: وأخذ رسول الله ﷺ ثوبه فوضعه على عليّ وفاطمة والحسن والحسين عليهم السلام، فقال﴿إنّما يريد الله ليذهب عنكم الرّجس أهل البيت ويطهّركم تطهيراً﴾.

قال: وشري عليّ نفسه ولبس ثوب رسول الله ﷺ ثمّ نام مكانه، وكان المشركون يرمونه بالحجارة.

وخرج النبي ﷺ في غزاة تبوك، فقال له عليّ: أأخرج معك؟ فقال: لا، فبكى عليّ فقال له: أما ترضى أن تكون منّي بمنزلة هارون من موسى إلّا أنّك لست بنبيّ، لا ينبغي أن أذهب إلّا وأنت خليفتي.

قال: وقال له رسول الله ﷺ: أنت وليّي في كلّ مؤمن بعدي.

قال: وسدّ أبواب المسجد غير باب عليّ، قال: فيدخل المسجد جنباً وهو طريقه ليس له طريق غيره.

وقال له: من كنت مولاه فإنّ مولاه عليّ.

It is transmitted in an unbroken chain of narrators from the Prophet ﷺ that he dispatched Abū Bakr with Sūrat al-Barā'a[95] to the Meccans. He went out with it for three.[96] Then he sent out ʿAlī after him saying, "Catch up to him and take it from him. You convey it." He did so. When Abū Bakr came back to the Prophet ﷺ he wept and said, "O Messenger of Allah, did something happen to me?"[97] He said, "No, but I was commanded that none could convey it but me or a man who is from me."

Another example is what was related by Akhṭab Khwārizm[98] going back to the Prophet ﷺ, who said: "O ʿAlī! Were someone to worship Allah — the Mighty, the Sublime — for as long as Nūḥ toiled among his people, and were he to have the equivalent amount in gold the weight of Mount Uḥud all of which he spent in the way of Allah, and were he to live so long that he performed a thousand pilgrimages to Mecca on foot, and then were he to die a martyr's death between Ṣafā' and Marwā, but was not loyal to you, O ʿAlī, he shall not so much as sniff the scent of Paradise, nor enter therein."[99]

Someone quipped to Salmān, "How intense your love is for ʿAlī!" He said, "I heard the Messenger of Allah ﷺ say, 'Whoever loves ʿAlī, has loved me; and whoever hates ʿAlī has hated me.'"[100]

Anas relates that the Messenger of Allah ﷺ said, "From the luminosity of the countenance of ʿAlī b. Abī Ṭālib Allah created 70,000 angels who are seeking forgiveness for him and those who love him until the day of judgement."[101]

the Ismāʿīlī scholar al-Qāḍī Abū Ḥanīfa al-Nuʿmān b. Muḥammad al-Tamīmī al-Maghribī, *Sharḥ al-akhbār fī faḍā'il al-a'immat al-aṭhār*, edited by Muḥammad Ḥusayn al-Ḥusaynī al-Jālālī (Qom: 1409/2008), 1:130–133. Numerous scholars have devoted their efforts over the centuries to the study of the transmission history of this *ḥadīth*. Notable later works include *ʿAbaqāt al-anwār* by Mīr Ḥāmid Ḥusayn Lakhnawī, *Kitāb al-ghadīr fī al-kitāb wa-l-sunna wa-l-adab* (Beirut: 1414/1994) by ʿAbd al-Ḥusayn Aḥmad al-Amīnī al-Najafī. Among classical Sunnī *ḥadīth* sources see: Aḥmad b. Ḥanbal, *al-Musnad*, 1:196, *ḥadīth* 651; 1: 265, *ḥadīth* 976; 1:266, *ḥadīth* 979; 1:332, *ḥadīth* 1327; 8:4208, *ḥadīth* 18771; 8:4209, *ḥadīth* 18772; 8:4430, *ḥadīth* 19587; 8:4436, *ḥadīth* 19610; 10:5461, *ḥadīth* 23495; al-Tirmidhī, *al-Jāmiʿ*, 2:948, *ḥadīth* 4078. Also compare Muslim b. al-Ḥajjāj, *al-Ṣaḥīḥ*, 2:1033, *ḥadīth* 6378.

95 Another name for Sūrat al-Tawba, the ninth Sūra of the Qur'ān.

96 The text only says "three" (*thalāthan*) without any further appellation.

97 He means to say, "was there something in me that made you change your mind?"

98 The title by which the Sunnī Ḥanafī Ashʿarī scholar al-Muwaffaq b. Aḥmad b. Muḥammad al-Makkī al-Khawārizmī (d. 568/1172) was known.

99 Al-Muwaffaq b. Aḥmad al-Khawārizmī, *al-Manāqib* (Qom: al-Nashr al-Islāmī, 1421/2000), 67–68, *ḥadīth* 40.

100 Al-Muwaffaq b. Aḥmad al-Khawārizmī, *al-Manāqib*, 69–70, *ḥadīth* 44.

101 Al-Muwaffaq b. Aḥmad al-Khawārizmī, *al-Manāqib*, 71, *ḥadīth* 47.

وعن النبيّ ﷺ مرفوعاً: أنّه بعث أبا بكر ببراءة إلى أهل مكّة فسار بها ثلاثاً، ثم قال لعليّ عليه السلام: الحقه فردّه وبلّغها أنت؛ ففعل، فلمّا قدم أبو بكر على النبي ﷺ بكى وقال: يارسول الله حدث فيّ شيءٌ؟ قال: لا، ولكن أمرت ألّا يبلّغه إلا أنا أو رجل منّي.

ومنها ما رواه أخطب خوارزم عن النبي ﷺ أنه قال: يا عليّ، لو أنّ عبداً عبد الله عزّ وجل مثل ما قام نوح في قومه وكان له مثل أحد ذهباً فأنفقه في سبيل الله ومدّ في عمره حتّى حج ألف عام على قدميه ثم قتل بين الصفا والمروة مظلوماً ثم لم يوالك يا عليّ لم يشمّ رائحة الجنّة ولم يدخلها.

وقال رجل لسلمان: ما أشدّ حبك لعليّ! قال: سمعت رسول الله ﷺ يقول: من أحبّ عليّاً فقد أحبّني، ومن أبغض عليّاً فقد أبغضني؛

وعن أنس قال: قال رسول الله ﷺ: خلق الله من نور وجه عليّ بن أبي طالب سبعين ألف ملك يستغفرون له ولمحبّيه إلى يوم القيامة.

Ibn ʿUmar related that Messenger of Allah ﷺ said, "Whoever loves ʿAlī, Allah will accept his prayers, his fasting, his supererogatory night prayers, and answers his supplications. Indeed, whoever loves ʿAlī, Allah will reward him for every drop of blood in his body with a city in Paradise. Indeed, whoever loves ʿAlī and whoever loves the Family of Muḥammad will be made safe from the accounting, the balance of deeds, and traversing the bridge over Hellfire. Indeed, whoever dies on the love of the Family of Muḥammad, I along with the prophets shall be his guarantor of Paradise. Indeed, whoever harbours enmity for the Family of Muḥammad shall arrive on the Day of Judgement stamped on his brow with the words: 'Forsaken of the Divine mercy.'"[102]

ʿAbdullāh b. Masʿūd related that he heard the Messenger of Allah ﷺ saying, "Whoever claims that he has believed in me and in that which I came with, but harbours enmity for ʿAlī, he is a liar and is not a believer."[103]

Abū Baraza related that one day when we were all seated with the Messenger of Allah ﷺ he said, "I swear by Him in whose Hand is my life! No one will withdraw a single footstep on the Day of Judgement without Allah — may He be glorified and exalted — asking him about four things: his years and how he past them, his body and in what he exerted it, his wealth and from what he acquired it and in what he spent it, and love for us, the People of the House." ʿUmar asked him, "What shall be the hallmark of love for you after you have passed on?" He then placed his hand upon the head of ʿAlī ؑ while facing him and said, "Truly, to love me after I have passed on is to love this person."[104]

ʿAbdullāh b. ʿUmar related that he heard the Messenger of Allah ﷺ say when he was asked, "In what manner of speech did Allah address you on the Night of the Heavenly Ascent?" He said, "He addressed in me in the manner of speech of ʿAlī b. Abī Ṭālib. I then thought to myself, O Lord, is it you addressing me or is it ʿAlī? He said to me, O Aḥmad! I am a thing unlike [other] things, I cannot be compared to persons, nor can I be described by form (*ashbāh*). I created you from My light, and ʿAlī from your light. I plumbed the inner recesses of your heart and found none more beloved to your heart than ʿAlī b. Abī Ṭālib. Thus, did I address you with in his manner of speech so that your heart might be tranquil."[105]

102 al-Muwaffaq b. Aḥmad al-Khawārizmī, *al-Manāqib*, 72–73, *ḥadīth* 51.
103 al-Muwaffaq b. Aḥmad al-Khawārizmī, *al-Manāqib*, 76, *ḥadīth* 57.
104 al-Muwaffaq b. Aḥmad al-Khawārizmī, *al-Manāqib*, 76, *ḥadīth* 58.
105 al-Muwaffaq b. Aḥmad al-Khawārizmī, *al-Manāqib*, 78, *ḥadīth* 61.

وعن ابن عمر، قال: قال رسول الله ﷺ: من أحبّ عليّا قبل الله منه صلاته وصيامه وقيامه واستجاب دعاءه، ألا ومن أحبّ عليّا أعطاه الله بكل عرق في بدنه مدينة في الجنّة، ألا ومن أحبّ آل محمّد أمن من الحساب والميزان والصراط، ألا ومن مات على حبّ آل محمّد فأنا كفيله بالجنّة مع الأنبياء، ألا ومن أبغض آل محمّد جاء يوم القيامة مكتوباً بين عينيه «آيس من رحمة الله».

وعن عبد الله بن مسعود قال: سمعت رسول الله ﷺ يقول: من زعم أنّه آمن بي وبما جئت به وهو يبغض عليّاً فهو كاذب ليس بمؤمن.

وعن أبي برزة قال: قال رسول الله ﷺ ونحن جلوس ذات يوم: والذي نفسي بيده لا يزول قدم عبد يوم القيامة حتّى يسأله تبارك وتعالى عن أربع: عن عمره فيم أفناه، وعن جسده فيم أبلاه، وعن ماله مما كسبه وفيم أنفقه، وعن حبّنا أهل البيت. فقال له عمر: فما آية حبّكم من بعدكم؟ فوضع يده على رأس عليّ عليه السلام وهو إلى جانبه فقال: إنّ حبّي من بعدي حبّ هذا.

وعن عبد الله بن عمر، سمعت رسول الله ﷺ وقد سئل: بأيّ لغة خاطبك ربّك ليلة المعراج؟ فقال: خاطبني بلغة عليّ بن أبي طالب، فألهمني أن قلت: يا ربّ أنت خاطبتني أم عليّ؟ فقال: يا أحمد، أنا شيء ليس كالأشياء لا أُقاس بالناس ولا أوصف بالأشباه، خلقتك من نوري وخلقت عليّا من نورك، فاطّلعت على سرائر قلبك فلم أجد إلى قلبك أحبّ من عليّ بن أبي طالب، فخاطبتك بلسانه كيما يطمئن قلبك؛

Ibn ʿAbbās related that the Messenger of Allah ﷺ said, "Were the gardens all to become pens, and the seas all to become ink, and all the Jinn to be employed in enumerating, and all humanity to be employed as scribes, they would be unable to count the merits of ʿAlī b. Abī Ṭālib."[106]

He also related that the Messenger of Allah ﷺ said, "Allah has given my brother ʿAlī merits in such abundance that they cannot be counted. Whoever mentions one of his merits assenting to it, Allah will forgive him his sins from the past and what is to come. Whoever writes down one of his merits, the angels will continue to seek forgiveness for him as long as the trace of that writing endures. Whoever listens to one of his merits, Allah will forgive him the sins he committed by listening. Whoever looks at the writing of one of his merits, Allah will forgive him the sins he committed by looking."

He also said, "Looking at the face of the Commander of the Faithful ʿAlī b. Abī Ṭālib is an act of worship. To mention him, is an act of worship. Allah will not accept the faith of his servant without his loyalty to him [i.e., to ʿAlī] and without his disavowal of his enemies [i.e., of the enemies of ʿAlī]." [107]

Hakīm narrated from his father through his grandfather from the Prophet ﷺ that he said, "Truly, the combat of ʿAlī b. Abī Ṭālib with ʿAmr b. ʿAbd Wudd on the Day of Khandaq exceeds in excellence all the actions of my *umma* until the Day of Judgement."

Saʿd b. Abī Waqqāṣ related that Muʿāwiya b. Abī Sufyān ordered him to curse [ʿAlī] and he refused to do so. He asked him, "What kept you from insulting the Father of Dust?"[108] He said: "Three things which the Messenger of Allah ﷺ had said keep me from ever cursing him. Had I had even one of them it would have been more beloved to me than the choicest of camels. I heard the Messenger of Allah ﷺ say to ʿAlī, having left him behind [in Medina] during one of his military expeditions, who said to him, 'O Messenger of Allah, would you leave me behind with the women and young boys?' To which the Messenger of Allah ﷺ said, 'Will you not be content with being in relation to me as was Hārūn to Mūsā — except that there shall be no prophet after me.'"

106 al-Muwaffaq b. Aḥmad al-Khawārizmī, *al-Manāqib*, 328, *ḥadīth* 341.

107 al-Muwaffaq b. Aḥmad al-Khawārizmī, *al-Manāqib*, 32–33, *ḥadīth* 2.

108 This was a title which was actually conferred upon ʿAlī by the Prophet himself However, it was employed derisively by his enemies. For original sources and discussion of these issues see Nebil Husayn, *Opposing the Imām. The Legacy of the Nawāṣib in Islamic Literature* (Cambridge: Cambridge University Press, 2021), 54–58 and 167–174.

وعن ابن عبّاس، قال: قال رسول الله ﷺ: لو أنّ الرياض أقلام والبحر مداد والجنّ حسّاب والإنس كتّاب ما أحصوا فضائل عليّ بن أبي طالب؛

وبالاسناد قال: قال رسول الله ﷺ: إن الله تعالى جعل لأخي عليّ فضائل لاتحصى كثرة، فمن ذكر فضيلة من فضائله مقرّاً بها غفر الله له ما تقدّم من ذنبه وما تأخّر؛ ومن كتب فضيلة من فضائله لم تزل الملائكة تستغفر له مابقي لتلك الكتابة رسم؛ ومن استمع فضيلة من فضائله غفر الله له الذنوب التي اكتسبها (بالاستماع، ومن نظر إلى كتاب من فضائله غفر الله له الذنوب التي اكتسبها) بالنظر؛

ثم قال: النظر إلى وجه أمير المؤمنين عليّ بن أبي طالب عبادة، وذكره عبادة؛ لا يقبل الله إيمان عبد إلّا بولايته والبراءة من أعدائه.

وعن حكيم عن أبيه عن جدّه عن النبي ﷺ أنّه قال: لمبارزة عليّ بن أبي طالب لعمرو بن عبد ود يوم الخندق أفضل من عمل أمّتي إلى يوم القيامة.

وعن سعد بن أبي وقّاص قال: أمر معاوية بن أبي سفيان سعداً بالسبّ فأبى، فقال: ما منعك أن تسبّ أبا تراب؟ فقال: ثلاث قالهنّ رسول الله ﷺ فلن أسبّه، لئن يكون لي واحدة منهنّ أحبّ إلي من حمر النّعم؛ سمعت رسول الله ﷺ يقول لعليّ وقد خلّفه في بعض مغازيه فقال له عليّ: يا رسول الله تخلّفني مع النساء والصبيان؟! فقال له رسول الله ﷺ: أما ترضى أن تكون منّي بمنزلة هارون من موسى، إلّا أنه لا نبيّ بعدي؟

"I also heard him say on the Day of Khaybar, 'Indeed, I shall certainly entrust the standard to one who loves Allah and His Messenger and whom Allah and His Messenger love.' So we were all craning our necks [looking here and there] when he said, 'Get me 'Alī!'' So he came, but his eyes were swollen over, so he spat in them and handed over the standard to him, and Allah granted him victory."

"Also, when the verse *Say: Let us then summon our sons and your sons*[109] was revealed the Messenger of Allah ﷺ summoned 'Alī, Fāṭima, Ḥasan, and Ḥusayn; and proclaimed, 'These are my Family.'"

'Āmir b. Wāthila relates that, "I was with 'Alī in the house on the Day of the Shūrā and heard him address those present saying, 'I will refute you all with arguments that no Arab nor Persian will be able to dispute.' He then began, 'I beseech you, all of you, in the Name of Allah! Is there amongst you a single one who professed the unicity of Allah the Exalted before me?' They said, 'O Allah! No.'

'I beseech you in the Name of Allah! Is there amongst you a single one but me who has a brother like my brother Ja'far al-Ṭayyār, soaring among the angels in Paradise?' They said, 'O Allah! No.'

'I beseech you in the Name of Allah! Is there amongst you a single one but me who has a paternal uncle like my paternal uncle Ḥamza, the Lion of Allah and the Lion of the Messenger of Allah, the Lord of the Martyrs?' They said, 'O Allah! No.'

'I beseech you in the Name of Allah! Is there amongst you a single one but me who has a wife like my wife Fāṭima Bint Muḥammad, Lady of the Women of Paradise?' They said, 'O Allah! No.'

'I beseech you in the Name of Allah! Is there amongst you a single one but me who is the father of two grandsons of the Prophet like Ḥasan and Ḥusayn, Princes of the Youths of Paradise?' They said, 'O Allah! No.'

'I beseech you in the Name of Allah! Is there amongst you a single one but me who had private audience with the Messenger of Allah ﷺ on ten separate occasions, giving alms before each audience?' They said, 'O Allah! No.'[110]

'I beseech you in the Name of Allah! Is there amongst you a single one but me to whom the Messenger of Allah ﷺ said: 'Whomsoever's master I am 'Alī is his master. O Allah! Befriend whomsoever befriends him and forsake whomsoever forsakes him. Let the one who has witnessed this convey to the one who has not?' They said, 'O Allah! No.'

109 Qur'ān 3:61.

110 This is a reference to Qur'ān 58:12.

وسمعته يقول يوم خيبر: لأعطينّ الراية رجلاً يحبّ الله ورسوله (ويحبّه الله ورسوله) . فتطاولنا فقال: ادعوا لي عليّاً؛ فأتاه وبه رمد فبصق في عينيه فدفع الراية إليه، ففتح الله عليه.

وأنزلت هذه الآية ﴿قل تعالوا ندع أبناءنا وأبناءكم﴾ دعا رسول الله ﷺ عليّاً وفاطمة وحسناً وحسيناً، فقال: اللّهمّ هؤلاء أهلي.

وعن عامر بن واثلة قال: كنت مع علي في البيت يوم الشورى فسمعت عليّا يقول لهم: لأحتجنّ عليكم بما لا يستطيع عربيّكم ولا عجميّكم تغيير ذلك، ثم قال: أنشدكم بالله أيها النفر جميعاً أفيكم أحد وحّد الله تعالى قبلي؟ قالوا: اللّهمّ لا.

قال: فأنشدكم بالله، هل فيكم أحد له أخ مثل أخي جعفر الطيّار في الجنّة مع الملائكة غيري؟ قالوا: اللهم لا.

قال: فأنشدكم بالله، هل فيكم أحد له عم مثل عمّي حمزة أسد الله وأسد رسوله سيّد الشهداء غيري؟ قالوا: اللّهمّ لا.

قال: فأنشدكم بالله، هل فيكم أحد له زوجة مثل زوجتي فاطمة بنت محمّد سيّدة نساء أهل الجنة غيري؟ قالوا: اللّهمّ لا.

قال: فأنشدكم بالله تعالى، هل فيكم أحد له سبطان مثل سبطيّ الحسن والحسين سيّدي شباب أهل الجنّة غيري؟ قالوا: اللّهمّ لا.

قال: فأنشدكم بالله، هل فيكم أحد ناجي رسول الله ﷺ عشر مرات وقدّم بين يدي نجواه صدقة غيري؟ قالوا: اللّهمّ لا.

قال: فأنشدكم بالله، هل فيكم أحد قال له رسول الله ﷺ: من كنت مولاه فعليّ مولاه، اللّهمّ وال من والاه وعاد من عاداه، ليبلغ الشاهد الغايب غيري؟ قالوا: اللّهمّ لا.

'I beseech you in the Name of Allah! Is there amongst you a single one but me to whom the Messenger of Allah ﷺ said: "O Allah! Bring to me the most beloved to You and me of your creation, one who loves You and me exceedingly, who can join me in eating this fowl." He came and ate with me?' They said, 'O Allah! No.'

'I beseech you in the Name of Allah! Is there amongst you a single one but me to whom the Messenger of Allah ﷺ said: "Indeed, I shall certainly entrust the standard to a man who loves Allah and His Messenger and whom Allah and His Messenger love. He shall not return [from the field of battle] without Allah granting victory at his hands," whereas others returned defeated?' They said, 'O Allah! No.'

'I beseech you in the Name of Allah! Is there amongst you a single one but me about whom the Messenger of Allah ﷺ said to the Banū Walīʿa: "Indeed, I shall truly send to you a man whose soul is like my soul, obedience to whom is obedience to me, defying whom is to defy me. He shall decide between you by the sword."' They said, 'O Allah! No.'

'I beseech you in the Name of Allah! Is there amongst you a single one but me about whom the Messenger of Allah ﷺ said: "Whoever says he loves me but harbours enmity against this man, he is a liar." They said, 'O Allah! No.'

'I beseech you in the Name of Allah! Is there amongst you a single one but me whom 3000 angels all at once saluted, including Jibrīl, Mīkāʾīl, and Isrāfīl, when I returned to the Messenger of Allah ﷺ with water from the well?"' They said, 'O Allah! No.'

'I beseech you in the Name of Allah! Is there amongst you a single one but me regarding whom a voice from heaven called out: "There is no sword but Dhū l-Fiqār,[111] and there is no noble warrior but ʿAlī!"' They said, 'O Allah! No.'

'I beseech you in the Name of Allah! Is there amongst you a single one but me to whom Jibrīl said: "This is none other than mutual sharing and co-equalising" To which the Messenger of Allah ﷺ said, "He is from me and I am from him." To which Jibrīl said: "And I am from the two of you?"' They said, 'O Allah! No.'

'I beseech you in the Name of Allah! Is there amongst you a single one to whom the Messenger of Allah ﷺ said: "You will fight the rebels, oppressors, and renegades (dubbed such by the Prophet himself) but me"?' They said, 'O Allah! No.'

111 This is how ʿAlī's sword was known.

قال: فأنشدكم بالله، هل فيكم أحد قال له رسول الله ﷺ: اللهم ائتنى بأحب الخلق إليك وإليّ، وأشدّهم لك حبّاً ولي حبّاً، يأكل معي هذا الطائر؛ فأتاه فأكل معه غيري؟ قالوا: اللّهمّ لا.

قال: فأنشدكم بالله، هل فيكم أحد قال له رسول الله ﷺ: لأعطينّ الراية رجلاً يحب الله ورسوله، ويحبه الله ورسوله، لا يرجع حتّى يفتح الله على يديه؛ إذ رجع غيري منهزماً غيري؟ قالوا: اللّهم لاّ.

قال: فأنشدكم بالله، هل فيكم أحد قال رسول الله ﷺ لبني وليعة: لتنتهنّ أو لأبعثنّ إليكم رجلا نفسه كنفسي طاعته طاعتي ومعصيته معصيتي يفصلكم بالسيف غيري؟ قالوا: اللّهمّ لا.

قال: فأنشدكم بالله، هل فيكم أحد قال رسول الله ﷺ: كذب من زعم أنّه يحبني ويبغض هذا غيري؟ قالوا: اللّهمّ لا.

قال: فأنشدكم بالله، هل فيكم أحد سلّم عليه في ساعة واحدة ثلاثة آلاف من الملائكة منهم جبرئيل وميكائيل وإسرافيل حيث جئت بالماء إلى رسول الله ﷺ من القليب غيري؟ قالوا: اللّهمّ لا.

قال: فأنشدكم بالله، هل فيكم أحد نودي به من السماء لاسيف إلّا ذوالفقار ولافتي إلّا علي غيري؟ قالوا: اللّهمّ لا.

قال: فأنشدكم بالله، هل فيكم أحد قال له جبرئيل: هذه هي المواساة، فقال رسول الله ﷺ: إنّه مني وأنا منه، فقال جبرئيل: وأنا منكما غيري؟ قالوا: اللّهمّ لا.

قال: فأنشدكم بالله، هل فيكم أحد قال له رسول الله ﷺ: تقاتل الناكثين والقاسطين والمارقين على لسان النبيّ ﷺ غيري؟ قالوا: اللّهمّ لا.

'I beseech you in the Name of Allah! Is there amongst you a single one to whom the Messenger of Allah ﷺ said: "It was *I* who fought on behalf of the revealed Qur'ān, but it is *you* who shall fight on behalf of the inner meaning of the Qur'ān" but me?' They said, 'O Allah! No.'

'I beseech you in the Name of Allah! Is there amongst you a single one for whom the Sun was caused to reverse course so as to allow him to say the afternoon prayer in its time but me?' They said, 'O Allah! No.'

'I beseech you in the Name of Allah! Is there amongst you a single one but me whom the messenger of Allah ﷺ ordered to take away Sūrat al-Barā'a from Abū Bakr, to which he said: "O Messenger of Allah, has some revelation been sent down about me regarding this?" He answered him saying, "None can convey it on my behalf but 'Alī"?' They said, 'O Allah! No.'

'I beseech you in the Name of Allah! Is there amongst you a single one about whom the Messenger of Allah said "None will love you but a believer, and none will hate you save a hypocrite" but me?' They said, 'O Allah! No.'

'I beseech you in the Name of Allah! Is there amongst you a single one for whom he shuttered all your doors leading into the Prophet's Mosque but left mine open, about which you all asked and the Messenger of Allah ﷺ told you, "It was not I who shuttered your doors nor I who opened his, but Allah who shuttered yours and opened his"?' They said, 'O Allah! No.'

'I beseech you in the Name of Allah! Is there amongst you a single one but me whom he called out for during the Battle of Ṭā'if to the exclusion of everyone else and he remained doing so to which you said that he calls out for him in place of us to which he said: "It is not I who called out to him, but Allah who called out to him."' They said, 'O Allah! No.'

'I beseech you in the Name of Allah! Do you not know that the Messenger of Allah ﷺ has said: "The truth is with 'Alī and 'Alī is with the truth. Whithersoever 'Alī turns the truth turns with him"?' They said, 'O Allah! Yes.'

'I beseech you in the Name of Allah! Do you not know that the Messenger of Allah ﷺ has said: "I am leaving behind in your midst the two weighty things, namely the Book of Allah and my Family. You shall never go astray so long as you hold fast to the two of them, nor shall the two be separated from one another until they reach me at the Fountain of Paradise"?' 'They said, 'O Allah! Yes.'

'I beseech you in the Name of Allah! Is there amongst you a single one who protected the Messenger of Allah ﷺ from the idolators by risking his life when he lay in his bed but me?' They said, 'O Allah! No.'

قال: فأنشدكم بالله، هل فيكم أحد قال له رسول الله ﷺ: إنّي قاتلت على تنزيل القرآن وتقاتل على تأويل القرآن غيري؟ قالوا: اللّهمّ لا.

قال: فأنشدكم بالله، هل فيكم أحد ردّت عليه الشمس حتى صلى العصر في وقتها غيري؟ قالوا: اللّهمّ لا.

قال: فأنشدكم بالله، هل فيكم أحد أمره رسول الله ﷺ أن يأخذ براءة من أبي بكر، فقال له أبو بكر: يا رسول الله، أنزل فيّ شيء؟ فقال له: إنه لا يؤدي عنّي إلا عليّ غيري؟ قالوا: اللّهمّ لا.

قال: فأنشدكم بالله، هل فيكم أحد قال له رسول الله ﷺ: لا يحبّك إلا مؤمن ولا يبغضك إلا منافق غيري؟ قالوا: اللّهمّ لا.

قال: فأنشدكم بالله، أتعلمون أنه أمر بسدّ أبوابكم وفتح بابي، فقلتم في ذلك، فقال رسول الله ﷺ: ما أنا سددت أبوابكم ولا أنا فتحت بابه، بل الله سدّ أبوابكم وفتح بابه غيري؟ قالوا: اللّهمّ لا.

قال: فأنشدكم بالله، أتعلمون أنه ناجاني في يوم الطائف دون الناس فأطال ذلك، فقلتم: ناجاه دوننا! فقال: ما أنا انتجيته، بل الله انتجاه غيري؟ قالوا: اللّهمّ لا.

قال: فأنشدكم بالله أتعلمون أن رسول الله ﷺ قال: الحق مع عليّ وعليّ مع الحقّ يدور الحقّ مع علي كيفما دار؟ قالوا: اللّهمّ نعم.

قال: فأنشدكم بالله، أتعلمون أن رسول الله ﷺ قال: إني تارك فيكم الثقلين كتاب الله وعترتي، لن تضلّوا ما استمسكتم بهما ولن يفترقا حتّى يردا على الحوض؟ قالوا: اللّهمّ نعم.

قال: فأنشدكم بالله، هل فيكم أحد وقى رسول الله ﷺ من المشركين بنفسه واضطجع في مضجعه غيري؟ قالوا: اللّهمّ لا.

'I beseech you in the Name of Allah! Is there amongst you a single one who engaged in one-on-one combat with 'Amr b. Wudd al-'Āmirī when he challenged you all to combat but me?' They said, 'O Allah! No.'

'I beseech you in the Name of Allah! Is there amongst you a single one but me regarding whom Allah revealed the Verse of Purification [i.e. Q33:33 known as *āyat al-taṭhīr*] in which he says: *Truly Allah only wishes to remove all impurity from you, O People of the House, and to purify you exceedingly.*' They said, 'O Allah! No.'

'I beseech you in the Name of Allah! Is there amongst you a single one about whom the Messenger of Allah ﷺ said, "You are the Lord of the Arabs" but me?' They said, 'O Allah! No.'

'I beseech you in the Name of Allah! Is there amongst you a single one to whom the Messenger of Allah ﷺ said, "I never asked Allah for anything without asking the like thereof for you" but me?' They said, 'O Allah! No.'

Another example is what was related by Abū 'Amr al-Zāhid, on the authority of Ibn 'Abbās who said: "'Alī has three qualities which are to be found in no other man but him. He it was who was the first amongst the Arabs and non-Arabs to pray with the Messenger of Allah ﷺ, he it was who bore his standard on every field of battle, he it was who persevered by his side in the Battle of Ḥunayn, and he it was who bathed him and placed him in his grave — may Allah pour forth His blessings upon them both."

On the authority of the Prophet ﷺ who said: "On the Night of the Ascent I passed by a people whose mouths had been ripped open, so I asked: 'O Jibrīl, who are they?' He said, 'They are the ones who cut people through backbiting.' Then I passed by a people making a clamour, so I asked: 'O Jibrīl, who are they?' He said: 'They are the unbelievers.' Then we took another path and once we had reached the fourth heaven I saw 'Alī performing *ṣalāt* and I said to Jibra'īl, 'Could it be that 'Alī has preceded us?' He said: 'No, this is not 'Alī.' I said: 'Then who is he?' He said: 'When the Angels who are Drawn Nigh heard of the merits of 'Alī ﵇, especially when you said: "... your status in relation to me is as the station of Hārūn in relation to Mūsā, except that there shall be no prophet after me"[112] they began to long for 'Alī, and so Allah created for them another angel in the image of 'Alī. When they long for 'Alī they gaze at that angel, and it is as though they gaze upon 'Alī.'

112 See Aḥmad b. Ḥanbal, *al-Musnad,* 1:386, *ḥadīth* 1566 and 1:367, *ḥadīth* 1481; Muslim b. al-Ḥajjāj, *al-Ṣaḥīḥ,* 2:1030, *ḥadīths* 6370, 6372, 6373 and 2:1031, *ḥadīth* 6374; Ibn Māja, *al-Sunan,* 21, *ḥadīths* 121, 122 and 22, *ḥadīth*. 126; al-Tirmidhī, *al-Jāmi',* 2:951, *ḥadīth* 4090 and 2:952, *ḥadīths* 4095, 4096.

قال: فأنشدكم بالله، هل فيكم أحد بارز عمرو بن ودّ العامري حيث دعاكم إلى البراز، غيري؟ قالوا: اللّهمّ لا.

قال: فأنشدكم بالله هل فيكم أحد أنزل الله فيه آية التطهير حيث يقول ﴿إنّما يريد الله ليذهب عنكم الرّجس أهل البيت ويطهّركم تطهيرا﴾ غيري؟ قالوا: اللّهمّ لا.

قال: فأنشدكم بالله، هل فيكم أحد قال له رسول الله ﷺ: أنت سيّد العرب غيري؟ قالوا: اللّهمّ لا.

قال: فأنشدكم بالله، هل فيكم أحد قال له رسول الله ﷺ: ما سألت الله شيئاً إلا سألت لك مثله غيري؟ قالوا: اللّهمّ لا.

ومنها ما رواه أبو عمر الزاهد عن ابن عبّاس قال: لعليّ أربع خصال ليس لأحد من الناس غيره: هو أوّل عربي وعجميّ صلّى مع رسول الله ﷺ، وهو الذي كان لواؤه معه في كل زحف، وهو الذي صبر معه يوم حنين، وهو الذي غسّله وأدخله قبره صلّى الله عليهما.

وعن النبي ﷺ قال: مررت ليلة المعراج بقوم تشرشر أشداقهم، فقلت: يا جبرئيل من هؤلاء؟ قال (هؤلاء الذين يقطعون الناس بالغيبة قال: مررت بقوم ضأضؤا فقلت: يا جبرئيل من هؤلاء؟ قال): هؤلاء الكفّار؛ قال: ثمّ عدلنا عن ذلك الطريق فلمّا انتهينا إلى السماء الرابعة رأيت عليّاً يصلّي فقلت لجبرئيل: (يا جبرئيل) أهذا عليّ قد سبقنا؟ قال: لا ليس هذا عليّاً. قلت: فمن هو؟ قال: إنّ الملائكة المقرّبين والملائكة الكروبيّين لمّا سمعت فضائل علي وبخاصة سمعت قولك فيه «أنت منّي بمنزلة هارون من موسى إلا أنّه لا نبيّ بعدي» اشتاقت إلى عليّ فخلق الله لها ملكاً على صورة علي، فإذا اشتاقت إلى علي نظرت إلى ذلك الملك، فكأنها قد رأت عليّا؛

On the authority of Ibn ʿAbbās, "One day when he was feeling particularly glad, the Chosen One ﷺ exclaimed: 'I am a chivalrous warrior, son of a chivalrous warrior, and the brother of a chivalrous warrior.'"

"By 'I am a chivalrous warrior' he meant the indisputable chivalrous warrior of the Arabs, that is to say their leader, and by 'son of a chivalrous warrior' he meant Ibrāhīm the Chosen Friend of Allah ﷺ — alluding to the statement of the Mighty, the Exalted: *We heard a young warrior make mention of them* [*i.e. their false gods*]*: he is known as Ibrāhīm*[113] — and by 'brother of a chivalrous warrior' he meant ʿAlī ﷺ — alluding to the statement of Jibraʾīl on the day of the Battle of Badr when he rose heavenward upon the victory and exclaimed in joy: 'There is no sword but Dhū l-Fiqār,[114] and there is no noble warrior but ʿAlī!'"

On the authority of Ibn ʿAbbās, "I saw Abū Dharr clutching the curtains of the Kaʿba exclaiming: 'He who knows me, knows me; and he that does not know me, I am Abū Dharr! Were you all to fast until you became as thin as bowstrings and prayed so much that you became bent as bows none of that will have done you any good unless you love ʿAlī ﷺ.'"

Another example is what was related by the compiler of *al-Firdaws* (*The Garden of Prophetic Traditions*),[115] on the authority of Muʿādh, on the authority of the Prophet ﷺ who said: "The love of ʿAlī b. Abī Ṭālib ﷺ is a merit which remains unharmed by any sin, and hating him is a sin which prevents benefit from any merit."

On the authority of Anas, "I was sitting with the Prophet ﷺ when ʿAlī happened to join us whereupon the Prophet ﷺ said; 'I and this one are the Proof of Allah against His creation.'"

On the authority of the Prophet ﷺ, "Had the people all been united in the love of ʿAlī, Allah would not have created the Fire."

113 Qurʾān 21:60.

114 This is how ʿAlī's sword was known.

115 Al-Daylamī, *al-Firdaws bi maʾthūr al-khiṭāb*; hereinafter referred to as *Firdaws al-akhbār*, 3:373, *ḥadīth* 5135.

وعن ابن عبّاس قال: إنّ المصطفى ﷺ قال ذات يوم وهو نشيط: أنا الفتى ابن الفتى أخو الفتى؛ قال: فقوله «أنا الفتى» يعني هو فتى العرب بإجماع، أي سيّدها، وقوله «ابن الفتى» يعني إبراهيم الخليل عليه السلام؛ من قوله عزّ وجل ﴿قالوا سمعنا فتى يذكرهم يقال له إبراهيم﴾ وقوله «أخو الفتى» يعني عليّا وهو قول جبرئيل في يوم بدر، ووقد عرج إلى السماء بالفتح وهو فرح وهو يقول: لا سيف إلّا ذو الفقار ولا فتى إلّا عليّ.

وعن ابن عبّاس قال: رأيت أبا ذر وهو متعلّق بأستار الكعبة وهو يقول: من عرفني فقد عرفني، ومن لم يعرفني فأنا أبو ذر، لو صمتم حتّى تكونوا كالأوتار وصلّيتم حتى تكونوا كالحنايا مانفعكم ذلك حتّى تحبّوا عليّاً؛

ومنها ما نقله صاحب الفردوس في كتابه عن معاذ عن النبي ﷺ قال: حبّ عليّ بن أبي طالب حسنة لا تضر معها سيّئة؛ وبغضه سيّئة لا تنفع معها حسنة. وعن ابن مسعود قال: حبّ آل محمّد خير من عبادة سنة، ومن مات عليه دخل الجنّة.

وعن أنس قال: كنت جالساً مع النبيّ ﷺ إذ أقبل عليّ فقال النبي ﷺ: أنا وهذا حجّة الله على خلقه.

وعن النبي ﷺ قال: لو اجتمع الناس على حبّ عليّ لم يخلق الله النار.

Another example is what was related by Abū ʿAbdullāh al-Ḥāfiẓ al-Shāfiʿī, giving his chain of transmission to Abū Baraza who said that the Messenger of Allah ﷺ said: "Truly Allah made a covenant with me regarding ʿAlī. I asked Him, 'O Lord make it clear to me.' He said to me: 'Pay heed!' I said: 'I pay heed.' He told me: "ʿAlī is the banner of guidance, the Imam of the those most near to Me, the light of those who obey Me, he is the word by which I have bound to Me the righteous, whoever loves him, has loved Me and whoever hates him has hated Me, give him, then, glad tidings of this!' When ʿAlī came, I gave him the glad tidings of this. He said: 'O Messenger of Allah! I am but a servant of Allah who is entirely in His grip. If He were to punish me, it would only be because of my misdeeds, and were that which you have given me glad tidings of to come about, then that is Allah's prerogative.' I said: 'O Allah, polish his heart and make faith his delight.'[116] Allah the Mighty and Sublime said: 'I have done with him thus.' Then it was made known to me that He would single him out with tribulations such that none of my Companions had ever experienced. I said to him: 'O Lord! He is my brother and friend!' He said to me: 'This is a matter which has been decreed. He shall be tried, and people shall be tried because of him.'" It was related by the author of *Ḥilyat al-awliyāʾ* (*The Adornment of Those Drawn Near to Allah*).

On the authority of ʿAmmār b. Yāsir, "The Messenger of Allah ﷺ said: 'To all who have believed in me and accepted [my message], I charge them with loyalty to ʿAlī b. Abī Ṭālib ؑ. Whoever is loyal to him, has been loyal to me and whoever is loyal to me has been loyal to Allah, the Mighty, the Sublime.'"

On the authority of Ibn ʿAbbās, "The Messenger of Allah ﷺ said: 'O ʿAlī! Whoever insults you has insulted me, and whoever insults me has insulted Allah, and whoever insults Allah, He shall throw him down prostrate upon his nostrils into the Fire.'"

The reports which have been related from the Adversaries are uncountable and this amount suffices this brief work.

As for the abominations of the band of men [who assumed the caliphate], the majority of their followers have related a great deal about that, so much so in fact that al-Kalbī even devoted an entire book to the disgraces of the Companions[117] and yet related not a single shortcoming ascribed the Ahl al-Bayt ؑ. Others besides him from amongst them related a great deal. We shall briefly mention some of these reports here.

---

116 The Arabic is *wa-jʿal rabīʿahu l-īmān* which literally means "and make faith his springtime."

117 See Abū l-Mundhir Hishām b. Muḥammad b. al-Sāʾib al-Kalbī (d. 204/819), *Mathālib al-ʿarab*, edited by Najāḥ al-Ṭāʾī (Beirut and London: Dār al-Hudā, 1419 /1998).

ومنها مارواه أبو عبد الله الحافظ الشافعي بإسناده عن أبي برزة قال: قال رسول الله ﷺ: إنّ الله عهد إليّ عهداً في عليّ فقلت: يا ربّ بيّنه لي، فقال: اسمع! فقلت: سمعت، فقال: إنّ عليّاً راية الهدى وإمام الأولياء ونور من أطاعني، وهو الكلمة التي ألزمتها المتّقين، من أحبّه أحبّني ومن أبغضه أبغضني، فبشّره بذلك؛ فجاء عليّ فبشّرته، فقال: يا رسول الله! أنا عبد الله في قبضته، فإن يعذّبني فبذنوبي، وإن يتّم لي الذي بشّرتني به فالله أولى بي؛ قال: فقلت: اللهم اجْلُ قلبه، واجعل ربيعه الإيمان! فقال الله عز وجل: فقد فعلت به ذلك. ثمّ إنه رفع إليّ أنّه سيخصّه من البلاء بشيء لم يخصّ به أحد من أصحابي، فقلت: يارب، أخي وصاحبي، فقال: إنّ هذا شيء قد سبق، إنّه مبتلى ومبتلى به. ورواه صاحب كتاب «حلية الأولياء».

وعن عمّار بن ياسر قال: قال رسول الله ﷺ: أوصي من آمن بي وصدّقني بولاية عليّ بن أبي طالب، من تولّاه فقد تولّاني، ومن تولّاني فقد تولى الله عزّ وجلّ.

وعن ابن عبّاس قال: قال رسول الله ﷺ: يا عليّ من سبّك فقد سبّني، ومن سبّني فقد سبّ الله، ومن سبّ الله أكبّه على منخريه في النار.

والأخبار الواردة من قبل المخالفين أكثر من أن تُحصى، لكن اقتصرنا في هذا المختصر على هذا القدر.

وأمّا المطاعن في الجماعة فقد نقل أتباعهم الجمهور منها شيئاً كثيراً، حتى صنّف الكلبي كتاباً كلّه في مثالب الصحابة، ولم يذكر فيه منقصة واحدة لأهل البيت عليهم السلام. وقد ذكر غيره منهم أشياء كثيرة، ونحن نذكر شيئاً يسيراً منها.

[The Abominations of Abū Bakr][118]

An example of this is what they relate regarding Abū Bakr. He said standing on the *minbar*: "The Prophet ﷺ was protected by virtue of revelation, but I have a devil which takes hold of me. If I stay on the straight and narrow help me, but if I falter correct me.[119] How can the Imāma be valid for a person who seeks the help of those over whom he rules to correct him, when it is they who are in need of him?

He also said: "Release me [from this charge] for I am not the best of you." Had his Imāma been valid, then him seeking release therefrom would have constituted a sin; and had it been invalid, it would have constituted an abomination anyway.

Also, ʿUmar said: "The swearing of allegiance to Abū Bakr was a precipitate affair (*falta*) whose evil was averted from the Muslims by Allah. Thus, kill whosoever should wish to go back to something like it."[120] Had his leadership (*imāma*) been valid, then how is it that whosoever should wish to go back to something like it deserves to be killed? Moreover, this would then entail abominable wrongdoing by ʿUmar. On the other hand if it was invalid, this would then entail abominable wrongdoing by both of them.

118 Compare this section with what ʿAllāma wrote in *Kashf al-Murād*, 504–511.

119 See the early Sunnī *ḥadīth* authority Abū Bakr ʿAbd al-Razzāq b. Humām al-Ṣanʿānī (d. 211/826), *al-Muṣannaf*, edited by Ḥabīb al-Raḥmān al-Aʿẓamī (Beirut: 1403/1983), 11: 336, *ḥadīth* 20701; the centenarian Sunnī *muḥaddith* Abū l-Qāsim Sulaymān b. Aḥmad b. Ayyūb al-Ṭabarānī (d. 360/970), *al-Muʿjam al-awsaṭ*, edited by Abū Muʿādh Ṭāriq b. ʿIwaḍullāh b. Muḥammad and Abū l-Faḍl ʿAbd al-Muḥsin b. Ibrāhīm al-Ḥusaynī (Cairo,: 1415 /1995), 8: 267, *ḥadīth* 8597; the Sunnī-Shāfiʿī *muḥaddith* Abū l-Qāsim ʿAlī b. al-Ḥasan, known as Ibn ʿAsākir (d. 571/1176), *Taʾrīkh Madīnat Dimishq*, edited by Muḥibb al-Dīn al-ʿAmrawī (Beirut: 1415/1995), 30: 303–304; and the Sunnī *ḥadīth* encyclopaedist ʿAlāʾ al-Dīn ʿAlī al-Muttaqī b. Ḥusām al-Dīn al-Hindī (d. 975 /1567), *Kanz al-ʿummāl* (Beirut: 1405/1985), 5:590, *ḥadīth* 14050.

120 The Shīʿī claim that the Caliphate was usurped by Abū Bakr and ʿUmar during the proceedings at the Saqīfa of Banū Sāʿida is related in detail by ʿUmar himself in many Sunnī sources. For example, see Abū Muḥammad ʿAbd al-Malik Ibn Hishām (d. 218 /833), *al-Sīrat al-nabawiyya*, edited by Muṣṭafā al-Saqā, Ibrāhīm al-Abyārī, and ʿAbd al-Ḥāfiẓ Shalabī (Cairo: n. d.), 2: 657–658; al-Ṭabarī (d. 310/921), *Taʾrīkh al-rusul wa- al-mulūk* (Cairo: 1960), 3:203–211 (= *Taʾrīkh al-rusul wa- al-mulūk*, edited by. M. J. de Goeje, *et al* [(Leiden: 1879–1901]), 1:1820–1829); and Ibn al-Athīr (d. 630/1233), *al-Kāmil fī l-tārīkh*, edited by Khalīl Maʾmūn Shīḥā (Beirut: 1422/2002), 2:300–307.

[مطاعن أبي بكر]

منها ماارووه عن أبي بكر أنّه قال على المنبر: إنّ النبي ﷺ كان يعصم بالوحي وإنّ لي شيطاناً يعتريني، فإن استقمت فأعينوني وإن زغت فقوّموني. وكيف تجوز إمامة من يستعين بالرعيّة على تقويمه مع أنّ الرعيّة تحتاج إليه؟

وقال: أقيلوني فلست بخيركم! فإن كانت إمامته حقاً كانت استقالته منها معصية. وإن كانت باطلة لزم الطعن. وقال عمر: كانت بيعة أبي بكر فلتة وقى الله المسلمين شرّها، فمن عاد إلى مثلها فاقتلوه. ولوكانت إمامته صحيحة لم يستحقّ فاعلها القتل، فيلزم تطرّق الطعن إلى عمر، وإن كانت باطلة، لزم الطعن عليهما معاً.

Abū Bakr said on his deathbed: "If only I had asked the Messenger of Allah ﷺ if the Anṣār had any right to this affair [i.e. the caliphate]."[121] This indicates that he doubted his leadership and that it had not come about correctly. In his death throes he exclaimed: "If only my mother had not given birth to me! Would that I were a straw in a brick!" Moreover, it has been related from the Prophet ﷺ that: "None face the throes of death without seeing his place in the Garden or the Fire."

Abū Bakr also said: "I wish that at the Covered Porch of Saqīfa that I had declared allegiance by putting my hand in the hand of one of the [other] two men and he could have been the Amīr and I the Vizier." This demonstrates that he was not fit and did not consider himself qualified for the Imāma.

When the Messenger of Allah ﷺ was ill with his final illness he repeated over and again: "Go out with the troops of Usāma! May the curse of Allah be upon the one who stays behind and does not join the troops of Usāma," and the three of them [i.e., Abū Bakr, ʿUmar, and ʿUthmān] remained with him, i.e., they remained behind] and Abū Bakr prevented ʿUmar from that.[122]

The Prophet ﷺ never entrusted Abū Bakr with a single [important] task in his lifetime. In fact, on one occasion he appointed ʿAmr b. al-ʿĀṣ over him, and Usāma on another, and when he dispatched him with Sūrat al-Barāʾa [also known as Sūrat al-Tawba; the 9th chapter of the Qurʾān], he had him called back on the third day after receiving a revelation from Allah the Exalted.[123] How, then, can a reasonable man be satisfied with him as Imam when even the Prophet ﷺ was not satisfied with him on the basis of a revelation from Allah the Exalted to convey ten verses from Sūrat al-Barāʾa?

121 See al-Ṭabarī, *Taʾrīkh al-rusul wa-l-mulūk,* 3:430–431 which corresponds to vol. 1, pp. 2140–2141 of the de Goeje edition wherein Abū Bakr is quoted expressing his life's regrets including his never having asked the Prophet who was to be his successor.

122 Ibn al-Athīr, *al-Kāmil fī l-tārīkh,* 2:309–11.

123 For example, during the Khaybar Campaign Abū Bakr, then ʿUmar were each dispatched by the Prophet with a contingent of troops to storm the Fortress of Khaybar only to be removed in succession due to their failure, followed by their replacement by ʿAlī who was victorious. On the latter see Ibn Hishām, *al-Sīrat al-nabawiyya,* 2:334–335; al-Ṭabarī, *Taʾrīkh al-rusul wa-l-mulūk,* 3:12–13 (=*Taʾrīkh al-rusul wa-l-mulūk,* edited by M. J. de Goeje *et al,* 1:1579–1581); and Ibn al-Athīr, *al-Kāmil fī l-tārīkh,* 2:200–201. Another example is of the Prophet appointing him to collect the alms (*ṣadaqāt*), again only to be dismissed by the Prophet because he coerced people to do this. On the latter see Muslim b. al-Ḥajjāj, *al-Ṣaḥīḥ,* 1:385: 2324 and Abū Dāwūd, *al-Sunan,* 1:279, *ḥadīth* 1625. Regarding the Sūrat al-Tawba incident, also see al-Ḥāfiẓ al-Ḥaskānī, *Shawāhid al-tanzīl li-qawāʿid al-tafḍīl,* 1:359–380.

وقال أبو بكر عند موته: ليتني كنت سألت رسول الله ﷺ هل للأنصار في هذا الأمر حقّ؟ وهذا يدلّ على أنّه في شكّ من إمامته ولم تقع صواباً. وقال عند احتضاره ليت أمّي لم تلدني! يا ليتني كنت تبنة في لبنة! مع أنهم نقلوا عن النبي ﷺ أنه قال: ما من محتضر يحتضر إلّا ويرى مقعده من الجنة أوالنار.

وقال أبو بكر: ليتني في ظلّة بني ساعدة ضربت يدي على يد أحد الرجلين، وكان هو الأمير وكنت الوزير! وهو يدلّ على أنّه لم يكن صالحاً يرتضي نفسه للإمامة.

وقال رسول الله ﷺ في مرض موته مرّة بعد أخرى، مكرراً لذلك «أنفذوا جيش أسامة! لعن الله المتخلف عن جيش أسامة»! وكان الثلاثة معه، ومنع أبو بكر عمر من ذلك.

وأيضاً لم يولّ النبي ﷺ أبا بكر عملاً ألبتّة في وقته، بل ولّى عليه عمرو بن العاص تارة وأسامة أخرى؛ ولمّا نفذه بسورة براءة ردّه بعد ثلاثة أيام بوحي من الله تعالى وكيف يرتضي العاقل إمامة من لايرتضيه النبي ﷺ بوحي من الله تعالى لأداء عشر آيات من براءة؟

Once he cut off the left hand of a thief because he did not know that it was the right hand which should ought to have been cut off.[124] He had Fujā'at al-Sulamī burned alive,[125] whereas the Prophet ﷺ had forbidden execution by conflagration, saying that "None may punish by fire save the Lord of Fire." Most of the rulings of the Sharī'a were hidden to him; for example, he was ignorant of the ruling regarding the estate of one who is without ascendants and descendants (*kalāla*)[126] and said: "I rule regarding it according to my opinion and if it hits the mark then it is from Allah, and if it is in error then it is from me and Satan." He ruled seventy different ways regarding the inheritance of grandmothers which shows the extent of his ignorance just how deficient he was in knowledge.[127]

124 Mālik b. Anas, *al-Muwaṭṭa'*, 328, *ḥadīth* 1534.

125 See al-Ṭabarī, *Ta'rīkh al-rusul wa-l-mulūk*, 3:264–265 and 430–431 (=*Ta'rīkh al-rusul wa-l-mulūk*, edited by M. J. de Goeje *et al*, 1:1903–1904 and 2140–2141); Abū l-Fidā' Ismā'īl b. Kathīr (d. 774/1372), *al-Bidāyā wa-l-nihāya*, 21 vols. in 20, edited by 'Abd al-Qādir al-Arna'ūṭ and Bashshār 'Awwād Ma'rūf (Doha: 1436/2016), 7:27. See also the Sunnī biographer Muḥammad b. Sa'd (d. 230/845), *al-Ṭabaqāt al-kubrā*, edited by Muḥammad 'Abd al-Qādir 'Aṭā (Beirut: 1376/1957), 7:278; Ibn 'Asākir, *Ta'rīkh Madīnat Dimishq*, 16:240; and the Sunnī Shams al-Dīn Muḥammad b. Aḥmad al-Dhahabī (d. 748/1374), *Siyar a'lām al-nubalā'*, 1:372. The last three sources indicate that the Khālid b. al-Walīd (d. 21/641) with the sanction of Abū Bakr burned everyone from the Banū Sulaym (the tribe of Fujā'at al-Sulamī) when they rose in opposition to the caliphate of Abū Bakr. This action of Khālid is explicitly cited as a juristic justification for such measures by the Sunnī-Ḥanbalī scholar Zayn al-Dīn 'Abd al-Raḥmān b. Shiḥab al-Dīn, known as Ibn Rajab al-Ḥanbalī (d. 795/1393) in his *Jāmī al-'ulūm wa-l-ḥikam*, edited by Māhir Yāsīn al-Faḥl (Damascus and Beirut: Dār Ibn Kathīr, 1429/2008), 366.

126 al-Muttaqī al-Hindī, *Kanz al-'ummāl*, 11:79–80, nr. 30691; the Zaydī-Shī'ī scholar Aḥmad b. Yaḥyā b. al-Murtaḍā (840/1437), *Kitāb Ṭabaqāt al-Mu'tazila*, edited by Susanna Diwald-Wilzer (Istanbul: 1960), 11.

127 Mālik b. Anas, *al-Muwaṭṭa'*, 184, *ḥadīths* 1080, 1081.

وقطع أبو بكر يسار سارق ولم يعلم أنّ القطع لليد اليمنى؛ وأحرق الفجاءة السلمي بالنار وقد نهى النبي ﷺ عن الاحراق بالنار، وقال: لا يعذّب بالنار إلا ربّ النار. وخفي عليه أكثر أحكام الشريعة، فلم يعرف حكم الكلالة؛ وقال: أقول فيها برأيي، فإن كان صواباً فمن الله وإن كان خطأ فمنّي ومن الشيطان. وقضى في الجدّ سبعين قضيّة، وهو يدل على قصوره في العلم.

What comparison, then, can be made between him and the one who said: "Ask me before you lose me! Ask me about the pathways of the heavens for I am more knowledgeable about them than I am of the pathways of the earth!"

Abū l-Buḥturī said: "I saw ʿAlī ﷺ ascending the *minbar* in Kufa and he was wearing the armour of the Messenger of Allah ﷺ, with the sword of the Messenger of Allah, clad in the turban of the Messenger of Allah ﷺ, and on his finger was the ring of the Messenger of Allah ﷺ. He took his seat on the *minbar*, exposed his chest and said: "Ask me before you lose me! Indeed, within my breast[128] alone there lies abundant knowledge! This is the flask of fragrant learning![129] This is the saliva of the Messenger of Allah ﷺ, this is what the Messenger of Allah ﷺ gave me to drink, a draught without any revelation being given to me. By Allah! Were you to set up a cushion for me I would have taken my seat upon it and given judgement to the People of the Torah from their Torah, and the People of the Gospel from their Gospel, until Allah would cause the Torah and the Gospel themselves to speak out saying: "ʿAlī has spoken the truth and given verdict according to what Allah revealed within us, whilst it is you all who merely recite the Book. Do you not use your intellect?'"

On the authority of al-Bayhaqī in his book with his chain of transmission from the Messenger of Allah ﷺ, "Whosoever wishes to gaze upon the knowledge of Ādam, the piety of Nūḥ, the gentle forbearance of Ibrāhīm, the awesome majesty of Mūsā, and the ascetic worship of ʿĪsā, then let him look at ʿAlī b. Abī Ṭālib ﷺ." Thus did he affirm all of that in him which was distributed among them.

128 The Arabic *bayna l-jawāniḥ* literally means "between the ribs."

129 The Arabic word *safaṭ* in *safaṭu l-ʿilm* signifies a container in which perfume is kept and is generally used to refer to a small box, the image being that just as the fragrance of a perfume spreads abundantly throughout a vast space from a tiny bottle, so too is the knowledge of ʿAlī b. Abī Ṭālib. See Ḥusayn al-Ḥusaynī al-Bīrjandī, *Gharīb al-ḥadīth fī Biḥār al-anwār* (Tehran: Wizārat-e Irshād ō Farhang-e Islāmī, 1379Sh), 387, col. 1 [citing Fakhr al-Dīn al-Ṭurayḥī's (d. 1085/1674) *Majmaʿ al-baḥrayn*]. According to Muḥammad b. ʿAbd al-Qādir al-Rāzī, *Mukhtār al-ṣiḥāḥ* (Beirut: Maktabat Lubnān Nāshirūn, 1995), 127, col. 1 it is Persian. According to Dehkhudā it derives from the Persian *sabad*, see his *Lughat-nāma farhang-e mutawassiṭ-e Dehkhudā* (Tehran: Intishārāt-e Dānishghāh-e Tihrān, 1385Sh), 2:1640, col. 1.

فأيّ نسبة له إلى من قال: سلوني قبل أن تفقدوني، سلوني عن طرق السماء فإنّي أعرف بها من طرق الأرض؟ قال أبو البحتري: رأيت عليّا صعد المنبر بالكوفة وعليه مدرعة كانت لرسول الله ﷺ، متقلّداً بسيف رسول الله، متعلماً بعمامة رسول الله ﷺ، في إصبعه خاتم رسول الله ﷺ، فقعد على المنبر وكشف عن بطنه فقال: سلوني قبل أن تفقدوني، فإنّما بين الجوانح منّي علم جمّ، هذا سفط العلم، هذا لعاب رسول الله ﷺ، هذا ما زقّني رسول الله ﷺ زقاً من غير وحي أُوحي إليّ، فوالله لو ثنيت لي وسادة فجلست عليها لأفتيت أهل التوراة بتوراتهم، ولأهل الإنجيل بإنجيلهم، حتى ينطق الله التوراة والإنجيل فتقول: صدق عليّ قد أفتاكم بما أنزل الله فيّ، وأنتم تتلون الكتاب أفلا تعقلون؟

وعن البيهقي في كتابه بإسناده عن رسول الله ﷺ قال: من أراد أن ينظر إلى آدم في علمه وإلى نوح في تقواه وإلى إبراهيم في حلمه وإلى موسى في هيبته وإلى عيسى في عبادته فلينظر إلى عليّ بن أبي طالب عليه السلام فأثبت له ما تفرّق فيهم.

Abū ʿAmr al-Zāhid said, quoting Abū l-ʿAbbās Thaʿlab: "We do not know of anyone exclaiming after [the demise of] his prophet 'Ask me' since the time of Shīth until Muḥammad except for ʿAlī; and indeed he *was* asked by men of high standing: Abū Bakr and ʿUmar, and others like them until questioning ceased. Yet, after all of that he still said [pointing to his chest]: 'O Kumayl b. Ziyād! Truly herein lies abundant knowledge! Would that I had found those worthy of bearing it!'"

Abū Bakr neglected the statutory punishments specified by Allah. Thus, he failed to chastise Khālid b. al-Walīd or implement the statutory punishment upon him after he killed Mālik b. Nuwayra, despite him being a Muslim, and proceeded to marry his wife the same night he killed him and bedded her even though ʿUmar advised him to execute him, but he did not agree to this.[130]

He opposed the order of Allah the Exalted in the matter of the inheritance of the daughter of the Prophet ﷺ and prevented her from [inheriting] the Grove of Fadak.[131]

He dubbed himself the "Successor of the Messenger of Allah" without him having designated him as his successor.

130 See al-Ṭabarī, *Taʾrīkh al-rusul wa-l-mulūk* (Cairo edn.), 3:276–280 (=*Taʾrīkh al-rusul wa-l-mulūk* [Leiden edn.], 1:1921–1929); Ibn al-Athīr, *al-Kāmil fī l-tārīkh*, 2:329–332.

131 This is a reference to a statement of Abū Bakr which he ascribed to the Prophet, namely *lā nūrathu* [sic.] *mā taraknā ṣadaqatun*. The latter is attested in many Sunnī sources from numerous narrators. In the interests of brevity, we shall cite the 9 instances we found in Aḥmad b. Ḥanbal, *al-Musnad*, 1:7, *ḥadīth* 10; 1:25, *ḥadīth* 59; 1:455, *ḥadīth* 1807; 1:112, *ḥadīth* 239; 1:117, *ḥadīth* 255; 1:144, *ḥadīth* 432; 11:6026, *ḥadīth* 25765; 11:6330, *ḥadīth* 26901. Regarding his denying her the Grove of Fadak see the following sources: Ibn Saʿd, *al-Ṭabaqāt*, edited by Eduard Sachau (Leiden: 1905–1940), vol. 2, pt. 2, 86; Ibn Shabba, *Taʾrīkh al-Madīnat al-Munawwara*, 196–202; al-Ṭabarī, *Taʾrīkh al-rusul wa-l-mulūk* (Cairo edn.), 3:207–208 (=*Taʾrīkh al-rusul wa-l-mulūk* [Leiden edn.], 1:1825). As for the Prophet having gifted it to her, see al-Ḥāfiẓ al-Ḥaskānī, *Shawāhid al-tanzīl li-qawāʿid al-tafḍīl*, 1:513–521; Aḥmad b. Yaḥyā b. Jābir al-Balādhurī (279/892), *Futūḥ al-buldān*, edited by Suhayl Zakkār (Beirut: 1412/1992), 38–39 and Jalāl al-Dīn al-Suyūṭī (d. 911/1505), *Tārīkh al-khulafāʾ*, edited by Qāsim al-Shammāʿī al-Rifāʿī and Muḥammad al-ʿUthmānī (Beirut: n. d.), 182.

قال أبو عمرو الزاهد: قال أبو العبّاس ثعلب: لا نعلم أحداً قال بعد نبيّه «سلوني» من شيث إلى محمّد إلّا عليّاً؛ فسأله الأكابر أبو بكر وعمر وأشباههما حتّى انقطع السؤال، ثم قال بعد هذا كله: يا كميل بن زياد! إنّ هاهنا لعلماً جمّا لو وجدت له حملة.

وأهمل أبو بكر حدود الله فلم يقتصّ من خالد بن الوليد ولا حدّه حين قتل مالك بن نويرة وكان مسلماً؛ وتزوّج امرأته من ليلة قتله وضاجعها. وأشار عليه عمر بقتله فلم يقبل.

وخالف أمر الله تعالى في توريث بنت النبي ﷺ ومنعها فدكاً. وتسمّى بخليفة رسول الله من غير أن يستخلفه.

[The Abominations of ʿUmar b. al-Khaṭṭāb]¹³²

Another example of this is what they relate regarding ʿUmar. Abū Nuʿaym al-Ḥāfiẓ related in his book *Ḥilyat al-awliyāʾ* (*The Adornment of the Saints*) that when he was in his death throes he said: "I wish I had been a goat for my people who fattened me up to their hearts content and then the best of them slaughtered me and that half of me would have been roasted and the other half cut into strips and dried and that they would have eaten me so that I could become excrement and not have been a human being."¹³³ Does this not amount to none other than the statement of Allah the Exalted: *and the unbeliever will say: "Would that I were dust!"*¹³⁴

He said to Ibn ʿAbbās when death approached: "Had I possessed an amount of gold equal to twice the whole earth I would have used it to ransom my soul out of foreboding of the departure [from this world]." This is similar to the All-Mighty's saying, "*Even if the wrongdoers were to possess everything in the world twice over, they would certainly offer it to ransom themselves from the horrible punishment on Judgment Day, for they will from Allah what they had never expected.*"¹³⁵

Let the impartial reasonable person then consider the statements of these two men as they were dying and compare it with the statements of ʿAlī ؑ: "When did he betray the beloveds: Muḥammad and his followers? When did he throw it! When did the worst of them rush forward!" And his words when he was dying: "By the Lord of the Kaʿba! I have attained to the supreme success!"

It has been related by the compilers of *al-Ṣiḥāḥ al-Sitta* (*The Six Rigorously Authenticated Books*) as related by Ibn ʿAbbās, that "When the Messenger of Allah was in his final illness he said: 'Bring me an inkwell and a clean writing surface so that I may write for you a document by virtue of which you can never go astray after me.' To this ʿUmar said: 'Truly the man talks nonsense. The Book of Allah suffices us.' A clamour arose and the Messenger of Allah ﷺ told them: 'All of you get out. It does not behove you to argue before me.'" Ibn ʿAbbās added, "What an enormous calamity came between us all and the document of the Messenger of Allah ﷺ."¹³⁶

---

132 Compare this section with what ʿAllāma wrote in *Kashf al-Murād*, 511–515.
133 Abū Nuʿaym al-Iṣfahānī, *Ḥilyat al-awliyāʾ wa-ṭabaqāt al-aṣfiyā* (Cairo: Maktabat al-Khānjī, 1351/1932), 52.
134 Qurʾān 78:40.
135 Qurʾān 39:47
136 Of the six books the event in question is recorded in the following: al-Bukhārī, *al-Jāmiʿ al-mus-*

[مطاعن عمر بن الخطّاب]

ومنها مارووه عن عمر: روى أبو نعيم الحافظ في كتاب «حلية الأولياء» أنّه لما احتضر قال يا ليتني كنت كبشاً لقومي فسمّوني ما بدا لهم، ثمّ جاءهم أحبّ قومهم إليهم فذبحوني فجعلوا نصفي شواء ونصفي قديداً فأكلوني، فأكون عذرة ولا أكون بشراً. هل هـذا إلّا مساوٍ لقول الله تعالى ﴿ويقول الكافر يا ليتني كنت تراباً﴾؟

وقال لابن عبّاس عند احتضاره: لو أنّ لي ملء الأرض ذهباً ومثله معه لأفتديت به نفسي من هول المطلع! وهذا مثل قوله تعالى ﴿ولو أنّ للّذين ظلموا ما في الأرض جميعاً ومثله معه لأفتدوا به من سوء العذاب﴾.

فلينظر المنصف العاقل قول الرجلين عند احتضارهما، وقول عليّ عليه السلام: متى ألقاها؟ متى يبعث أشقاها؟ متى ألقى الأحبّة محمّداً وحزبه؟ وقوله حين قتل: فزت وربّ الكعبة!

وروى صاحب الصحاح السبعة في السّتة من مسند ابن عبّاس أن رسول الله صلى الله عليه وآله قال في مرض موته: ائتوني بدواة وبياض لأكتب لكم كتاباً لا تضلّون به من بعدي، فقال عمر: إنّ الرجل ليهجر، حسبنا كتاب الله! وكثر اللّغط فقال رسول الله صلى الله عليه وآله: اخرجوا عنّي لا ينبغي التنازع لديّ؛ فقال ابن عبّاس: الرزيّة كلّ الرزيّة ما حال بيننا وبين كتاب رسول الله صلى الله عليه وآله.

When the Messenger of Allah ﷺ passed away, ʿUmar said: "I swear by Allah, Muḥammad has not died and will not die until he has cut off men's hands and feet!" It was only after Abū Bakr had rebuked him and recited to him *Verily you will die and so will they*[137] and *if he dies or is killed*[138] that he said: "It is as though I had never even heard this verse."[139]

When Fāṭima admonished Abū Bakr regarding the Grove of Fadak, he prepared for her a document in which he returned it to her but as she left, ʿUmar met her on the way and tore up the document.[140] She then prayed that end befall him at the hands of Abū Luʾluʾ.

He rendered null and void the punishments stipulated by Allah. Thus, he did not implement the punishment of al-Mughīra b. Shuʿba. He used to give to the widows of the Prophet ﷺ out of the public treasury what was more than their fair share.[141] He used to give ʿĀʾisha and Ḥafṣa 10,000 dirhams annually. He also changed the injunction of Allah regarding combining the *ʿumra* with the Hajj in the season of the Hajj with one set of *ṭawāf* and *saʿī* (*ḥajj al-tamattuʿ*) as well as the temporary marriage (*nikāḥ al-mutʿa*).[142]

He had little knowledge of legal rulings of Sacred Law. Thus he ruled for stoning a pregnant woman, then ʿAlī ؑ said to him: "Even if you have justification against her, you have none against the child she carries." So, he did not do it and said, "Were it not for ʿAlī, ʿUmar would have been destroyed!"[143]

---

nad al-ṣaḥīḥ, 1:30: 114, 2:887: 4475–4476, 3: 1176: 5731, 3:1486: 7454; cf. Jamāl al-Dīn al-Mizzī, *Tuḥfat al-ashrāf*, 5517, 5841; Muslim b. al-Ḥajjāj, *al-Ṣaḥīḥ*, 2:701–702: 4319–4322; Abū Dāwūd, *al-Sunan*, 2:527: 3031.

137 Qurʾān 39:30.
138 Qurʾān 3:144.
139 See Ibn Hishām, *al-Sīrat al-nabawiyya*, 4:655–656. This work was originally authored by Muḥammad b. Isḥāq (d. 218/833) and this is the recension made by Ibn Hishām. The original work of Ibn Isḥāq no longer survives in its entirety and all that remains of the original work are scattered quotations in other works, such as in the Qurʾān commentary by Abū Jaʿfar Muḥammad b. Jarīr al-Ṭabarī (d. 310/921).
140 See Abū Jaʿfar Muḥammad b. Yaʿqūb al-Kulaynī (d. 329/941), *al-Uṣūl min al-kāfī*, 2 vols., edited by ʿAlī Akbar al-Ghaffārī (Tehran: Dār al-Kutub al-Islamiyya, 1388/1968), 1:543.
141 According to ʿAbd al-Razzāq al-Ṣanʿānī, *al-Muṣannaf*, 11:99–100, nr. 20036 ʿUmar assigned 12,000 dirhams *per annum* for each of the wives, except Ṣafiyya and Juwayriya who each received 6,000 *per annum*. Aḥmad b. Ḥanbal, *al-Musnad*, 6:3418–3419, *ḥadīth* 16150 indicates that the wives each received 10,000 *per annum* except Ṣafiyya, Juwayriya, and Maymūna but that then he increased their amounts after ʿĀʾishah intervened by saying that the Prophet treated them all equally.
142 See for example Muslim b. al-Ḥajjāj, *al-Ṣaḥīḥ*, 1:571, *ḥadīths* 3482, 3483.
143 See for example the Sunnī *ḥadīth* scholar Abū ʿUmar Yūsuf b. ʿAbdullāh b. ʿAbd al-Barr al-Qurṭubī (d. 463/1070), *al-Istīʿāb fī maʿrifat al-aṣḥāb*, edited by ʿAbd al-Ghanī Muḥammad ʿAlī Mistū (Beirut: 1431/2010), 2:208.

وقال عمر لمّا مات رسول الله ﷺ: والله ما مات محمّد ولا يموت حتّى يقطع أيدي رجال وأرجلهم! فلما نبّهه أبو بكر وتلا عليه ﴿إنّك ميّت﴾ وقوله ﴿أفإن مات أو قتل﴾ قال: كأنّي ما سمعت بهذه الآية.

ولمّا وعظت فاطمة عليها السلام أبابكر في فدك كتب لها بها كتاباً وردّها عليها، فخرجت من عنده فلقيها عمر فخرق الكتاب، فدعت عليه بما فعله أبو لؤلؤة به.

وعطّل حدّ الله تعالى فلم يحدّ المغيرة بن شعبة، وكان يعطي أزواج النبي ﷺ من بيت المال أكثر ممّا ينبغي؛ فكان يعطي عائشة وحفصة في كلّ سنة عشرة آلاف درهم وغيّر حكم الله تعالى في المتعتين.

وكان قليل المعرفة بالأحكام: أمر برجم حامل فقال له عليّ عليه السلام: إن كان لك عليها سبيل فلا سبيل لك على ما في بطنها فأمسك، وقال: لولا عليّ لهلك عمر.

He ruled for stoning an insane woman, then ʿAlī ؉ said to him: "Insane people are not to be held accountable for what they do until sanity returns to them." So, he did not do it and said, "Were it not for ʿAlī, ʿUmar would have been destroyed!"[144]

He once said in a public speech: "Whoever stipulates an extortionate dowry, I will put it in the public treasury!" Then a woman said to him, "How can you prevent us from what Allah has granted us in the His Book where he says *even if you have given her a quintal of gold*."[145] To this he said: "Everyone knows the law better than ʿUmar, even secluded women."[146]

He did not implement the punishment of Qudāma b. Maẓʿūn for consuming alcohol because he recited to him the verse *those who believe and do right actions are not to be blamed for anything they have consumed*. Then ʿAlī said to him, "This verse does not apply to Qudāma." And he ordered him to flog him, but he did not know how many lashes, so the Commander of the Faithful ؉ told him 80 lashes because when someone drinks, he becomes drunk, and when drunk he speaks nonsense, and when he speaks nonsense, he lies.

He once summoned a pregnant woman and she miscarried from fear of him. The Companions said to him, "We find you to have acted within propriety and not be at fault." He then asked the Commander of the Faithful ؉ who said that he owed her damages for the child.

Two women disputed over a child and he did not know how to rule. So he turned to the Commander of the Faithful ؉ who sent for the two women and addressed them both, but neither would go back on her claim. So, he said, "Bring me a saw!" The two said to him: "What will you do?" He said: "I will cut him into two, then each of you can take a half." One of them agreed, but the other one said, "Allah! Allah! O Abū l-Ḥasan, if you must do so then let her have him." At this he said to her, "Allah is Most Great! He is truly your son and not her's. Had he been hers her heart would have been moved for him." She then admitted the truth lay with the other woman. ʿUmar was overjoyed at this and he prayed for the Commander of the Faithful ؉.

---

144 Ibid.
145 Qurʾān 4:20.
146 See for example the Sunnī *muḥaddith* Abū Bakr Aḥmad b. al-Ḥusayn b. ʿAlī al-Bayhaqī (458/1065), *al-Sunan al-kubrā*, edited by Muḥammad ʿAbd al-Qādir ʿAṭā (Beirut: 1424/2003), 7:380, no. 14336.

وأمر برجم مجنونة فقال له عليّ عليه السلام: إنّ القلم رفع عن المجنون حتى يفيق فأمسك وقال: لولا عليّ لهلك عمر.

وقال في خطبة له: من غالى في مهر امرأة جعلته في بيت المال، فقالت له امرأة: كيف تمنعنا ما أعطانا الله تعالى في كتابه حيث قال ﴿وآتيتم إحداهنّ قنطاراً﴾ فقال: كلّ أفقه من عمر حتّى المخدّرات.

ولم يحدّ قدامة بن مظعون في الخمر لأنّه تلا عليه ﴿ليس على الّذين آمنوا وعملو الصّالحات جناح فيها طعموا﴾ فقال له عليّ: ليس قدامة من أهل هذه الآية، وأمره بحدّه فلم يدركم يحدّه، فقال له أمير المؤمنين: حدّه ثمانين؛ إنّ شارب الخمر إذا شربها سكر، وإذا سكر هذي، وإذا هذي افترى.

وأرسل إلى حامل يستدعيها فأجهضت خوفاً، فقال له الصحابة: نراك مؤدّباً ولا شيء عليك؛ ثمّ سأل أمير المؤمنين فأوجب الدية على عاقلته.

وتنازعت إمرأتان في طفل فلم يعلم الحكم، وفزع فيه إلى أمير المؤمنين فاستدعى المرأتين ووعظهما فلم ترجعا فقال: ائتوني بمنشار! فقالت المرأتان له: ما تصنع؟ قال: أقدّه نصفين تأخذ كل واحدة نصفاً، فرضيت إحداهما وقالت الأخرى: الله الله يا أبا الحسن، إن كان لا بدّ من ذلك قد سمحت به لها، فقال: الله أكبر، هو ابنك دونها. ولو كان ابنها لرقت عليه فاعترفت الأخرى أنّ الحقّ مع صاحبتها، ففرح عمر ودعا لأمير المؤمنين.

He once ruled that a woman be stoned who had just given birth six months prior. Then ʿAlī told him: "And what if I oppose you with the Book of Allah the Exalted, who says: *and his bearing and weaning take thirty months*[147] and said *mothers should nurse their children for two full years*[148] so he let her go."

He used to be bewildered by the rulings of Sacred Law. He gave one hundred different rulings regarding the inheritance of grandmothers.[149] He used to exercise preference in matters of the division of the spoils of war and allowances whereas Allah had stipulated equality. He used to give rulings based on whim, surmise, and conjecture.

He rendered the matter of succession one of consultation after him and opposed the one who had preceded him by not leaving the matter for the people to decide, nor did he explicitly designate an Imam to succeed him. He even regretted that Sālim, the client of Ḥudhayfa, was not available and about whom he said, "Were he alive I would have no reservations about him." He said this in the presence of ʿAlī ﷺ. So, he assembled a group comprised of inferiors and one who was superior, whereas it is the right of the superior to come before the inferior. He then found fault with each person put forward by the consultation indicating his unwillingness to follow the Muslims in his death as they had followed him in his life. He then imposed on them the condition that the Imāma should be confined to one of six people, then he changed his mind and said four, then three, then one and he left it up to ʿAbd al-Raḥmān b. ʿAwf to decide even after he had described him as weak and inept. The he said, "If it comes down to the Commander of the Faithful and ʿUthmān, then do what they both agree on, and if it comes down to three, then it shall come down to the three which includes ʿAbd al-Raḥmān b. ʿAwf." He did this because he knew that ʿAlī and ʿUthmān would never both agree on anything and that ʿAbd al-Raḥmān b. ʿAwf would never rule against his kinsman ʿUthmān who was his cousin. Finally, he stipulated that if they deliberated for more than three days then all of them would be executed even though their number included the so-called "Ten Who were Promised Paradise" as well as the execution of anyone who opposed ʿAbd al-Raḥmān. Naturally, all of this is opposed to the religion.

147 Qurʾān 46:15.

148 Qurʾān 2:233.

149 See Ibn Abī l-Ḥadīd (d. 656/1258), *Sharḥ Nahj al-Balāgha*, edited by Ḥusayn al-Aʿlamī (Beirut: Muʾassasat al-Aʿlamī, 1425/2004), 12:356–359 and al-Sharīf al-Murtaḍā, *al-Shāfī fī l-imāma*, edited by ʿAbd al-Zahrāʾ al-Ḥusaynī al-Khaṭīb (Tehran: Muʾassasat al-Ṣādiq), 4:193–199. See Muslim b. al-Ḥajjāj, *al-Ṣaḥīḥ*, 2:689–690, *ḥadīth* 4235; 2:1272, *ḥadīth*s 7745–7746.

وأمر برجم إمرأة ولدت لستّة أشهر، فقال له عليّ: إن خاصمتك بكتاب الله خصمتك! إنّ الله تعالى يقول: ﴿وحمله وفصاله ثلاثون شهراً﴾، وقال: ﴿والوالدات يرضعن أولادهنّ حولين كاملين﴾ فخلّى سبيلها.

وكان يضطرب في الأحكام، فقضى في الجدّ بمائة قضيّة وكان يفضّل في الغنيمة والعطاء، وأوجب الله تعالى التسوية؛ وقال بالرأي والحدس والظنّ وجعل الأمر شورى من بعده وخالف فيه من تقدّمه؛ فإنّه لم يفوّض الأمر فيه إلى اختيار الناس، ولا نصّ على إمام بعده؛ بل تأسّف على سالم مولى حذيفة وقال: لو كان حيّاً لم يختلجني فيه شك وأمير المؤمنين عليّ حاضر. وجمع في من يختار بين المفضول والفاضل، ومن حقّ الفاضل التقدّم على المفضول. ثمّ طعن في كلّ واحد من اختاره للشورى، وأظهر أنّه يكره أن يتقلّد أمر المسلمين ميتاً كما تقلّده حيّاً؛ ثم تقلّده بأن جعل الإمامة في ستّة ثمّ ناقض فجعلها في أربعة، ثمّ في ثلاثة، ثمّ في واحد؛ فجعل إلى عبد الرحمن بن عوف الاختيار بعد أن وصفه بالضعف والقصور؛ ثمّ قال: إن اجتمع أمير المؤمنين وعثمان فالقول ما قالاه، وإن صاروا ثلاثة ثلاثة فالقول للذين فيهم عبد الرحمن، لعلمه أنّ عليّاً وعثمان لا يجتمعان على أمر وأنّ عبد الرحمن لا يعدل بالأمر عن أخيه وهو عثمان وابن عمّه؛ ثم أمر بضرب أعناقهم إن تأخّروا عن البيعة ثلاثه أيام، مع أنّهم عندهم من العشرة المبشّرة بالجنّة، (وأمر بقتل من خالف الأربعة منهم)، وأمر بقتل من خالف الثلاثة الذين منهم عبد الرحمن وكلّ ذلك مخالف للدين.

He said to ʿAlī ※: "If you come to power, and this will not happen, then you will lead them on the shining path," and this indicates that they had no intention of letting him come to power.

He said to ʿUthmān, "If you come to power you will impose the rule of Banū Umayya upon the necks of the people, and if you do this they will surely kill you," and this indicates that he wished him to be killed.

وقال لعلّي عليه السلام: إن ولّيتها وليسوا فاعلين لتركبنّهم على المحجّة البيضاء؛ وفيه إشارة إلى أنّهم لا يولّونه إيّاها .

وقال لعثمان: إن ولّيتها لتركبن آل أبي معيط على رقاب الناس، ولئن فعلت لتقتلنّ؛ وفيه إشارة إلى الأمر بقتله .

[The Abominations of ʿUthmān b. ʿAffān][150]

As for ʿUthmān he appointed those who were unworthy of governorship over the affairs of the Muslims.[151] Some of them even went so far as to openly commit moral depravities and some of them treason. He divided up the regions among his relatives, and even though he was reproached many times he did not change his ways.

He appointed al-Walīd b. ʿUqba [as a governor] who went so far as to consume alcohol and lead the people in prayer while he was drunk.

He appointed Saʿīd b. al-ʿĀṣ over Kufa who [treated the people so unfairly] that the people of Kufa drove him out of the city.

He appointed ʿAbdullāh b. Abī Sarḥ over Egypt and he oppressed the people. He wrote to him telling him to secretly continue in the position even though publicly he had written the opposite of that, and he ordered him to kill Muḥammad b. Abī Bakr.

He appointed Muʿāwiya over Syria and he committed the transgressions which he committed.

He appointed ʿAbdullāh b. ʿĀmir over Iraq who perpetrated the unspeakable acts which he perpetrated.

He appointed Marwān to his post and gave him the keys of his affairs and gave him his seal which led to the killing of ʿUthmān [himself] and the spread of chaos in the Muslim *umma* as is well known.

He used to curry favour with his family by showering them with much wealth from the public treasury of the Muslims. He gave to four people from Quraysh to whom he married his daughters 400,000 dirhams and gave Marwan a million dirhams.

150 Compare this section with what ʿAllāma wrote in *Kashf al-Murād*, 515–517. Also, an extremely important source for the key events of ʿUthmān's rule is Aḥmad b. Yaḥyā b. Jābir al-Balādhurī (279/892), *Ansāb al-ashrāf*, edited by Suhayl Zakkār and Riyāḍ Ziriklī (Beirut: n.d.), 6:99–229.

151 al-Balādhurī, *Ansāb al-ashrāf*, 6:133–138, 166–167.

[مطاعن عثمان بن عفّان]

وأمّا عثمان فإنّه ولّى أمور المسلمين من لا يصلح للولاية، حتّى ظهر من بعضهم الفسوق ومن بعضهم الخيانة؛ وقسّم الولايات بين أقاربه، وعوتب على ذلك مراراً فلم يرجع.

واستعمل الوليد بن عقبة حتّى ظهر منه شرب الخمر، وصلّى بالناس وهو سكران. واستعمل سعيد بن العاص على الكوفة، فظهر منه ما أدّى إلى أن أخرجه أهل الكوفة منها.

وولّى عبد الله بن أبي سرح مصر حتّى تظلّم منه أهلها، وكاتبه أن يستمرّ على ولايته سرّاً، خلاف ما كتب إليه جهراً، وأمره بقتل محمّد بن أبي بكر.

وولّى معاوية الشام، فأحدث من الفتن ما أحدث. وولّى عبد الله بن عامر العراق ففعل من المناكير ما فعل.

وولّى مروان أمره وألقى إليه مقاليد أموره، ودفع إليه خاتمه، فحدث من ذلك قتل عثمان؛ فحدث من الفتنة بين الأمّة ما حدث. وكان يؤثر أهله بالأموال الكثيرة من بيت مال المسلمين حتى أنّه دفع إلى أربعة نفر من قريش زوجّهم بناته أربع مائة ألف دينار، ودفع إلى مروان ألف ألف دينار.

Ibn Mas'ūd used to denounce him and accused him of unbelief. When he learned of this he had him beaten to death.¹⁵² He had 'Ammār beaten until he got a hernia.¹⁵³ The Prophet ﷺ had said about him that "I see 'Ammār being whipped. He will be killed by the seditious party, and they will be barred from my intercession on the Day of Judgement." 'Ammār used to denounce him.

The Messenger of Allah ﷺ had banished al-Ḥakam b. Abī l-'Āṣ from Medina along with his son Marwān and they remained banished throughout his life, and then Abū Bakr's life, and then 'Umar's, but when 'Uthmān rose to power he gave him sanctuary and allowed him to return to Medina. He made Marwān his secretary and deputy even though Allah has stated: *You will not find those who believe in Allah and the Last Day loving those who oppose Allah and his Prophet.*¹⁵⁴

He exiled Abū Dharr to Rabdha and had him savagely beaten¹⁵⁵ even though the Prophet ﷺ had said about him: "The sky has never covered nor has the earth ever supported a man more honest in speech than Abū Dharr." He also said: "Indeed Allah the Exalted has revealed to me that he loves four of my Companions and has commanded me to love them." He was asked: "Who are they O Messenger of Allah?" so he said: "'Alī is their master, then Salmān, Miqdād, and Abū Dharr."

He allowed the rulings of Sacred Law to become null-and-void. Thus, he did not execute 'Ubaydullāh b. 'Umar when he murdered al-Hurmuzān who had become the client of the Commander of the Faithful ؇ after he became a Muslim. Indeed, the Commander of the Faithful ؇ would look for 'Ubaydullāh in order to impose retribution on him, but he sought refuge with Mu'āwiya.¹⁵⁶ He also did not implement the punishment for consuming alcohol on al-Walīd b. 'Uqba.¹⁵⁷ Finally, the Commander of the Faithful ؇ imposed the punishment on him saying, "The punishment of Allah will not be made void while I am present."

---

152 al-Balādhurī, *Ansāb al-ashrāf,* 6:148, 167. He also had burned Ibn Mas'ūd's personal copy of the Qur'ān. This was part of the larger policy of 'Uthmān of having all personal copies which had not been made in accordance with the master copy he established (*muṣḥaf al-imām*) and of which various authorised copies were made and sent out to the major outposts of the expanding Muslim empire (the exact number and the exact cities in question varies in the sources). Regarding the burning of these personal codices the best Sunnī source is perhaps Abū Bakr 'Abdullāh b. Abī Dāwūd b. Sulaymān al-Sijistānī (the son of the *muḥaddith* also known as Abū Dāwūd), *Kitāb al-maṣāḥif* (Beirut: 1405 /1995), 19–34.
153 al-Balādhurī, *Ansāb al-ashrāf,* 6:161–165, 209.
154 Qur'ān 58:22.
155 al-Balādhurī, *Ansāb al-ashrāf,* 6:166–171.
156 al-Balādhurī, *Ansāb al-ashrāf,* 6:138–146.
157 Ibid.

وكان ابن مسعود يطعن عليه ويكفّره، ولمّا علم ضربه حتّى مات؛ وضرب عمّاراً حتّى صار به فتق؛ وقد قال فيه النبي ﷺ: عمّار جلدة بين عيني تقتله الفئة الباغية؛ لا أنالهم الله شفاعتي يوم القيامة. وكان عمّار يطعن عليه.

وطرد رسول الله ﷺ الحكم بن أبي العاص عمّ عثمان عن المدينة ومعه ابنه مروان، فلم يزل طريداً هو وابنه في زمن النبي ﷺ وأبي بكر وعمر، فلمّا ولي عثمان آواه وردّه إلى المدينة وجعل مروان كاتبه وصاحب تدبيره، مع أنّ الله تعالى قال: ﴿لا تجد قوماً يؤمنون بالله﴾ ـالآية.

ونفى أبا ذر إلى الربذة وضربه ضرباً وجيعاً، مع أنّ النبي ﷺ قال في حقّه: ما أقلّت الغبراء ولا أظلّت الخضراء على ذي لهجة أصدق من أبي ذر؛ وقال: إنّ الله تعالى أوحى إليّ أنه يحبّ أربعة من أصحابي وأمرني بحبّهم، فقيل له: من هم يا رسول الله؟ قال: عليّ سيّدهم، وسلمان والمقداد وأبو ذر.

وضيّع حدود الله، فلم يقد عبيد الله بن عمر حين قتل الهرمزان مولى أمير المؤمنين بعد إسلامه، وكان أمير المؤمنين يطلب عبيد الله لإقامة القصاص عليه، فلحق بمعاوية وأراد أن يعطّل حدّ الشرب في الوليد بن عقبة حتّى حدّه أمير المؤمنين؛ وقال: لا يبطل حدّ الله وأنا حاضر.

He added the second call-to-prayer (*adhān*) on Friday, which is a reprehensible innovation in religion (*bid'a*), but it has now acquired the status of a normal practice. All of the Muslims opposed him so much that he finally ended up being killed.[158] They denounced his actions. They said to him: "You were absent from the Battle of Badr, fled the field during the Battle of Uḥud, and were not present at the Oath of Riḍwān."[159] Reports of all that are more numerous than can be reckoned.

It has been mentioned by al-Shahrastānī[160] — who is a staunch foe of the Imāmī Shī'a — that the locus of all corruption [in human history] after Satan's doubt was the discord that arose during the final illness of the Prophet ﷺ. The first instance of conflict occurred during his final illness as recorded by al-Bukhārī with his chain of transmission back to Ibn 'Abbās who said, "When the illness from which the Prophet died become severe he said: 'Bring an inkwell and writing material so that I might write for you a document by virtue of which you will never go astray after me.' Then 'Umar said: 'Surely your companion is talking nonsense! The Book of Allah suffices us.' At this a clamour arose and the Prophet ﷺ said: 'Go away. It is unbecoming that there should be discord in my presence.'"[161]

The second instance was also during his final illness. He said: "Make ready the troops of Usāma! May the curse of Allah be upon those who do not join with him." A group of them said: "It is incumbent upon us to obey his command" as Usāma had already left Medina, but others said: "His illness has become severe, and our hearts cannot bear to leave him."

The third instance was after his death. 'Umar said: "Whoever says that Muḥammad has died, I will kill him with this sword of mine. Indeed, he has but risen to heaven as did 'Īsā son of Maryam." Abū Bakr said: "He who used to worship Muḥammad, know that Muḥammad has died; and he that worships the deity of Muḥammad, indeed He is Alive and never dies."

158 The many reports regarding the death of 'Uthmān and the events leading up to it and afterwards have been collected by al-Balādhurī, *Ansāb al-ashrāf*, 6:209–229.

159 See al-Bukhārī, *al-Jāmi' al-musnad al-ṣaḥīḥ*, 2:609, *ḥadīth* 3167; 2:729, *ḥadīth* 3745; 2:807, *ḥadīth* 4115 and al-Tirmidhī, *al-Jāmi'* 2: 946, *ḥadīth* 4071. In all of these *ḥadīths* the narrators confirm Uthman's absence at these pivotal events in the history of Islam, but try to offer various excuses for this. However, they at no time deny that he was not present.

160 Al-Ḥillī paraphrases what follows until the end of the section from the work of Muḥammad b. 'Abd al-Karīm al-Shahrastānī (d. 548/1153), *al-Milal wa-l-niḥal*, edited by Sa'īd al-Ghānimī (Beirut and Baghdad: Manshūrāt al-Jamal, 2013), 100–105.

161 See al-Bukhārī, *al-Jāmi' al-musnad al-ṣaḥīḥ*, 1:30, *ḥadīth* 114, 2:887, *ḥadīths* 4475–4476, 3:1176, *ḥadīth* 5731, 3:1486, *ḥadīth* 7454; cf. Jamāl al-Dīn al-Mizzī, *Tuḥfat al-ashrāf*, entries 5517, 5841. The event is also alluded to in Muslim b. al-Ḥajjāj, *al-Ṣaḥīḥ*, 2:701–702, *ḥadīths* 4319–4322 and Abū Dāwūd, *al-Sunan*, 2:527, *ḥadīth* 3031.

وزاد الأذان الثاني يوم الجمعة وهي بدعة وصار سنّة إلى الآن، وخالفه المسلمون كلهم حتّى قتل، وعابوا فعاله وقالوا له: غبت عن بدر وهربت يوم أحد ولم تشهد بيعة الرضوان؛ والأخبار في ذلك أكثر من أن تُحصى.

وقد ذكر الشهرستاني وهو أشدّ المبغضين على الإماميّة أنّ مثار الفساد بعد شبهة إبليس الاختلافات الواقعة في مرض النبي ﷺ؛ فأوّل تنازع وقع في مرضه فيما رواه البخاري بإسناده إلى ابن عبّاس قال: لمّا اشتدّ بالنبيّ مرضه الذي توفيّ فيه قال: ائتوني بدواة وقرطاس اكتب لكم كتاباً لا تضلّوا بعدي، فقال عمر: إنّ صاحبكم ليهجر؛ حسبنا كتاب الله! وكثر اللّغط فقال النبي ﷺ: قوموا عنّي لا ينبغي عندي التنازع.

والخلاف الثاني في مرضه ﷺ أنه قال: جهّزوا جيش أسامة! لعن الله من تخلّف عنه. فقال قوم: يجب علينا امتثال أمره، وأسامة قد برز عن المدينة، وقال قوم: اشتدّ مرضه ولا يسع قلوبنا المفارقة.

والثالث في موته ﷺ قال عمر: من قال أنّ محمّداً قد مات قتلته بسيفي هذا، وإنّما رفع إلى السماء كما رفع عيسى بن مريم. وقال أبو بكر: من كان يعبد محمّداً فإنّ محمّداً قد مات، ومن كان يعبد إله محمّد فإنّه حيّ لا يموت.

The fourth instance was with respect to the leadership (*imāma*) [of the Muslim community after the Prophet's demise]. The greatest matter of dispute among the *umma* is the dispute over Imāma. There has been no religious doctrine over which swords have been repeatedly drawn in every age than the doctrine of Imāma. The Muhājirūn and the Anṣār differed, with the latter saying: "Appoint a leader (*amīr*) from us and from amongst yourselves a leader also." They agreed on their leader Saʿd b. ʿUbāda al-Anṣārī, but ʿUmar who, along with Abū Bakr, arrived later at the Saqīfa of Banī Sāʿida[162] extended his hand to Abū Bakr in allegiance and the people followed suit. [Later] ʿUmar described it saying: "It was a precipitate affair (*falta*), but Allah prevented its evil, so whoever would go back to something like it, let him be killed." During this time the Commander of the Faithful ﷺ was preoccupied with what the Prophet ﷺ had discharged him to do in preparing him for burial and tending his grave, and thus he and those who were with him did not give allegiance.

The fifth instance concerns the grove of Fadak and inheriting from the Prophet ﷺ which was repudiated by Abū Bakr through a narration of his own from the Prophet ﷺ: "We the assembly of the Prophets do not have heirs. What we leave behind is alms."[163]

The sixth instance has to do with the killing of those who refused the *zakāt*. Abū Bakr fought them. In the days of his rule, ʿUmar strove to release the prisoners who had been taken and to return the property taken from them and releasing those who had been imprisoned.

The seventh instance was Abū Bakr designating ʿUmar as his successor. Among the people was one who said: "You have imposed upon us one who is rough and hard of heart."

162 *Saqīfa* in Arabic means a "covered porch" or "portico," a meeting place of the Banū Sāʿida.

163 See Wilferd Madelung, *The Succession to Muḥammad. A Study of the Early Caliphate* (Cambridge: Cambridge University press, 1997), Excursus 2 ("The Inheritance of Muḥammad"), 360–363.

الرابع في الإمامة، وأعظم خلاف بين الأمّة خلاف الإمامة؛ إذ ما سلّ سيف في الإسلام على قاعدة دينية مثل ما سلّ على الإمامة في كلّ زمان، واختلف المهاجرون والأنصار. فقالت الأنصار منّا أمير ومنكم أمير، واتّفقوا على رئيسهم سعد بن عبادة الأنصاري؛ فاستدرك عمر وأبو بكر بأن حضرا سقيفة بني ساعدة ومدّ عمر يده إلى أبي بكر بايعه فبايعه الناس، وقال عمر: إنّها كانت فلتة وقى الله شرّها ! فمن عاد إلى مثلها فاقتلوه، وأمير المؤمنين مشغول بما أمره النبي ﷺ من دفنه وتجهيزه وملازمة قبره، وتخلّف هو وجماعة عن البيعة.

الخامس في فدك والتوارث عن النبي ﷺ ودفعها أبو بكر بروايته عن النبي ﷺ نحن معاشر الأنبياء لانورّث ما تركناه صدقة.

والسادس في قتال مانعي الزكاة، فقاتلهم أبو بكر واجتهد عمر في أيام خلافته فردّ السبايا والأموال إليهم وأطلق المحبوسين.

السابع في تنصيص أبي بكر على عمر بالخلافة، فمن الناس من قال: ولّيت علينا فظاً غليظاً.

The eighth instance has to do with the matter of the consultation, because of which, after much wrangling, they settled on 'Uthmān. Many differences arose. Among these was his allowing al-Ḥakam b. Abī l-'Āṣ of the Banū Umayya to return to Medina after he had been banished by the Messenger of Allah and was even known as "the one banished by the Messenger of Allah" ﷺ, and despite the fact that he had petitioned both Abū Bakr and 'Umar during their rule and had been refused by them, and 'Umar had even had him removed a further forty miles from where he had been in Yemen. Among these is also his exile of Abū Dharr to Rabdha, his daughter marrying Marwan b. al-Ḥakam and giving him one fifth of the war booty of Africa, an amount which reached 200,000 dinars. Among these is his amnesty of 'Abdullāh b. Sa'd b. Abī Sarḥ, this after the Prophet ﷺ had ordered him to be executed if found, and appointing him over Egypt, and his appointing of 'Abdullāh b. 'Āmir over Basra resulting in him doing there what he did. His military commanders were Mu'āwiya b. Abī Sufyān in Syria, Sa'īd b. al-'Āṣ in Kufa, and after him 'Abdullāh b. 'Āmir, and al-Walīd b. 'Uqba in Basra.

The ninth instance was in the time of the Commander of the Faithful ؊ after agreement upon him had been reached and after the allegiance had been given to him. Firstly, the rising up of Ṭalḥa and Zubayr from Mecca, then their taking 'Ā'isha to Basra, then fighting against him [i.e., 'Alī] in what became known as the Battle of the Camel, the differences which arose between him and Mu'āwiya resulting in the Battle of Ṣiffīn, 'Amr b. al-'Āṣ leaving Abū Mūsā al-Ash'arī, similarly his differences with the evil renegades at Nahrawān. In every single case, 'Alī was with the truth and the truth was with 'Alī.

In his time also their emerged those who rebelled against him and opposed him, people such as al-Ash'ath b. Qays, and Mas'ūd b. Mudhakkā al-Tamīmī, Zayd b. Ḥusayn al-Ṭā'ī, and others. In his time also a group with extreme beliefs [i.e., the *ghulāt*] came into existence, people such as 'Abdullāh b. Saba'. And innovations and misguidance came into being from both sides and the saying of the Prophet ﷺ was seen to come true: "Two kinds of person will come to destruction regarding you: One who exceeds the bounds in devotion to you, and one who transgresses the limits in aversion to you."

Objectively consider, then, the words of this man [i.e., al-Shahrastānī]. Did not the cause for [all this] chaos issue forth from these three men, or are they innocent?

الثّامن في أمر الشورى، واتّفقوا بعد الاختلاف على إمامة عثمان، ووقعت اختلافات كثيرة؛ منها ردّه الحكم بن أميّة إلى المدينة بعد أن طرده رسول الله، وكان يسمّى طريد رسول الله ﷺ؛ وبعد أن تشفّع إلى أبي بكر وعمر أيّام خلافتها فما أجابا إلى ذلك، ونفاه عمر من مقامه باليمن أربعين فرسخاً. ومنها نفيه أبا ذر إلى الربذة، وتزويجه مروان بن الحكم ابنته، وتسليمه خمس غنائم أفريقية له، وقد بلغت مائتي ألف دينار. ومنها إيواؤه عبد الله بن سعد بن أبي سرح بعد أن أهدر النبيّ ﷺ دمه، وتوليته إيّاه مصر، وتوليته عبد الله بن عامر البصرة حتّى أحدث فيها ما أحدث. وكان أمراء جنوده معاوية بن أبي سفيان عامل الشام، وسعيد بن العاص عامل الكوفة، وبعده عبد الله بن عامر، والوليد بن عقبة عامل البصرة.

التّاسع في زمن أمير المؤمنين بعد الاتّفاق عليه وعقد البيعة له؛ فأوّلاً خروج طلحة والزبير إلى مكّة، ثم حمل عائشة إلى البصرة، ثم نصب القتال معه - ويعرف ذلك بحرب الجمل - والخلاف بينه وبين معاوية وحرب صفّين، ومغادرة عمرو بن العاص أبا موسى الأشعري، وكذا الخلاف بينه وبين الشراة المارقين بالنهروان؛ وفي الجملة كان عليّ مع الحقّ والحقّ معه.

وظهر في زمانه الخوارج عليه مثل الأشعث بن قيس ومسعود بن مذكي التميمي وزيد بن حصين الطائي وغيرهم. وظهر في زمانه الغلاة كعبد الله بن سبأ. ومن الفريقين ابتدأت البدعة والضلالة؛ وصدق فيه قول النبيّ ﷺ يهلك فيك اثنان: محبّ غال ومبغض قال.

فانظر بعين الإنصاف إلى كلام هذا الرجل، هل خرج موجب الفتنة عن المشائخ أو تعدّاهم؟

Section 3:
On the Proofs establishing the Imāma of the Commander of the Faithful ʿAlī b. Abī Ṭālib after the Messenger of Allah

الفصل الثّالث
في الأدلّة الدّالة على
إمامة أمير المؤمنين عليّ بن أبي طالب
بعد رسول الله ﷺ

The proofs in this regard are many, indeed even innumerable, however we shall mention the most important of these and have divided this section into [four] "ways."

The First Way: Rational Proofs

The First

It is necessary that the Imam be infallible, and when that is proven it follows that the Imam can be none but ʿAlī.

The first premise: Man, by nature, is a political animal.[1] He cannot live in isolation since for his survival he is in need of food, clothing, and shelter and these cannot be secured by himself alone, rather he is in need of the assistance of others who in turn need each other in order to establish a social order. Whereas one can expect to find mutual struggle and strife amidst human beings in society in as much as each person needs something or another which belongs to or is provided by another, and his desire may compel him to rest it from him by force and by doing wrong to him, thereby leading to turmoil and disorder giving rise to chaos, thus, it is a must to put in place an infallible Imam to prevent them from oppression and crossing the bounds, restraining them from overpowering and coercing others, dispensing justice to the oppressed from the oppressors, securing the rights due to everyone. Such a person cannot be given over to falling into error, or succumbing to inadvertence, or committing sins, otherwise then he too would be in need of an Imam; for the need to appoint an Imam derives from this very propensity of the *umma* for error, and were he subject to error then he too would be in need of an Imam, unless he is infallible, in which case he is the Imam. Otherwise, this would lead to an infinite regress.

The second premise is obvious since neither Abū Bakr, nor ʿUmar, nor ʿUthmān have ever been regarded as infallible,[2] and ʿAlī *was* infallible. It follows, therefore, that he was the Imam.

1 This is a very ancient idea. He means to say that human beings, by nature, socially organise themselves into a polity. The locution "man is a political animal (ζῷον πολιτικόν, *zoon politikon*)" was formulated by Aristotle, *Politics*, Bk. I, 1253a. Such notions of man by nature living in a community or polity are also found in Confucius' notion of *ren* (仁), see his *Analects* (*Lúnyǔ*), Book IV (*Li ren* 里仁). The argument for the necessity of the Imam may well have been influenced by that of Avicenna in *The Metaphysics of the Healing. A parallel English-Arabic text translated, introduced, and annotated by Michael E. Marmura* (Provo, Utah: Brigham Young University Press, 2005), Book 10, *passim*.

2 Indeed, no group in Islamic history has ever regarded them as having been so.

الأدّلة في ذلك كثيرة لاتحصى لكن نذكر المهمّ منها وتنظمه أربعة مناهج:

المنهج الأوّل: في الأدّلة العقليّة وهي خمسة:

الأوّل:

إنّ الإمام يجب أن يكون معصوماً، ومتى كان كذلك كان الإمام هو عليّ.

أمّا المقدّمة الأولى فلأنّ الإنسان مدنيّ بالطبع لا يمكن أن يعيش منفرداً لافتقاره في بقائه إلى مأكل وملبس ومسكن لا يمكن أن يفعلها بنفسه؛ بل يفتقر إلى مساعدة غيره بحيث يفزع كلّ منهم لما يحتاج إليه صاحبه حتّى يتم نظام النوع. ولمّا كان الاجتماع في مظنّة التغالب والتناوش فإنّ كلّ واحد من الأشخاص قد يحتاج إلى ما في يد غيره، فتدعوه قوّته الشهوية إلى أخذه وقهره عليه وظلم فيه؛ فيؤدّي ذلك إلى وقوع الهرج والمرج وإثارة الفتن. فلا بدّ من نصب إمام معصوم يصدهم عن الظلم والتعدّي ويمنعهم عن التغلّب والقهر، وينتصف للمظلوم من الظالم ويوصل الحقّ إلى مستحقّه، لا يجوز عليه الخطأ ولا السهر ولا المعصية، وإلّا لأفتقر إلى إمام آخر؛ لأنّ العلّة المحوجة إلى نصب الإمام هو جواز الخطأ على الأمّة، فلو جاز الخطأ عليه لأحتاج إلى إمام؛ فإن كان معصوماً كان هو الإمام وإلّا لزم التسلسل.

وأما المقدّمة الثانية فظاهرة؛ لأنّ أبا بكر وعمر وعثمان لم يكونوا معصومين اتّفاقاً. وعليّ معصوم، فيكون هو الإمام.

The Second

The Imam must be explicitly designated [by the Prophet ﷺ]. Whereas we have already established the invalidity of the Imam's selection by choice, since the group doing the choosing are no more worthy than the others for whom they are doing the choosing, and that this leads to conflict and slaughter, thus choosing the Imam in this fashion leads to the very worst forms of strife. For these reasons, and in order to avoid even the slightest strife, we argued for the necessity of appointing an Imam [by designation] in the first place. Yet, it is a matter of consensus that there is none amongst their leaders who was explicitly designated [by the Prophet ﷺ] but ʿAlī, therefore he is the Imam.

الثاني:

إنّ الإمام يجب أن يكون منصوصاً عليه؛ لِمَا بيّنا من بطلان الاختيار وأنّه ليس بعض المختارين (لبعض الأمّة أولى من البعض) المختار للآخر، ولأدائه إلى التنازع والتناحر فيؤدي نصب الإمام إلى أعظم أنواع الفساد التي لأجل إعدام الأقلّ منها أوجبنا نصبه؛ وغير عليّ من أئمّتهم لم يكن منصوصاً عليه بالإجماع، فتعيّن أن يكون هو الإمام.

On the Proofs establishing the Imāma of the Commander of the Faithful 'Alī b. Abī Ṭālib after the Messenger of Allāh

The Third

The Imam must have a full and complete mastery of the Sharīʿa[3] since revelation ceased with the death of the Prophet ﷺ and since the Book and the Sunna do not spell out every detail of all rulings applying to every particular case arising until the Day of Judgement. Therefore, there must be an Imam appointed by Allah, the Exalted, safeguarded from mistakes and errors in order that he not leave some injunctions unfulfilled or add to them, wilfully or inadvertently. And it is a matter of consensus that there was none such as this but ʿAlī ؓ.

---

3   The Arabic reads *ḥāfiẓan li l-sharʿ*. The term *ḥāfiẓan* here means more than just "uphold," "safeguard," or protect, rather it means that the person in question is a master of the Sacred Law in the sense of knowing it all by heart.

الثالث:

إنّ الإمام يجب أن يكون حافظاً للشرع لانقطاع الوحي بموت النبي ﷺ وقصورالكتاب والسنّة عن تفاصيل أحكام الجزئيّات الواقعة إلى يوم القيامة؛ فلا بدّ من إمام (منصوب) من الله تعالى معصوم من الزلل والخطأ، لئلا يترك بعض الأحكام أو يزيد فيها عمداً أو سهواً. وغير عليّ لم يكن كذلك بالإجماع.

The Fourth

Allah is capable of putting in place an infallible Imam. The need of the world [for an Imam] demands this, and there is no harm or detriment in his appointment. Thus he, the Imam, must be put in place, and it is a matter of consensus that there was no such person but ʿAlī ﷺ. Thus it follows that the Imam must be none other than ʿAlī ﷺ. As for His capacity to do so, it is evident, as is the need of the world [for an Imam]. For we have already established the occurrence of conflict in the world [without an Imam]. As for the absence of any detriment or harm in his appointment, this too is evident for it is without him that harm arises. As for the necessity of his being appointed, this follows from His capacity and motivation for doing so, as well as the absence of anything preventing Him [from that], thus He must do it.

الرابع:

إنّ الله تعالى قادر على نصب إمام معصوم، والحاجة للعالم داعية إليه ولا مفسدة فيه، فيجب نصبه؛ وغير عليّ لم يكن كذلك إجماعاً . فتعيّن أن يكون الامام هو عليّ. أمّا القدرة فظاهرة، وأمّا الحاجة فظاهرة أيضاً؛ لِمَا بيّنّا من وقوع التنازع بين العالم. وأمّا انتفاء المفسدة فظاهر أيضاً؛ لأنّ المفسدة لازمة لعدمه. وأمّا وجوب نصبه فلأن عند ثبوت القدرة والداعي وانتفاء الصارف يجب الفعل.

The Fifth

The Imam must be better than his subjects over whom he exercises authority, and, as will be established at length, ʿAlī ﷺ was the most excellent person of the age. Thus, since it is established by both reason and revelation that it is reprehensible to prefer the inferior to the superior, he was the Imam. Allah, the Exalted, has said: *Is not he who guides to the Truth more worthy of being followed, or he who finds not the way unless he himself be guided? What is the matter with you? How do you judge?*[4]

4 Qurʾān 10:35.

الخامس:

إن الإمام يجب أن يكون أفضل من رعيّته، وعليّ أفضل أهل زمانه على ما يأتي فيكون هو الإمام لقبح تقديم المفضول على الفاضل عقلا ونقلاً. قال الله تعالى: ﴿أفمن يهدي إلى الحقّ أن يتّبع أمن لا يهدي إلّا أن يهدى فما لكم كيف تحكمون﴾.

The Second Way: Qur'ānic Evidence for the Imāma of ʿAlī b. Abī Ṭālib

Demonstration 1[5]

The statement of the Exalted: ﴿*Your guardian can only be Allah; and His Messenger and the faithful who establish the prayer and give zakāt while bowing down*﴾.[6] It is a matter of consensus that it was revealed regarding ʿAlī.

Al-Thaʿlabī said, through his chain of transmission to Abū Dharr who said: "I heard the Messenger of Allah with these very two [ears], and if it is not true let me be made deaf, and I saw him with these very two [eyes], and if it is not true let me be made blind saying: "ʿAlī is the leader of the righteous and the one who does battle with the unbelievers. Victorious is the one who aids him in victory and disgraced is the one who would disgrace him.' As for me, one day I prayed the noon prayer behind the Messenger of Allah and a beggar was begging in the mosque, but no one gave him anything. The beggar raised his hand toward the sky and said: 'O Allah! Bear witness that I begged in the mosque of the Messenger of Allah and no one gave me anything. At this point ʿAlī was in the bowing posture of prayer (*rukūʿ*), and he gestured with the ring finger of his right hand — in which he was wearing a ring — whereupon the beggar came forward and took the ring off his ring finger and the Prophet noticed this. When he had concluded his prayer, he gazed heavenward and said: 'O Allah! Mūsā beseeched you saying: *My Lord open my heart, and make my task easy for me, and loosen the knot from my tongue so that they will understand my words, and appoint for me a vizier from my family, Hārūn my brother. And add through him to my strength and let him share my task*'.[7] Then Allah revealed to him a verse from the Qur'ān declaring *We will reinforce you with your brother and by Our Signs will give*

5 A number of works have been written on the verses of the Qur'ān that were revealed regarding ʿAlī. Among the most comprehensive of these is by the Sunnī Ḥanafī scholar ʿUbaydullāh b. ʿAbdullāh b. Aḥmad, known as al-Ḥāfiẓ al-Ḥaskānī (fl. 5th/11th cen.), *Shawāhid al-tanzīl li-qawāʿid al-tafḍīl*, edited by Muḥammad Bāqir al-Maḥmūdī (Qom?: Majmaʿ Iḥyāʾ al-Turāth al-Islāmī, 1427/2006). In what follows each demonstration will be referenced to this work, followed by references to the works explicitly cited by ʿAllāma. However, in some cases there is no reference in *Shawāhid al-tanzīl*. For this first demonstration see the latter, 1:249–289 and al-Ḥāfiẓ Abū Nuʿaym al-Iṣfahānī, *al-Nūr al-mushtaʿal*, 61–85.

6 Qur'ān 5:55.

7 Qur'ān 20:25–32.

المنهج الثّاني: في الأدلّة المأخوذة من القرآن والبراهين الدّالة على إمامة عليّ عليه السلام من الكتاب العزيز

وهي أربعون برهاناً:

الأول:

قوله تعالى: ﴿إنّما وليّكم الله ورسوله والّذين ءامنوا الّذين يقيمون الصّلاة ويؤتون الزكاة وهم راكعون﴾، وقد أجمعوا على أنّها نزلت في عليّ عليه السلام.

قال الثعلبي بإسناده إلى أبي ذرّ قال: سمعت رسول الله صلى الله عليه وآله بهاتين وإلا فصمّتا، ورأيته بهاتين وإلا فعميتا، يقول: عليّ قائد البررة وقاتل الكفرة منصورٌ من نصره مخذولٌ من خذله؛ أما إنّي صلّيت مع رسول الله صلى الله عليه وآله يوماً صلاة الظهر فسأل سائل في المسجد فلم يعطه أحد شيئاً فرفع السائل يده إلى السماء وقال: اللهمّ اشهد أنّي سألت في مسجد رسول الله صلى الله عليه وآله فلم يعطني أحد شيئاً! وكان عليّ راكعاً فأومأ إليه بخنصره اليمني وكان يتختّم بها. فأقبل السائل حتّى أخذ الخاتم من خنصره وذلك بعين النبيّ صلى الله عليه وآله. فلمّا فرغ من صلاته رفع رأسه إلى السماء وقال: اللهمّ إن موسى سألك فقال ﴿ربّ اشرح لي صدري ويسّر لي أمري واحلل عقدة من لساني يفقهوا قولي * واجعل لّي وزيراً من أهلي * هارون أخي أشدد به أزري * وأشركه في أمري﴾

you both such authority that they will not be able to lay a hand on you.[8] [And he said:] 'O Allah! I am Muḥammad, your prophet and your sincerely devoted servant! O Allah! Open then my heart and make my task easy for me, and appoint for me a vizier from my family, ʿAlī, my brother, and add through him to my strength!'" Abū Dharr continues: "No sooner had the Messenger of Allah ﷺ spoken these words that Jibrīl ﷺ descended upon him from on High and said: 'O Muḥammad! Recite!' To which he said: 'What am I to recite?' He said: 'Recite *Your guardian can only be Allah; and His Messenger and the faithful who establish the prayer and give zakāt while bowing down.*'"[9]

The Shāfiʿī *faqīh* Ibn al-Maghāzilī al-Wāsiṭī records via his chain of transmission form Ibn ʿAbbās that this verse was revealed regarding ʿAlī ﷺ.[10] The term 'guardian' (*walī*) refers to the one who has the right to administer affairs freely. Thus, his authority is established in this verse just as it is established for Allah and His Messenger ﷺ.

8 Qurʾān 28:35

9 Unfortunately, this portion is missing from *ThM. ThVE*, fol. 463a, ln.12–25.

10 There are actually five *ḥadīth*, in all, related by Ibn al-Maghāzilī about this event. See Ibn al-Maghāzilī, *Manāqib Ahl al-bayt*, 369–375, *ḥadīth*s 359–363.

فأنزل عليه قرآنا ناطقاً ﴿سنشدّ عضدك بأخيك ونجعل لكما سلطاناً فلا يصلون إليكما بآياتنا﴾ اللّهم وأنا محمّد نبيّك وصفيّك؛ اللّهم فاشرح لي صدري ويسّر لي أمري واجعل لي وزيراً من أهلي عليّا اشدد به ظهري! قال أبو ذرّ: فما استتمّ رسول الله ﷺ حتّى نزل عليه جبرئيل من عند الله تعالى فقال: يا محمّد إقرأ، قال: وما أقرأ؟ قال: إقرأ ﴿إنّما وليّكم الله ورسوله والذين آمنوا الّذين يقيمون الصّلاة ويؤتون الزّكاة وهم راكعون﴾.

ونقل الفقيه ابن المغازلي الواسطي الشافعي عن ابن عبّاس أنّ هذه الآية نزلت في عليّ، والوليّ هو المتصرّف وقد أثبت له الولاية في الآية كما أثبتها الله تعالى لنفسه ولرسوله ﷺ.

Demonstration 2[11]

The statement of the Exalted: *O Messenger! Make known what was revealed to you from your Lord, for if you do not, you will not have conveyed His message, and Allah will protect you from the people.*[12] They [i.e., scholars] agree that it was revealed regarding ʿAlī ﷺ.

It is narrated by the Ḥāfiẓ Abū Nuʿaym,[13] who is from the mainstream Sunnī scholars (*al-jumhūr*), through his chain of transmission from ʿAṭiyya who said, "This verse was revealed to the Messenger of Allah ﷺ regarding ʿAlī b. Abī Ṭālib ﷺ."

From the *Tafsīr* of al-Thaʿlabī:[14] "It means *make known what was revealed to you from your Lord* about the merits of ʿAlī. Thus, when this verse was revealed, the Messenger of Allah ﷺ took hold of the hand of ʿAlī and said: 'Whosoever's master I am, ʿAlī is his master.'" [15]Whereas there is no dispute that the Prophet ﷺ is the master of Abū Bakr, and ʿUmar, and all the other Companions, it then follows that ʿAlī ﷺ too must be their master; therefore, he must be the Imām.

11 *Shawāhid al-tanzīl li-qawāʿid al-tafḍīl,* 1:294–305.

12 Qurʾān 5:3.

13 Al-Ḥāfiẓ Abū Nuʿaym al-Iṣfahānī, *al-Nūr al-mushtaʿal,* 86–88.

14 Unfortunately, this portion is missing from MSS Maḥmūdiyya 98–107. MS Veliyüddin Efendi 130, fol.468b, ln.18–21.

15 This is the Ḥadīth of Ghadīr Khumm or "Ḥadīth al-Walāya". ʿAllāma refers to this *ḥadīth* many times. See Ibn ʿUqda al-Kūfī (d. 322/94), *Kitāb al-wilāya*, edited by ʿAbd al-Razzāq Muḥammad Ḥusayn Ḥirz al-Dīn (Qom: 1421/2000), 155–255. On him, see the monograph-length introduction to the aforementioned work, 9–152. This edition is a reconstruction based on surviving quotations in still extant primary sources of a work by Ibn ʿUqda containing all of the narrations of the *ḥadīth* of Ghadīr Khumm known to him. This reconstructed work contains narrations by 98 different companions of the Prophet. An eminent Sunnī contemporary of Ibn ʿUqda, namely the jurist, Qurʾān commentator, and historian Abū Jaʿfar Muḥammad b. Jarīr al-Ṭabarī (d. 310/921), also devoted a work entitled *Kitāb al-Ghadīr* to the large number of narrations of this *ḥadīth* which has subsequently been lost. However, there are references to it in works contemporaneous with him, for example see the Ismāʿīlī scholar al-Qāḍī Abū Ḥanīfa al-Nuʿmān b. Muḥammad al-Tamīmī al-Maghribī, *Sharḥ al-akhbār fī faḍāʾil al-aʾimmat al-aṭhār*, edited by Muḥammad Ḥusayn al-Ḥusaynī al-Jālālī (Qom: 1409/2008), 1:130–133. Numerous scholars have devoted their efforts over the centuries to the study of the transmission history of this *ḥadīth*. Notable later works include *ʿAbaqāt al-anwār* by Mīr Ḥāmid Ḥusayn Lakhnawī; Abd al-Ḥusayn Aḥmad al-Amīnī al-Najafī, *Kitāb al-ghadīr fī l-kitāb wa-l-sunnah wa-l-adab* (Beirut: 1414/1994). Among classical Sunnī *ḥadīth* sources see: Aḥmad b. Ḥanbal, *al-Musnad,* 1:196, *ḥadīth* 651; 1:265, *ḥadīth* 976; 1:266, *ḥadīth* 979; 1:332, *ḥadīth* 1327; 8:4208, *ḥadīth* 18771; 8:4209, *ḥadīth* 18772; 8:4430, *ḥadīth* 19587; 8:4436, *ḥadīth* 19610; 10:5461, *ḥadīth* 23495; al-Tirmidhī, *al-Jāmiʿ*, 2:948:4078. Also compare Muslim b. al-Ḥajjāj, *al-Ṣaḥīḥ*, 2:1033, *ḥadīth* 6378.

البرهان الثاني:

قوله تعالى: ﴿يا أيها الرّسول بلّغ ما أنزل إليك من ربّك وإن لّم تفعل فما بلغت رسالته والله يعصمك﴾.

اتّفقوا على نزولها في عليّ عليه السلام.

وروى أبو نعيم الحافظ من الجمهور بإسناده عن عطيّة قال: نزلت هذه الآية على رسول الله ﷺ في عليّ (بن أبي طالب).

ومن تفسير الثعلبي قال: معناه بلّغ ما أنزل إليك من ربّك في فضل عليّ فلمّا نزلت هذه الآية أخذ رسول الله ﷺ بيد عليّ وقال: من كنت مولاه فعليّ مولاه، والنبي ﷺ مولى أبي بكر وعمر وباقي الصحابة بالإجماع فيكون عليّ مولاهم فيكون هو الإمام؛

Also from the *Tafsīr* of al-Thaʿlabī:[16] "When the Messenger of Allah ﷺ was at Ghadīr Khumm,[17] he called the people together. Once they had assembled he took hold of ʿAlī's hand and said: 'Whosoever's master I am, ʿAlī is his master.' The news of that spread far and wide throughout the land until it reached al-Ḥārith b. Nuʿmān al-Fihrī. He set out for the Messenger of Allah ﷺ on his she-camel until he reached the Valley of al-Abṭaḥ, dismounted, tied his she-camel there, and came to the Prophet ﷺ who was surrounded by his Companions."

"He said to him: 'O Muḥammad! You commanded us by the authority of Allah to bear witness that there is no god but Allah, and that you are the Messenger of Allah, and we accepted this from you. You commanded us to pray five times a day, and we accepted this from you. You commanded us to fast for a month [i.e. the Month of Ramaḍān], and we accepted this from you. You commanded us to give obligatory alms from our wealth [i.e., the annual *zakāt*], and we accepted this from you. You commanded us to embark on the pilgrimage to the House [i.e. the Hajj], and we accepted this from you. Then, you were not satisfied with this until you raised aloft the arm of the son of your uncle and preferred him over us exclaiming "Whomsoever's master I am, ʿAlī is his master." Is this from you or from Allah?'"

"He said to him: 'I swear by Him than other there is no god but He, that it is none other than the command of Allah.'"

"At this al-Ḥārith b. al-Nuʿmān turned away going toward his mount while saying: 'O Allah! If what Muḥammad says is true, then cause stones from on high to strike us or send upon us a painful torment.' No sooner had he reached her [i.e. his she-camel] but Allah struck him with a stone. It hit the top of his skull and came out his rear end, killing him. Allah the Exalted then revealed: *A questioner asked about a punishment bound to happen, which none can repel from the unbelievers* [...]"[18]

This account has also been narrated by al-Naqqāsh,[19] one of the mainstream Sunnī scholars, in his commentary on the Qurʾān.

16 Unfortunately, this portion is missing from MSS Maḥmudiyya 98–107. MS Veliyüddin Efendi 130, fol.468b, ln.18–21.

17 Using classical Arabic geographical sources such as Yāqūt al-Ḥamawī's *Muʿjam al-buldān*, 2:389–390 and ʿAbd al-Muʾmin al-Baghdādi's *Marāṣid al-iṭṭilāʿ*, 483, 985 and modern maps, I conclude that the present-day location of Ghadīr Khumm is about 164 km to the North of Mecca, or about 450 km to the South of Medina, and that it is 26 km to the East of the modern settlement Rābigh toward the South-East which would put it at about 8 km to the East of the present mosque of the *mīqāt* of al-Juḥfa. I found the coordinates of the latter to be 22 degrees, 42 minutes, 18 seconds North; by 39 degrees, 8 minutes, 50 seconds East.

18 Qurʾān 70:1-2.

19 Muḥammad b. al-Ḥasan b. Muḥammad b. Ziyād b. Hārūn b. Jaʿfar, Abū Bakr al-Naqqāsh (d. 351/962). His *tafsīr* was entitled *Shifāʾ al-ṣudūr* (*Healing for the Hearts*); see Ibn Kathīr, *al-Bidāyā wa-l-nihāya* (Beirut: Maktabat al-Maʿārif, 1410/1990), 11:242–243.

ومن تفسير الثعلبي قال: لمّا كان رسول الله ﷺ بغدير خمّ نادى الناس فاجتمعوا فأخذ بيد عليّ فقال: من كنت مولاه فعليّ مولاه، فشاع ذلك وطار في البلاد، وبلغ ذلك الحارث بن النعمان القهري فأتى رسول الله ﷺ على ناقته حتّى (أتى الأبطح، فنزل عن ناقته) فأناخها وعقلها، وأتى النبيّ ﷺ وهو في ملأ من أصحابه فقال: يا محمّد ! أمرتنا عن الله أن نشهد أن لا إله إلّا الله وأنّك رسول الله فقبلناه منك ! وأمرتنا أن نصلّي خمساً فقبلناه منك ! وأمرتنا أن نصوم شهراً فقبلناه منك ! وأمرتنا أن نزكّي أموالنا فقبلناه منك ! وأمرتنا أن نحجّ البيت فقبلناه ! ثم لم ترض بهذا حتّى رفعت بضبعي ابن عمّك ففضّلته علينا وقلت «من كنت مولاه فعليّ مولاه» . وهذا شيء منك أم من الله ؟

فقال: والذي لا إله إلّا هو إنه من أمر الله .

فولّى الحارث بن النعمان يريد راحلته وهو يقول: اللّهمّ إن كان ما يقول محمّد حقّاً فأمطر علينا حجارة من السماء أو ائتنا بعذاب أليم. فما وصل إليها حتى رماه الله بحجر فسقط على هامته وخرج من دبره فقتله؛ وأنزل الله تعالى ﴿سأل سائل بعذاب واقع * للكافرين ليس له دافع﴾ .

قد روى هذه الرواية النّقاش من علماء الجمهور في تفسيره.

Demonstration 3[20]

The statement of the Exalted: *This day have I perfected for you your religion and completed My favour unto you and have chosen for you as religion al-Islam.*[21]

It is narrated by the Abū Nuʿaym[22] through his chain of transmission to Abū Saʿīd al-Khudrī who said, "The Messenger of Allah ﷺ called the people to gather round ʿAlī at Ghadīr Khumm. He ordered the thorns to be swept away from under the trees and took ʿAlī by the hands and raised his arms up [so high] that people could see the whiteness under the arms of the Messenger of Allah ﷺ. They did not leave until Allah had revealed this verse: *This day have I perfected for you your religion and completed My favour unto you and have chosen for you as religion al-Islam.* Then the Messenger of Allah ﷺ said, 'Allah is Most Great for having perfected the religion, completed the favour, and the choice of the Lord of my message and the authority of ʿAlī after me.' Then he said: 'Whomsoever's master I am, ʿAlī is his master. O Allah! Be a friend to whomever is a friend to him, and an enemy to whomever is an enemy to him! Support whomever supports him and disgrace whomever would disgrace him.'"

20 al-Ḥāfiẓ al-Ḥaskānī, *Shawāhid al-tanzīl li-qawāʿid al-tafḍīl*, 1:237–247.

21 Qur'ān 5:65.

22 al-Ḥāfiẓ Abū Nuʿaym al-Iṣfahānī, *al-Nūr al-mushtaʿal*, 56–60.

البرهان الثالث:

قوله تعالى: ﴿اليوم أكملت لكم دينكم وأتممت عليكم نعمتي ورضيت لكم الإسلام دينا﴾.

روى أبو نعيم بإسناده إلى أبي سعيد الخدري قال: إنّ النبي ﷺ دعا الناس إلى عليّ في غدير خمّ وأمر بما تحت الشجر من الشوك (فقمّ ودعا) عليّاً فأخذ بضبعيه فرفعها حتّى نظر الناس إلى بياض إبطي رسول الله ﷺ؛ ثم لم يتفرّقوا حتى نزلت هذه الآية: ﴿اليوم أكملت لكم دينكم وأتممت عليكم نعمتي ورضيت لكم الإسلام ديناً﴾. فقال رسول الله ﷺ: الله أكبر على إكمال الدين وإتمام النعمة ورضاء الربّ برسالتي وبالولاية لعليّ من بعدي، ثمّ قال: من كنت مولاه فعليّ مولاه؛ اللهمّ وال من والاه وعاد من عاداه وانصر من نصره واخذل من خذله؛

'Alī b. Abī Ṭālib after the Messenger of Allāh

Demonstration 4[23]

The statement of the Exalted: *By the star as it falls. Your companion has neither erred, nor is he deceived.*[24]

It is narrated by the Shāfiʿī *faqīh* Ibn al-Maghāzilī through his chain of transmission to Ibn ʿAbbās who said, "I was sitting with the young men of the Banū Hāshim in the presence of the Prophet ﷺ when we saw a shooting-star. The Messenger of Allah ﷺ then said: 'Whosoever's house this shooting-star lands on shall be my legatee after me.' The young men of the Banū Hāshim got up to look, and behold that the star landed on the house of ʿAlī b. Abī Ṭālib ؑ. They said: 'O Messenger of Allah ﷺ, you have erred in the love you have for ʿAlī.' Then Allah the Exalted sent down *By the star as falls. Your companion has neither erred, nor is deceived.*[25]

---

23 al-Ḥāfiẓ al-Ḥaskānī, *Shawāhid al-tanzīl li-qawāʿid al-tafḍīl*, 2:325–330.
24 Qurʾān 53:1–2.
25 Ibn al-Maghāzilī, *Manāqib Ahl al-bayt*, 368–369, *ḥadīth* 358. He relates the same through his chain of transmission from Anas on 332–333, *ḥadīth* 318.

البرهان الرابع:

قوله تعالى: ﴿والنّجم إذا هوى * ما ضلّ صاحبكم وما غوى﴾ .

روى الفقيه عليّ بن المغازلي الشافعي بإسناده عن ابن عباس قال: كنت جالساً مع فتية من بني هاشم عند النبيّ ﷺ إذ انقضّ كوكب. فقال رسول الله ﷺ: من انقضّ هذا النجم في منزله فهو الوصيّ من بعدي! فقام فتية من بني هاشم فنظروا فإذا الكوكب قد انقضّ في منزل عليّ بن أبي طالب. قالوا يا رسول الله قد غويت في حبّ عليّ! فأنزل الله تعالى ﴿والنّجم إذا هوى * ماضلّ صاحبكم وماغوى﴾ .

Demonstration 5[26]

The statement of the Exalted: *Truly Allah only wishes to remove all impurity from you, O People of the House, and to purify you exceedingly.*[27]

Aḥmad b. Ḥanbal narrated in his *Musnad* on the authority of Wāthila b. al-Asqaʿ[28] who said, "I sought out ʿAlī ﷺ at his house, but Fāṭima said: 'He left to get the Messenger of Allah ﷺ.' Then the two of them came back and went in. I followed them in. He seated ʿAlī on his left, Fāṭima on his right, and Ḥasan and Ḥusayn in front of him. Then he draped them with his garment and said: 'Truly Allah only wishes to remove all impurity from you, O People of the House! O Allah! These are my People! O Allah! They are the most worthy!'"

On the authority of Umm Salama who said: "The Prophet ﷺ was in his house when Fāṭima came to him with a vessel in which there was some soup. He said to her: 'Call me your husband and your two sons.' Then ʿAlī, Ḥasan and Ḥusayn ﷺ came and joined them. They sat down and had some of the soup. He and them were seated upon a sheet beneath which was a cloak from Khaybar spread on to the earthen floor. I was in an anteroom praying when Allah the Exalted revealed this verse: *Truly Allah only wishes to remove all impurity from you, O People of the House, and to purify you exceedingly.* He then took the ends of the cloak and draped them with it. Next, he took his hand and pointed toward the sky and said: 'These are the People of my House and those dear to me! O Allah! Remove from them all impurity and purify them exceedingly.' He then said it again. I asked him: 'Am I amongst them, O Messenger of Allah?' He said: 'You will be well. You will be well.'"

26 al-Ḥāfiẓ al-Ḥaskānī, *Shawāhid al-tanzīl li-qawāʿid al-tafḍīl*, 2:15–172; al-Ḥāfiẓ Abū Nuʿaym al-Iṣfahānī, *al-Nūr al-mushtaʿal*, 175–187.

27 Qurʾān 33:33.

28 See Aḥmad b. Ḥanbal, *al-Musnad*, 7:3758, *ḥadīth* 17262.

البرهان الخامس:

قوله تعالى: ﴿إنّما يريد الله ليذهب عنكم الرّجس أهل البيت ويطهّركم تطهيرا﴾ .

روى أحمد بن حنبل في (مسنده عن) واثلة بن الأسقع قال: طلبت عليّا في منزله فقالت فاطمة: ذهب (يأتي برسول) الله ﷺ، فجاءا جميعاً فدخلا ودخلت معها . فأجلس علياً عن يساره وفاطمة عن يمينه والحسن والحسين بين يديه، ثم التفع عليهم ثوبه وقال: إنما يريد الله ليذهب عنكم الرجس أهل البيت؛ اللّهمّ إنّ هؤلاء أهلي؛ اللهمّ هؤلاء أحقّ .

وعن أمّ سلمة قالت: إنّ النبيّ ﷺ كان في بيتها فأتته فاطمة ببرنة فيها حريرة فدخلت بها عليه، قال: ادعي لي زوجك وابنيك، قالت: فجاء عليّ وحسن وحسين فدخلوا فجلسوا يأكلون من تلك الحريرة، وهو وهم على منام له على دكّان تحته كساء خيبري. قالت: وأنا في الحجرة أصلّي فأنزل الله تعالى هذه الآية ﴿إنّما يريد الله ليذهب عنكم الرّجس أهل البيت ويطهّركم تطهيرا﴾ . قالت: فأخذ فضل الكساء وكساهم به ثم أخرج يده فألوى بها إلى السماء وقال: هؤلاء أهل بيتي وخاصّتي؛ اللهم فأذهب عنهم الرجس وطهّرهم تطهيراً؛ وكرر ذلك. قالت: فأدخلت رأسي وقلت: وأنا معكم يا رسول الله؟ قال: إنّك إلى خير (إنّك إلى خير) .

In this verse is evidence of infallibility which is emphasized by the Arabic particle *innamā* which comes before the subject and this is further strengthened by the letter *lām* before the predicate, as well as exclusively addressing the *ahl al-bayt* and the repetition contained in *yuṭahirrakum* and emphasis again in *taṭhīran*. Other than them, none are infallible, thus the Imāma belongs to ʿAlī. Moreover, he claimed it in many of his statements, such as "I swear by Allah that Ibn Abī Quḥāfa [i.e. Abū Bakr] has adorned himself with it [i.e. the Imāma] like a shirt while he knows too well that my relation to it is like the that of the axis to a millstone."[29] The removal of impurity from him is established [by this verse], thus he must speak the truth, so [by this statement of his] he is the Imam.

Demonstration 6[30]

The statement of the Exalted: *In houses which Allah has allowed to be built in which His Name is invoked* [...][31]

It was narrated by al-Thaʿlabī[32] through his chain of transmission to Anas b. Mālik and Burayda that the Messenger of Allah ﷺ recited this verse and a man stood up and asked: "What houses are these, O Messenger of Allah ﷺ?" He said: "The houses of the Prophets." Then Abū Bakr stood up and asked, "O Messenger of Allah ﷺ, is this house among them?" He meant the house of ʿAlī and Fāṭima. He said: "Yes, it is among the best of them."

The verse goes onto speak of "men not distracted from the remembrance of Allah" and this indicates their superlative character. Thus, ʿAlī is the Imam. Were it not so this would have entailed the superiority of the inferior over the superior.

29 A very famous quote from the celebrated third sermon (*khuṭba*) of the *Nahj al-balāgha* (*The Peak of Eloquence*), a collection of the sermons, letters, and aphorisms of ʿAlī b. Abī Ṭālib compiled by al-Sharīf al-Raḍī (d. 406/1015) and known as *al-Shaqshaqiyya*. Modern editions typically expurgate the explicit reference to Abū Bakr, i.e., "Ibn Abī Quḥāfa," and replace it with "so-and-so" (*fulān*). See, for example, *Nahj al-balāgha*, edited by Subḥī Ṣāliḥ (Qom: Manshūrāt Dār al-Hijra, 1412/192), 48 and *Nahj al-balāgha*, edited by Muḥammad ʿAbduh (Beirut: al-Maktabat al-ʿAṣriyya, 1424/2003), 32.

30 al-Ḥāfiẓ al-Ḥaskānī, *Shawāhid al-tanzīl li-qawāʿid al-tafḍīl*, 1:617–619.

31 Qurʾān 24:36.

32 Unfortunately, this portion is missing from MSS Maḥmudiyya 98–107. MS Veliyüddin Efendi 132, fol. 991b, ln.19–25 to fol. 992a, ln. 1.

وفي هذه الآية دلالة على العصمة مع التأكيد بلفظ «إنّما» وبإدخال «اللام» في الخبر والاختصاص في الخطاب بقوله «أهل البيت» والتكرير بقوله «يطهّركم» والتأكيد بقوله «تطهيراً»؛ وغيرهم ليس بمعصوم فتكون الإمامة في عليّ. ولأنه ادّعاها في عدّة من أقواله، كقوله: «والله لقد تقمّصها ابن أبي قحافة (وهو يعلم) أنّ محلّي منها محلّ القطب من الرحي» وقد ثبت نفي الرجس عنه فيكون صادقاً، فيكون هو الإمام؛

البرهان السادس:

قوله تعالى ﴿في بيوت أذن الله أن ترفع﴾ الآية.

قال الثعلبي بإسناده عن أنس بن مالك وبريدة قالا: قرأ رسول الله ﷺ هذه الآية فقام رجل فقال: أيّ بيوت هذه يا رسول الله؟ فقال: بيوت الأنبياء؛ فقام إليه أبو بكر فقال: يا رسول الله ﷺ هذا البيت منها؟ يعني بيت عليّ وفاطمة. قال: نعم، من أفاضلها.

وصف فيها الرجال بما يدلّ على أفضليّتهم، فيكون عليّ هو الإمام وإلّا لزم تقديم المفضول على الفاضل.

Demonstration 7[33]

The statement of the Exalted: *Say: I seek no recompense for this save love of [my] relatives.*[34]

Aḥmad narrated in his *Musnad* through Ibn ʿAbbās. He said: "When *Say: I seek no recompense for this save love of [my] relatives* was revealed they said, "O Messenger of Allah, who are your relatives whom we are obligated to love?" He said: "ʿAlī, Fāṭima, and their two sons ﷺ. The same is found in the *tafsīr* of al-Thaʿlabī[35] and the like in Bukhārī and Muslim.[36] This does not apply to the three Companions besides ʿAlī. Thus, ʿAlī is superior and must be the Imam, for opposing him would constitute not loving him and obeying his commands is to love him, therefore obeying him is obligatory and that is the meaning of Imāma.

33 al-Ḥāfiẓ al-Ḥaskānī, *Shawāhid al-tanzīl li-qawāʿid al-tafḍīl*, 2:257–261; al-Ḥāfiẓ Abū Nuʿaym al-Iṣfahānī, *al-Nūr al-mushtaʿal*, 207–215.

34 Qurʾān 42:23.

35 MS Maḥmudiyya 105, fol.65b, ln. 10–16; MS Veliyüddin Efendi 133, fol. 1262a, ln. 1–5.

36 This *ḥadīth* does not seem to be in the *Musnad* of Aḥmad b. Ḥanbal, however it is mentioned by him in his *Faḍāʾil al-ṣaḥāba*, 2:669, 1141. As for the reference to the *ḥadīth* collections of Bukhārī and Muslim, I did not find it in the latter, however it is does occur in al-Bukhārī, *al-Jāmiʿ al-musnad al-ṣaḥīḥ*, 2:691, 3537; 2:999, 4867 as well as in al-Tirmidhī, *al-Jāmiʿ*, 2:832, 3560; cf. *Tuḥfat al-ashrāf*, 5731. In the case of the two occurrences in Bukhārī and the single one in Tirmidhī, the expression "ʿAlī, Fāṭima, and their two sons' does not occur but rather *qurbā Muḥammad* (the close relations of Muḥammad). These three are all narrated from Ibn ʿAbbās via Ṭāwūs (d. ca. 106 AH or sometime after 110 AH) in the form of an exchange between Saʿīd b. Jubayr (executed by al-Ḥajjāj b. Yusuf in 95 AH) and Ibn ʿAbbās. Both Ṭāwus and Saʿīd b. Jubayr related *ḥadīth* from Ibn ʿAbbās. However, the version in *Faḍāʾil al-ṣaḥāba* does have the expression "ʿAlī, Fāṭima, and their two sons" and is narrated from Ibn ʿAbbās directly via Saʿīd b. Jubayr. The discrepancy in these versions is peculiar, to say the least, since the meaning of one and the same Qurʾānic verse (42:23) is being explained. On Ṭāwūs, see al-Mizzī, *Tahdhīb al-kamāl*, 13:357–374, entry 2958 and on Saʿīd b. Jubayr see ibid., 10:358–376, entry 2245.

البرهان السابع:

قوله تعالى: ﴿قل لّا أسألكم عليه أجراً إلّا المودّة في القربى﴾

روى أحمد في مسنده عن ابن عبّاس قال: لمّا نزل ﴿قل لّا أسألكم عليه أجراً إلّا المودّة في القربى﴾ قالوا: يا رسول الله، من قرابتك الّذين وجبت علينا مودّتهم؟ قال: علي وفاطمة وابناهما؛ وكذا في تفسير الثعلبي، ونحوه في الصحيحين. وغير عليّ من الصحابة الثلاثة لا تجب مودّته فيكون عليّ أفضل، فيكون هو الإمام؛ لأنّ مخالفته تنافي المودّة وامتثال أوامره يكون مودّة، فيكون واجب الطاعة؛ وهو معنى الإمامة.

Demonstration 8[37]

The statement of the Exalted: *And among the people there is* [*also*] *a kind of person who would willingly sell his own self in order to earn the pleasure of Allah* [...][38]

Al-Thaʿlabī said:[39] When the Messenger of Allah ﷺ set out on the Hijra, he left behind ʿAlī b. Abī Ṭālib to pay off his loans and to return the things that people had entrusted to his care. He ordered him to sleep in his bed the night that he left for the cave. By this time that idolators had surrounded the house. He said to him: "O ʿAlī! Cover yourself with my green Haḍramī cloak and sleep on my bed. No harm shall come to you from them, by the will of Allah, the Mighty, the Sublime." He did so and then Allah, the Mighty, the Sublime, revealed to Jibraʾīl and Mīkāʾīl: "I have made the two of you brothers to one another and made the life of one of you longer than the life of the other. Which of you then would prefer life for his companion?" Each chose the other. Allah then revealed to them, "You are like ʿAlī b. Abī Ṭālib. I made him and Muḥammad to be brothers to one another, and ʿAlī slept in his bed willing to sacrifice himself and give his life. Descend, then, the both of you and protect him from his enemies." So they went down and Jibraʾīl stood at his head and Mīkāʾīl stood at his feet. Jibraʾīl said: "How fortunate is the like of you, O Ibn Abī Ṭālib! Allah boasts of you to the angels. Thus did Allah reveal to His Messenger, as he was migrating toward Medina, regarding ʿAlī b. Abī Ṭālib ﵇: *And among the people there is* [*also*] *a kind of person who would willingly sell his own self in order to earn the pleasure of Allah* [...][40]

Ibn ʿAbbās related that this verse was revealed regarding ʿAlī b. Abī Ṭālib ﵇ when the Prophet ﷺ fled from the idolators toward the cave.

This is a merit which is not established for anyone else, thus it indicates his superiority over all the Companions, therefore he is the Imam.

37 al-Ḥāfiẓ al-Ḥaskānī, *Shawāhid al-tanzīl li-qawāʿid al-tafḍīl*, 1:145–154.

38 Qurʾān 2:207.

39 MS Maḥmudiyya 99, fol. 64b, ln.19 to fol. 65a, ln. 1–19; MS Veliyüddin Efendi 130, fol. 138b, ln. 19–25.

40 Qurʾān 2:207.

البرهان الثامن:

قوله تعالى: ﴿ومن النّاس من يشري نفسه أبتغاء مرضاة الله﴾.

قال الثعلبي: إنّ رسول الله ﷺ لمّا أراد الهجرة خلّف عليّ بن أبي طالب لقضاء ديونه وردّ الودائع التي كانت عنده. وأمره ليلة خرج إلى الغار وقد أحاط المشركون بالدار أن ينام على فراشه، فقال له: يا عليّ اتّشح ببردي الحضرمي الأخضر ونم على فراشي، فإنّه لا يخلص إليك منهم مكروه إن شاء الله عزّ وجل؛ ففعل ذلك. فأوحى الله عز وجل إلى جبرئيل وميكائيل: إنّي قد آخيت بينكما وجعلت عمر أحدكما أطول من عمر الآخر، فأيّكما يؤثر صاحبه بالحياة؟ فاختار كلاهما الحياة. فأوحى الله عز وجل إليها: ألا كنتما مثل عليّ بن أبي طالب، آخيت بينه وبين محمّد فبات على فراشه يفديه بنفسه ويؤثره بالحياة؛ اهبطا إلى الأرض فاحفظاه من عدوّه فنزلا. فكان جبرئيل عند رأسه وميكائيل عند رجليه، فقال جبرئيل: بخّ بخّ من مثلك يابن أبي طالب يباهي الله بك الملائكة! فأنزل الله على رسوله وهو متوجّه إلى المدينة في شأن عليّ بن أبي طالب ﴿ومن النّاس من يشري نفسه ابتغاء مرضاة الله﴾.

(وقال ابن عبّاس: إنّها نزلت في عليّ بن أبي طالب) لمّا هرب النبي ﷺ من المشركين إلى الغار.

وهذه فضيلة لم تحصل لغيره تدلّ على أفضليته على جميع الصحابة، فيكون هو الإمام.

Demonstration 9[41]

The statement of the Exalted: *If anyone argues with you about him [Jesus, son of Mary] after the knowledge that has come to you, say, "Come! Let us call our sons and your sons, our women and your women, our souls and your souls, and then let us supplicate humbly and ardently and invoke the curse of Allah upon those who lie."*[42]

It is related by the majority of scholars that *our sons* refers to Ḥasan and Ḥusayn, that *our women* refers to Fāṭima عليها السلام and *our souls* refers to ʿAlī b. Abī Ṭālib عليه السلام and this verse is the most clear evidence of the Imāma of ʿAlī عليه السلام since the Exalted designated him as the *soul* of the Messenger of Allah ﷺ, and since unification cannot be intended it must be equality of status that is intended, and since his authority extends over all, so too does that of he who is equal to him in status.

Moreover, were there some other group of persons which included one equal to him in status and more noble than them for the acceptance of supplications, Allah would have then ordered him to appear with them for here he was in a state of need, and were they to have been superior, then their Imāma would have been established.

The clear evidence of this verse is only lost on those whom Satan has overwhelmed and taken total control of their hearts and caused them to love the world, which is only attained by preventing the worthy from attaining their rights.

41 al-Ḥāfiẓ al-Ḥaskānī, *Shawāhid al-tanzīl li-qawāʿid al-tafḍīl*, 1:183–200; al-Ḥāfiẓ Abū Nuʿaym al-Iṣfahānī, *al-Nūr al-mushtaʿal*, 49–60.

42 Qurʾān 3:61.

البرهان التاسع:

قوله تعالى: ﴿فمن حاجّك فيه من بعد ما جاءك من العلم فقل تعالوا ندع أبناءنا وأبناءكم ونساءنا ونساءكم وأنفسنا وأنفسكم ثم نبتهل فنجعل لعنة الله على الكاذبين﴾.

نقل الجمهور كافّة أنّ ﴿أبناءنا﴾ إشارة إلى الحسن والحسين، و﴿نساءنا﴾ إشارة إلى فاطمة، و﴿أنفسنا﴾ إشارة إلى عليّ بن أبي طالب. وهذه الآية أدلّ دليل على ثبوت الإمامة لعليّ؛ لأنّه تعالى قد جعله نفس رسول الله ﷺ والاتّحاد محال، فينبغي المراد المساوي. وله ﷺ الولاية العامّة فكذا لمساويه.

وأيضاً لوكان غير هؤلاء مساوياً لهم أو أفضل منهم في استجابة الدعاء لأمره الله تعالى بأخذهم معه؛ لأنّه في موضع الحاجة. وإذا كانوا هم الأفضل تعيّنت الإمامة فيهم.

وهل تخفى دلالة هذه الآية على المطلوب إلّا على من استحوذ الشيطان عليه وأخذ بمجامع قلبه، وخيل له حب الدنيا التي لا ينالها إلّا بمنع أهل الحقّ عن حقّهم.

Demonstration 10

The statement of the Exalted: *Ādam received words from his Lord* [...].[43]

The Shāfiʿī *faqīh* Ibn al-Maghāzilī narrates through his chain of transmission from Ibn ʿAbbās who said, "The Prophet ﷺ was asked about the words which Ādam received from his Lord by virtue of which he was forgiven. He said: 'He asked Him by the right of Muḥammad, ʿAlī, Fāṭima, Ḥasan, and Ḥusayn to forgive him, and thus did He forgive him.'"

This is a merit that none among the Companions share with him, therefore he is the Imam due to his equality with the Prophet in respect of interceding with Allah, the Exalted.

Demonstration 11

The statement of the Exalted: *"Behold! I am making you an Imam over all mankind." He asked, "And from among my descendants?"*[44]

It is narrated by the Shāfiʿī *faqīh* Ibn al-Maghāzilī on the authority of ʿAbdullāh b. ʿAbbās that the Messenger of Allah ﷺ said: "Calling [people to Allah] has now passed over to me and to ʿAlī. Neither one of us ever prostrated before an idol. Thus, did He take me as [His] prophet, and ʿAlī as [His] legatee."[45] This is a prooftext pertaining to this [verse].

43 Qurʾān 2:37.

44 Qurʾān 2:124.

45 Ibn al-Maghāzilī, *Manāqib Ahl al-bayt*, 342–343, *ḥadīth* 327.

البرهان العاشر:

قوله تعالى: ﴿فتلقّى آدم من ربّه كلمات﴾.

روى الفقيه ابن المغازلي الشافعي بإسناده عن ابن عبّاس قال: سُئل النبي ﷺ عن الكلمات التي تلقّاها آدم من ربّه فتاب عليه، قال: سأله بحقّ محمّد وعليّ وفاطمة والحسن والحسين إلّا تبتَ عليّ فتاب عليه.

وهذه فضيلة لم يلحقه أحد من الصحابة فيها فيكون هو الإمام لمساواته النبي ﷺ في التوسّل به إلى الله تعالى.

البرهان الحادي عشر:

قوله تعالى: ﴿إنّي جاعلك للنّاس إماماً قال ومن ذرّيتي﴾.

روى الفقيه ابن المغازلي الشافعي عن عبد الله بن مسعود قال: قال رسول الله ﷺ: انتهت الدعوة إليّ وإلى عليّ، لم يسجد أحدنا لصنم قطّ؛ فاتّخذني نبيّاً واتخذ عليّا وصيّاً. وهذا نصّ في الباب.

ʿAlī b. Abī Ṭālib after the Messenger of Allāh

Demonstration 12[46]

The statement of the Exalted: *Indeed, those who believe and do good works, the Infinitely Compassionate will endow with love.*[47]

The Ḥāfiẓ Abū Nuʿaym[48] narrates through his chain of transmission from Ibn ʿAbbās who said, "This was revealed regarding ʿAlī. By *love* is meant love for him in the hearts of the believers."

From the *Tafsīr* of al-Thaʿlabī:[49] "On the authority of al-Barāʾ b. ʿĀzib who said, 'The Messenger of Allah said to ʿAlī b. Abī Ṭālib: "O ʿAlī! Say, 'O Allah! establish for me a covenant with you, and place love within the hearts of the believers.'" So Allah the Exalted revealed: *Indeed, those who believe and do good works, the Infinitely Compassionate will endow with love.*"

This is a merit that is not found among any of the Companions but him, therefore he is superior to them and must be the Imam.

Demonstration 13

The statement of the Exalted: *You are but a warner and to every people there is a guide.*[50]

From the *Firdaws al-akhbār* (*The Garden of Prophetic Traditions*): On the authority of Ibn ʿAbbās who said, "The Messenger of Allah said: 'I am the warner and ʿAlī is the guide. O ʿAlī! It is through you that those who are on guidance received guidance.'"[51] The like thereof is narrated by Abū Nuʿaym.[52] This statement explicitly establishes authority and Imāma.

---

46 al-Ḥāfiẓ al-Ḥaskānī, *Shawāhid al-tanzīl li-qawāʿid al-tafḍīl*, 1:543–557.
47 Qurʾān 19:96.
48 Al-Ḥāfiẓ Abū Nuʿaym al-Iṣfahānī, *al-Nūr al-mushtaʿal*, 129–137.
49 Unfortunately, this portion in missing from MSS Maḥmudiyya 98–107. MS Veliyüddin Efendi 132, fol. 901b, ln. 21–25 to fol. 902a, ln 1–2.
50 Qurʾān 13:7.
51 This tradition does not appear in the modern edition of the al-Daylamī, *Firdaws al-akhbār*, however the 13th/19th century scholar al-Qandōzī (d. 1294/1877) cites it from the latter in his *Yanābīʿ al-mawwada li-dhawī l-qurbā* (Baghdad: Manshūrāt al-Maktabat al-Ḥaydariyya, 1384/1965), 1:211.
52 al-Ḥāfiẓ Abū Nuʿaym al-Iṣfahānī, *al-Nūr al-mushtaʿal*, 117–24.

البرهان الثاني عشر:

قوله تعالى: ﴿إنّ الّذين آمنوا وعملوا الصّالحات سيجعل لهم الرّحمن ودّا﴾ .

روى الحافظ أبو نعيم بإسناده إلى ابن عبّاس قال: نزلت في عليّ قال: والودّ محبّته في قلوب المؤمنين.

وعن تفسير الثعلبي عن البراء بن عازب قال: قال رسول الله ﷺ لعليّ بن أبي طالب يا عليّ قل اللهمّ اجعل لي عندك عهداً واجعل لي في صدور المؤمنين مودّة! فأنزل الله تعالى ﴿الّذين آمنوا وعملوا الصّالحات سيجعل لهم الرّحمن ودّاً﴾ .

ولم يثبت لغيره من الصحابة ذلك، فيكون أفضل منهم، فيكون هو الإمام.

البرهان الثالث عشر:

قوله تعالى: ﴿إنّما أنت منذر ولكلّ قوم هاد﴾ . من كتاب الفردوس عن ابن عبّاس قال: قال رسول الله ﷺ: أنا المنذر وعليّ الهادي، وبك يا عليّ يهتدى المهتدون؛ ونحوه رواه أبو نعيم. وهو صريح في ثبوت الولاية والإمامة.

Demonstration 14[53]

The statement of the Exalted: *And call them to a halt, for they must be questioned.*[54]

From Ḥāfiẓ Abū Nuʿaym,[55] on the authority of al-Shaʿbī, on the authority of Ibn ʿAbbās who said, "He [i.e. Messenger of Allah ﷺ] said regarding the statement of the Exalted: *And call them to a halt, for they must be questioned* that what was meant is that they must be questioned about the authority of ʿAlī b. Abī Ṭālib." The same is found in *Firdaws al-akhbār* (*The Garden of Prophetic Traditions*) on the authority of Abū Saʿīd al-Khudrī, on the authority of the Prophet ﷺ.

If they are to be questioned about ʿAlī's authority, then it follows that his authority is an established fact. Moreover, it is not so for any of the Companions but him. Therefore, he is superior and must be the Imam.

Demonstration 15[56]

The statement of the Exalted: *and you shall truly know them by their manner of speech.*[57]

Abū Nuʿaym al-Ḥāfiẓ[58] has related via his chain of transmission from Abū Saʿīd al-Khudrī regarding the statement of the Exalted: *and you shall truly know them by their manner of speech*: "That is to say by their hatred of ʿAlī." This has not been established for any of the other Companions. Thus, he is superior to them and therefore it is he who is the Imam.

53 al-Ḥāfiẓ al-Ḥaskānī, *Shawāhid al-tanzīl li-qawāʿid al-tafḍīl*, 2:195–199.
54 Qurʾān 37:24.
55 al-Ḥāfiẓ Abū Nuʿaym al-Iṣfahānī, *al-Nūr al-mushtaʿal*, 196–199.
56 al-Ḥāfiẓ al-Ḥaskānī, *Shawāhid al-tanzīl li-qawāʿid al-tafḍīl*, 2:296–298.
57 Qurʾān 47:30.
58 al-Ḥāfiẓ Abū Nuʿaym al-Iṣfahānī, *al-Nūr al-mushtaʿal*, 227–229.

البرهان الرابع عشر:

قوله تعالى: ﴿وقفوهم إنّهم مسئولون﴾ . من طريق الحافظ أبي نعيم عن الشعبي عن ابن عبّاس قال في قوله تعالى: ﴿وقفوهم إنّهم مسئولون﴾ قال: عن ولاية عليّ بن أبي طالب؛ وكذا في كتاب الفردوس عن أبي سعيد الخدري عن النّبي ﷺ. وإذا سئلوا عن الولاية وجب أن تكون ثابتة له ولم يثبت لغيره من الصحابة ذلك، فيكون أفضل فيكون هو الإمام.

البرهان الخامس عشر:

قوله تعالى: ﴿ولتعرفنّهم في لحن القول﴾ .

روى أبو نعيم الحافظ بإسناده عن أبي سعيد الخدري في قوله تعالى: ﴿ولتعرفنّهم في لحن القول﴾ قال: ببغضهم عليّا . ولم يثبت لغيره من الصحابة ذلك فيكون أفضل منهم فيكون هو الإمام.

Demonstration 16[59]

The statement of the Exalted: *and the Foremost are indeed the Foremost! Those are the Ones Brought Near.*[60]

It is narrated by the Ḥāfiẓ Abū Nuʿaym on the authority of Ibn ʿAbbās who said regarding this verse: "The foremost of this *umma* is ʿAlī b. Abī Ṭālib."[61]

It is narrated by the Shāfiʿī *faqīh* Ibn al-Maghāzilī, on the authority of Mujāhid, on the authority of Ibn ʿAbbās regarding His statement: *and the Foremost are indeed the Foremost!*, he said: The foremost in relation to Mūsā was Yūshaʿ b. Nūn, and the foremost in relation to ʿĪsā was Ṣāḥib Yāsīn, and the foremost in relation to Muḥammad ﷺ was ʿAlī."[62]

This merit is not established for any one from amongst the Companions but him, therefore he must be the Imam.

59 al-Ḥāfiẓ al-Ḥaskānī, *Shawāhid al-tanzīl li-qawāʿid al-tafḍīl*, 2:341–347.
60 Qurʾān 56:10–11.
61 al-Ḥāfiẓ Abū Nuʿaym al-Iṣfahānī, *al-Nūr al-mushtaʿal*, 240–244.
62 Ibn al-Maghāzilī, *Manāqib Ahl al-bayt*, 380–381, *ḥadīth* 370.

البرهان السادس عشر:

قوله تعالى: ﴿والسّابقون السّابقون أولئك المقرّبون﴾.

روى أبو نعيم الحافظ، عن ابن عبّاس، قال في هذه الآية: سابق هذه الأمّة عليّ بن أبي طالب.

وروى الفقيه ابن المغازلي الشافعي عن مجاهد عن ابن عبّاس في قوله: ﴿والسّابقون السّابقون﴾ قال: سبق يوشع بن نون إلى موسى و(صاحب يس) إلى عيسى، وسبق عليّ إلى محمّد ﷺ.

وهذه الفضيلة لم تثبت لغيره من الصحابة، فيكون هو الإمام.

Demonstration 17[63]

The statement of the Exalted: *Those who have believed, and migrated, and striven with their wealth and their lives in the path of Allah have the highest rank with Allah.*[64]

It is narrated by Razīn b. Muʿāwiya[65] in *al-Jamʿ bayna l-ṣiḥāḥ al-sitta* (*The Ḥadīths found in All Six of the Rigorously Authenticated Books*) that it was revealed regarding ʿAlī ﷺ when Ṭalḥa b. Shayba and al-ʿAbbās were boasting [about themselves].

This is a merit which is not established for any one from amongst the Companions but him, therefore he is superior and must be the Imam.

63 al-Ḥāfiẓ al-Ḥaskānī, *Shawāhid al-tanzīl li-qawāʿid al-tafḍīl*, 1:381–393.

64 Qurʾān 9:19-21. There appears to be an error in this edition. It is clear from the context as well from another work by ʿAllāma, namely *Nahj al-ḥaqq wa-kashf al-ṣidq* (*The Pathway of Truth and the Unveiling of Veracity*), that what is in question is in fact verses 19 through 21 of Sūrat al-Tawba (the 9th Sūra of the Qurʾān). In the latter work, the same tradition regarding ʿAlī is quoted as is here.

65 Abū l-Ḥasan Razīn b. Muʿāwiya b. ʿAmmār al-ʿAbdarī was an Andalusian *ḥadīth* scholar from Saragossa who died in 524/1129 or 535/1140. His *al-Jamʿ bayna l-ṣiḥāḥ al-sitta* remains, to the best of my knowledge, in manuscript and includes the five well-known Sunnī collections but replaces the sixth, namely the *Sunan* of Ibn Māja, with the *al-Muwaṭṭaʾ* of Mālik. Thus, it is also known by the title *Kitāb al-Tajrīd fī l-jamʿ bayna l-Muwaṭṭaʾ wa-l-ṣiḥāḥ al-khamsa*. Another title is *Tajrīd al-ṣiḥāḥ al-sitta fī l-ḥadīth*. See Etan Kohlberg, *A Medieval Muslim Scholar at Work. Ibn Ṭāwūs and his Library* (Leiden: E. J. Brill, 1992), 201. I have not been able to locate this reference in these six works. A number of *ḥadīths* in this regard are, however, quoted in *Shawāhid al-tanzīl* cited above as well as in al-Ḥāfiẓ Abū Nuʿaym al-Iṣfahānī, *al-Nūr al-mushtaʿal*, 98–101.

البرهان السابع عشر:

قوله تعالى: ﴿الذين آمنوا وهاجروا وجاهدوا في سبيل الله بأموالهم وأنفسهم أعظم درجة عند الله﴾ الآيات.

روى رزين بن معاوية في الجمع بين الصحاح الستّة أنّها نزلت في عليّ لمّا افتخر طلحة بن شيبة والعبّاس.

وهذه فضيلة لم تحصل لغيره من الصحابة، فيكون أفضل فيكون هو الإمام.

'Alī b. Abī Ṭālib after the Messenger of Allāh

Demonstration 18[66]

The statement of the Exalted: *O you who believe! When you consult the Messenger in private precede your private consultation by giving alms [to the poor] [...]*.[67]

From Ḥāfiẓ Abū Nuʿaym, on the authority of Ibn ʿAbbās who said, "Allah made forbidden consulting the Messenger of Allah ﷺ without preceding it by the giving of alms [to the poor]. However, they were too miserly to give alms before consulting him, but ʿAlī gave alms, and no one else from among the Muslims did so."[68]

From the *Tafsīr* of al-Thaʿlabī:[69] Ibn ʿUmar said, "ʿAlī ؏ had three things even one of which if I had it would have been more beloved to me than the choicest of camels. His marriage to Fāṭima, his being entrusted with the battle-flag during the Battle of Khaybar, and his being singled out by the verse of consultation."

It is narrated by Razīn b. Muʿāwiya in *al-Jamʿ bayna l-Ṣiḥāḥ al-sitta* (*The Ḥadīths found in All Six of the Rigorously Authenticated Books*),[70] on the authority of ʿAlī ؏, "No one acted upon this verse but me, and it is through me that Allah the Exalted lightened this burden from the *umma*."

This indicates his superiority and his being most worthy of the Imāma.

---

66 al-Ḥāfiẓ al-Ḥaskānī, *Shawāhid al-tanzīl li-qawāʿid al-tafḍīl*, 2:363–383.
67 Qurʾān 58:12.
68 al-Ḥāfiẓ Abū Nuʿaym al-Iṣfahānī, *al-Nūr al-mushtaʿal*, 249–252.
69 MS Maḥmudiyya 106 fol. 82a, ln.7–9 and fol. 81b ln. 11 to fol. 82a, ln. 1–6; MS Veliyüddin Efendi 133, fol. 1425a, ln. 1–3 and fol. 1424b, ln. 1–25 (i.e. whole page).
70 I have not been able to locate this reference in these six works. However, this statement of ʿAlī is recorded in Ibn al-Maghāzilī, *Manāqib Ahl al-bayt*, 387, ḥadīth 378.

البرهان الثامن عشر:

قوله تعالى: ﴿يا أيها الّذين آمنوا إذا ناجيتم الرسول﴾ الآية.

من طريق الحافظ أبي نعيم إلى ابن عبّاس قال: إنّ الله حرم كلام رسول الله ﷺ إلّا بتقديم الصدقة وبخلوا أن يتصدّقوا قبل كلامه، وتصدّق عليّ ولم يفعل ذلك أحد من المسلمين غيره؛

ومن تفسير الثعلبي قال ابن عمر: كان لعليّ ثلاثة، لوكانت لي واحدة منهنّ كانت أحبّ إليّ من حمر النّعم: تزويجه بفاطمة وإعطاؤه الراية يوم خيبر وآية النجوى.

وروى رزين العبدري في الجمع بين الصحاح الستّة عن عليّ: ما عمل بهذه الآية غيري، وبي خفّف الله تعالى عن هذه الأمّة وهذا يدلّ على أفضليّته عليهم فيكون أحقّ بالإمامة.

'Alī b. Abī Ṭālib after the Messenger of Allāh

Demonstration 19[71]

The statement of the Exalted: *And ask those We sent before you as messengers* [...].[72]

Ibn 'Abd al-Barr said — and Abū Nu'aym also recorded this[73] — "When the Prophet ﷺ was made to journey by night [to al-Quds and rose heavenward therefrom] Allah the Exalted made him enter into the presence of the [previous] prophets and said to him: 'Ask them, O Muḥammad, on what were you all sent forth.' They said: 'We were sent forth on bearing witness that there is no deity but Allah, acknowledging your prophethood, and the authority of 'Alī b. Abī Ṭālib.'"

This is an explicit affirmation of the Imāma of 'Alī ؑ.

Demonstration 20[74]

The statement of the Exalted: *And that receptive ears might retain it.*[75]

From the *Tafsīr* of al-Tha'labī: "The Messenger of Allah ﷺ said: 'O 'Alī, I asked Allah, the Mighty, the Sublime, to make your ears such.'"[76]

From Abū Nu'aym who said, the Messenger of Allah ﷺ said: 'O 'Alī, Allah, the Mighty, the Sublime, ordered me to draw close to you and to teach you in order that you might retain [what you are taught], and then this verse was revealed. So it is you who personify *receptive ears retentive* of knowledge.[77]

This merit is not established for anyone but him, therefore he must be the Imam.

---

71 al-Ḥāfiẓ al-Ḥaskānī, *Shawāhid al-tanzīl li-qawā'id al-tafḍīl*, 2:269–272.
72 Qur'ān 43:45.
73 I have not been able to locate either of these references. However, the incident is alluded to in al-Muwaffaq b. Aḥmad al-Khawārizmī, *al-Manāqib*, 312 ḥadīth 312.
74 al-Ḥāfiẓ al-Ḥaskānī, *Shawāhid al-tanzīl li-qawā'id al-tafḍīl*, 2:421–442.
75 Qur'ān 69:12.
76 MS Maḥmudiyya 106, fol.175b, ln. 18 to fol. 176, ln. 3; MS Veliyüddin Efendi 133, fol. 1506b, ln. 19–25.
77 al-Ḥāfiẓ Abū Nu'aym al-Iṣfahānī, *al-Nūr al-mushta'al*, 266–272.

البرهان التاسع عشر:

قوله تعالى: ﴿وأسأل من أرسلنا من قبلك من رسلنا﴾.

قال ابن عبد البرّ وأخرجه أبو نعيم أيضاً قال: إنّ النبي ﷺ ليلة أسري به جمع الله تعالى بينه وبين الأنبياء ثم قال له: سلهم يا محمّد على ماذا بعثتم؟ فقالوا: بعثنا على شهادة أن لا إله إلا الله وعلى الإقرار بنبوّتك والولاية لعليّ بن أبي طالب.

وهذا تصريح بثبوت الإمامة لعليّ عليه السلام.

البرهان العشرون:

قوله تعالى: ﴿وتعيها أذن واعية﴾.

في تفسير الثعلبي قال: قال رسول الله ﷺ: سالت الله عزّ وجل أن يجعلها أذنك يا عليّ.

ومن طريق أبي نعيم قال: قال رسول الله ﷺ: يا عليّ! إنّ الله عزّ وجلّ أمرني أن أدنيك وأعلّمك لتعي وأنزلت هذه الآية أذن واعية، فأنت أذن واعية للعلم.

وهذه الفضيلة لم تحصل لغيره، فيكون هو الإمام.

On the Proofs establishing the Imāma of the Commander of the Faithful ʿAlī b. Abī Ṭālib after the Messenger of Allāh

Demonstration 21[78]

The Sūra of *Hal atā*.[79]

From the *Tafsīr* of al-Thaʿlabī citing various chains of transmission:[80] Ḥasan and Ḥusayn both fell ill and were thus visited by their grandfather, the Messenger of Allah ﷺ as well as most of the Arabs. They said: "O Abū l-Ḥasan [a respectful way to address ʿAlī]! You should make a vow for your two sons to get better." So he vowed that if they got well he would fast for three days, as did their mother Fāṭima ؑ along with their handmaid Fiḍḍa, and both of them recovered. While the Household of Muḥammad was not entirely empty, they did not have much either, so ʿAlī ؑ borrowed three measures of grain. Fāṭima ؑ ground it and made from it five loaves, a loaf for each of them. ʿAlī ؑ offered the *maghrib* prayer with the Prophet ﷺ and then came home. When the food was placed before him, all of a sudden a needy person came to the door and said: "Peace be unto you, O Household of Muḥammad, I am a needy man from amongst the needy Muslims! Feed me, may Allah feed you from the table spreads of the Garden!" ʿAlī ؑ heeded his plea and ordered that he be given food. Thus, did they pass both their day and their night having tasted nothing but clear water.

The next day Fāṭima ؑ prepared another measure of bread, and ʿAlī offered the prayer with the Prophet ﷺ and went home. When the food was placed before him, all of a sudden a needy person came to the door and said: "Peace be unto you, O Household of Muḥammad, I am a needy man from amongst the needy Migrants! My father was martyred in the Battle of al-ʿAqaba! Feed me, may Allah feed you from the table spreads of the Garden!" ʿAlī ؑ heeded his plea and ordered that he be given food. Thus, did they pass a second day and a second night having tasted nothing but clear water.

---

78 al-Ḥāfiẓ al-Ḥaskānī, *Shawāhid al-tanzīl li-qawāʿid al-tafḍīl*, 2:459–481.

79 This is the 76th Sūra of the Qurʾān and is known as Sūrat al-Insān as well as Sūrat al-Dahr or simply by its opening words, as here, *Hal atā*. The full form is *hal atā ʿalā l-insāni ḥīnun min al-dahri lam yakun shayʾan madhkūran* ("Has there ever come upon man any period of time in which he was a thing unremembered?").

80 MS Maḥmudiyya 107, fol. 15b, ln.14 to fol. 18, ln. 19; MS Veliyüddin Efendi 133, fol. 1549b, ln. 14 to fol. 1551b, ln. 23.

البرهان الحادي والعشرون:

سورة ﴿هل أتى﴾.

في تفسير الثعلبي من طرق مختلفة قال: مرض الحسن والحسين عليهما السلام فعادهما جدّهما رسول الله ﷺ وعامّة العرب، فقالوا له: يا أبا الحسن لو نذرت على ولديك! فنذر صوم ثلاثة أيام، وكذا نذرت أمّهما فاطمة وجاريتهم فضّة، فبرءا وليس عند آل محمّد قليل ولا كثير، فاستقرض عليّ ثلاثة أصوع من شعير. فقامت فاطمة إلى صاع فطحنته واختبزت منه خمسة أقراص، لكلّ واحد منهم قرصاً، وصلّى عليّ مع النبيّ ﷺ المغرب ثم أتى المنزل. فوضع الطعام بين يديه إذ أتاهم مسكين فوقف بالباب، فقال: السلام عليكم أهل بيت محمّد، مسكين من مساكين المسلمين، أطعموني أطعمكم الله من موائد الجنّة! فسمعه عليّ فأمر بإعطائه، فأعطوه الطعام ومكثوا يومهم وليلهم لم يذوقوا شيئاً إلّا الماء القراح.

فلمّا أن كان اليوم الثاني قامت فاطمة فاختبزت صاعاً وصلّى عليّ مع النبي ﷺ ثمّ أتى المنزل، فوضع الطعام بين يديه فأتاهم يتيم فوقف بالباب، وقال: السلام عليكم أهل بيت محمد، يتيم من أولاد المهاجرين استشهد والدي يوم العقبة؛ أطعموني أطعمكم الله من موائد الجنّة! فسمعه عليّ فأمر بإعطائه، فأعطوه الطعام ومكثوا يومين وليلتين لم يذوقوا شيئاً إلّا الماء القراح.

On the third day Fāṭima ground another measure of grain and prepared bread and ʿAlī offered the prayer with the Prophet and went home. When the food was placed before him, all of a sudden a captive came to the door and said: "Peace be unto you, O Household of Muḥammad, I was taken captive, my hands have been tied, and they do not feed me! Feed me, for I am a captive of Muḥammad, may Allah feed you from the table spreads of the Garden!" ʿAlī heeded his plea and ordered that he be given food. Thus, did they pass a third day and a third night having tasted nothing but clear water.

When the fourth day came and they had fulfilled their vow, ʿAlī took Ḥasan by his right hand and Ḥusayn by his left hand and came to the Messenger of Allah and they were all trembling like little chicks from the severity of hunger. When the Prophet saw this he said: "O Abū l-Ḥasan! How severe is that which I see in you! Take me with you to the house of my daughter Fāṭima. They went to her and she was in her prayer-niche. Her belly had joined her back out of the severity of hunger and her eyes had become sunken in. When the Prophet saw her he exclaimed: "Succour, O Allah! Relief, O Allah! The Household of Muḥammad is dying of hunger!" Then Jibraʾīl descended upon Muḥammad and said: "O Muḥammad! Receive that which Allah has conferred upon your Household!" "And what is that?" he asked. So, he recited to him *Has there ever come upon man any period of time in which he was a thing unremembered?*

This indicates the manifold merits unprecedented for anyone else prior or after. Thus, he is superior to all others and is the Imam.

Demonstration 22[81]

The statement of the Exalted: *He who brings the truth and he who confirms it* [...].[82]

From Abū Nuʿaym, narrating from Mujāhid regarding the statement of the Exalted: *He who brings the truth and he who confirms it*, it refers to ʿAlī b. Abī Ṭālib.[83]

Also from the Shāfiʿī scholar [Ibn al-Maghāzilī], narrating from Mujāhid regarding the statement of the Exalted: *He who brings the truth and he who confirms it*, it means Muḥammad brought it and it was confirmed by ʿAlī.[84] Thus, this is a merit for which he has been singled out and so he is the Imam.

81 al-Ḥāfiẓ al-Ḥaskānī, *Shawāhid al-tanzīl li-qawāʿid al-tafḍīl*, 2:214–217.

82 Qurʾān 39:33.

83 al-Ḥāfiẓ Abū Nuʿaym al-Iṣfahānī, *al-Nūr al-mushtaʿal*, 204–205.

84 Ibn al-Maghāzilī, *Manāqib Ahl al-bayt*, 336, *ḥadīth* 322.

فلمّا كان اليوم الثالث قامت فاطمة إلى الصاع الثالث فطحنته واختبزته، وصلّى عليّ مع النبيّ ﷺ ثمّ أتى المنزل، فوضع الطعام بين يديه إذ أتاهم أسير فوقف بالباب، فقال: السلام عليكم أهل بيت محمّد، تأسروننا وتشدّوننا ولا تطعمونا ؟ أطعموني فإنّي أسير محمّد، أطعمكم الله على موائد الجنّة ! فسمعه عليّ فأمر بإعطائه، فأعطوه الطعام ومكثوا ثلاثة أيام ولياليها لم يذوقوا شيئاً إلا الماء القراح.

فلمّا كان اليوم الرابع وقد وفّوا نذرهم أخذ عليّ الحسن بيده اليمنى والحسين بيده اليسرى وأقبل على رسول الله ﷺ وهم يرتعشون كالفراخ من شدّة الجوع. فلمّا بصر به النبى ﷺ قال: يا أبا الحسن، ما أشد ما يسوءني ما أرى بكم انطلق بنا إلى منزل ابنتي فاطمة، فانطلقوا إليها وهي في محرابها قد لصق ظهرها ببطنها من شدّة الجوع وغارت عيناها . فلمّا رآها النبيّ ﷺ قال: واغوثاه بالله أهل بيت محمّد يموتون جوعاً . فهبط جبرئيل على محمّد ﷺ فقال: يا محمّد، خذ ما هنّاك الله في أهل بيتك؛ قال: وما أخذ ياجبرئيل ؟ فأقرأه ﴿هل أتى على الإنسان﴾ .

وهي تدلّ على فضائل جمّة لم (يسبق إليها) أحد ولا يلحقه أحد، فيكون أفضل من غيره فيكون هو الإمام.

البرهان الثاني والعشرون:

قوله تعالى: ﴿الّذي جاء بالصّدق وصدّق به﴾ .

من طريق أبي نعيم عن مجاهد في قوله تعالى: ﴿والذي جاء بالصّدق﴾: محمّد ﴿وصدّق به﴾ قال: عليّ بن أبي طالب.

ومن طريق الفقيه الشافعي عن مجاهد في قوله تعالى: ﴿والّذي جاء بالصّدق وصدّق به﴾ قال: جاء به محمّد، وصدّق به عليّ. وهذه فضيلة اختصّ بها فيكون هو الإمام.

'Alī b. Abī Ṭālib after the Messenger of Allāh

Demonstration 23[85]

The statement of the Exalted: *He it is who supports you with his help and with the believers.*[86]

From Abū Nuʿaym, narrating from Abū Hurayra, "The Messenger of Allah ﷺ said: 'Inscribed on the [Divine] Throne are the words: There is no deity but Allah, Alone, no partner has He. Muḥammad is My servant and My messenger whom I have supported with ʿAlī b. Abī Ṭālib. And that is stated in His book as well: *He it is who supports you with his help and with the believers*, which is a reference to ʿAlī b. Abī Ṭālib. This is one of his greatest merits which no one else possesses, so he is the Imam.'"[87]

Demonstration 24[88]

The statement of the Exalted: *O Prophet! Allah is Sufficient for you and those of the believers who follow you.*[89]

From Abū Nuʿaym, who said: "It was revealed regarding ʿAlī b. Abī Ṭālib."[90]

This is a merit which is not established for any one from amongst the Companions but him, therefore he must be the Imam.

Demonstration 25

The statement of the Exalted: *Allah will bring forward a people whom He loves and who love Him.*[91]

Al-Thaʿlabī said: "It was revealed regarding ʿAlī b. Abī Ṭālib ؑ."[92]

This indicates that he is superior and therefore he must be the Imam.

---

85 al-Ḥāfiẓ al-Ḥaskānī, *Shawāhid al-tanzīl li-qawāʿid al-tafḍīl*, 1:349–357.
86 Qurʾān 8:62.
87 al-Ḥāfiẓ Abū Nuʿaym al-Iṣfahānī, *al-Nūr al-mushtaʿal*, 89–91
88 al-Ḥāfiẓ al-Ḥaskānī, *Shawāhid al-tanzīl li-qawāʿid al-tafḍīl*, 1:358–481.
89 Qurʾān 8:64.
90 al-Ḥāfiẓ Abū Nuʿaym al-Iṣfahānī, *al-Nūr al-mushtaʿal*, 92–93.
91 Qurʾān 5:54.
92 Unfortunately, this portion in missing from MSS Maḥmudiyya 98–107. MS Veliyüddin Efendi 130, fol. 462a, ln. 15.

البرهان الثالث والعشرون:

قوله تعالى: ﴿هو الّذي أيدك بنصره وبالمؤمنين﴾.

من طريق أبي نعيم عن أبي هريرة قال: قال رسول الله ﷺ: مكتوب على العرش «لا إله إلا الله وحده لاشريك له، محمّد عبدي ورسولي أيدته بعليّ بن أبي طالب»، وذلك قوله تعالى في كتابه: ﴿هو الّذي أيدك بنصره وبالمؤمنين﴾ يعني عليّ بن أبي طالب. وهذه من أعظم الفضائل التي لم تحصل لغيره، فيكون هو الإمام.

البرهان الرابع والعشرون:

قوله تعالى: ﴿أيها النّبي حسبك الله ومن اتّبعك من المؤمنين﴾.

من طريق أبي نعيم قال: نزلت في عليّ بن أبي طالب.

وهذه فضيلة لم تحصل لأحد من الصحابة غيره، فيكون هو الإمام.

البرهان الخامس والعشرون:

قوله تعالى: ﴿فسوف يأتي الله بقوم يحبّهم ويحبّونه﴾.

قال الثعلبي: إنّها نزلت في عليّ عليه السلام. وهذا يدلّ على أنّه أفضل، فيكون هو الإمام.

Demonstration 26[93]

The statement of the Exalted: *Those who have faith in Allah and His Messengers — such people are the truly sincere* [...][94]

It is narrated by Aḥmad b. Ḥanbal through his chain of transmission to Ibn Abī Laylā, on the authority of his father: "The Messenger of Allah ﷺ said: *The truly sincere* are three: Ḥabīb b. Mūsā al-Najjār, the believer of the Āl Yāsīn, who said *O my people! Follow the messengers!*[95] Then Ḥazaqīl, the believer of the Āl Firʿawn, who said: *Will you slay a man for saying: Allah is my Lord*?[96] Then ʿAlī b. Abī Ṭālib ؑ and he is the best of them."[97]

The like thereof was also narrated by the Shāfiʿī *faqīh* Ibn al-Maghāzilī[98] as well as the compiler of the *Firdaws al-akhbār* (*The Garden of Prophetic Traditions*).[99]

This is a merit which indicates that he is the Imam.

Demonstration 27[100]

The statement of the Exalted: *Those who spend their wealth by night and day, in secret and in the open.*[101]

From Ḥāfiẓ Abū Nuʿaym through his chain of transmission to Ibn ʿAbbās, who said: "It was revealed about ʿAlī b. Abī Ṭālib ؑ. He had four dirhams. He gave away one dirham at night. and in the day a dirham, and a dirham in secret, and a dirham in the open.[102] Such was recorded by al-Thaʿlabī in his *Tafsīr*.[103]

This did not apply to anyone but ʿAlī ؑ. Thus, he is superior and is the Imam.

93 al-Ḥāfiẓ al-Ḥaskānī, *Shawāhid al-tanzīl li-qawāʿid al-tafḍīl*, 2:355–359; al-Ḥāfiẓ Abū Nuʿaym al-Iṣfahānī, *al-Nūr al-mushtaʿal*, 245–247.

94 Qurʾān 57:19.

95 Qurʾān 36:20.

96 Qurʾān 40:28.

97 Aḥmad b. Ḥanbal, *Faḍāʾil al-ṣaḥāba* 2:627, *ḥadīth* 1072.

98 Ibn al-Maghāzilī, *Manāqib Ahl al-bayt*, 313–314 *ḥadīth* 298.

99 al-Daylamī, *Firdaws al-akhbār*, 2:421, *ḥadīth* 3866.

100 al-Ḥāfiẓ al-Ḥaskānī, *Shawāhid al-tanzil li-qawāʿid al-tafḍīl*, 1:163–175.

101 Qurʾān 2:274.

102 al-Ḥāfiẓ Abū Nuʿaym al-Iṣfahānī, *al-Nūr al-mushtaʿal*, 43–48.

103 MS Maḥmudiyya 99, fol. 192b, ln.8–14; MS Veliyüddin Efendi 130, fol. 212b, ln. 10–14.

البرهان السادس والعشرون:

قوله تعالى: ﴿الّذين آمنوا بالله ورسله أولئك هم الصّدّيقون﴾.

روى أحمد بن حنبل بإسناده إلى ابن أبي ليلى عن أبيه قال: قال رسول الله ﷺ: الصديقون ثلاثة: حبيب بن موسى النّجار مؤمن آل يس الذي قال ﴿ياقوم اتّبعوا المرسلين﴾، وحزقيل مؤمن آل فرعون الذي قال ﴿أتقتلون رجلا أن يقول ربيّ الله﴾، وعليّ بن أبي طالب الثالث، وهوأفضلهم.

ونحوه رواه الفقيه ابن المغازلي الشافعي وصاحب كتاب الفردوس.

وهذه فضيلة تدلّ على إمامته.

البرهان السابع والعشرون:

قوله تعالى: ﴿الّذين ينفقون أموالهم باللّيل والنّهار سرّا وعلانية﴾.

من طريق أبي نعيم الحافظ بإسناده إلى ابن عبّاس قال: نزلت في عليّ، كان معه أربعة دراهم فأنفق بالليل درهماً وبالنهار درهماً وفي السرّ درهماً وفي العلانية درهماً؛ وكذا رواه الثعلبي في تفسيره.

ولم يحصل لغير عليّ ذلك، فيكون أفضل فيكون هو الإمام.

Demonstration 28

It has been related by Aḥmad b. Ḥanbal: "On the authority of Ibn ʿAbbās who said: There is not a single instance of *O you who believe!* in the Qurʾān without ʿAlī being its chief, its prince, its nobleman, and its master." Allah has even rebuked Muḥammad in the Qurʾān, but He only has ever mentioned ʿAlī with praise."[104]

This indicates ʿAlī's pre-eminence [over the other Companions], therefore it is he who is the Imam.

Demonstration 29

The statement of the Exalted: *Indeed Allah and His angels bless the Prophet; O you who have faith! Invoke blessings on him and salute him with a worthy salutation.*[105]

From the *Ṣaḥīḥ* (*The Rigorously Authenticated Collection*) of al-Bukhārī, on the authority of Kaʿb b. ʿUjra who said: "We asked the Messenger of Allah ﷺ how are we to bless you, the Household (*ahl al-bayt*), for Allah has [only] taught us how to salute you. He said: 'Say *Allāhummā ṣallī ʿalā Muḥammadin wa-ʿalā Āli Muḥammadin kamā ṣallayta ʿalā Ibrāhīma wa-Āli Ibrāhīma innaka ḥamīdun majīd* (O Allah bless Muḥammad and the Household of Muḥammad as you blessed Ibrāhīm and the Household of Ibrāhīm. Indeed, You are truly the Ever-Praised, the Ever-Glorified).'"[106]

From the *Ṣaḥīḥ* (*The Rigorously Authenticated Collection*) of Muslim it is related that it was asked: "O Messenger of Allah! As for saluting you, we understand how to do it, but how are we to bless you? He said, 'Say *Allāhummā ṣallī ʿalā Muḥammadin wa-ʿalā Āli Muḥammadin kamā ṣallayta ʿalā Ibrāhīma wa-Āli Ibrāhīma* (O Allah bless Muḥammad and the Household of Muḥammad as you blessed Ibrāhīm and the Household of Ibrāhīm).'"[107]

There is no doubt that ʿAlī is the best of the Household of Muḥammad and therefore he is the most worthy of the Imāma.

104 Aḥmad b. Ḥanbal, *Faḍāʾil al-Ṣaḥāba*, 2:654, 1114. See also al-Muwaffaq b. Aḥmad al-Khawārizmī, *al-Manāqib*, 266–267 *ḥadīth* 249 and al-Ḥāfiẓ Abū Nuʿaym al-Iṣfahānī, *Ḥilyat al-awliyāʾ*, 1:64.

105 Qurʾān 33:56.

106 See al-Bukhārī, *al-Jāmiʿ al-musnad al-ṣaḥīḥ*, 3:1292, 6431; cf. Jamāl al-Dīn al-Mizzī, *Tuḥfat al-ashrāf*, 11113.

107 Muslim b. al-Ḥajjāj, *al-Ṣaḥīḥ*, 1:172, 935; cf. Jamāl al-Dīn al-Mizzī, *Tuḥfat al-ashrāf*, 11113.

البرهان الثامن والعشرون:

ما رواه أحمد بن حنبل عن ابن عبّاس قال: ليس من آية في القرآن ﴿يا أيها الّذين آمنوا﴾ إلّا وعليّ رأسها وأميرها وشريفها وسيّدها؛ ولقد عاتب الله عزّ وجل أصحاب محمّد ﷺ في القرآن وماذكر عليّاً إلّا بخير.

وهذا يدلّ على أنّه أفضل، فيكون هو الأمام.

البرهان التاسع والعشرون:

قوله تعالى: ﴿إنّ الله وملائكته يصلون على النّبيّ يا أيها الّذين آمنوا صلّوا عليه وسلّموا تسليماً﴾.

من صحيح البخاري عن كعب بن عجرة قال: سألنا رسول الله ﷺ فقلنا: يا رسول الله كيف الصلاة عليكم أهل البيت، فإن الله قد علّمنا كيف نسلّم؟ قال: قولوا اللّهمّ صلّ على محمّد وعلى آل محمّد كما صلّيت على إبراهيم وآل إبراهيم إنّك حميد مجيد.

ومن صحيح مسلم قلنا: يا رسول الله، أمّا السلام عليك فقد عرفناه، فكيف الصلاة عليك؟ فقال: قولوا اللّهمّ صلّ على محمّد وآل محمّد كما صلّيت على إبراهيم وآل إبراهيم.

ولاشكّ في أنّ عليّاً أفضل آل محمد، فيكون أولى بالإمامة.

'Alī b. Abī Ṭālib after the Messenger of Allāh

Demonstration 30[108]

The statement of the Exalted: *He has let loose the two seas, meeting together.*[109]

From the *Tafsīr* of al-Thaʿlabī[110] and from Abū Nuʿaym,[111] on the authority of Ibn ʿAbbās regarding the statement of the Exalted: *He has let loose the two seas, meeting together*, he said: "ʿAlī and Fāṭima, *betwixt the two is a barrier which they do not pass* means the Prophet ﷺ, *there comes forth from the two of them pearl and coral* means Ḥasan and Ḥusayn ؑ."

None amongst the Companions has this merit, therefore he is most worthy of the Imāma.

Demonstration 31[112]

The statement of the Exalted: *and he who possesses knowledge of the Book.*[113]

From Ḥāfiẓ Abū Nuʿaym,[114] on the authority of Ibn al-Ḥanafiyya who said: "It refers to ʿAlī b. Abī Ṭālib ؑ."

In the *Tafsīr* of al-Thaʿlabī, on the authority of ʿAbdullāh b. Salām: "I asked who is the one meant by *he who possesses knowledge of the Book*? I was told: 'ʿAlī b. Abī Ṭālib.'"

This indicates his superiority and that he is therefore the Imam.

---

108 al-Ḥāfiẓ al-Ḥaskānī, *Shawāhid al-tanzīl li-qawāʿid al-tafḍīl*, 2:333–339.
109 Qurʾān 55:19.
110 MS Maḥmudiyya 106, fol. 36b, ln. 14 to fol. 37a, ln. 1; MS Veliyüddin Efendi 133, fol. 1397a, ln. 21–25 to fol. 1397b, ln. 1.
111 al-Ḥāfiẓ Abū Nuʿaym al-Iṣfahānī, *al-Nūr al-mushtaʿal*, 236–239.
112 al-Ḥāfiẓ al-Ḥaskānī, *Shawāhid al-tanzīl li-qawāʿid al-tafḍīl*, 1:473–478.
113 Qurʾān 13:43.
114 al-Ḥāfiẓ Abū Nuʿaym al-Iṣfahānī, *al-Nūr al-mushtaʿal*, 125–128.

البرهان الثلاثون:

قوله تعالى: ﴿مرج البحرين يلتقيان﴾.

من تفسير الثعلبي وطريق أبي نعيم عن ابن عبّاس في قوله تعالى: ﴿مرج البحرين يلتقيان﴾، قال: عليّ وفاطمة، ﴿بينهما برزخ لا يبغيان﴾ النبيّ ﷺ، ﴿يخرج منهما اللؤلؤ والمرجان﴾، الحسن والحسين؛

ولم يحصل لغيره من الصحابة هذه الفضيلة، فيكون أولى بالإمامة.

البرهان الحادي والثلاثون:

قوله تعالى: ﴿ومن عنده علم الكتاب﴾.

من طريق الحافظ أبي نعيم عن ابن الحنفيّة قال: هو عليّ بن أبي طالب.

وفي تفسير الثعلبي عن عبد الله بن سلام، قلت: من هذا الذي عنده علم الكتاب؟ فقال: إنّما ذلك عليّ بن أبي طالب.

وهذا يدل أنّه أفضل، فيكون هو الإمام.

On the Proofs establishing the Imāma of the Commander of the Faithful ʿAlī b. Abī Ṭālib after the Messenger of Allāh

Demonstration 32

The statement of the Exalted: *on the Day when Allah will not disgrace the Prophet and those who had believed along with him.*[115]

The Ḥāfiẓ Abū Nuʿaym relates in a chain of transmission going back to Ibn ʿAbbās, who said: "The first person to be adorned with the adornments of the Garden will be Ibrāhīm because of his deep intimacy with Allah, then Muḥammad because he is the choicest of Allah's servants, and then ʿAlī will be conducted between the two of them to the Garden." Then Ibn ʿAbbās recited *on the Day when Allah will not disgrace the Prophet and those who had believed along with him* and said, "It means ʿAlī and his followers."[116]

This indicates that he is superior to others and is thus the Imam.

Demonstration 33[117]

The statement of the Exalted: *Truly those who believe and do good works — it is they who are the best of creatures.*[118]

It is narrated by the Ḥāfiẓ Abū Nuʿaym on the authority of Ibn ʿAbbās who said, "When this verse was revealed the Messenger of Allah said to ʿAlī: 'This means you and your supporters. You and your supporters shall come forward on the Day of Judgement pleased and Allah will be pleased with you, but your enemies will be come forth wretched with the wrath of Allah upon them.'"[119]

If he is *the best of creatures,* then he must necessarily be the Imam.

---

115 Qurʾān 66:8.
116 al-Ḥāfiẓ Abū Nuʿaym al-Iṣfahānī, *al-Nūr al-mushtaʿal*, 262–265.
117 al-Ḥāfiẓ al-Ḥaskānī, *Shawāhid al-tanzīl li-qawāʿid al-tafḍīl*, 2:535–551.
118 Qurʾān 98:7.
119 al-Ḥāfiẓ Abū Nuʿaym al-Iṣfahānī, *al-Nūr al-mushtaʿal*, 273–278.

البرهان الثاني والثلاثون:

قوله تعالى: ﴿يوم لا يخزي الله النّبي والّذين آمنوا معه﴾.

روى أبو نعيم مرفوعاً إلى ابن عبّاس قال: أوّل من يكسى من حلل الجنّة إبراهيم عليه السلام لخلّته من الله، ومحمّد ﷺ لأنه صفوة الله، ثمّ عليّ يُزف بينهما إلى الجنان. ثم قرأ ابن عبّاس ﴿يوم لا يخزي الله النّبيّ والّذين آمنوا معه﴾؛ قال: عليّ وأصحابه.

وهذا يدلّ على أنّه أفضل من غيره، فيكون هو الإمام.

البرهان الثالث والثلاثون:

قوله تعالى: ﴿إنّ الّذين آمنوا وعملوا الصّالحات أولئك هم خير البريّة﴾.

روى الحافظ أبو نعيم بإسناده إلى ابن عبّاس، قال: لمّا نزلت هذه الآية قال رسول الله ﷺ لعليّ: هم أنت وشيعتك؛ تأتي أنت وشيعتك يوم القيامة راضين مرضيين، ويأتي عدوّك غضاباً مقمحين.

وإذا كان خير البريّة، وجب أن يكون هو الإمام.

'Alī b. Abī Ṭālib after the Messenger of Allāh

Demonstration 34[120]

The statement of the Exalted: *And He it is Who created man from water, and has appointed for him kindred by blood and kindred by marriage [...]*[121]

From the *Tafsīr* of al-Thaʿlabī, on the authority of Ibn Sīrīn who said: "It was revealed about the Prophet ﷺ and ʿAlī b. Abī Ṭālib. He gave Fāṭima in marriage to ʿAlī. He is the one who is a man created from water and who was appointed kindred by blood and by marriage for your Lord is All-Powerful."[122]

This has not been established for anyone but him, so he is superior, and thus must be the Imam.

Demonstration 35[123]

The statement of the Exalted: *O ye who believe! Be mindful of Allah, and be with the truthful.*[124]

Allah has made standing by the truthful to be obligatory upon us, and this is only established for those who are infallible, since others may lie. Thus, it must refer to ʿAlī ؑ since there is no infallible amongst the four but him.

In a *ḥadīth* recorded by Abū Nuʿaym, on the authority of Ibn ʿAbbās: "It was revealed about ʿAlī ؑ."[125]

Demonstration 36[126]

The statement of the Exalted: *and bow along with those who bow.*[127]

From Abū Nuʿaym, on the authority of Ibn ʿAbbās: "It was revealed about the Messenger of Allah ﷺ and ʿAlī ؑ in particular. They are the first to have prayed and bowed."[128]

This indicates his superiority and establishes his Imāma.

---

120   al-Ḥāfiẓ al-Ḥaskānī, *Shawāhid al-tanzīl li-qawāʿid al-tafḍīl*, 1:623–624.
121   Qurʾān 25:54.
122   Unfortunately, this portion in missing from MS Maḥmudiyya 98–107. MS Veliyüddin Efendi 132, fol. 1010a, ln. 4–14.
123   al-Ḥāfiẓ al-Ḥaskānī, *Shawāhid al-tanzīl li-qawāʿid al-tafḍīl*, 1:405–409.
124   Qurʾān 9:119.
125   al-Ḥāfiẓ Abū Nuʿaym al-Iṣfahānī, *al-Nūr al-mushtaʿal*, 102–105.
126   al-Ḥāfiẓ al-Ḥaskānī, *Shawāhid al-tanzīl li-qawāʿid al-tafḍīl*, 1:130–134.
127   Qurʾān 2:43.
128   al-Ḥāfiẓ Abū Nuʿaym al-Iṣfahānī, *al-Nūr al-mushtaʿal*, 40–42.

البرهان الرابع والثلاثون:

قوله تعالى: ﴿وهو الّذي خلق من الماء بشراً فجعله نسباً وصهراً﴾.

في تفسير الثعلبي عن ابن سيرين قال: نزلت في النبيّ ﷺ وعليّ بن أبي طالب. زوّج فاطمة عليّا. وهو الذي خلق من الماء بشراً فجعله نسباً وصهراً وكان ربّك قديراً؛

ولم يثبت لغيره ذلك فكان أفضل، فكان هو الإمام.

البرهان الخامس والثلاثون:

قوله تعالى: ﴿ياأيها الّذين آمنوا اتّقوا الله وكونوا مع الصّادقين﴾.

أوجب الله تعالى علينا الكون (مع المعلوم فيهم) الصدق، وليس إلّا المعصوم؛ لتجويز الكذب في غيره، فيكون هو عليّا؛ إذ لا معصوم من الأربعة سواه.

في حديث أبي نعيم عن ابن عباس: إنّها نزلت في عليّ عليه السلام.

البرهان السادس والثلاثون:

قوله تعالى: ﴿واركعوا مع الرّاكعين﴾.

من طريق أبي نعيم عن ابن عبّاس: أنّها نزلت في رسول الله ﷺ وعليّ خاصّةً، وهما اوّل من صلّى وركع.

وهو يدل على أفضليّته، فيدل على إمامته.

On the Proofs establishing the Imāma of the Commander of the Faithful 'Alī b. Abī Ṭālib after the Messenger of Allāh

Demonstration 37[129]

The statement of the Exalted: *And appoint for me a vizier from my family.*[130]

From Abū Nuʿaym, on the authority of Ibn ʿAbbās: "The Prophet ﷺ took ʿAlī by the hand and then took me by the hand and then led us in four units of prayer. He then raised his hands skyward in supplication and prayed: 'O Allah! Mūsā son of ʿImrān asked it of you, and I Muḥammad, Your Prophet too ask you to expand my breast, to relieve the knot in my tongue and make my speech understood, and to appoint for me a vizier from my family, ʿAlī b. Abī Ṭālib ؏ my brother. To fortify my support through him and to make him a part of my affair.'" Ibn ʿAbbās then said: "I then heard a caller cry out: 'O Aḥmad! You have been granted that which you ask.' And this is affirmed in the Book.[131]

---

129 al-Ḥāfiẓ al-Ḥaskānī, *Shawāhid al-tanzīl li-qawāʿid al-tafḍīl*, 1:559–571.
130 Qurʾān 20:29.
131 al-Ḥāfiẓ Abū Nuʿaym al-Iṣfahānī, *al-Nūr al-mushtaʿal*, 138–141.

البرهان السابع والثلاثون:

قوله تعالى: ﴿واجعل لّي وزيراً﴾ .

من طريق أبي نعيم عن ابن عبّاس قال: أخذ النبيّ ﷺ بيد عليّ بن أبي طالب وبيدي ونحن بمكّة، وصلى أربع ركعات ثم رفع يده إلى السماء فقال: اللّهمّ إنّ موسى بن عمران سألك، وأنا محمّد نبيّك أسألك أن تشرح لي صدري وتحلل عقدة من لساني يفقهوا قولي واجعل لي وزيراً من أهلي عليّ بن أبي طالب أخي؛ اشدد به أزري وأشركه في أمري. قال ابن عبّاس: فسمعت منادياً ينادي يا أحمد ! قد أوتيت ما سألت. وهذا نصّ في الباب.

Demonstration 38[132]

The statement of the Exalted: *As brethren, face to face, [they rest] on couches raised.*[133]

From the *Musnad* of Aḥmad b. Ḥanbal with his chain of narration back to Zayd b. Abī Awfā[134] who said, "I came upon the Messenger of Allah ﷺ in his mosque and mention was made of the account of the mutual brotherhood pact instituted by the Messenger of Allah ﷺ among his Companions when ʿAlī was to have said: 'My spirit went out of me, and my back was broken when I saw what you had done with all of your Companions except for me, and I thought, if this is because you are upset with me, then you are kind and have the last word.' The Messenger of Allah ﷺ said: 'I swear by the One who sent me as a Prophet, I have kept you for none but me, for your station in relation to me is as the station of Hārūn in relation to Mūsā, except that there shall be no prophet after me.[135] You are my brother and my confidant. You shall be with me in my palace in the Garden with my daughter Fāṭima and you are my brother and confidant.' Then the Messenger of Allah ﷺ recited the verse: *As brethren, face to face, on couches raised* loving one another for the sake of Allah, gazing at each other." Mutual brotherhood demands congenerity and similarity. Since ʿAlī ؑ was singled out for brotherhood with the Messenger of Allah ﷺ, he is the Imam.

132 al-Ḥāfiẓ al-Ḥaskānī, *Shawāhid al-tanzīl li-qawāʿid al-tafḍīl*, 1:487–492.

133 Qurʾān 15:47.

134 Aḥmad b. Ḥanbal, *al-Musnad*, 1:386, *ḥadīth* 1566; 1:367, *ḥadīth* 1481.

135 See Aḥmad b. Ḥanbal, *al-Musnad*, 1:386, *ḥadīth* 1566 and 1:367, *ḥadīth* 1481; Muslim b. al-Ḥajjāj, *al-Ṣaḥīḥ*, 2:1030, *ḥadīth*s 6370, 6372, 6373 and 2:1031, *ḥadīth* 6374; Ibn Māja, *al-Sunan*, 21, *ḥadīth*s 121, 122 and p22, *ḥadīth* 126; al-Tirmidhī, *al-Jāmiʿ* 2:951, *ḥadīth* 4090 and 2:952, *ḥadīth*s 4095 and 4096.

البرهان الثامن والثلاثون:

قوله تعالى: ﴿إخواناً على سرر متقابلين﴾.

من مسند أحمد بن حنبل بإسناده إلى زيد بن أبي أوفى قال: دخلت على رسول الله ﷺ مسجده، فذكر عليه قصّة مؤاخاة رسول الله ﷺ بين أصحابه، فقال عليّ: لقد ذهبت روحي وانقطع ظهري حين فعلت بأصحابك مافعلت غيري؛ فإن كان هذا من سخط عليّ فلك العقبى والكرامة. فقال رسول الله ﷺ: والذي بعثني بالحقّ نبيّاً ما اخترتك إلّا لنفسي، فأنت منّي بمنزلة هارون من موسى إلّا أنّه لا نبيّ بعدي؛ وأنت أخي ورفيقي وأنت معي في قصري في الجنّة مع ابنتي فاطمة؛ وأنت أخي ورفيقي؛ ثمّ تلا رسول الله ﷺ: ﴿إخواناً على سرر متقابلين﴾ المتحابّون في الله ينظر بعضهم إلى بعض. والمؤخاة تستدعي المناسبة والمشاكلة، فلمّا اختصّ عليّ بمؤاخاة رسول الله ﷺ كان هو الإمام.

Demonstration 39

The statement of the Exalted: *When your Lord brought forth from the Children of Adam, from their loins, their descendants* [...][136]

From the *Firdaws al-akhbār* (*The Garden of Prophetic Traditions*) by Ibn Shīrawayh,[137] tracing it back to Ḥudhayfa b. al-Yamān who said: "The Messenger of Allah ﷺ said: 'Were people to know when ʿAlī was dubbed "the Commander of the Faithful" they would not have denied his superiority. He was given the title "the Commander of the Faithful" when Ādam was between spirit and body. Allah the Mighty the Sublime has said: *When your Lord brought forth from the Children of Adam, from their loins, their descendants and made them bear witness over themselves* [*saying*]*: Am I not your Lord?* The angels said: 'We bear witness', and then Allah said: 'I am your Lord, Muḥammad is your prophet and ʿAlī is your *amīr*.'" This statement speaks for itself.

136 Qur'ān 7:173.

137 Al-Daylamī, *Firdaws al-akhbār*, 3:354, *ḥadīth* 5066 which is supported in the same volume by 3:283 *ḥadīth* 4851 which indicates that ʿAlī and the Prophet Muḥammad were a single light in the presence of Allah 14,000 years before the creation of Ādam and it was only after his creation that the one light was divided. The latter tradition, related by Salmān al-Fārisī, is also found in Aḥmad b. Ḥanbal, *Faḍā'il al-ṣaḥāba*, 2:662, *ḥadīth* 1130; Sibṭ Ibn al-Jawzī (d. 656/1258), *Tadhkirat khawāṣṣ al-umma fī khaṣā'is al-a'imma*, 46–47 and al-Sayyid ʿAlī al-Ḥusaynī al-Mīlānī, *Nafaḥāt al-azhār fī khulāṣat ʿAbaqāt al-anwār* (Qom?: 1414/1993), vol. 5, *passim*. Although al-Mīlānī, unlike the previous two who are Sunnī, is a Shīʿī scholar in the work cited only Sunnī sources are cited. In Shīʿī sources not only ʿAlī, but his wife Fāṭima, their two sons Ḥasan and Ḥusayn and often the next nine descendants of the latter are all subsumed within the pre-existing Light of Muḥammad. See Muḥammad Bāqir al-Majlisī (d. 1111/1699), *Biḥār al-anwār* (Tehran; Dār al-Kutub al-Islamiyya, 1376/1957) 23:305–324, 25:1–99.

البرهان التاسع والثلاثون:

قوله تعالى: ﴿وإذ أخذ ربّك من بني آدم من ظهورهم ذرّيتهم﴾ الآية.

من كتاب الفردوس لابن شيرويه يرفعه عن حذيفة بن اليمان قال: قال رسول الله ﷺ: لو يعلم الناس متى سمّي عليّ أمير المؤمنين ما أنكروا فضله. سمّي أمير المؤمنين وآدم بين الروح والجسد؛ قال الله عزّ وجلّ: ﴿وإذ أخذ ربّك من بني آدم من ظهورهم ذرّيتهم وأشهدهم على أنفسهم ألست بربّكم﴾ قالت الملائكة: بلى فقال تبارك وتعالى أنا ربّكم ومحمّد نبيكم وعليّ أميركم. وهوصريح في الباب.

On the Proofs establishing the Imāma of the Commander of the Faithful 'Alī b. Abī Ṭālib after the Messenger of Allāh

Demonstration 40

The statement of the Exalted: *Truly Allah is his Protector and so are Jibrīl and every righteous believer and, furthermore, the angels too will come to his support.*[138]

The commentators [on the Qur'ān] are in agreement that *every righteous believer* is a reference to 'Alī. Abū Nu'aym[139] relates with his chain of transmission to Asmā' bt. 'Umays who said, "I heard the Messenger of Allah recite this verse *and if you assist one another against him truly Allah is his Protector and so are Jibrīl and every righteous believer and, furthermore, the angels too will come to his support.* He said: '*Every righteous believer* is a reference to 'Alī.'"

This exclusive characterization by this verse establishes his superiority and thus he must be the Imam.

Verses of this sort are many and we have confined ourselves to what we have thus far mentioned in the interests of brevity.

---

138 Qur'ān 66:4.
139 al-Ḥāfiẓ Abū Nu'aym al-Iṣfahānī, *al-Nūr al-mushta'al*, 257–261.

البرهان الأربعون:

قوله تعالى: ﴿فإنّ الله هو مولاه وجبريل وصالح المؤمنين والملائكة بعد ذلك ظهير﴾.

أجمع المفسّرون على أنّ صالح المؤمنين هوعليّ، وروى أبو نعيم بإسناده إلى أسماء بنت عميس قالت: سمعت رسول الله ﷺ يقرأ هذه الآية ﴿وإن تظاهرا عليه فإنّ الله هو مولاه وجبريل وصالح المؤمنين﴾. قال: صالح المؤمنين عليّ بن أبي طالب.

واختصاصه بذلك يدلّ على أفضليّته، فيكون هو الإمام.

والآيات المذكورة في هذا المعنى كثيرة، اقتصرنا على ما ذكرناه للاختصار.

The Third Way: Evidence From the Sunna Related From the Prophet

The First

What has been transmitted by everyone that when the verse *And warn the nearest of your kinsfolk*[140] was revealed the Messenger of Allah ﷺ gathered the Banū ʿAbd al-Muṭṭalib in the house of Abū Ṭālib, and they were forty men in all, and gave instructions that a lamb shoulder should be roasted for them along with a measure of wheat, and a measure of yoghurt, and that they would eat and drink seated all together. So they all ate from what was a small amount until they were satiated and they were surprised at this, and it was clear that this was a sign of his prophethood. Then he said to them: "O Banū ʿAbd al-Muṭṭalib! Allah has sent me to the whole of creation, and to you in particular and has said to me *And warn the nearest of your kinsfolk*. I am inviting you all to accept two simple phrases which though they roll lightly off the tongue, they are heavy in the scale of deeds. You will possess thereby the Arabs and non-Arabs and will rule through them over the nations and will enter by them into Paradise and will be saved by them from Hell. These are: to bear witness that there is no deity but Allah and that I am the Messenger of Allah. Who, then, will answer my call and support me in this and become thereby my brother, my legatee, my vizier, my heir, and my successor after me?" None of them uttered a word.

The Commander of the Faithful said: "I will, O Messenger of Allah, support you in this." "He said, 'Sit down,' and repeated his appeal to the group a second time. They remained silent and I stood up and repeated what I had said the first time, but he said, 'Sit down.' Then he repeated his appeal to the group a third time. No one uttered so much as a single letter. So, I stood up and said, I will, O Messenger of Allah, support you in this. Then he said, 'Sit down, for you shall be my brother, my legatee, my vizier, my heir, and my successor after me.'"

All of them jumped to their feet and said to Abū Ṭālib: "Let us congratulate you today for having entered the religion of your nephew who has made your son an *amīr* over you!"

140 Qurʾān 26:214.

المنهج الثالث في
الأدلّة المستندة [إلى السنّة] المنقولة عن النبيّ ﷺ

وهي اثنا عشر:

الأوّل:

ما نقله الناس كافّة، أنّه لمّا نزل قوله تعالى: ﴿وأنذر عشيرتك الأقربين﴾ جمع رسول الله ﷺ بني عبد المطّلب في دار أبي طالب وهم أربعون رجلاً؛ وأمر أن يصنع لهم فخذ شاة مع مدّ من البر ويعدّ لهم صاعاً من اللبن، وكان الرجل منهم يأكل الجذعة في مقعد واحد ويشرب الفرق من الشراب في ذلك المقام. فأكلت الجماعة كلّها من ذلك اليسير حتّى شبعوا (ولم يتبيّن ما أكلوا) . فبهرهم بذلك وتبيّن لهم آية نبوّته. ثم قال: يا بني عبد المطلب! إنّ الله بعثني بالحق إلى الخلق كافّة وبعثني إليكم خاصّة! فقال: ﴿وأنذر عشيرتك الأقربين﴾، وأنا أدعوكم إلى كلمتين خفيفتين على اللسان ثقيلتين في الميزان، تملكون بها العرب والعجم وتنقاد لكم بها الأمم وتدخلون بها الجنّة وتنجون بها من النار: شهادة أن لا إله إلّا الله وأنّي رسول الله؛ فمن يجبني إلى هذا الأمر ويوازرني على القيام به يكن أخي وصيّي ووزيري ووارثي وخليفتي من بعدي؟ فلم يجب أحد منهم.

فقال أمير المؤمنين: أنا يارسول الله أوازرك على هذا الأمر! فقال: اجلس! ثمّ أعاد القول على القوم ثانية فأصمتوا وقمت فقلت مثل مقالتي الأولى، فقال: اجلس! ثمّ أعاد على القوم مقالته ثالثة فلم ينطق أحد منهم بحرف، فقمت فقلت: أنا أؤازرك يا رسول الله على هذا الأمر! فقال: اجلس فأنت أخي ووصيّي ووزيري ووارثي وخليفتي من بعدي.

فنهض القوم وهم يقولون لأبي طالب: ليهنك اليوم أن دخلت في دين ابن أخيك، فقد جعل ابنك أميراً عليك.

The Second

There is a widely-attested report from the Prophet ﷺ that when the verse *O Messenger convey what has been revealed to you from your Lord*[141] came down, he addressed the people at Ghadīr Khumm and said to all who were present: "O people! Am I not more worthy of you than your own selves?" To which they said: "Yes!" And then he said: "Whomsoever's master I am, ʿAlī is his master. O Allah! Be a friend to whomever is a friend to him, and an enemy to whomever is an enemy to him! Support whomever supports him and disgrace whomever would disgrace him."

ʿUmar said to him: "Congratulations! Congratulations! You have become my master and the master of every believer, man and woman."

The term "master" (*mawlā*) here means the one who is more worthy of disposing affairs as is indicated by his having prefaced what he said with "Am I not more worthy of you than your own selves?"

The Third

The statement of the Prophet ﷺ: "Your status in relation to me is as the station of Hārūn in relation to Mūsā, except that there shall be no prophet after me?"[142] establishes for him all of the ranks that Hārūn derived from Mūsā without exception. Included among the aggregate of qualities that belong to Hārūn is that he was Mūsā's designated successor. Had he survived him, he would also have been his successor, otherwise this would have entailed a shortcoming in him [i.e., in Mūsā] in as much he was his successor when he was alive but briefly absent [when he went up the mountain] and this would apply even more after his death.

141 Qurʾān 4:67.

142 See Aḥmad b. Ḥanbal, *al-Musnad*, 1:386, *ḥadīth* 1566 and 1:367, *ḥadīth* 1481; Muslim b. al-Ḥajjāj, *al-Ṣaḥīḥ*, 2:1030, *ḥadīth*s 6370, 6372, 6373 and 2:103, *ḥadīth* 6374; Ibn Māja, *al-Sunan*, 21, *ḥadīth*s 121, 122 and 22, *ḥadīth* 126; al-Tirmidhī, *al-Jāmiʿ*, 2:951, *ḥadīth* 4090 and 2:952, *ḥadīth*s 4095, 4096.

الثاني:

الخبر المتواتر عن النبيّ ﷺ أنّه لمّا نزل قوله تعالى: ﴿يا أيّها الرسول بلّغ ما أنزل إليك من ربّك﴾ خطب الناس في غدير خم وقال للجمع كلّه: أيّها الناس! ألست أولى منكم بأنفسكم!؟ قالوا: بلى! قال: فمن كنت مولاه فهذا عليّ مولاه، اللّهمّ وال من والاه وعاد من عاداه وانصر من نصره واخذل من خذله!

فقال له عمر: بخ! بخ! أصبحت مولاي ومولى كلّ مؤمن ومؤمنة.

والمراد بالمولى هنا الأولى بالتصرّف لتقدّم التقرير منه ﷺ بقوله ألست أولى منكم بأنفسكم؟

الثالث:

قوله ﷺ: أنت منّي بمنزلة هارون من موسى إلّا أنّه لا نبيّ بعدي. أثبت له جميع منازل هارون من موسى للاستثناء، ومن جملة منازل هارون أنّه كان خليفة لموسى؛ ولو عاش بعده لكان خليفة أيضاً وإلّا لزم تطرّق النقص إليه. ولأنه خليفة مع وجوده وغيبته مدّة يسيرة، وبعد موته وطول الغيبة أولى بأن يكون خليفته.

The Fourth

The Prophet ﷺ appointed him to take his place in Medina even though he was only going to be absent briefly. This proves that he is his successor after his death as well, for it is a matter of consensus that no one else but ʿAlī ؑ ever took his place in his lifetime and he never removed him from governing Medina [in his absence], thus he must be his successor there [i.e. in Medina] after his death as well; and it would have to be unanimously conceded that if he is his successor over Medina then he must be his successor elsewhere as well.

The Fifth

It has been recorded by all of the mainstream [Sunnī] scholars that the Prophet ﷺ said to the Commander of the Faithful: "You are my brother, my legatee, my successor after me, and the one who shall establish my religion." This is an explicit designation.

الرابع:

إنّه ﷺ استخلفه على المدينة مع قصر مدّة الغيبة، فيجب أن يكون (له خليفة) بعد موته؛ وليس غير عليّ (خليفة له في حال حياته) إجماعاً؛ لأنّه لم يعزله عن المدينة، فيكون خليفة له بعد موته فيها؛ وإذا كان خليفة في المدينة كان خليفة في غيرها إجماعاً.

الخامس:

ما رواه الجمهور بأجمعهم عن النبيّ ﷺ انّه قال لأمير المؤمنين: أنت أخي ووصيّي وخليفتي من بعدي وقاضي ديني، وهو نصّ في الباب.

The Sixth: The Pact of Mutual Brotherhood

It is related by Anas who said, "On the day of the mutual imprecation (*mubāhala*) the Prophet ﷺ established a mutual brotherhood pact between the Muhājirūn and the Anṣār and ʿAlī remained standing by himself watching what was happening and no one was appointed brother to him, so he left with tears in his eyes. The Prophet ﷺ noticed he was gone and said: "What happened to Abū l-Ḥasan?" They said: "He left with tears in his eyes." So he said: "O Bilāl! Go and bring him."

So he went to him and he had gone into his house with tears in his eyes. Fāṭima said to him: "Why are you crying! May Allah not cause your eyes to shed tears!" He said: "The Prophet ﷺ appointed to everyone a brother amongst the Muhājirūn and the Anṣār and I remained standing alone. He saw me and recognized me but did not assign anyone to me." She said: "May Allah not make you sad. No doubt he has only saved you for himself."

Bilāl then cried out, "O ʿAlī! Answer the call of the Prophet ﷺ!"

So he came to the Prophet ﷺ who asked him: "What made you cry, O Abū l-Ḥasan?" He said: "You appointed brothers between the Muhājirūn and the Anṣār and I remained standing alone and you saw me and recognized me but did not assign anyone to me." He said: "I have only saved you for myself. Would it not make you happy to be the brother of your prophet?" he said: "Indeed it would O Messenger of Allah."

So, he took him by the hand, placed him on the *minbar* and said: "O Allah! Indeed, this one is from me and I am from him, indeed his station in relation to me is as the station of Hārūn in relation to Mūsā. Whomsoever's master I am, ʿAlī is his master." Thus, ʿAlī left glad of heart and ʿUmar followed behind him saying: "Congratulations! Congratulations! You have become my master and the master of every believer."

The mutual brotherhood pact indicates his superiority and thus he must be the Imam.

السادس: المؤاخاة

روى أنس قال: لمّا كان يوم المباهلة وآخى النبيّ ﷺ بين المهاجرين والأنصار وعليّ واقف يراه ويعرف مكانه ولم يؤاخ بينه وبين أحد؛ فانصرف عليّ باكي العين (فافتقده النبي ﷺ فقال: ما فعل أبو الحسن؟ قالوا: انصرف باكي العين) قال: يا بلال! اذهب فأت به.

فمضى إليه وقد دخل منزله باكي العين، فقالت فاطمة: ما يبكيك لا أبكى الله عينيك؟ قال: آخى النبي ﷺ بين المهاجرين والأنصار وأنا واقف يراني ويعرف مكاني ولم يؤاخ بيني وبين أحد. قالت: لا يحزنك الله لعلّه إنّما دخرك لنفسه.

فقال بلال: يا عليّ! أجب النبيّ ﷺ!

فأتى النبي ﷺ فقال: ما يبكيك يا أبا الحسن؟ فقال: آخيت بين المهاجرين والأنصار (يا رسول الله) وأنا واقف تراني وتعرف مكاني ولم تؤاخ بيني وبين أحد؛ قال: إنّما ادّخرتك لنفسي! ألا يسرّك أن تكون أخا نبيّك؟ قال: بلى يا رسول الله، أنّى لي بذلك.

فأخذ بيده فأرقاه المنبر فقال: اللّهم إنّ هذا منّي وأنا منه؛ ألا إنّه منّي بمنزلة هارون من موسى؛ ألا من كنت مولاه فهذا عليّ مولاه؛ فانصرف عليّ قرير العين فاتّبعه عمر فقال: بخّ! بخّ! يا أبا الحسن! أصبحت مولاي ومولى كلّ مؤمن.

والمؤاخاة تدلّ على الأفضليّة، فيكون هو الإمام.

'Alī b. Abī Ṭālib after the Messenger of Allāh

The Seventh

It has been recorded by all of the mainstream [Sunnī] scholars that when the Prophet ﷺ had laid siege the Fortress of Khaybar for 29 nights the standard was passed to the Commander of the Faithful ؏ who was suffering from swelling in his eyes which was preventing him from taking part in battle. So the Messenger of Allah ﷺ summoned Abū Bakr and told him to take the standard. He took it and went out with a band of Muhājirūn and did his utmost but could do nothing and came back defeated.

The next day 'Umar was given the task. He went out a short distance but returned rebuking his companions with cowardice. The Prophet ﷺ then asked for 'Alī ؏. He was told that his eyes were swollen over. He said: "Bring him to me and you will see a man who loves Allah and His Messenger and who is loved by Allah and His Messenger and does not retreat."

They brought him 'Alī. He spat in his hand and wiped over his eyes and head and the swelling was gone. He gave him the battle flag and Allah granted them victory at his hand fighting heartily. His describing him in this way indicates that this applies to none but him which establishes his superiority and that he is the Imam.

The Eighth: The Report of the Fowl[143]

It has been recorded by all of the mainstream [Sunnī] scholars that the Prophet ﷺ was brought a fowl and said: "O Allah! May the most beloved of Your creation join me in eating this fowl." 'Alī then came to the door and knocked. Anas b. Mālik told him: "The Prophet ﷺ is busy with something. Go away." Then the Prophet ﷺ prayed again as he had done the first time, and 'Alī knocked on the door. Anas said: "Did I not say that the Prophet ﷺ is busy with something. Go away." Then the Prophet ﷺ prayed again as he had done the first two times, and 'Alī knocked on the door even harder than the first two times. The Prophet ﷺ heard Anas say to him that he was busy, so he told him to allow him to enter. He said: "O 'Alī, what delayed you?" He said: "I was here but Anas turned me away, then I came back a third time but Anas turned me away." So he said to him: "O Anas! What behoved you to do that?" He said: "I wanted your supplication to be fulfilled in someone from the Anṣār." He said: "O Anas, is there any among the Anṣār better than 'Alī?" If he is the most beloved of Allah's creation, then he must be the Imam.

---

143 al-Tirmidhī, *al-Jāmi'*, 2:948: *ḥadīth*s 4077 and 4078.

السابع:

ماروواه الجمهور كافّة أنّ النبيّ ﷺ لما حاصر خيبر تسعاً وعشرين ليلة وكانت الراية لأمير المؤمنين، فلحقه رمد أعجزه عن الحرب وخرج مرحب يتعرّض للحرب؛ فدعا رسول الله ﷺ أبا بكر فقال له: خذ الراية؛ فأخذها في جمع من المهاجرين فاجتهد ولم يغن شيئاً ورجع منهزماً.

فلمّا كان من الغد تعرض لها عمر فسار غير بعيد، ثم رجع يجّبن أصحابه. فقال النبي ﷺ: جيئوني بعلي فقيل: إنّه ارمد. فقال: أرونيه تروني رجلا يحبّ الله ورسوله ويحبّه الله ورسوله ليس بفرار.

فجاءوه بعلي فتفل في يده ومسحها على عينيه ورأسه فبرئ، وأعطاه الراية، ففتح الله على يده وقتل مرحباً؛ ووصفه عليه السلام بهذا الوصف يدل على انتفائه عن غيره، وهو يدلّ على أفضليّته فيكون هو الإمام.

الثامن: خبر الطائر

روى الجمهور كافّة أنّ النبيّ ﷺ أتي بطائر فقال: اللهم ائتني بأحبّ خلقك إليّ يأكل معي من هذا الطائر. فجاء عليّ فدقّ الباب، فقال أنس بن مالك: إنّ النبي ﷺ على حاجة فانصرف. ثم قال النبى ﷺ كما قال أوّلاً، فدقّ عليّ الباب فقال أنس: أو لم أقل لك أنّ النبي ﷺ على حاجة؟ فانصرف. فقال النبى ﷺ كما قال في الأوليين فجاء عليّ فدقّ الباب أشدّ من الأوليين، فسمعه النبي ﷺ وقد قال له أنس أنّه على حاجة، فأذن له بالدخول وقال: يا عليّ ما أبطأك عنّي؟ قال: جئت فردّني أنس، ثم جئت فردّني، ثم جئت الثالثة فردّني؛ فقال: يا أنس ما حملك على هذا؟ فقال: رجوت أن يكون الدّعاء لأحد من الأنصار. فقال: يا أنس! أفي الأنصار خير من عليّ؟! أوفي الأنصار أفضل من عليّ؟!؟ وإذا كان أحبّ الخلق إلى الله تعالى وجب أن يكون هو الإمام.

'Alī b. Abī Ṭālib after the Messenger of Allāh

The Ninth

It has been recorded by the mainstream [Sunnī] scholars that the Prophet ﷺ ordered his Companions to salute 'Alī by referring to him with the title "the Commander of the Faithful". He said: "He is the Lord of the Muslims, the Imam of the Righteous, the Commander of those of Shining Countenance." And he said: "He is the master of every believer after me." And he said in his favour: "Indeed, 'Alī is from me and I am from him, and he is the master of every believing man and woman." Thus, 'Alī must be after him just as he said he would be. These explicit statements establish the fact [that he is the Imam].

The Tenth

It has been recorded by the mainstream [Sunnī] scholars that the Prophet ﷺ said: "I am leaving behind in your midst that which if you hold fast to them, you will never go astray: The Book of Allah and my Household, my Family. The two shall never be separated from one another until they reach me at the Fountain of Paradise." He also said: "The likeness of my Household amongst you is like the Ark of Noah. Whoever comes aboard is saved, and whoever does not drowns." This proves the necessity of following what his Household say and that their master is 'Alī ؈, thus it is necessary to follow him in everything. Therefore, he must be the Imam to the exclusion of any of the other Companions.

التاسع:

ما رواه الجمهور من أنّه ﷺ أمر أصحابه بأن يسلّموا على عليّ بإمرة المؤمنين؛ وقال: إنّه سيّد المسلمين وإمام المتّقين وقائد الغرّ المحجّلين؛ وقال: هذا وليّ كلّ مؤمنٍ بعدي. وقال في حقّه: إنّ عليّاً منّي وأنا منه، وهو وليّ كلّ مؤمن ومؤمنة. فيكون عليّ بعده كذلك، وهذه نصوص في الباب.

العاشر:

ما رواه الجمهور من قول النبي ﷺ: إنّي تارك فيكم ما إن تمسّكتم به لن تضلّوا: كتاب الله وعترتي أهل بيتي ولن يفترقا حتّى يردا عليّ الحوض. وقال ﷺ: مثل أهل بيتي فيكم مثل سفينة نوح، من ركبها نجا ومن تخلّف عنها غرق. وهذا يدلّ على وجوب التمسّك بقول أهل بيته، وسيّدهم عليّ، فيكون واجب الطاعة على الكلّ، فيكون هو الإمام دون غيره من الصحابة.

The Eleventh

It has been recorded by the mainstream [Sunnī] scholars that it is obligatory to love him and be loyal to him.

Aḥmad b. Ḥanbal records in his *Musnad* that the Messenger of Allah ﷺ took Ḥasan and Ḥusayn by the hand and said: "Whoever loves me, and loves these two, and loves their father, and loves their mother shall join me in my rank on the Day of Judgement."[144]

It was related by Ibn Khālawayh, on the authority of Ḥudhayfa who said: "The Messenger of Allah said: 'He who wishes to hold fast to the ruby sceptre which Allah created with His own hand to which he said "Be!" let him be loyal to ʿAlī b. Abī Ṭālib after me.'"

It was related by Abū Saʿīd who said: "The Messenger of Allah said to ʿAlī: 'Love for you is faith. Hate for you is hypocrisy. The first to enter the Garden will be those who love you. The first to enter the Fire will be those who hate you. He has made you worthy of this, for you are from me and I am from you and there shall be no Prophet after me.'"

On the authority of Shaqīq b. Salama, on the authority of ʿAbdullāh who said: "I saw the Messenger of Allah ﷺ while taking the hand of ʿAlī b. Abī Ṭālib saying: 'This is my master [over you] and I am his master. I am an enemy of whoever is his enemy, and at peace with whoever is at peace with him.'"

It was related by Akhṭab Khawārizmī, on the authority of Jābir who said: "The Messenger of Allah ﷺ said: 'Jibraʾīl came to me from Allah the Mighty, the Sublime bearing a green paper on which was written in silver: "Truly, I have made incumbent upon My creation the love of ʿAlī b. Abī Ṭālib. So, convey this to them on my behalf."'"[145]

Reports of this kind from those who oppose us are so numerous as to be beyond reckoning and they indicate his superiority and his being worthy of the Imāma.

144 Aḥmad b. Ḥanbal, *al-Musnad,* 1:182, *ḥadīth* 586 (ʿAlī b. Abī Ṭālib).
145 al-Muwaffaq b. Aḥmad al-Khawārizmī, *al-Manāqib,* 66, *ḥadīth* 37.

الحادي عشر:

مارواه الجمهور من وجوب محبّته وموالاته.

روى أحمد بن حنبل في مسنده أنّ رسول الله ﷺ أخذ بيده حسن وحسين، وقال: من أحبّني وأحبّ هذين وأباهما وأمّها كان معي في درجتي يوم القيامة.

وروى ابن خالويه عن حذيفة قال: قال رسول الله ﷺ: من أحبّ أن يتمسّك بقصبة الياقوت التي خلقها الله تعالى بيده ثمّ قال لها: كوني فكانت، فليتولّ عليّ بن أبي طالب من بعدي.

وعن أبي سعيد قال: قال رسول الله ﷺ لعليّ: حبّك إيمان وبغضك نفاق؛ وأوّل من يدخل الجنة محبّك وأوّل من يدخل النار مبغضك، وقد جعلك أهلا لذلك؛ فأنت منّي وأنا منك ولا نبيّ بعدي.

وعن شقيق بن سلمة عن عبد الله قال: رأيت رسول الله ﷺ وهو آخذ بيد عليّ بن أبي طالب وهو يقول: هذا وليّي وأنا وليّه، عاديت من عادى وسالمت من سالم.

وروى أخطب خوارزم عن جابر قال: قال رسول الله ﷺ: جاءني جبرئيل من عند الله عزّ وجلّ بورقة خضراء مكتوب فيها ببياض إنّي افترضت محبّة عليّ بن أبي طالب على خلقي فبلّغهم ذلك عنّي.

والأخبار في ذلك لا تُحصى كثرة من طرق المخالفين، وهذا يدلّ على أفضليّته واستحقاقه للإمامة.

The Twelfth

It has been recorded by Akhṭab Khawārizmī with his chain of transmission to Abū Dharr al-Ghifārī who said: "The Messenger of Allah ﷺ said: 'Whoever puts in place of ʿAlī someone else as caliph after me is an unbeliever and has declared war on Allah and His Messenger. Whoever doubts ʿAlī is an unbeliever.'"[146]

On the authority of Anas who said: "I was with the Prophet ﷺ and he saw ʿAlī coming ؑ and said: 'I and this one are the proof against my *umma* on the Day of Judgement.'"

On the authority of Muʿāwiya b. Ḥīdat al-Qurashī who said: "I heard the Prophet ﷺ saying to ʿAlī ؑ: 'O ʿAlī! I am not exaggerating when I say that whoever dies hating you dies a Jew or a Christian.'"

The Imāmī Shīʿa say: When we see our adversary relate the likes of these *ḥadīth*, and we have related all of this many times over through our own reliable transmitters, we have no choice but to accept them and it is forbidden to leave them aside.

146 This *ḥadīth* does not appear in the published version of the *Manāqib* of al-Khawārizmī. However, it is to be found in the *Manāqib* of Ibn al-Maghāzilī, 107–108, *ḥadīth* 70.

الثاني عشر:

روى أخطب خوارزم بإسناده إلى أبي ذر الغفاري قال: قال رسول الله ﷺ: من ناصب عليّا الخلافة بعدي فهو كافر وقد حارب الله ورسوله، ومن شكّ في عليّ فهو كافر. وعن أنس قال: كنت عند النبيّ ﷺ فرأى عليّا مقبلاً فقال: أنا وهذا حجّة على أمتي يوم القيامة.

وعن معاوية بن حيدة القشيري قال: سمعت النبيّ ﷺ يقول لعليّ: يا عليّ! لا يبالي من مات وهو يبغضك مات يهوديّاً أونصرانيّاً.

قالت الإماميّة: إذا رأينا المخالف لنا يورد مثل هذه الأحاديث ونقلنا نحن أضعافها عن رجالنا الثقات، وجب علينا المصير إليها وحرم العدول عنها.

The Fourth Way: Evidence For His Imāma Based On His States

The First

He was the foremost of ascetics after the Messenger of Allah ﷺ. He had made a triple repudiation of the world.[147] His food typically consisted of unground barely and he used to keep it sealed so that the two Imams [i.e. Ḥasan and Ḥusayn] would not put dust in it. He used to wear a short, rough garment. His shirt had been patched so many times that a person would be ashamed to patch it again. His sword strap was made of palm fibre and so were his shoes.

Akhṭab Khawārizmī[148] relates from ʿAmmār who said: "I heard the Messenger of Allah ﷺ saying: 'O ʿAlī! Truly Allah the Exalted has adorned you with an adornment with which he has not adorned any of his servants with more beloved to him than this: he has made you to renounce the world, he has made it hateful in your eyes, he has made the poor dear to you and you are content with them as your followers and they are content with you as their Imam. O ʿAlī! Blessed is he who loves you and believes in you and cursed is he who hates you and denies you. As for the one who loves you, they are your brothers in religion and will join you in Paradise, and the one who hates you and denies you, he deserves to be placed by Allah in the station of the liars on the Day of Judgement.'"

Suwayd b. Ghafla said: "I went to ʿAlī b. Abī Ṭālib ؓ in the afternoon. I found him seated in front of a bowl of very sour yoghurt which I could smell because it was so sour. He had in his hand a piece of bread and I could see bits of wheat husk on his face as he occasionally broke the bread with his hands, and sometimes when he could not do so he placed it on his knee to break it and then put it in the yoghurt. He said to me: 'Come close to me so that I can pour some of our food for you.' I told him that I was fasting. So he said: 'I heard the Messenger of Allah ﷺ saying: "Whoever is prevented from eating a food he likes because he is fasting, it is incumbent on Allah to feed him from the food of Paradise and give him to drink from its beverages."'"

---

147   The Arabic expression indicates a "triple divorce."
148   al-Muwaffaq b. Aḥmad al-Khawārizmī, *al-Manāqib*, 116, ḥadīth 126.

المنهج الرابع في الأدلّة على إمامته المستنبطة من أحواله عليه السلام

وهي اثنا عشر:

الأوّل:

انّه كان أزهد الناس بعد رسول الله صلى الله عليه وآله - وطلّق الدنيا ثلاثاً وكان قوته جريش الشعير؛ وكان يختمه لئلاّ يضع الإمامان عليهما السلام فيه أدماً؛ وكان يلبس خشن الثياب قصيرها، ورقع مدرعته حتّى استحيى من راقعها . وكان حمائل سيفه من اللّيف وكذا نعله .

روى أخطب خوارزم عن عمّار قال: سمعت رسول الله صلى الله عليه وآله يقول: يا عليّ! إنّ الله تعالى زيّنك بزينة لم يزيّن العباد بزينة (أحبّ إليه) منها - زهّدك في الدنيا وبغّضها إليك، وحبّب إليك الفقراء، فرضيت بهم أتباعاً ورضوا بك إماماً؛ يا عليّ! طوبى لمن أحبّك وصدق عليك، والويل لمن أبغضك وكذب عليك؛ أمّا من أحبّك وصدق عليك فإخوانك في دينك وشركاؤك في جنّتك؛ وأمّا من أبغضك وكذب عليك فحقيق على الله تعالى يوم القيامة أن يقيمه مقام الكذّابين.

قال سويد بن غفلة: دخلت على عليّ بن أبي طالب القصر فوجدته جالساً بين يديه صحفة فيها لبن حازر أجد ريحه من شدّة حموضته. وفي يديه رغيف أرى قشار الشعير في وجهه وهو يكسر بيده أحياناً، فإذا غلبه كسره بركبته فطرحه فيه. فقال: ادن فأصيب من طعامنا هذا! فقلت: إنّي صائم! فقال: سمعت رسول الله صلى الله عليه وآله يقول: من منعه الصيام من طعام يشتهيه كان حقّاً على الله أن يطعمه من طعام الجنّة ويسقيه من شرابها .

"I said to his servant girl who was standing near him, 'O Fiḍḍa! Woe unto you! Do you not fear Allah regarding this old man! Do you not sift the grain for him? I see that it [i.e. the bread] is very coarse.' She said: 'He has already told us not to sift the grain for him.' He said: 'What did you say to her?' So I told him. He said: 'I swear by my father and by my mother, [I am one for whom] no grain will be sifted, nor who shall have his fill of unsifted barely bread for three days until Allah takes his soul.'"

One day he bought two garments of rough cloth. He let [his servant] Qanbar choose one of them and he wore the other one. He found the sleeves to be too long, so he just cut them.

Ḍirār b. Ḍamra said: "I went to see Muʿāwiya after the murder of ʿAlī, the Commander of the Faithful ﷺ, and I asked him to describe ʿAlī to me." He said: 'Leave me alone!' but I pressed him and so he said: 'If I must, then I swear by Allah that he was far-sighted, exceedingly strong, decisive in speech, just in judgement, knowledge burst forth from him, uttering wisdom from every side, averse to the world and its blandishments, accustomed to the night and its isolation, much given to weeping, much given to contemplation. He would wring his hands and reproach himself. He preferred clothing of rough fabric and of food the same. He lived among us like one of us. If he was called, he would answer. If we invited him, he would join us. As for us, despite his befriending us and being close to us we almost never spoke to him out of awe for him. He greatly respected people of religion and used to befriend the poor. The strong did not covet his retribution, nor did the weak fear his justice. I bear witness by Allah that once I saw him somewhere when the night had spread its gloom and the stars had come out. He was clutching his beard grieving like one utterly broken, weeping bitterly saying: "O world! Tempt someone else! Do you dare to come to me or seek me out! How remote is such a thing! How remote is such a thing! I have thrice repudiated you and there is no going back! Your life is short, your significance minor, your existence base! Ah! How little is the provision, and how long is the journey, and how desolate is the path!"' Then Muʿāwiya wept and said: 'May Allah have mercy on Abū l-Ḥasan! It is thus that he was. How was your love for him?' I said it was as the love of Mūsā's mother for Mūsā. He asked: 'How was your grief for him?' I said it was like the grief of a mother who had her own child slaughtered in front of her, unceasing tears and unending pain."

In short, none attained to the degree of such ascesis whether before him or after him, and if he was the most ascetic of men he must be the Imam since he who is inferior cannot be so.

قال: فقلت لجاريته وهي قائمة بقرب منه: ويحك يا فضّة! ألا تتقين الله في هذا الشيخ؟ (ألا تنخلون) له طعاماً ممّا أرى فيه من النخالة؟ فقالت: لقد تقدّم إلينا ألّا ننخل له طعاماً. قال: ماقلت لها؟ فأخبرته فقال: بأبي وأمّي من لم ينخل له طعام ولم يشبع من خبز البرّ ثلاثة أيام حتّى قبضه الله عزّ وجلّ.

واشترى يوماً ثوبين غليظين فخيّر قنبراً فيها، فأخذ واحداً ولبس هو الآخر؛ ورأى في كمّه طولاً عن أصابعه فقطعه.

قال ضرار بن ضمرة: دخلت على معاوية بعد قتل عليّ أمير المؤمنين فقال: صِفْ لي عليّا. فقلت: أعفني! فقال: لابدّ أن تصفه. فقلت: أما إذ لا بدّ فإنّه كان والله بعيد المدى شديد القوى، يقول فصلاً ويحكم عدلاً، يتفجّر العلم من جوانبه وتنطق الحكمة من نواحيه. يستوحش من الدنيا وزهرتها ويأنس بالليل ووحشته. غزير العبرة، طويل الفكرة (يقلّب كفّه ويعاتب نفسه)؛ يعجبه من اللباس ما خشن ومن الطعام ماجشب. وكان فينا كأحدنا يجيبنا إذا سألناه ويأتينا إذا دعوناه. ونحن والله مع تقريبه لنا وقربه منّا لا نكاد نكلّمه هيبة له؛ يعظّم أهل الدين ويقرّب المساكين؛ لا يطمع القويّ في باطله ولا ييأس الضعيف من عدله. فأشهد بالله لقد رأيته في بعض مواقفه وقد أرخى الليل سدوله، وغارت نجومه، قابضاً على لحيته يتململ تململ السليم ويبكي بكاء الحزين؛ ويقول: يا دنيا غرّي غيري، أَبي تعرّضتِ أم لي تشوّقتِ؟! هيهات! هيهات! قد أبنتك ثلاثاً لا رجعة فيها؛ فعمرك قصير، وخطرك يسير، وعيشك حقير، آه من قلّة الزاد وبعد السفر ووحشة الطريق! فبكى معاوية وقال: رحم الله أبا الحسن! كان.. والله... كذلك. (قال معاوية: كيف كان حبّك له؟ قال: كحبّ أمّ موسى لموسى. قال:) فما حزنك عليه يا ضرار؟ قال: حزن من ذبح ولدها في حجرها فلا ترقأ عبرتها ولا يسكن حزنها.

وبالجملة، فزهده لم يلحقه أحد فيه ولا يسبقه أحد إليه عليه السلام. وإذا كان أزهد الناس، كان هو الإمام لامتناع تقدّم المفضول عليه.

The Second

He was the most worshipful of men. He would spend the day in fasting and pass the night in prayer and supplication. It is from him that the people learned the night prayer and the supererogatory devotions of daytime along with most of the recommended devotions and supplications with which one can fill one's day. He used to offer 1,000 units of optional prayer over the course of the day and the night and never left the night prayer even during one of the nights of the Battle of Ṣiffīn, known as *laylat al-harīr* [when some 10,000 people are reported to have perished].

Ibn ʿAbbās said: "I saw him in wartime intently watching the movement of the Sun. So, I said to him: 'O Commander of the Faithful, what are you doing?' He said: 'I am watching for when the Sun will start casting a shadow so that I can pray.' I said to him: 'At a time like this?' He said: 'We are but fighting them for the sake of prayer.'"

Thus, he never neglected prayer as soon as it became time for it even in the most difficult circumstances. Whenever he needed to have arrowheads extracted from his wounds, he would wait until he began praying during which time he was intently focused on Allah, the Exalted, and unaware of anything but him, not perceiving the pain of what was happening to him.

He combined both the prayer and the *zakāt* by giving alms when he was bowing down in prayer, and Allah revealed a verse about this which is recited in the Qur'ān, and he gave alms out of his food and the food of his family for three days consecutively until the verse of *hal atā* was revealed about them. He would give alms day and night, openly and in secret. He sought private audience with the Messenger of Allah and gave alms beforehand, so Allah revealed a verse about it.[149] He manumitted a thousand slaves through the labour of his own hand. He used to hire out himself for labour and spend what he earned on the Messenger of Allah ﷺ who was surrounded in the quarter of the Hollow of Banū Ṭālib.

149 Qur'ān 58:12.

الثاني:

أنّه عليه السلام كان أعبد الناس، يصوم النهار ويقوم الّليل. ومنه تعلّم الناس صلاة الليل ونوافل النهار، وأكثر العبادات والأدعية المأثورة عنه تستوعب الوقت. وكان يصلّي في نهاره وليلته ألف ركعة، ولم يخل بصلاة الليل حتى في ليلة الهرير.

قال ابن عباس: رأيته في حربه وهو يرقب الشمس، فقلت: يا أمير المؤمنين ماذا تصنع؟ فقال: انظر إلى الزوال لأصلّي. فقلت: في هذا الوقت؟! فقال: إنّما نقاتلهم على الصلاة.

فلم يغفل عن فعل العبادة في أوّل وقتها في أصعب الأوقات، وكان إذا أريد إخراج شيء من الحديد من جسده ترك إلى أن يدخل في الصلاة فيبق متوجّها إلى الله تعالى غافلاً عمّا سواه، غير مدرك للآلام التي تفعل به.

وجمع بين الصلاة والزكاة فتصدّق وهو راكع، فأنزل الله تعالى فيه قرآناً يتلى؛ وتصدّق بقوته وقوت عياله ثلاثة أيام حتّى أنزل فيه وفيهم ﴿هل أتى﴾، وتصدّق ليلاً ونهاراً وسرّا وجهاراً. وناجى الرسول فقدّم بين يدي نجواه صدقة فأنزل الله تعالى فيه قرآناً؛ وأعتق ألف عبد من كسب يده، وكان يؤجر نفسه وينفق على رسول الله ﷺ في الشّعب. وإذا كان أعبد الناس كان أفضل، فيكون هو الإمام.

On the Proofs establishing the Imāma of the Commander of the Faithful 'Alī b. Abī Ṭālib after the Messenger of Allāh

The Third

He was the most knowledgeable of men after the Messenger of Allah ﷺ. The Messenger of Allah ﷺ said: "The most sound in judgement among you is 'Alī." Judgement necessarily implies knowledge and religion. It is in this regard that Allah revealed the verse *and that receptive ears might remember it*[150] because he was the utmost in intelligence and insight, ever attentive to learning. He constantly spent all his time with the Messenger of Allah, who was the most perfect of men, intensely following him day and night, from his childhood until the Messenger of Allah ﷺ passed away. The Prophet ﷺ has said: "Learning from a young age is like carving onto stone." Thus, his knowledge was more abundant than that of others due to the perfection of receptivity and the perfection of the efficient cause. It is from him that people derived the sciences.

As for the science of Arabic grammar (*naḥw*), he is its founder. He said to Abū l-Aswad al-Duʾalī: "Speech consists of three elements: the noun, the verb, and the particle [...]" and he taught him the modes of inflection.

As for the science of Islamic law (*fiqh*), all of the legal scholars ultimately go back to him. As for the Imāmiyya, this is obvious because they took their knowledge from him through his descendants. The same is true for the others as well. As for the followers of Abū Ḥanīfa, such as Abū Yūsuf, Muḥammad [Ibn al-Ḥasan al-Shaybānī], and Zufar [b. al-Hudhayl al-ʿAnbarī al-Tamīmī], they studied with Abū Ḥanīfa, and al-Shāfiʿī studied with Muḥammad b. al-Ḥasan and Mālik, so his knowledge of law goes back to the two of them. As for Aḥmad b. Ḥanbal, he studied with al-Shāfiʿī, so his knowledge of law goes back to him; and al-Shāfiʿī's knowledge of law stretches back to Abū Ḥanīfa [through Muḥammad b. al-Ḥasan] and, in turn, Abū Ḥanīfa studied with al-Ṣādiq, who studied with al-Bāqir, who studied with Zayn al-ʿĀbidīn, who studied with his father, who studied with ʿAlī ؑ. As for Mālik, he studied with Rabīʿa al-Raʾy, and he studied with ʿIkrima, who studied with ʿAbdullāh b. ʿAbbās who was a pupil of ʿAlī ؑ.

As for the science of Islamic theology (*kalām*), he is its origin. The people derived benefit from his sermons. Everyone is his pupil in this. Indeed, the Muʿtazila go back to Wāṣil b. ʿAṭāʾ who is their leader. He was a pupil of Abū Hāshim ʿAbdullāh b. Muḥammad b. al-Ḥanafiyya. Abū Hāshim was the pupil of his father, and his father was a pupil of ʿAlī ؑ. As for the Ashʿarīs, they are pupils of Abū l-Ḥasan ʿAlī b. Abī Bishr al-Ashʿarī, who was a pupil of Abū ʿAlī al-Jubbāʾī, and he is the teacher of the teachers of the Muʿtazila.

---

150 Qurʾān 69:12.

الثالث:

أنّه عليه السلام كان أعلم الناس بعد رسول الله ﷺ. قال رسول الله ﷺ: أقضاكم عليّ – والقضاء يستلزم العلم والدين. وفيه نزل قوله تعالى: ﴿وتعيها أذن واعية﴾. ولأنّه كان في غاية الذكاء والفطنة، شديد الحرص على التعلّم؛ ولازم رسول الله الذي هو أكمل الناس ملازمة شديدة ليلا ونهاراً من صغره إلى وفاة رسول الله ﷺ. وقال ﷺ: العلم في الصّغر كالنقش في الحجر؛ فيكون علومه أكثر من علوم غيره لحصول القابل الكامل والفاعل التامّ، ومنه استفاد الناس العلم.

أمّا النحو فهو واضعه؛ قال لأبي الأسود الدؤلي: الكلام كلّه ثلاثة أشياء: اسم وفعل وحرف. . . وعلّمه وجوه الإعراب.

وأمّا الفقه فالفقهاء كلّهم يرجعون إليه؛ أمّا الإمامية فظاهر؛ لأنّهم أخذوا علمهم منه ومن أولاده. وأمّا غيرهم فكذلك. أمّا أصحاب أبي حنيفة كأبي يوسف ومحمد وزفر فإنّهم أخذوا عن أبي حنيفة، والشافعيّ قرأ على محمد بن الحسن وعلى مالك، فرجع فقهه إليهما؛ وأمّا أحمد بن حنبل فقرأ على الشافعيّ فرجع فقهه إليه؛ وفقه الشافعّي راجع إلى (أبي حنيفة) وأبو حنيفة قرأ على على الصادق، والصادق قرأ على الباقر، والباقر قرأ على زين العابدين، وزين العابدين قرأ على أبيه، وأبوه قرأ على عليّ عليه السلام. وأمّا مالك فقرأ على ربيعة الرأي، وقرأ ربيعة على عكرمة، وعكرمة على عبد الله بن عبّاس، وعبد الله بن عبّاس تلميذ عليّ.

وأمّا علم الكلام فهوأصله؛ ومن خطبه استفاد الناس، وكلّ الناس تلاميذه: فإنّ المعتزلة انتسبوا إلى واصل بن عطاء وهو كبيرهم، وكان تلميذ أبي هاشم عبد الله بن محمد بن الحنفيّة، وأبو هاشم تلميذ أبيه، وأبوه تلميذ عليّ؛ والأشعريّة تلامذة أبي الحسن عليّ بن أبي بشر الأشعري، وهو تلميذ أبي علي الجبائي، وهو شيخ من شيوخ المعتزلة.

As for the science of Qur'ānic interpretation (*tafsīr*), it goes back to him because Ibn 'Abbās was his pupil in this science. Ibn 'Abbās said: "The Commander of the Faithful spoke to me about the meaning of the letter *bā'* in *bi-smillāhi l-raḥmāni l-raḥīm* [in the Name of Allah, the Infinitely Compassionate, the Ever Merciful] from nightfall until dawn."

As for the science of the spiritual path (*ṭarīqa*), it is ascribed to him for all of the Sufis trace the patched cloak of the path to him.

As for the science of eloquence (*faṣāḥa*), he is its well-spring. It has even been said that his speech is above the speech of the creation, but below the speech of the Creator. It is from him that the orators have learned their craft.

He said: "Ask me before you lose me! Ask me about the pathways of the heavens for I am more knowledgeable about them even than I am of the pathways of the earth!" It is to him that the Companions would turn to with their problems. Many instances of the cases brought to 'Umar have been recorded about which he said: "Were it not for 'Alī, 'Umar would have been destroyed." He clarified many difficult questions. Two people once came to him, one of whom had had five loaves of bread and the other had had three. They had sat down to eat only to be joined by a third man. When they had eaten the third man gave them 8 dirhams. The one who had had more loaves said he was entitled to 5 dirhams. The second man refused and so they came to 'Alī ﷺ. He said: "I will be equitable." He said: "O Commander of the Faithful! My right is greater, and I wish for rights to be upheld." He said: "If that is the case then take one dirham and give him the rest."

Once two men, unbeknownst to one another, lay in succession with a slave girl within a single interval of purity. She became pregnant and the matter was vague. So, the two came to him. He told them to draw lots and the Messenger of Allah ﷺ approved of this course of action. He said: "Praise be to Allah who made us, the Ahl al-Bayt, of those who rule according to the ways of Dāwūd," by which he meant judging by divine inspiration.

Once a slave girl rode on the back of a second and was then prodded with a stick by a third. The one who was riding fell down and died. He ruled that two-thirds of her blood money be paid by the one who prodded her and the one she was riding and the Prophet ﷺ approved it.

وعلم التفسير إليه يعزى؛ لأن ابن عبّاس كان تلميذه فيه، قال ابن عبّاس: حدّثني أمير المؤمنين من تفسير الباء من «بسم الله الرحمن الرحيم» من أوّل الليل إلى آخره.

وأمّا علم الطريقة، فإليه منسوب؛ فإنّ الصوفية كلّهم يسندون الخرقة إليه.

وأمّا علم الفصاحة فهو منبعه، حتّى قيل في كلامه أنّه فوق كلام المخلوق ودون كلام الخالق، ومنه تعلّم الخطباء.

وقال: «سلوني قبل أن تفقدوني! سلوني عن طرق السماء فإنّي أعلم بها من طرق الأرض!» وإليه يرجع الصحابة في مشكلاتهم، و(رووا في عمر) قضايا كثيرة قال فيها: «لولا عليّ لهلك عمر». وأوضح كثيراً من المشكلات: جاء إليه شخصان كان مع أحدهما خمسة أرغفة ومع الآخر ثلاثة، فجلسا يأكلان. فجاءهما ثالث فشاركها، فلمّا فرغوا رمى لها ثمانية دراهم، فطلب صاحب الأكثر خمسة، فأبى عليه صاحب الأقلّ فتخاصما ورجعا إلى عليّ فقال: قد أنصفك، فقال: يا أمير المؤمنين إنّ حقّي أكثر وأنا أريد مرّ الحقّ، فقال: إذا كان كذلك فخذ درهماً واحداً وأعطه الباقي.

ووقع مالكا جارية عليها جهلا في طهر واحد، فحملت فأشكل الحال، فترافعا إليه، فحكم بالقرعة، فصوّبه رسول الله ﷺ وقال: الحمد لله الذي جعل لنا أهل البيت من يقضي على سنن داود، يعني به القضاء بالإلهام.

وركبت جارية أخرى فنخستها ثالثة، فوقعت الراكبة فماتت. فقضى بثلثي ديتها على الناخسة والقامصة، وصوّبه النبيّ ﷺ

A cow killed a donkey. The respective owners took their dispute to Abū Bakr. He said: "A beast killed another beast, there is no penalty on the owner." Then they went to ʿUmar, who gave the same ruling. Then they went to ʿAlī ﷺ who said: "If the cow went into the stable of the donkey, then the owner of the cow owes the owner of the donkey the value of the donkey, but if it was the donkey who went into the stable of the cow and killed it, then there shall be no penalty on its owner." Then the Prophet ﷺ said: "ʿAlī b. Abī Ṭālib has judged between you by the decree of Allah the Mighty, the Sublime." Marvellous accounts of this sort are many. If he was the most knowledgeable, then he must be the Imam in accordance with the statement of the Exalted: *Who has more right to be followed, he who guides to the truth, or he who cannot guide unless he is himself guided? What is the matter with you? How to you reach your judgement?*[151]

The Fourth

He was the most courageous of men. It was by his sword that the foundations of Islam were made firm, and the pillars of faith firmly planted. Nowhere did he ever meet with defeat. Nor did he ever strike a blow with his sword except that it cut. He always remained firm defending the honour of the Messenger of Allah ﷺ and never fled, unlike the others.

He defended him by putting himself at risk and when he passed the night in his bed covered with his garment so that the idolators took him to be him – for they had resolved to murder the Messenger of Allah ﷺ. They had been watching him closely and lay in wait fully armed for the break of dawn to openly kill him and so that the responsibility for shedding his blood would fall upon all the tribes, and thus the Banū Hāshim would not be able to avenge him by opposing them all. That was how the Messenger of Allah ﷺ ended up being saved, peace was preserved, and thereby was made possible the goal of calling people to Islam. Thus, when morning came the group sought to murder him, their plans were overturned, and they dispersed once they realized it was him. Thus did their plans came to naught and their scheme was thwarted.

In the Battle of Badr — which was the very first battle [in Islam] just 18 months after his having arrived in Medina and he was only 27 years old — he single-handedly killed 36 of their men, which is more than half of the casualties they took, and he also took part in the rest of the hostilities as well.

151 Qurʾān 10:35.

وقتلت بقرة حماراً، فترافع المالكان إلى أبي بكر، فقال: بهيمة قتلت بهيمة، لا شيء على ربّهما ! ثم مضيا إلى عمر فقضى بذلك أيضاً، ثم مضيا إلى عليّ فقال: إن كانت البقرة دخلت على الحمار في منامه، فعلى ربّهما قيمة الحمار لصاحبه، وإن كان الحمار دخل على البقرة في منامها فقتلته فلا غرم على صاحبها ! فقال النبي ﷺ: لقد قضى عليّ بن أبي طالب بينكما بقضاء الله عزّ وجلّ؛ والأخبار العجيبة في ذلك لا تحصى كثرة، وإذا كان أعلم وجب أن يكون هو الإمام لقوله تعالى: ﴿أفمن يهدي إلى الحقّ أحقّ أن يتّبع أمّن لايهدي إلّا أن يهدى فما لكم كيف تحكمون﴾

الرابع:

أنّه كان أشجع الناس، وبسيفه ثبتت قواعد الإسلام وتشيّدت أركان الإيمان؛ ما انهزم في موطن قطّ ولا ضرب بسيفه إلّا قطّ، وطالما كشف الكرب عن وجه رسول الله ﷺ ولم يفرّ كما فرّ غيره.

ووقاه بنفسه لمّا بات على فراشه مستتراً بإزاره، فظنّه المشركون. وقد اتّفقوا على قتل رسول الله ﷺ أنّه هو، فأحدقوا به وعليهم السلاح يرصدون طلوع الفجر ليقتلوه ظاهراً، فيذهب دمه؛ لمشاهدة بني هاشم قاتليه من جميع القبائل، ولا يتمّ لهم الأخذ بثاره لإشتراك الجماعة في دمه، ويعود كلّ قبيل إلى رهطه، وكان ذلك سبب حفظ دم رسول الله ﷺ، وتمّت السلامة، وانتظم به الغرض في الدعاء إلى الملّة. فلمّا أصبح القوم وأرادوا الفتك به ثار إليهم فتفرّقوا عنه حين عرفوه، وانصرفوا وقد ضلّت حيلتهم وانتقض تدبيرهم.

وفي غزاة بدر وهي أوّل الغزوات كانت على رأس ثمانية عشر شهراً من قدومه المدينة، وعمره سبعة وعشرون سنة، قتل عليه السلام منهم ستة وثلاثين رجلاً بانفراده، وهم أعظم من نصف المقتولين، وشرك في الباقين.

On the Proofs establishing the Imāma of the Commander of the Faithful 'Alī b. Abī Ṭālib after the Messenger of Allāh

In the Battle of Uḥud, the people fled leaving the Prophet alone, all except for 'Alī b. Abī Ṭālib. A small group of them did come back, including 'Āṣim b. Thābit, Abū Dujāna, and Sahl b. Ḥunayf. 'Uthmān appeared three days later and the Messenger of Allah said: "You truly fled a long way indeed!"

The angels were in awe of the perseverance and resolve of 'Alī. Jibra'īl said as he was rising toward Heaven: "There is no sword but Dhū l-Fiqār,[152] and there is no noble warrior but 'Alī!" It was 'Alī who killed most of the idolators in this battle and victory was gained at his hands.

Qays b. Sa'd narrated from his father who said: "I heard 'Alī say: 'In the Battle of Uḥud I suffered 16 blows and fell to the ground from four of them. A man of beautiful countenance and fragrant smell came to me, took me by the arm and stood me up. Then he said: "Advance toward them for you are obeying Allah and His Messenger and both of them are pleased with you."' 'Alī said: 'When I came to the Messenger of Allah, I told him what happened and he said: "O 'Alī! Do you not know who the man was?"' He said: 'No, but it looked like Diḥya al-Kalbī.' He said: 'O 'Alī! May Allah cool your eyes! That was Jibra'īl.'"

In the Battle of the Confederates, which is also known as the Battle of the Ditch, once the Messenger of Allah had finished preparing the ditch, the Quraysh advanced with Abū Sufyān at their head along with Kināna and the people of Tihāma 10,000 strong. Ghaṭafān also advanced, followed by the people of Najd, and they fell on the Muslims from all sides as He, May He be exalted, said: *When they came at you from above and from below.*[153] The Prophet came out with the Muslims 3,000 strong, but with the ditch between them. The idolators had allied with the Jews and had become haughty due to their numbers and the support of the Jews.

'Amr b. Wudd and 'Ikrima b. Abī Jahl rode out and crossed a narrow point of the ditch to the Muslim side and made a challenge for one-on-one combat. 'Alī rose up and accepted, but the Prophet said: "That is 'Amr b. Wudd." So he went silent. Then he made a challenge a second and a third time. Each time 'Alī would stand up, but the Prophet would say: "That is 'Amr b. Wudd." The fourth time, he gave him permission.

'Alī said to him: "You had sworn an oath to Allah that no man from Quraysh would call out to you for a battle to the death without you taking his life, but I call you to Islam!" He said: "I have no need for it." He said: "I call you [then] to dismount and fight." He said: "I do not want to have to kill you." 'Alī said: "But I do want to kill you!"

---

152 This is how 'Alī's sword was known.
153 Qur'ān 33:10.

وفي غزاة أحد انهزم الناس كلّهم عن النبيّ ﷺ إلّا عليّ بن أبي طالب وحده، ورجع إلى رسول الله ﷺ نفر يسير أوّلهم عاصم بن ثابت وأبو دجانة وسهل بن حنيف، وجاء عثمان بعد ثلاثة أيام، فقال له رسول الله ﷺ : لقد ذهبت فيها عريضة.

وتعجّبت الملائكة من ثبات عليّ، وقال جبرئيل وهو يعرج إلى السماء «لا سيف إلّا ذو الفقار ولا فتى إلّا عليّ»؛ وقتل عليّ أكثر المشركين في هذه الغزاة، وكان الفتح فيها على يديه عليه السلام.

روى قيس بن سعد عن أبيه، قال: سمعت عليّا يقول: أصابتني يوم أحد ستّ عشرة ضربة، سقطت إلى الأرض في أربع منهنّ؛ فجاءني رجل حسن الوجه (حسن الكلم) طيّب الريح، فأخذ بضبعي فأقامني. ثم قال: أقبل عليهم فإنّك في طاعة الله وطاعة رسوله، فهما عنك راضيان؛ قال عليّ: فأتيت رسول الله ﷺ فأخبرته فقال: ياعليّ! أما تعرف الرجل؟ قلت: لا، ولكن شبّهته بدحية الكلبي؛ فقال: يا عليّ! أقرّ الله عينك، كان جبرئيل!

وفي غزاة الأحزاب وهي غزاة الخندق لمّا فرغ رسول الله ﷺ من عمل الخندق أقبلت قريش يقدمها أبو سفيان، وكنانة وأهل تهامة في عشرة آلاف؛ وأقبلت غطفان ومن تبعها من أهل نجد، ونزلوا من فوق المسلمين ومن تحتهم كما قال تعالى: ﴿إذ جاؤوكم من فوقكم ومن أسفل منكم﴾. فخرج النبيّ ﷺ بالمسلمين وهم ثلاثة آلاف، وجعل الخندق بينهم، واتّفق المشركون مع اليهود وطمع المشركون بكثرتهم وموافقة اليهود.

وركب عمرو بن ودّ وعكرمة بن أبي جهل ودخلوا من مضيق في الخندق إلى المسلمين وطلب المبارزة. فقام عليّ وأجابه، فقال له النبيّ ﷺ: إنه عمرو فسكت، ثمّ طلب المبارزة ثانياً وثالثاً، وكلّ ذلك يقوم عليّ ويقول له النبي ﷺ: إنّه عمرو، فأذن له في الرابعة.

فقال له عليّ: كنت عاهدت الله ألّا يدعوك رجل من قريش إلى إحدى خلّتين إلّا أخذتها منه، وأنا أعودك إلى الإسلام؛ قال: لا حاجة لي بذلك، قال أدعوك إلى النزال! قال: ما أحبّ أن أقتلك. فقال له عليّ: ولكنّي أحبّ أن أقتلك!

On the Proofs establishing the Imāma of the Commander of the Faithful ʿAlī b. Abī Ṭālib after the Messenger of Allāh

ʿAmr became furious, got off his horse, and the two walked toward one another. ʿAlī ؏ killed him and [later] killed his son. ʿIkrima was defeated as were the rest of the idolators. It was about this that the Messenger of Allah ﷺ said: "ʿAlī's killing ʿAmr b. Wudd was more excellent than the worship of all the *jinn* and mankind combined."

In the Battle of the Banū Naḍīr, ʿAlī ؏ killed the archer who shot at the tent of the Prophet ﷺ, and afterwards killed another ten of their men and they were defeated.

In the Battle of al-Silsila, a Bedouin came and told the Prophet ﷺ that a group of Arabs wished for him to pass the night [with them] in Medina. So he said: "Who will take the valley?" Abū Bakr said: "I'll do it." So, he gave him the battle flag and 700 men. When he got there, they said to him, "Go back to him and tell him that they are too many." So, they went back.

The next day the Prophet ﷺ said: "Who will take the valley?" ʿUmar said: "I'll do it, O Messenger of Allah." So, he gave him the battle flag and he did as the first had done.

On the third day the Prophet ﷺ said: "Where is ʿAlī b. Abī Ṭālib." He said: "Here I am, O Messenger of Allah." So, he gave him the battle flag. He reached them after the morning prayer. He killed six or seven of them and the remaining were [also] defeated. Allah himself swears in the Qurʾān by what the Commander of the Faithful achieved: *By the charging horses as they pant.*[154]

In the Battle of the Banū Muṣṭaliq, he killed Mālik and his son and took many prisoners including Juwayriya bt. al-Ḥārith b. Abī Ḍirār. The Prophet ﷺ took her as a wife. Her father came the same day and said: "O Messenger of Allah, my daughter is a noble woman. She cannot be a made a captive." So he gave the command that she be allowed to choose and she chose the Prophet of Allah ﷺ. He said: "Well done." Then [her father] said: "My daughter! Do not shame your people!" She said: "I have chosen Allah and His Messenger."

---

154 Qurʾān 100:1.

فحمي عمرو ونزل عن فرسه وتجاولا، فقتله عليّ وولده وانهزم عكرمة؛ ثمّ انهزم باقي المشركين واليهود. وعنه قال رسول الله ﷺ: قتل عليّ لعمرو بن ودّ أفضل من عبادة الثقلين.

وفي غزاة بني النضير قتل عليّ رامي قبّة النبيّ ﷺ بسهم، وقتل بعده عشرة منهم فانهزموا.

وفي غزاة السلسلة وفي غزاة جاء أعرابي فأخبر النبيّ ﷺ أنّ جماعة من العرب قصدوا أن يبيّتوا النبيّ ﷺ بالمدينة، فقال ﷺ: من للوادي؟ فقال أبو بكر: أنا له، فدفع إليه اللواء وضمّ إليه سبعمائة؛ فلمّا وصل إليهم قالوا له: ارجع إلى صاحبك فإنّا في جمع كثير فرجع.

فقال في اليوم الثاني من للوادي؟ فقال عمر: أنا ذا يا رسول الله، فدفع إليه الراية، ففعل كالأوّل.

فقال ﷺ: في اليوم الثالث: أين عليّ بن أبي طالب؟ فقال: أنا ذا يارسول الله، فدفع إليه الراية فمضى إلى القوم فلقيهم بعد صلاة الصبح، فقتل منهم ستّة أوسبعة وانهزم الباقون. وأقسم الله تعالى (بفعل أمير المؤمنين) فقال ﴿والعاديات ضبحاً﴾ السورة.

وقتل من بني المصطلق مالكاً وابنه، وسبى كثيراً من جملتهم جويرية بنت الحارث بن أبي ضرار، فاصطفاها النبيّ ﷺ فجاء أبوها في ذلك اليوم، فقال: يا رسول الله ابنتي كريمة لا تسبى، فأمره بأن يخيّرها (فاختارت النبيّ صلى الله عليه وآله) فقال: أحسنت وأجملت. ثم قال: يا بنيّة لا تفضحي قومك! فقالت: اخترت الله ورسوله!

Victory in the Battle of Khaybar was at the hands of the Commander of the Faithful ﷺ. The Prophet ﷺ had given the battle flag to Abū Bakr, who came back defeated; then to 'Umar, who came back defeated; and then to 'Alī ﷺ. He was suffering from a swelling in his eyes. So, he spat in his eyes and then he went out and killed many of them and the rest of them were routed and closed the gate of the fortress on them. The Commander of the Faithful dealt with it and ripped off the entire gate using it as bridge over the moat, and twenty men had been holding back the gate. The Muslims stormed the fortress and gained booty. 'Alī ﷺ said: "I swear by Allah! I did not rip off the door of Khaybar with mere physical strength, but by spiritual power." The conquest of Mecca was also due to him.

In the Battle of Ḥunayn, the Prophet ﷺ went out facing them with 10,000 Muslims. Abū Bakr saw them and said: "Today we cannot be defeated because we are so many." Yet, they were routed, and no one remained with the Prophet ﷺ except nine people of the Banū Hāshim and Ayman b. Umm Ayman. The Commander of the Faithful ﷺ stood in front of him striking blows with his sword and killed forty idolators and they were routed.

The Fifth

His predictions of the unseen and prognostications of future events before they happened. When Ṭalḥa and Zubayr sought his permission to go to Mecca for the lesser pilgrimage (*'umra*) he predicted thus: "No, by Allah they do not intend the lesser pilgrimage, but rather intend to set out for Basra." And so it proved to be.

When he was seated at Dhī Qār taking the oaths of allegiance he said that "A thousand men shall come to you from Kufa, no less and no more, who shall swear allegiance unto death." And so it was and the last of them was Uways al-Qaranī.

وفي غزاة خيبر كان الفتح فيها على يد أمير المؤمنين. دفع صلى الله عليه وآله الراية إلى أبي بكر فانهزم، ثمّ إلى عمر فانهزم، ثمّ إلى عليّ وكان أرمد العين فتفل في عينه. وخرج فقتل مرحباً فانهزم الباقون وغلّقوا عليهم الباب، فعالجه أمير المؤمنين فقلعه وجعله جسراً على الخندق - كان الباب يغلقه عشرون رجلا - ودخل المسلمون الحصن ونالوا الغنائم؛ وقال عليه السلام: والله ماقلعت باب خيبر بقوّة جسمانية بل بقوّة ربّانيّة. وكان فتح مكّة بواسطته.

وفي غزاة حنين خرج رسول الله ﷺ متوجّها إليهم في عشرة آلاف من المسلمين، فعاينهم أبو بكر وقال: لن تغلب اليوم من كثرة؛ فانهزموا ولم يبق مع النبيّ ﷺ غير تسعة من بني هاشم وأيمن ابن أم أيمن، وكان أمير المؤمنين بين يديه يضرب بالسيف وقتل من المشركين أربعين (نفراً فانهزموا).

الخامس:

إخباره بالغائب والكائن قبل كونه. فأخبر بأنّ طلحة والزبير لمّا استأذناه في الخروج إلى العمرة: «لا والله ما يريدان العمرة وإنما يريدان البصرة»؛ فكان كما قال.

وأخبر وهو (بذي قار جالس لأخذ البيعة: يأتيكم من قبل الكوفة ألف رجل لا يزيدون ولا ينقصون، يبايعوني) على الموت، فكان كذلك، وكان آخرهم أويس القرني.

He predicted that Dhī l-Thadiya would be killed, and so it was. Someone told him that a band had crossed [the canal] during the Battle of Nahrawān and he said: "They have not crossed." He was told this again and said, "They have not crossed, I swear by Allah, there shall they make their stand." And so it was. He predicted the murder of his own noble self. He told Juwayriya bt. Mushīr that the damned one would cut off his hands and feet and crucify him. This is exactly what Muʿāwiya did with him. He told Mītham al-Tammār that he would be crucified at the door of ʿAmr b. Ḥurayth, the tenth one of ten [to be crucified there] and that his would be the shortest stake. He even showed him the palm tree that would be used for his crucifixion.[155] That is exactly how it came to be.

He told Rushayd al-Hajarī that his hands and feet would be cut off, his tongue cut out, and that he would be crucified, and that is what happened. He told Kumayl b. Ziyād that Ḥajjāj would kill him, and that is what happened; and that Ḥajjāj would slaughter Qanbar, and so it was. He told al-Barāʾ b. ʿĀzib: "My son Ḥusayn will be killed and none will come to his aid." It happened as he said. He also predicted where he would be killed.

He predicted the rule of the Abbasid dynasty and that the Turks would rest control of their rule from them. He said: "The rule of the Abbasids will be easy with no difficulty, even if the Turks, Daylamites, the Indians, Berbers, and Ṭaylasānites unite to bring down their rule they will not be able to bring it down, not until their clients and officials attack them and the rule of the Turks comes upon them. They shall come from where their rule began. They will not pass through a city without conquering it. No banner will be raised against them without being brought down. Woe unto whoever opposes them for they shall continue until they conquer. This will last until victory will be granted to one of my descendants who will speak the truth and act in accord with it." This is exactly what happened for Hülegü (Hulākū) came forth from the direction of Khurasan, and it is from there that the Abbasid dynasty began when Abū Muslim al-Khurāsānī gave them his allegiance.

155 On the Umayyad's macabre penchant for crucifixion, see the study of Sean Anthony, *Crucifixion and Death as Spectacle. Umayyad Crucifixion in Late Antique Context* (New Haven, Connecticut: American Oriental Society, 2014).

وأخبر بقتل ذي الثدية وكان كذلك. وأخبره شخص بعبور القوم في قضيّة النهروان، فقال: لم يعبروا، ثم أخبره آخر بذلك فقال: لم يعبروه وإنه الله لمصرعهم، فكان كذلك. وأخبر بقتل نفسه الشريفة. وأخبر جويرية بن مسهر بأنّ اللعين يقطع يديه ورجليه ويصلبه، ففعل به معاوية ذلك. وأخبر ميثم التّمار بأنّه يصلب على باب عمرو بن حريث عاشر عشرة، وهو أقصرهم خشبة، وأراه النخلة التي يصلب عليها؛ فوقع كذلك.

وأخبر رشيد الهجري بقطع يديه ورجليه وصلبه وقطع لسانه فوقع. وأخبر كميل بن زياد بأنّ الحجّاج يقتله فوقع. وإنّ قنبراً يذبحه الحجّاج فوقع. وقال للبراء بن عازب: «إنّ ابني الحسين يقتل ولا تنصره» فكان كما قال، وأخبر بموضع قتله.

وأخبر بملك بني العبّاس وأخذ الترك الملك منهم، فقال: «ملك بني العبّاس يسر لا عسر فيه، لو اجتمع عليهم الترك والديلم والسند والهند والبربر والطيلسان على أن يزيلوا ملكهم لما قدروا أن يزيلوه، حتى يشدّ عنهم مواليهم وأرباب دولتهم، ويسلّط عليهم ملك من الترك يأتي عليهم من حيث بدأ ملكهم، لا يمرّ بمدينة إلّا فتحها، ولا ترفع له راية إلّا نكّسها، الويل الويل لمن ناواه، فلا يزال كذلك حتّى يظفر، ثمّ يدفع بظفره إلى رجل من عترتي يقول بالحقّ ويعمل به». وكان الأمر كذلك حيث ظهر هولاكو من ناحية خراسان، ومنه ابتدأ ملك بني العبّاس؛ حيث بايع لهم أبو مسلم الخراساني.

The Sixth: His Prayers were answered

Once he prayed against Busr b. Arṭāt that Allah should remove his reason, and he lost his senses. He prayed that Eleazer should go blind, and he went blind. He prayed that Anas be afflicted with leprosy when he refused to acknowledge the event of Ghadīr Khumm, and he was so afflicted[156] and that Zayd b. Arqam should go blind, and he did.

The Seventh

On the way to Ṣiffīn his companions came down with extreme thirst. So he took them in a slightly different direction until they saw a monastery. They called out to the occupant and asked him for water. He replied that there was no source of water for another two miles and that were it not for the fact that the water was brought to him each month, an amount just enough to suffice him for a month, he would have died of thirst. Then the Commander of the Faithful pointed to a place near the monastery and ordered it to be excavated. They found a huge stone and were unable to budge it, yet he managed to do it alone. Then they drank water [from the well that was uncovered]. The monk came out to him and asked, "Are you a prophet sent forth or an angel drawn nigh?" He said, "No, none but the legatee of the Messenger of Allah ﷺ," and he became a Muslim at his hand. He told him: "This monastery was built on the hope of this stone being extracted and the water under it being brought out, but many before me have passed without them being able to find the one who could do it." The monk became one of those who was martyred along with him. The poet al-Sayyid al-Ḥimyarī versified the incident in his golden ode.

156 See Ibn Qutayba, *al-Maʿārif*, edited by Tharwat ʿUkkāsha (Cairo: Dār al-Maʿārif 1981), 580.

السادس: أنّه كان مستجاب الدعاء

دعا على بسر بن أرطاة بأن يسلبه الله عقله؛ فخولط فيه. ودعا على العيزار بالعمى فعمي ودعا على أنس بن مالك لمّا كتم شهادته بالبرص، فأصابه وعلى زيد بن أرقم بالعمى فعمي.

السابع:

أنّه لمّا توجّه إلى صفّين لحق بأصحابه عطش شديد فعدل بهم قليلاً، فلاح لهم دير، فصاحوا بساكنه وسألوه عن الماء فقال: بيني وبينه أكثر من فرسخين، ولولا أني أتى بما يكفيني كلّ شهر على التقصير لتلفت عطشاً؛ فأشار أمير المؤمنين إلى مكان قريب من الدير وأمر بكشفه فوجدوا صخرة عظيمة فعجزوا عن إزالتها فقلعها وحده. ثم شربوا المساء (فنزل إليه الراهب وقال له: أنت نبيّ مرسل أوملك مقرّب؟) قال: لا، ولكنّي وصيّ رسول الله ﷺ، فأسلم على يده وقال: إنّ هذا المدير بني على طلب قالع هذه الصخرة ومخرج الماء من تحتها، وقد مضى جماعة قبلي ولم يدركوه؛ وكان الراهب من جملة من استشهد معه، ونظم القصّة السيّد الحميري في قصيدته المذهبة.

The Eighth

It has been related by the mainstream [Sunnī] scholars that when the Prophet ﷺ embarked upon the expedition against the Banū Muṣṭaliq he went off the trail until nightfall and he made camp in a rugged valley. Jibraʾīl ؑ came down in the middle of the night and told him that a band of unbelieving *jinn* had made this valley their home and wanted to do harm to him and his Companions. So he called ʿAlī ؑ and prayed over him and ordered him to enter the valley, so [he did so and] killed them.

The Ninth

The Sun reversed its course for him on two occasions. The first was in the time of the Prophet ﷺ and the second after him.

As for the first occasion, it is related by Jābir and Abū Saʿīd al-Khudrī that one day Jibraʾīl came down to the Messenger of Allah ﷺ calling for him from Allah, the Exalted. When the revelation overwhelmed him, he supported himself using ʿAlī's thigh as a pillow and did not lift his head up again until the Sun had gone down, thus causing ʿAlī to have offered the *ʿaṣr* prayer by gestures [while seated thus]. When the Prophet ﷺ awoke, he said to him: "Ask Allah, the Exalted, to make the Sun go back so that you may offer the *ʿaṣr* prayer standing." He supplicated and the Sun went back, and he offered the *ʿaṣr* prayer standing.

As for the second time, it was when he wanted to cross the Euphrates at Babel and many of his companions became preoccupied with helping their animals cross, so he offered the *ʿaṣr* prayer among a small group of his companions and many of them ended up missing it and they made a point of it, so he asked Allah to make the Sun go back, and it did. The poet al-Sayyid al-Ḥimyarī versified it in his golden ode:

The Sun went back to its place when the time
of the prayer had passed and the Sun was about to set

So much so that its light shone in its time
until the afternoon then it set as a star sets

And once again it went back to its place in Babel
and this never happened for anyone else among the Arabs

الثامن:

مارواه الجمهور أنّ النبيّ ﷺ لمّا خرج إلى بني المصطلق جنب عن الطريق وأدركه الليل، فنزل بقرب واد وعر فهبط جبرئيل عليه السلام آخر الليل وأخبره أنّ طائفة من كفّار الجن قد استوطنوا الوادي يريدون كيده وإيقاع الشرّ بأصحابه، فدعا بعليّ وعوّذه وأمره بنزول الوادي فقتلهم عليه السلام

التاسع:

رجوع الشمس له مرتين، إحداهما في زمن النبيّ ﷺ والثانية بعده. أمّا الأولى فروى جابر وأبو سعيد الخدري أنّ رسول الله ﷺ نزل عليه جبرئيل يوماً يناجيه من عند الله تعالى، فلمّا تغشّاه الوحي توسّد فخذ أمير المؤمنين عليه السلام فلم يرفع رأسه حتّى غابت الشمس؛ فصلّى عليّ العصر بالإيماء. فلمّا استيقظ النبي ﷺ قال له: سل الله تعالى يردّ عليك الشمس لتصلّي العصر قائماً؛ فدعا فردّت الشمس فصلّى العصر قائماً. وأمّا الثانية فلمّا أراد أن يعبر الفرات ببابل اشتغل كثير من أصحابه بتعبير دوابّهم، وصلّى بنفسه في طائفة من أصحابه العصر وفاتت كثيراً منهم، فتكلّموا في ذلك فسأل الله تعالى ردّ الشمس فردّت. ونظمه السيد الحميري في قصيدته المذهّبة فقال:

ردّت عليه الشمس لمّا فاته — وقت الصلاة وقد دنت للمغرب
حتّى تبلّج نورها في وقتها — للعصر ثمّ هوت هُوِيَّ الكوكب
وعليه قد رُدّت ببابل مرّة — أخرى وما رُدّت لخلق معرب

The Tenth

It has been related by the scholars of biography that once the waters near Kufa rose and they feared a flood and they came frightened to the Commander of the Faithful ﷺ. So, he rode out on the mule of the Messenger of Allah ﷺ and the people went out with him. He went down to the shore of the Euphrates and prayed. Then he supplicated and struck the surface of the water with the staff he held in his hand. The waters receded and left in their wake a vast quantity of fish who spoke giving salutations to him. Yet, none of the salamanders, eels, and the like spoke. They asked him about that, and he replied: "Allah caused to speak to me only those fish which are ritually clean to eat, and made silent those which he made forbidden, ritually unclean and remote."

The Eleventh

A group of the biographers has related that once ʿAlī ﷺ was giving a sermon from the *minbar* of Kufa when a serpent appeared and began to ascend the *minbar*.[157] The people were afraid and wanted to kill it, but he stopped them. It addressed him and then descended. The people asked him about it. He told them: "He is a ruler from amongst the rulers of the *jinn*. He was perplexed about a case, and I clarified it for him." The people of Kufa named the gate from which he had entered the "Gate of the Serpent." The Banū Umayya [later] wanted to efface memory of this merit so they put an elephant in that place for a long time until it became known as the "Gate of the Elephant."

157 See al-Sayyid Hāshim al-Baḥrānī, *Madīnat al-maʿājiz* (Beirut: 1422/2002), 1:65–66.

العاشر:

ماروواه أهل السيرة أنّ الماء زاد في الكوفة وخافوا الغرق، ففزعوا إلى أمير المؤمنين فركب بغلة رسول الله ﷺ وخرج الناس معه. فنزل على شاطىء الفرات فصلّى ثم دعا وضرب صفحة الماء بقضيب في يده فغاض الماء. وسلّم عليه كثير من الحيتان، ولم ينطق الجرّي والزمّار والمار ماهي، فسئل عن ذلك، فقال: أنطق الله لي ما طهر من السموك، وأصمت ما حرّمه ونجّسه وأبعده.

الحادي عشر:

روى جماعة أهل السيرة أنّه عليه السلام كان يخطب على منبر الكوفة، فظهر ثعبان فرقى المنبر؛ فخاف الناس وأرادوا قتله فمنعهم، فخاطبه ثمّ نزل، فسأل الناس عنه فقال: إنّه حاكم من حكّام الجنّ التبس عليه قضيّة فأوضحتها له. وكان أهل الكوفة يسمّون الباب الذي دخل منه «باب الثعبان»، فأراد بنو أميّة إطفاء هذه الفضيلة، فنصبوا على ذلك الباب فيلا مدّة طويلة حتّى سمّي «باب الفيل».

'Alī b. Abī Ṭālib after the Messenger of Allāh

The Twelfth

Virtues pertain either to the soul, the body, or are external [to both]. Taking the first two possibilities, they either adhere to some person himself or to someone else. The Commander of the Faithful embodies all of these.

As for the virtues of soul which apply to him, they are such as his knowledge, his ascesis, his generosity, his forbearance; these are all too well-known to have been hidden. Those which apply to someone else are also similar to that, such as the many sciences coming from him and others deriving benefit from him. Similarly, his physical virtues such as his worship, his bravery, his giving alms, etc. As for the external virtues, these are such as his lineage, which no one else shares with him, due to his proximity to the Messenger of Allah ﷺ and his being given in marriage to his daughter the Lady of Womankind.

Akhṭab Khawārizmī, one of the most eminent of Sunnī scholars, has related through his chain of transmission back to Jābir who said, "When 'Alī married Fāṭima, it was Allah who had given him in marriage to her from above the Seven Heavens. Jibrā'īl performed the ceremony and Mīkā'īl along with Isrāfīl stood as witnesses amidst 70,000 angels. Allah revealed to the tree of Ṭūbā to shower them with what was in it of pearls and precious stones, and it did so. Allah revealed to the wide white-eyed and dark black pupiled maidens of heaven to gather them up [i.e., these pearls and precious stones] and so shall they remain doing so exchanging these as gifts until the Day of Judgement. And he related many traditions of this sort.[158]

His children were also the most noble of people after the Messenger of Allah and their father.

On the authority of Ḥudhayfa b. al-Yamān who said: "I saw the Prophet ﷺ take Ḥusayn b. 'Alī ؏ and say: 'O people! This is Ḥusayn b. 'Alī. Know him and honour him! I swear by Allah that his grandfather is dearer to Allah than the grandfather of Yūsuf b. Ya'qūb, peace be upon them both. This is Ḥusayn b. 'Alī. His grandfather will be in the Garden, and his grandmother is in the Garden, and his mother will be in the Garden, and his father will be in the Garden, and his paternal uncle is in the Garden, and his maternal uncle is in the Garden, and his maternal aunt is in the Garden, and his brother will be in the Garden, and he will be in the Garden, and those who love him will be in the Garden, and those who love those who love him will be in the Garden.'"

---

158   A number of *ḥadīth*s are cited in al-Muwaffaq b. Aḥmad al-Khawārizmī's *al-Manāqib* which support this, and it seems that 'Allāma has combined them together. See al-Muwaffaq b. Aḥmad al-Khawārizmī, *al-Manāqib*, 337–342, *ḥadīth*s 358, 360–363.

الثاني عشر:

الفضائل إمّا نفسانيّة أوبدنيّة أوخارجيّة؛ وعلى التقديرين الأوّلين فإمّا أن تكون متعلّقة بالشخص نفسه أو بغيره، وأمير المؤمنين جمع الكلّ.

أمّا فضائله النفسانيّة المتعلّقة به كعلمه وزهده وكرمه وحلمه فهي أشهر من أن تخفى؛ والمتعلّقه بغيره كذلك كظهور العلوم عنه واستفادة غيره منه وكذا فضائله البدنية كالعبادة والشجاعة والصدقة. وأما الخارجيّة فكالنسب، ولم يلحقه أحد فيه لقربه من رسول الله ﷺ وتزويجه إياه بإبنته سيّدة النساء؛ وقد روى أخطب خوارزم من كبار السنّة بإسناده عن جابر قال: لمّا تزوّج عليّ فاطمة زوّجه الله إياها من فوق سبع سماوات، وكان الخاطب جبرئيل، وكان ميكائيل وإسرافيل في سبعين ألفاً من الملائكة شهوداً؛ فأوحى الله تعالى إلى شجرة طوبى أن انثري ما فيك من الدرّ والجواهر ففعلت، وأوحى الله تعالى إلى الحور العين أن «القطن» فلقطن، فهنّ يتهادين بينهنّ إلى يوم القيامة؛ وأورد أخباراً كثيرة في ذلك. وكان أولاده عليهم السلام أشرف الناس بعد رسول الله ﷺ وبعد أبيهم عليه السلام.

وعن حذيفة بن اليمان قال: رأيت النبيّ ﷺ آخذاً بيد الحسين بن عليّ عليه السلام وقال: أيها الناس، هذا الحسين بن عليّ، الا فاعرفوه وفضّلوه، فوالله لجدّه أكرم على الله من جدّ يوسف بن يعقوب عليه السلام؛ هذا الحسين بن عليّ جدّه في الجنّة، وجدّته في الجنّة، وأمّه في الجنّة، وأبوه في الجنّة، وعمّه في الجنّة، وعمّته في الجنّة، وخاله في الجنّة، وخالته في الجنّة، وأخوه في الجنّة، وهو في الجنّة، ومحبّوهم في الجنة، ومحبّو محبّيهم في الجنّة؛

On the authority of Ḥudhayfa b. al-Yamān who said: "Once I passed the night with the Prophet ﷺ and I saw someone with him. He said: 'Did you see that?' I said, 'Yes, I did, O Messenger of Allah.' He said: 'That was an angel who had not come to me since I had been sent as a prophet. He came to me from Allah to give me glad tidings of Ḥasan and Ḥusayn being the masters of the youths of Paradise.'"

Such traditions are many. Muḥammad b. al-Ḥanafiyya was a noble learned man, so much so that some even claimed the Imāma for him.

وعن حذيفة بن اليمان قال: بتُّ عند النبيّ ﷺ ذات ليلة فرأيت عنده شخصاً. فقال لي: هل رأيت؟ قلت: نعم يا رسول الله. قال: هذا ملك لم ينزل إليّ منذ بعثت، أتاني من الله فبشّرني أنّ الحسن والحسين سيّدا شباب أهل الجنّة.

والأخبار في ذلك كثيرة. وكان محمد بن الحنفيّة فاضلاً عالماً حتّى ادّعى قوم فيه الإمامة.

Section 4: On the Imāma of the Remaining Twelve Imams

الفصل الرابع
في إمامة باقي الأئمة الاثنا عشر

In this regard we have recourse to various means of establishing this.

The first of these is by of explicit designation and this is a matter of widely transmitted and corroborated tradition (*tawātur*) among the Shīʿa in the most far-flung lands from generation-to-generation from the time of the Prophet 🌹 that he said to Ḥusayn 🌸: "This son of mine is an Imam, the son of an Imam, the brother of an Imam, and the progenitor of nine Imams, the ninth of whom shall be The One Who Will Rise Up. His name shall be identical to mine. His patronym shall be identical to mine. He shall fill the Earth with justice and equity just as aforetime it had been filled with oppression and tyranny." Ibn ʿUmar has narrated that the Messenger of Allah 🌹 said: "At the end of time there shall come forth a man from my progeny. His name shall be identical to mine. His patronym shall be identical to mine. He shall fill the world with justice just as aforetime it had been filled with tyranny. He is none other than The Guided One." It was transmitted by the Ḥanbalī scholar Ibn al-Jawzī from [the *Sunan* of] Abū Dāwūd (d. 275/888) and the *Ṣaḥīḥ* of al-Tirmidhī (d. 279/892).

Secondly, we have already established that there must be an infallible Imam in every age, and, moreover, that as a matter of unanimous consensus none but them — upon whom be peace — are infallible.

Thirdly, the merits possessed by each one of them necessitates that each one of them be an Imam.

لنا في ذلك طرق:

أحدها النصّ، وقد تواترت به الشيعة في بلاد المتباعدة خلفاً عن سلف من النبيّ ﷺ أنّه قال للحسين: هذا ابني إمامٌ ابنُ إمامٍ أخُو إمامٍ أبو أئمّةٍ تسعة، تاسعهم قائمهم اسمه اسمي وكنيته كنيتي يملأ الأرض عدلاً وقسطاً كما ملئت ظلمًا وجوراً. وقد روى ابن عمر قال: قال رسول الله ﷺ: يخرج في آخر الزمان رجل من ولدي اسمه كاسمي وكنيته كنيتي يملأ الأرض عدلاً كما ملئت جوراً، فذلك هو المهدي. رواه ابن الجوزي الحنبلي عن أبي داود وصحيح الترمذي.

الثاني أنّا قد بيّنا أنّه يجب في كلّ زمان إمام معصوم (وغير هؤلاء إجماعاً ليس بمعصوم).

الثالث: الفضائل التي اشتمل كلّ واحد منهم عليها، الموجبة لكونه إماماً.

Section 5:
Those Who Were Put Forward Do Not Qualify as Imams

الفصل الخامس
في أنّ من تقدّمه لم يكن إماماً

This is established by several facts.

Fact 1

The statement of Abū Bakr: "I have a devil which takes hold of me. So, if I am upright then cooperate with me, and if I deviate then set me straight." Yet among the duties of an Imam is to guide the public, so how is it that he is sought guidance from them?

Fact 2

The statement of 'Umar: "The swearing of allegiance to Abū Bakr was a precipitate affair (*falta*) — may Allah avert its evil — thus kill whomsoever should wish to go back to something like it." The admission that it was a precipitate affair indicates that it did not emerge based on a right decision. His beseeching Allah to avert its evil and then commanding the death of those who should wish to go back to something like it, all of these, necessarily indict him.

Fact 3

Their being deficient in knowledge and their having recourse to 'Alī ؑ in most judgements.

Fact 4

The acts which they perpetrated, and we have already presented most of these.

Fact 5

The statement of Allah: *the oppressors shall have no part in My covenant* indicates that the covenant of the Imāma does not extend to the oppressor or to the unbeliever, due to His statement *and the unbelievers are none other than oppressors*. Moreover, there is no doubt that each of them were unbelievers and worshipped idols before the Prophet ﷺ came forth.

ويدلّ عليه وجوه:

الأول:

قول أبي بكر: إنّ لي شيطاناً يعتريني، فإن استقمت فأعينوني، وإن زغت فقوّموني. ومن شأن الإمام تكميل الرعيّة، فكيف يطلب منهم الكمال؟!

الثاني:

قول عمر: كانت بيعة أبي بكر فلتة (وقى الله المسلمين شرّها، فمن عاد إلى مثلها فاقتلوه!) وكونها فلتة يدل على أنّها لم تنبع عن رأي صحيح، ثم سأل وقاية شرّها، ثمّ أمر بقتل من يعود إلى مثلها؛ وكلّ ذلك يوجب الطعن فيه.

الثالث:

قصورهم في العلم، والإلتجاء في أكثر الأحكام إلى عليّ عليه السلام

الرابع:

الوقائع الصادرة عنهم، وقد تقدّم أكثرها.

الخامس:

قوله تعالى: ﴿لا ينال عهدي الظّالمين﴾ أخبر بأنّ عهد الإمامة لا يصل إلى الظالم والكافر؛ لقوله تعالى: ﴿والكافرون هم الظّالمون﴾ ولا شكّ في أنّ الثلاثة كانوا كفّاراً يعبدون الأصنام إلى أن ظهر النبي صلى الله عليه وآله

Fact 6

The statement of Abū Bakr: "Release me [from this charge] for I am not the best of you." Had he really been an Imam it would have been impossible to seek to be relieved [of the office].

Fact 7

The statement of Abū Bakr on his death bed: "I wish that I had asked the Messenger of Allah ﷺ if the Anṣār had any right to this affair." This indicates his own doubts about the validity of the allegiance given to him, although it was he himself who denied the Anṣār [this very option] on the Day of Saqīfa when they said: "Let there be an *amīr* from amongst us, and an *amīr* from amongst you," basing himself on what was related from the Messenger of Allah ﷺ: "The Imams shall be from the Quraysh."

Fact 8

His statement during his [final] illness: "I wish that I had left the house of Fāṭima alone and not raided it, and I wish that under the canopy of the Saqīfa I had given my hand [in allegiance] to one of the [other] two men [besides myself, i.e. either ʿUmar b. al-Khaṭṭāb or Abū ʿUbayda al-Jarrāḥ] so that he would have become the *amīr* and I could then have been the vizier." This establishes that he attacked the house of Fāṭima ﷺ when the Commander of the Faithful, Zubayr, and others were gathered there, and establishes that he saw others to be more qualified than himself.

Fact 9

The Messenger of Allah ﷺ had made ready the troops of Usāma and had repeatedly ordered that they should be deployed — and this [deployment] was to include Abū Bakr, ʿUmar, and ʿUthmān — but not the Commander of the Faithful ﷺ because he ﷺ wanted to prevent them from seizing the *khilāfa* after him, but they did not obey his order.

السادس:

قول أبي بكر: أقيلوني فلست بخيركم! ولوكان إماماً لم يجز له طلب الإقالة.

السابع:

قول أبي بكر عند موته: «ليتني كنت سألت رسول الله ﷺ هل للأنصار في هذا الأمر حق». وهذا يدلّ على شكّه في صحة بيعة نفسه مع أنّه الذي دفع الأنصار يوم السقيفة لمّا قالوا: «منّا أمير ومنكم أمير» بما رواه عن رسول الله ﷺ: «الأئمّة من قريش».

الثامن:

قوله في مرضه: «ليتني كنت تركت بيت فاطمة لم أكشفه، وليتني في ظلّة بني ساعدة كنت ضربت على يد أحد الرجلين فكان هوالأمير وكنت الوزير». وهذا يدلّ على إقدامه على بيت فاطمة عند اجتماع أمير المؤمنين والزبير وغيرهما فيه، وعلى أنّه كان يرى الفضل لغيره لا لنفسه.

التاسع:

أنّ رسول الله ﷺ جهزّ جيش أسامة وكرّر الأمر بتنفيذه، وكان فيهم أبو بكر وعمر وعثمان، ولم ينفذ أمير المؤمنين عليه السلام لأنه ﷺ أراد منعهم من التوثّب على الخلافة بعده، فلم يقلبوا منه.

Fact 10

The Prophet ﷺ never appointed Abū Bakr to any position of authority always appointing others rather than him.

Fact 11

He ﷺ sent him forth to deliver the message of Sūrat al-Barā'a [the ninth Sūra of the Qur'ān also known as al-Tawba] only to dispatch 'Alī ؑ with the order for him to return and to relinquish the task to him. How then can one who was not even qualified to convey a Sūra, or even a part thereof, be qualified for the general Imāma which encompasses conveying judgements to the entire Muslim community (*umma)*?

Fact 12

The claim of 'Umar that "Muḥammad did not die," which indicates the paucity of his knowledge. He also commanded a pregnant woman to be stoned but 'Alī ؑ prevented him, prompting him to say: "Were it not for 'Alī, 'Umar would have perished," not to mention other instances of rulings in which he erred and came up with novel judgements.

Fact 13

'Umar introduced communal *tarāwīḥ* prayers, even though the Prophet ﷺ had said: "O people! Truly offering the supererogatory nocturnal prayers during the month of Ramaḍān communally is an innovation, and the forenoon prayer (*al-ḍuḥā*) is an innovation. Thus, do not gather together in groups at night in the month of Ramaḍān for supererogatory prayers, and do not pray the forenoon prayer (*al-ḍuḥā*). For indeed, a small act from the Prophetic norm (*sunna*) is better than many acts which are innovations. Indeed, every innovation [in religion] is error, and every error's path leads to the Fire." When 'Umar went out one night in the month of Ramaḍān he saw lanterns in the mosques and asked, "What is this?" He was told, "People have gathered together for supererogatory prayers," to which he said, "An innovation, and what a fine innovation it is!" Thus, he [even] admitted it to be an innovation.

العاشر:

أنّ النبيّ ﷺ لم يولّ أبا بكر شيئاً من الأعمال وولّى غيره.

الحادي عشر:

انّه ﷺ أنفذه لأداء سورة براءة ثمّ أنفذ إليه عليّا وأمره بردّه وأن يتولّى هو ذلك، ومن لا يصلح لأداء سورة أو بعضها كيف يصلح للإمامة العامّة المتضمّنة لأداء الأحكام إلى جميع الأمّة؟!

الثاني عشر:

قول عمر: أنّ محمّداً لم يمت! وهو يدلّ على قلّة علمه، وأمر برجم حامل فنهاه عليّ، فقال: «لولا عليّ لهلك عمر». وغير ذلك من الأحكام التي غلط فيها وتلوّن فيها.

الثالث عشر:

أبدع التراويح مع أنّ النبيّ ﷺ قال: يا أيها الناس، إنّ الصلاة بالليل في شهر رمضان في النافلة جماعة بدعة، وصلاة الضحى بدعة، ألا فلا تجمعوا ليلا في شهر رمضان في النافلة، ولا تصلّوا صلاة الضحى، فإنّ قليلاً في سنّة خير من كثير في بدعة، ألا وإنّ كلّ بدعة ضلالة، وكلّ ضلالة سبيلها إلى النار؛ وخرج عمر في شهر رمضان ليلا فرأى المصابيح في المساجد. فقال: ما هذا؟ فقيل له: إنّ الناس قد اجتمعوا لصلاة التطوّع، فقال: «بدعة ونعمت البدعة»، فاعترف بأنّها بدعة.

Fact 14

'Uthmān committed acts which were forbidden to the extent that all the Muslims rejected him, and more people ended up agreeing on killing him than had agreed on his Imāma as well as the Imāma of his two associates.

الرابع عشر:

أنّ عثمان فعل أموراً لا يجوز فعلها، حتّى أنكر عليه المسلمون كافّة وأجمعوا على قتله أكثر من إجماعهم على إمامته وإمامة صاحبيه.

Section 6:
Invalidating their Proofs for the Imāma of Abū Bakr

الفصل السادس
في نسخ حججهم على إمامة أبي بكر

The have presented a variety of arguments.

[Argument 1]

The first of these being the consensus.

The response to this is that a group from amongst the Banū Hāshim did not agree to it, as well as a group of prominent Companions such as Salmān, Abū Dharr, ʿAmmār, Ḥudhayfa, Saʿd b. ʿUbāda, Zayd b. Arqam, and Khālid b. Saʿīd b. al-ʿĀṣ. Moreover, even his own father repudiated it saying, "Whom have the people appointed?" He was told, "Your son," to which he replied, "And what of the two weak ones" — by which he was alluding to ʿAlī and ʿAbbās. They said: "They were busy preparing the Messenger of Allah for burial, and so they [i.e., the people] were of the opinion that your son is the eldest of the Companions," to which he quipped, "But *I* am older than he is!"

Furthermore, the whole tribe of Banū Ḥanīfa did not present their *zakāt* to him and so he declared them to be apostates, killed them, and took them prisoner. ʿUmar objected to this and released the prisoners during his reign as caliph.

Also, consensus on its own does not amount to evidence, rather those involved in arriving at some consensus must rely on some evidence (*dalīl*) based on which they arrive at some judgement on which they then agree, otherwise they are in error. Such evidence may either be rational (*ʿaqlī*) — and there is no purely rational justification for his Imāma — or transmitted (*naqlī*), but according to them the Prophet ﷺ died without making any directive (*waṣiyya*) or explicit designation (*naṣṣ*) of his [i.e. Abū Bakr's] Imāma and the Qurʾān is [also] silent about it. Therefore, even if [such a] consensus came about, it was in error, and this repudiates the argument.

Also, in considering consensus one must either take into account the views of the whole *umma*, and of course this did not occur, or the consensus of the people of Medina or some of them, and indeed most of the people agreed on the murder of ʿUthmān.

Also, each individual member of the *umma* is open to error, so what is to prevent them from arriving at a false consensus?

Also, we have already established the explicitly affirmed designation of the Commander of the Faithful as Imam [by the Prophet ﷺ]. Thus, if they arrived at a consensus that goes against this, they are in error, since any consensus in the face of an explicit text is invalid for them.

احتجّوا بوجوه:

الأوّل: الإجماع

والجواب منع الإجماع؛ فإنّ جماعة من بني هاشم لم يوافقوا على ذلك وجماعة من أكابر الصحابة؛ كسلمان وأبي ذر والمقداد وعمّار وحذيفة وسعد بن عبادة وزيد بن أرقم وأسامة بن زيد و(خالدبن سعيد بن العاص) حتّى أنّ أباه أنكر ذلك وقال: من استخلف الناس؟ فقالوا: ابنك، فقال: وما فعل المستضعفان؟ إشارة إلى عليّ والعبّاس؟ فقالوا: اشتغلوا بتجهيز رسول الله؛ ورأوا أنّ ابنك أكبر الصحابة سنّاً، فقال: أنا أكبر منه!

و[كَـــ]بني حنيفة كافّة، لم يحملوا الزكاة إليه حتّى سمّاهم أهل الردّة وقتلهم وسباهم، وأنكر عمر عليه وردّ السبايا أيام خلافته.

وأيضاً الإجماع ليس أصلاً في الدلالة، بل لا بدّ أن يستند المجمعون إلى دليل على الحكم حتّى يجمعوا عليه، وإلّا كان خطأ؛ وذلك الدليل إمّا عقليّ، وليس في العقل دلالة على إمامته؛ وإمّا نقليّ، وعندهم أنّ النبيّ ﷺ مات عن غير وصيّة ولا نصّ على إمامته، والقرآن خال منه، فلو كان الإجماع متحققاً كان خطأ، فتنتفي دلالته.

وأيضاً الإجماع إمّا أن يعتبر فيه قول كل الأمة، ومعلوم أنّه لم يحصل؛ بل ولا إجماع أهل المدينة أوبعضهم، وقد أجمع أكثر الناس على قتل عثان.

وأيضاً كلّ واحد من الأمّة يجوز عليه الخطاء، فأيّ عاصم لهم عن الكذب عند الاجماع؟

وأيضاً قد بيّنا ثبوت النصّ الدالّ على إمامة أمير المؤمنين، فلو أجمعوا على خلافه كان خطأ لأنّ الإجماع الواقع على خلاف النصّ يكون خطأ عندهم.

[Argument 2]

The second of these is what they relate from the Prophet ﷺ that he said: "Follow the two who come after me, Abū Bakr and 'Umar."

The response to this is that this narration cannot be used as a proof-text for Imāma, since following jurists does not entail that they are Imams.

Also, Abū Bakr and 'Umar differed in many rulings, thus it is impossible to follow both of them.

Also, this contradicts what they relate of his having [also] said: "My Companions are like stars, whomsoever you follow, you will have been guided" because they have a consensus that all of them [i.e., the Companions] were not Imams.

الثاني:

ما رووه عن النبيّ ﷺ أنّه قال: اقتدوا باللّذين من بعدي أبي بكر وعمر.

والجواب المنع من الرواية من دلالتها على الإمامة، فإنّ الاقتداء بالفقهاء لا يستلزم كونهم أئمّة.

وأيضاً فإنّ أبا بكر وعمر اختلفا في كثير من الأحكام، فلا يمكن الاقتداء بها.

وأيضاً فإنّه معارض بما رووه من قوله: «أصحابي كالنجوم بأيهم اقتديتم اهتديتم»، مع إجماعهم على انتفاء إمامتهم.

[Argument 3]

The third of these is what has been related regarding his merits, such as the verse of the cave (*āyat al-ghār*), the statement of the Exalted: *He who is truly the most mindful of Allah will be spared from that fire,*[1] the statement of the Exalted: *Tell those bedouin Arabs who stayed behind: 'In time you will be called upon to face a people of mighty power'*[2] where Abū Bakr is understood to be the one who will call them, that he was the intimate of the Messenger of Allah ﷺ at al-ʿArīsh on the Day of Badr, that he spent on the Prophet ﷺ, and that he came forward to lead the prayer.

The response to this is that he has no merit for merely having been in the cave, for he could have had him accompany him in order to prevent him from potentially disclosing the matter [of the Prophet's a clandestine departure from Mecca]. Also, the Qurʾānic verse in question points to his being deficient for it says *grieve not,* which indicates his weakness, impatience, complete lack of certitude in Allah, complete lack of gratitude for accompanying the Prophet ﷺ and complete lack of certitude in Allah's ordainment and decree, for if grief had constituted obedience it would have been impossible that the Prophet ﷺ would forbid it, and if it is a sin then what they are citing as a merit actually becomes a disgrace. Also, whenever the descent of tranquillity upon the Messenger of Allah ﷺ is mentioned in the Qurʾān the believers are mentioned along with him, except in this one instance and there can be no defect greater than this.

As for the statement of the Exalted: *He who is truly the most mindful of Allah,* what is being referred to is that Abū l-Daḥdāḥ purchased a palm tree from someone for his neighbour and the Prophet ﷺ had offered a palm tree in paradise to the one who owned the palm tree, but he refused; and when Abū l-Daḥdāḥ learned of this he purchased it with a garden he owned and presented it to his neighbour, and so the Messenger of Allah ﷺ gave him a garden in paradise in lieu of that.

1 Qurʾān 92:17.
2 Qurʾān 48:16.

الثالث:

ماورد منه من الفضائل كآية الغار، وقوله تعالى: ﴿وسيجنّبها الأتقي﴾، وقوله تعالى: ﴿قل للمخلّفين من الأعراب ستدعون إلى قوم أولي بأس شديد﴾ والداعي هو أبو بكر، وكان أنيس رسول الله ﷺ في العريش يوم بدر، وأنفق على النبي ﷺ وتقدّم في الصلاة.

والجواب أنّه لا فضيلة له في الغار لجواز أن يستصحبه حذراً منه لئلا يظهر أمره. وأيضاً فإنّ الآية تدل على نقصه؛ لقوله ﴿لا تحزن﴾، فإنّه يدلّ على خوره وقلّة صبره وعدم يقينه بالله تعالى وعدم رضاه (لمساواته للنبيّ) ﷺ وبقضاء الله وقدره، لأنّ الحزن إن كان طاعة استحال أن ينهى النبيّ ﷺ عنه، وإن كان معصية كان ما ادّعوه فضيلة رذيلة. وأيضاً فإنّ القرآن حيث ذكر إنزال السكينة على رسول الله ﷺ شرك معه المؤمنين، إلّا في هذا الموضع ولا نقص أعظم منه.

وأمّا قوله تعالى ﴿وسيجنّبها الأتقى الّذي﴾ فإنّ المراد به أنّ أبا الدحداح حيث اشترى نخلة شخص لأجل جاره، وقد عرض النبيّ ﷺ على صاحب النخل نخلة في الجنّة فأبى، فسمع أبو الدحداح فاشتراها (ببستان له) ووهبها للجار؛ فجعل له رسول الله ﷺ بستاناً عوضها في الجنّة.

As for the statement of the Exalted: *those who stayed behind will say,*[3] He intended those who were not present during [the Treaty of] Ḥudaybiyya, but who [thereafter] wished to take a portion of the spoils of the Battle of Khaybar, but Allah forbade them with His statement *Say: You will not follow us* [...][4] for He had specified the spoils of the Battle of Khaybar for those who had been present at [the Treaty of] Ḥudaybiyya, it was then that He said: *Tell those bedouin Arabs who stayed behind: 'In time you will be called upon to face a people of mighty power'*[5] by which He meant "We will call upon you in time to do battle with a people of formidable strength." Indeed, the Prophet ﷺ called them to many a battle, such as Mu'ta, Ḥunayn, Tabūk, and others, and in each instance the one who called was the Messenger of Allah ﷺ.

It is also possible that the person meant thereby is ʿAlī ؑ since it was he who fought the rebels (*nākithīn*), oppressors (*qāsiṭīn*), and renegades (*māriqīn*), and their obeying ʿAlī was submission (*islām*) to his ﷺ pronouncement "O ʿAlī, your battles are my battles" and to make war on the Prophet is unbelief (*kufr*).

As for his having been his intimate at al-ʿArīsh during the Battle of Badr, this is no distinction, for the ﷺ Prophet being the intimate of Allah renders any other intimate superfluous, however the Prophet ﷺ realized that sending him into battle would ruin things. Indeed, he fled the field many times in subsequent battles. Who then is better: the one who sits on the sidelines of combat, or the one who strives in the path of Allah risking his life and wealth?

As for his having spent money on the Prophet ﷺ it is a lie because he was not a wealthy man. His father was extremely poor and used to beg daily at the table of ʿAbdullāh b. Jadʿān for a morsel of food for his subsistence. Had Abū Bakr been wealthy, surely he would have provided for him.

In the pre-Islamic period Abū Bakr was a teacher of small boys and in the Islamic period a tailor.

And when he assumed power over the Muslims, the people told him to leave tailoring, to which he said that he needed to earn a living and so they earmarked three dirhams a day for him from the public treasury, whereas the Prophet ﷺ was wealthy prior to the Hijra due to the wealth of Khadīja and he was not in need of war or the outfitting of troops. After the Hijra, Abū Bakr in no way possessed anything at all.

3 Qur'ān 48:11.

4 Qur'ān 48:15.

5 Qur'ān 48:16.

وأمّا قوله تعالى: ﴿سيقول لك المخلّفون﴾ فإنّه أراد الذين تخلّفوا عن الحديبية، والتمس هؤلاء أن يخرجوا إلى غنيمة خيبر فمنعهم الله بقوله: ﴿قل لن تتّبعونا﴾ الآية، لأنّه تعالى جعل غنيمة خيبر لمن شهد الحديبية. ثم قال ﴿قل للمخلّفين من الأعراب ستدعون﴾ يريد أنّه سندعوكم فيما بعد إلى قتال قوم أولي بأس شديد، وقد دعاهم النبيّ ﷺ إلى غزوات كثيرة، كمؤتة وحنين وتبوك وغيرها، وكان الداعي رسول الله ﷺ.

وأيضاً جاز أن يكون عليّاً، حيث قاتل الناكثين والقاسطين والمارقين، وكان رجوعهم إلى طاعته إسلاماً لقوله: «يا عليّ حربك حربي» وحرب رسول الله ﷺ كفر.

وأمّا كونه أنيسه في العريش يوم بدر فلا فضل فيه؛ لأن النبيّ ﷺ كان أنسه بالله تعالى مغنياً له عن كلّ أنيس، لكن لمّا عرف النبيّ ﷺ أنّ أمره لأبي بكر بالقتال يؤدّي إلى فساد الحال حيث هرب عدّة مرات في غزواته. فأيما أفضل: القاعد عن القتال أو المجاهد بنفسه وماله في سبيل الله؟

وأمّا إنفاقه على رسول الله ﷺ فكذب؛ لأنّه لم يكن ذا مال؛ فإنّ أباه كان فقيراً في الغاية، وكان ينادي على مائدة عبد الله بن جدعان بمدّ في كلّ يوم يقتات به. فلو كان أبو بكر غنياً لكفى أباه.

وكان أبو بكر في الجاهليّة معلماً للصبيان، وفي الإسلام كان خيّاطاً.

ولمّا ولي أمر المسلمين منعه الناس من الخياطة، فقال: إنّي أحتاج إلى القوت! فجعلوا له في كلّ يوم ثلاثة دراهم من بيت المال، والنبيّ ﷺ كان قبل الهجرة غنيّاً بمال خديجة. ولم يحتج إلى الحرب وتجهيز الجيوش؛ وبعد الهجرة لم يكن لأبي بكر شيء البتة (على حالٍ من الأحوال).

Furthermore, had he spent then necessarily some portion of the Qur'ān would have come down mentioning it such as *Hal atā* in the case of ʿAlī ﷺ. It is a known fact that the Prophet ﷺ was more noble than the people to whom ʿAlī gave alms, and since the wealth which they allege that he spent was supposed to have been larger than what ʿAlī spent, the fact that nothing of the Qur'ān was revealed in this regard points to this transmission being a lie.

As for his having been put forward for the prayer it is wrong. When Bilāl made the *adhān* it was ʿĀ'isha who ordered Abū Bakr to be brought forward. As the Prophet ﷺ regained consciousness and heard the *takbīr*, he asked who is leading the prayer and they said Abū Bakr, whereupon he said: "Take me outside!" He came out supported on either side by ʿAlī and al-ʿAbbās. He pushed him aside from the *qibla* and removed him from the prayer and led it himself.

This, then, is the quality of their evidence. Let, then, the intelligent man look with even-handedness while intending to seek the truth rather than follow passion and leaving behind imitation of fathers and grandfathers. For Allah ﷻ has forbidden that in His Book, and let not the world divert him from conveying the truth to those who deserve it, and not withhold from the one who deserves that which is his right. This is the last of that which we wished to set out in this introductory work and Allah is the guarantor of truth.

I finished copying it in Jumādā al-Ulā in the year nine and seven hundred [709 H][6] in the region of Khurāsān. This was written by [al-]Ḥasan b. Yūsuf [b.] al-Muṭahhar [al-Ḥillī], the author of this work, and all praise is due to Allah, the Lord of the Worlds. Benedictions upon the Master of all the Messengers — Muḥammad, and upon his noble, immaculate Family.

6 Approximately October 1309 CE.

ثمّ لو أنفق لوجب أن ينزل فيه قرآن كما نزل في عليّ عليه السلام ﴿هل أتى﴾، ومن المعلوم أنّ النبيّ صلى الله عليه وآله كان أشرف من الذين تصدّق عليهم أمير المؤمنين عليه السلام، والمال الذي يدّعون إنفاقه كان أكثر، فحيث لم ينزل شيء دلّ على كذب النقل.

وأمّا تقدّمه في الصلاة فخطأ؛ لأنّ بلالاً لمّا أذّن بالصلاة أمرت عائشة أن يقدّم أبو بكر، فلمّا افاق النبيّ صلى الله عليه وآله سمع التكبير، فقال: من يصلّي بالناس؟ فقالوا أبو بكر، فقال: أخرجوني! فخرج بين عليّ عليه السلام والعبّاس، فنحاه عن القبلة وعزله عن الصلاة وتولّى هو الصلاة.

فهذا حال أدلّة هؤلاء؛ فلينظر العاقل بعين الإنصاف ويقصد طلب الحقّ دون اتّباع الهوى، ويترك تقليد الآباء والأجداد؛ فقد نهى الله تعالى في كتابه عن ذلك، ولا تلهيه الدنيا عن إيصال الحقّ إلى مستحقّه، ولا يمنع المستحقّ عن حقّه. فهذا آخر ما أردنا إثباته في هذه المقدّمة والله الموفّق للصواب.

فرغت من تسويده في جمادى الأول من سنة تسع وسبعمائة بناحية خراسان، وكتب حسن بن يوسف المطهّر مصنّف الكتاب، والحمد لله ربّ العالمين وصلّى الله على سيّد المرسلين محمّد وآله الطيّبين الطاهرين.

Bibliography

المصادر والمراجع

Primary literature

ʿAbd al-Bāqī, Muḥammad Fuʾād. *Al-Muʿjam al-mufahras li-alfāẓ al-Qurʾān al-Karīm.* Cairo: Dār al-Ḥadīth, 1407/1988.

Abū Dāwūd (=Abū Dāwūd Sulaymān b. al-Ashʿath b. Shaddād al-Azdī). *Al-Sunan.* 2 vols. Vaduz, Lichtenstein: Thesaurus Islamicus Foundation, 2000.

Abū l-Ḥasan al-Ashʿarī. *Maqālāt al-islāmiyyīn.* 2 vols. Edited by Muḥammad ʿAbd al-Ḥamīd Muḥyī al-Dīn. Beirut and Sidon: al-Maktabat al-ʿAṣriyya, 1411/1990.

Abū Nuʿaym al-Iṣfahānī (=al-Ḥāfiẓ Abū Nuʿaym Aḥmad b. Abdullāh al-Iṣfahānī). *Ḥilyat al-awliyāʾ wa-ṭabaqāt al-aṣfiyāʾ.* 10 vols. in 5. Cairo: Maktabat al-Khānjī, 1351/1932.

———. *Al-Nūr al-mushtaʿal min Kitāb Mā nuzila min al-Qurʾān fī ʿAlī ʿalayhī l-salām.* Edited by Muḥammad Bāqir al-Maḥmūdī. Qom: Wizārat al-Irshād al-Islāmī, 1406/1986.

Aḥmad b. Ḥanbal. *Faḍāʾil al-Ṣaḥāba.* 2 vols. Edited by Waṣīyyullāh b. Muḥammad ʿAbbās. Mecca: Jāmiʿat Umm al-Qurā, 1403/1983.

———. *Al-Musnad.* 14 vols. Vaduz, Lichtenstein: Thesaurus Islamicus Foundation, 2006.

al-Amīnī, Abd al-Ḥusayn Aḥmad. *Kitāb al-ghadīr fī l-kitāb wa-l-sunna wa-l-adab.* 11 vols. Beirut: n.p., 1414/1994.

Avicenna (=Ibn Sīnā). *The Metaphysics of the Healing. A parallel English-Arabic text translated, introduced, and annotated by Michael E. Marmura.* Provo, Utah: Brigham Young University Press, 2005.

al-Baghdādi, ʿAbd al-Muʾmin (=Ṣafī al-Dīn ʿAbd al-Muʾmin b. ʿAbd al-Ḥaqq). *Marāṣid al-iṭṭilāʿ ʿalā asmāʾ al-amkinat wa-l-biqāʿ.* Edited by ʿAlī Muḥammad al-Bījāwī. Beirut: Dār al-Maʿrifa, 1373/1954.

al-Baḥrānī, al-Sayyid Hāshim. *Madīnat al-maʿājiz.* 5 vols. Beirut: Muʾassasat al-Nuʿmān, 1422/2002.

al-Balādhurī, Aḥmad b. Yaḥyā b. Jābir. *Futūḥ al-buldān = Liber Expungnationis Regionum.* Edited by M. J. de Goeje. Leiden: E. J. Brill, 1866 (=*The Origins of the Islamic State.* Translated by Phillip K. Hitti. New York: Columbia University Press, 1916).

al-Bīrjandī, Ḥusayn al-Ḥusaynī. *Gharīb al-ḥadīth fī Biḥār al-anwār.* Tehran: Wizārat-i Irshād u Farhang-i Islāmī, 1379/[2000].

al-Bukhārī, Abū ʿAbdullāh Muḥammad b. Ismāʿīl. *Al-Jāmiʿ al-musnad al-ṣaḥīḥ al-mukhtaṣar.* 3 vols. Vaduz, Lichtenstein: Thesaurus Islamicus Foundation, 2000.

al-Daylamī, Shīrawayh b. Shahrdār. *Al-Firdaws bi-maʾthūr al-khiṭāb.* 6 vols. Edited by Muḥammad al-Saʿīd b. Basyūnī Zaghlūl. Beirut: Dār al-Kutub al-ʿIlmiyya, 1406/1986.

Dihkhudā, ʿAlī-Akbar. *Lughat-nāma farhang-i mutawassiṭ-i Dihkhudā.* Tehran: Intishārāt-i Dānishghāh-i Tihrān, 1385/[2006].

al-Faḍl b. Shādhān al-Azdī al-Naysabūrī. *Al-Iḍāḥ*. Edited by al-Sayyid Jalāl al-Dīn al-Ḥusaynī al-Urmawī. Tehran: Tehran University Press, 1351/[1972].

al-Farazdaq. *Dīwān al-Farazdaq*. 2 vols. Edited by Karam al-Bustānī (Beirut: Dār Bayrūt, 1404/1984 (=*Dīwān al-Farazdaq*. Edited by ʿAlī Fāʿūr. Beirut: Dār al-Kutub al-ʿIlmiyya, 1407/1987).

al-Firōzābādī, Majd al-Dīn Muḥammad b. Yaʿqūb. *Al-Qāmūs al-muḥīṭ*. Beirut: Muʾassasat al-Risāla 1407/1987.

al-Ḥafiẓ al-Ḥaskānī (=ʿUbaydullāh b. ʿAbdullāh b. Aḥmad). *Shawāhid al-tanzīl li-qawāʿid al-tafḍīl*. 3 vols. Edited by Muḥammad Bāqir al-Maḥmūdī. [Qom?]: Majmaʿ Iḥyāʾ al-Turāth al-Islāmī, 1427/2006.

al-Ḥākim al-Naysābūrī. *Al-Mustadrak ʿalā l-ṣahīhayn*. 5 vols. Edited by Muṣṭafā ʿAbd al-Qādir ʿAṭā. Beirut: Dār al-Kutub al-ʿIlmiyya, n.d.; reprint of Ḥaydarābād: Dārʾirat al-Maʿārif al-Niẓāmiyya, 1342/1923.

al-Ḥillī, al-Ḥasan b. Yūsuf b. al-Muṭahhar (=al-ʿAllāma al-Ḥillī). *Kashf al-murād fī sharḥ Tajrīd al-iʿtiqād*. Edited by Ḥasan Ḥasanzādah al-Āmulī. Qom: Muʾassasat al-Nashr al-Islāmī al-Tābiʿa li-Jamāʿat al-Mudarrisīn bi-Qum al-Musharrafa, 1422/2002.

Ibn ʿAbd al-Barr (=Abū ʿUmar Yūsuf b. ʿAbdullāh). *Al-Istīʿāb fī maʿrifat al-aṣḥāb*. 3 vols. Beirut: al-Maktabat al-ʿAṣriyya, 1431/2010 (=*al-Istīʿāb fī maʿrifat al-aṣḥāb*. 3 vols. Edited by ʿAbd al-Ghanī Muḥammad ʿAlī Mistū. Beirut: 1431/2010).

Ibn Abī l-Ḥadīd. *Sharḥ Nahj al-balāgha*. 21 vols. in 11. Edited by Ḥusayn al-Aʿlamī. Beirut: Muʾassasat al-Aʿlamī, 1425/2004.

Ibn ʿAsākir (=Abū l-Qāsim ʿAlī b. al-Ḥasan). *Taʾrīkh Madīnat Dimishq*. Edited by Muḥibb al-Dīn al-ʿAmrawī. 80 vols. Beirut: Dār al-Fikr, 1415/1995.

Ibn al-Athīr (=ʿIzz al-Dīn Abū l-Ḥasan ʿAlī b. Muḥammad). *Al-Kāmil fī l-tārīkh*. 10 vols. Edited by Khalīl Maʾmūn Shīḥā. Beirut: Dār al-Maʿrifa, 1422/2002.

———. *Usd al-ghāba fī maʿrifat al-ṣaḥāba*. 5 vols. Edited by Khalīl Maʾmūn Shīḥā. Beirut: Dār al-Maʿrifa, 1428/2007.

Ibn Hishām (=Abū Muḥammad ʿAbd al-Malik b. Hishām). *Al-Sīrat al-nabawiyya*. 4 vols. in 2. Edited by Muṣṭafā al-Saqā, Ibrāhīm al-Abyārī and ʿAbd al-Ḥāfiẓ Shalabī. Cairo: Dār al-Qiblā, n.d.

Ibn Kathīr (=Abū l-Fidāʾ Ismāʿīl b. Kathīr). *Al-Bidāyā wa-l-nihāya*. 21 vols. in 20. Edited by ʿAbd al-Qādir al-Arnaʾūṭ and Bashshār ʿAwwād Maʿrūf. Damascus and Beirut:Dār Ibn Kathīr, 1436/2016.

Ibn al-Maghāzilī (=Abū l-Ḥasan ʿAlī b. Muḥammad al-Jallābī). *Manāqib Ahl al-Bayt*. Edited by Muḥammad Kāẓim al-Maḥmūdī. Tehran: Markaz al-Taḥqīqāt wa-l-Dirāsāt al-Tābiʿ li-l-Majmaʿ al-ʿIlmī li-l-Taqrīb bayna l-Madhāhib al-Islāmiyya, 1427/2006.

Ibn Māja (=Abū ʿAbdullāh Muḥammad b. Yazīd b. Māja al-Qazwīnī al-Ribʿī). *Al-Sunan*. Vaduz, Lichtenstein: Thesaurus Islamicus Foundation, 2006.

Ibn al-Murtaḍā (=Aḥmad b. Yaḥyā b. al-Murtaḍā). *Kitāb Ṭabaqāt al-Muʿtazila*. Edited by Susanna Diwald-Wilzer. Wiesbaden: Franz Steiner Verlag, 1961.

Ibn Qutayba. *Al-Maʿārif*. Edited by Tharwat ʿUkkāsha. Cairo: Dār al-Maʿārif, 1981.

Ibn Rajab al-Ḥanbalī (=Zayn al-Dīn ʿAbd al-Raḥmān b. Shiḥab al-Dīn). *Jāmī al-ʿulūm wa-l-ḥikam*. Edited by Māhir Yāsīn al-Faḥl. Damascus and Beirut: Dār Ibn Kathīr, 1429/2008 (= *Jāmī al-ʿulūm wa-l-ḥikam*. 2 vols. Edited by Shuʿayb al-Arnaʾūṭ and Ibrāhīm Bajis. Beirut: Muʾassasat al-Risāla, 1419/1999).

Ibn Saʿd (= Muḥammad b. Saʿd Kātib al-Wāqidī). *Al-Ṭabaqāt*. Edited by Eduard Sachau. Leiden: E. J. Brill, 1905–1940 (= *Al-Ṭabaqāt al-kubrā*. Edited by Muḥammad ʿAbd al-Qādir ʿAṭā. Beirut: n.p., 1376/1957).

Ibn Shabba (=ʿUmar b. Shabba). *Taʾrīkh al-Madīnat al-Munawwara*. Edited by Fahīm Maḥmūd Shaltut. Beirut: Dār al-Turāth, 1410/1990.

Ibn ʿUqda al-Kūfī. *Kitāb al-wilāya*. Edited by ʿAbd al-Razzāq Muḥammad Ḥusayn Ḥirz al-Dīn. Qom: Intishārāt-i Dalīl, 1421/2000.

al-Kalbī (= Abū l-Mundhir Hishām b. Muḥammad b. al-Sāʾib). *Mathālib al-ʿarab*. Edited by Najāḥ al-Ṭāʾī. Beirut and London: Dār al-Hudā, 1419/1998.

al-Kulaynī, Abū Jaʿfar Muḥammad b. Yaʿqūb. *Al-Uṣūl min al-kāfī*. 2 vols. Edited by ʿAlī Akbar al-Ghaffārī. Tehran: Dār al-Kutub al-Islamiyya, 1388/1968.

al-Maḥallī, Jalāl al-Dīn al-Maḥallī and Jalāl al-Dīn al-Suyūṭī. *Tafsīr al-Jalālayn*. Cairo: Dār al-Qalam, 1385/1966.

al-Majlisī, Muḥammad Bāqir b. Muḥammad Taqī. *Biḥār al-anwār al-jāmiʿa li-durar akhbār al-aʾimmat al-aṭhār*. 110 vols. Tehran: Dār al-Kutub al-Islamīyya, 1376/1957.

Mālik b. Anas. *Al-Muwaṭṭa*. Vaduz, Lichtenstein: Thesaurus Islamicus Foundation, 2000.

al-Mīlānī, al-Sayyid ʿAlī al-Ḥusaynī. *Nafaḥāt al-azhār fī khulāṣat ʿAbaqāt al-anwār*. 12 vols. Qom: Mihr, 1414/1993.

Mirrīkh, ʿĀdil Muḥammadd Masʿūd. *Al-ʿArabiyyat al-qadīma wa-lahjātuhā: dirāsa muqārana bayn alfāẓ al-muʿjam al-sabaʾī wa-alfāẓ lahjāt ʿArabiyya qadīma: al-Gibbāliyya wa-l-Mihriyya*. Abu Dhabi: al-Majmaʿ al-Thaqāfī, 1421/2000.

al-Mizzī, Jamāl al-Dīn Abū l-Ḥajjāj Yūsuf. *Tahdhīb al-kamāl fī asmāʾ al-rijāl*. Edited by Bashshār ʿAwwād Maʿrūf. Beirut: Muʾassasat al-Risālā, 1422/2002.

Muslim (=Abū l-Ḥusayn Muslim b. al-Hajjāj al-Naysābūrī). *Al-Jāmiʿ al-ṣaḥīḥ*. 2 vols. Vaduz, Lichtenstein: Thesaurus Islamicus Foundation, 2000.

al-Muttaqī al-Hindī (=Alāʾ al-Dīn ʿAlī al-Muttaqī b. Ḥusām al-Dīn al-Hindī). *Kanz al-ʿummāl*. 18 vols. Beirut: Muʾassasat al-Risāla, 1405/1985.

al-Muwaffaq al-Khawārizmī (=al-Muwaffaq b. Aḥmad b. Muḥammad al-Makkī al-Khawārizmī). *Al-Manāqib*. Qom: al-Nashr al-Islāmī, 1421/2000.

al-Qāḍī al-Nuʿmān (=Qāḍī Abū Ḥanīfa al-Nuʿmān b. Muḥammad al-Tamīmī al-Maghribī). *Sharḥ al-akhbār fī faḍā'il al-a'immat al-aṭhār*. 3 vols. Edited by Muḥammad Ḥusayn al-Ḥusaynī al-Jālālī. Qom: Mu'assasat al-Nashr al-Islāmī al-Tābi'a li-Jamā'at al-Mudarrisīn bi-Qum al-Musharrafa, 1409.

al-Qandōzī, Sulaymān b. Ibrāhīm. *Yanābī' al-mawwada li-dhawī l-qurbā*. 2 vols. in 1. 7th edn. Baghdad: Manshūrāt al-Maktabat al-Ḥaydariyya, 1384/1965.

al-Rāfi'ī, Abū l-Qāsim 'Abd al-Karīm b. Muḥammad. *Al-'Azīz sharḥ al-Wajīz*. Edited by 'Alī Muḥammad Mu'awwaḍ and 'Ādil Aḥmad 'Abd al-Mawjūd. Beirut: Dār al-Kutub al-'Ilmiyya, 1417/1997.

al-Rāghib al-Iṣfahānī (=al-Ḥusayn b. Muḥammad). *Al-Mufradāt fī gharīb al-Qur'ān*. Edited by Muḥammad Sa'īd al-Kaylānī. Beirut: Dār al-Ma'rifa, 1418/1997.

al-Rāzī, Muḥammad b. 'Abd al-Qādir. *Mukhtār al-ṣiḥāḥ*. Beirut: Maktabat Lubnān Nāshirūn, 1995.

al-Ṣan'ānī, Abū Bakr 'Abd al-Razzāq b. Humām. *Al-Muṣannaf*. 12 vols. Edited by Ḥabīb al-Raḥmān al-A'ẓamī. Beirut: Al-Maktab al-Islāmī, 1403/1983.

al-Shahrastānī, Muḥammad b. 'Abd al-Karīm. *Al-Milal wa-l-niḥal*. Edited by Sa'īd al-Ghānimī. Beirut and Baghdad: Manshūrāt al-Jamal, 2013.

al-Sharīf al-Murtaḍā (='Alam al-Hudā 'Alī b. al-Ḥusayn al-Mūsawī). *Al-Shāfī fī l-imāma*. 4 vols in 2. Edited by al-Sayyid 'Abd al-Zahrā' al-Ḥusaynī al-Khaṭīb. Tehran: Mu'assasat al-Ṣādiq, 1426/2005.

Sibṭ Ibn al-Jawzī. *Tadhkirat khawāṣṣ al-umma fī khaṣā'is al-a'imma*. Edited by al-Sayyid Muḥammad Ṣādiq Baḥr al-'Ulūm. Tehran: Maktabat Nineveh al-Ḥadītha, n.d.

al-Sijistānī, Abū Bakr 'Abdullāh b. Abī Dāwūd b. Sulaymān b. al-Asha'ath. *Kitāb al-Maṣāḥif*. Beirut: Dār al-Kutub al-'Ilmiyya, 1405/1985.

al-Shinqīṭī, Aḥmad b. Amīn. *Sharḥ al-Mu'allaqāt al-'ashar wa-akhbār shu'arā'ihā*. Beirut: Dār al-Kitāb al-'Arabī, 1405/1986.

Shubbar, al-Sayyid 'Abdullāh. *Tafsīr al-Qur'ān al-Karīm*. Beirut: al-A'lamī, 1415/1995.

al-Suyūṭī, Aḥmad b. Yaḥyā b. Jābir al-Jalāl al-Dīn. *Tārīkh al-khulafā'*. Edited by Qāsim al-Shammā'ī al-Rifā'ī and Muḥammad al-'Uthmānī. Beirut: n.p., n.d.

al-Ṭabarānī, Abū l-Qāsim Sulaymān b. Aḥmad b. Ayyūb. *Al-Mu'jam al-awsaṭ*. 10 vols. Edited by Abū Mu'ādh Ṭāriq b. 'Iwaḍullāh b. Muḥammad and Abū l-Faḍl 'Abd al-Muḥsin b. Ibrāhīm al-Ḥusaynī. Cairo: Dār al-Ḥaramayn, 1415 /1995.

———. *Al-Mu'jam al-kabīr*. Edited by Sa'd b. 'Abdullāh al-Ḥumayyid and Khālid b. 'Abd al-Raḥmān al-Juraysī. Beirut: n.p., n.d.

al-Ṭabarī, Abū Ja'far Muḥammad b. Jarīr. *Ta'rīkh al-rusul wa-l-mulūk*. Edited by M. J. de Goeje *et al.* Leiden: 1879–1901 (=*Ta'rīkh al-rusul wa-l-mulūk*. Edited by Muḥammad Abū l-Faḍl Ibrāhīm. Cairo: Dār al-Ma'ārif, 1960).

al-Ṭabāṭabā'ī, al-Sayyid Muḥammad Ḥusayn (=al-'Allāma al-Ṭabāṭabā'ī). *Tafsīr al-Mīzān*. 20 vols. Qom: Mu'assasat al-Nashr al-Islāmī al-Tābi'a li Jamā'at al-Mudarrisīn bi-Qum al-Musharrafa, n.d.

al-Thaʿlabī, Abū Isḥāq Aḥmad b. Muḥammad b. Ibrāhīm. *Al-Kashf wa-l-bayān ʿan tafsīr al-Qurʾān*. MSS Maḥmudiyya 98, 99, 100, 101, 102, 103, 104, 105, 106, 107, Medina, Kingdom of Saudi Arabia, Maktabat al-Madīnat al-Munawwara al-ʿĀmma; MSS Veliyüddin Efendi 130, 131, 132, 133, İstanbul, Türkiye Cumhuriyeti, Süleymaniye Yazma Eser Kütüphanesi.

al-Tirmidhī, Abū ʿĪsā Muḥammad b. ʿĪsā b. Sawra. *Al-Jāmiʿ al-mukhtaṣar min al-sunan*. 2 vols. Vaduz, Lichtenstein: Thesaurus Islamicus Foundation, 2000.

Yāqūt al-Ḥamawī (= Shihāb al-Dīn Yāqūt b. ʿAbdullāh). *Muʿjam al-buldān*. 7 vols. Beirut: Dār Ṣādir, 1416/1995.

al-Zamakhsharī, Abū l-Qāsim Mahmūd b. ʿUmar b. Muḥammad. *Asās al-Balāgha*. Beirut: Dār Ṣadir, 1399/1979.

———. *Al-Kashshāf ʿan ḥaqāʾiq al-tanzīl wa-ʿuyūn al-aqāwīl fī wujūh al-taʾwīl*. 4 vols. Beirut: Dār al-Maʾrifa, n.d.

———. *Rabīʿ al-abrār*. 5 vols. Edited by ʿAbd al-Amīr Munnā. Beirut: al-Aʿlamī, 1412/1192.

al-Zawzanī, al-Ḥusayn b. Aḥmad b. al-Ḥusayn. *Sharḥ al-Muʿallaqāt al-sabʿ*. Cairo: n.p., n.d.

Secondary literature

Anthony, Sean. *Crucifixion and Death as Spectacle. Umayyad Crucifixion in Late Antique Context*. New Haven, Connecticut: American Oriental Society, 2014.

Aristotle. *Politics*. In *The Complete Works of Aristotle*. 2 vols. Edited by Jonathan Barnes. Princeton: Princeton University Press, 1984.

Biblia Graeca Septuaginta. Edited by Alfred Rahlfs. London: United Bible Societies, 2013.

Biblia Hebraica Stuttgartensia. Rev. edn. Edited by K. Elliger and W. Rudolph Stuttgart: Deutsche Bibelgesellschaft, 1977.

Biblia Sacra Vulgata. 3rd edn. Edited by Robert Weber and Roger Gryson. Stuttgart: Deutsche Bibelgesellschaft, 1994.

Bosworth, Clifford Edmund. *The New Islamic Dynasties. A Chronological and Genealogical Manual*. New York: Columbia University Press, 1996.

Brown, Francis, C. A. Driver, and Charles A Briggs. *A Hebrew and English Lexicon of the Old Testament with an Appendix containing the Biblical Aramaic based on the Lexicon of William Gesenius as translated by Edward Robinson*. Oxford: Clarendon Press, 1951.

Confucius. *Confucius: Confucian Analects, The Great Learning, and the Doctrine of the Mean*. Translated by James Legge. New York: Dover Publications Inc., 1971; reprint of orig. 1893 edition by Oxford University Press.

El Omari, Racha. *The Theology of Abū l-Qāsim al-Balkhī/al-Kaʿbī (d. 319/931)*. Leiden: E. J. Brill, 2016.

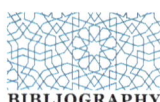

Encylopaedia Judaica, 16 vols. Jerusalem: Encyclopaedia Judaica, 1972.

Goldziher, Ignaz. *Muslim Studies*. 2 vols. Translated and edited by S. M. Stern. Chicago: Aldine-Atherton, 1971.

———. *The Ẓāhirīs: Their Doctrine and their History. A Contribution to the History of Islamic Theology*. Translated and edited by Wolfgang Behn. Leiden: E. J. Brill, 2008.

Ḥamishah Ḥamushei Torah ʿim perūsh Rashī: ʾUnqelōs, Saʿadyāh Gaōn, ʾEven ʿĒzrāʾ. 5 vols. Jerusalem: Derekh Khadmonim, 1989-90.

Höfner, Maria. *Altsüdarabische Grammatik*. Leipzig: Otto Harrassowitz, 1942.

Husayn, Nebil. *Opposing the Imām. The Legacy of the Nawāṣib in Islamic Literature*. Cambridge: Cambridge University Press, 2021.

Jafri, S. H. M. *The Origins and Early Development of Shīʿa Islam*. Beirut: Librairie du Liban, 1979.

Kamali, Hashim. *Principles of Islamic Jurisprudence*. Revised edition. Cambridge, UK: Islamic Texts Society, 1991.

Kohlberg, Etan. *A Medieval Muslim Scholar at Work. Ibn Ṭāwūs and his Library*. Leiden: E. J. Brill, 1992.

———. "An Unusual Shīʿī isnād," *Israel Oriental Studies* 5 (1975):142–149 (article VIII in his anthology *Belief and Law in Imāmī Shīʿism*. Aldershot: Variorum Reprints, 1991).

Madelung, Wilfred. *The Succession to Muḥammad. A Study of the Early Caliphate*. Cambridge: Cambridge University Press, 1997.

———. "Shīʿī Attitudes to Women as reflected in Fiqh." In *Society and Sexes in Medieval Islam*. Edited by A. Lutfi al-Sayyid-Marsot. Malibu, California: Undena Publications, 1979.

NASA. "Catalog of Solar Eclipses 601 CE to 700 CE." https://eclipse.gsfc.nasa.gov/SEcat5/SE0601-0700.html.

OED = *The Oxford English Dictionary*. 20 vols. 2nd edn. Oxford: Clarendon Press, 1989.

Peshīṭṭā. London: United Bible Societies, 1979.

Powers, David S. *Studies in Qurʾān and Ḥadīth. The Formation of the Islamic Law of Inheritance*. Berkeley, California: University of California Press, 1986.

Ricks, Stephen D. *Lexicon of Inscriptional Qatabanian*. Rome: Editrice Pontificio Istituto Biblico, 1989.

Saleh, Walid A. *The Formation of the Classical Tafsīr Tradition. The Qurʾān Commentary of al-Thaʿlabī* (d. 427/1035). Leiden: E. J. Brill, 2004.

Schliefer, J. "Fadak" in *Encyclopaedia of Islam*, First Edition, 3:35.

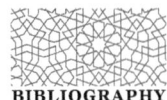

Ṣiddīqī, Muḥammad Zubayr. *Ḥadīth Literature. Its Origin, Development and Special Features*. Cambridge: Islamic Texts Society, 1993.

Steinbrüchel, A. *Tafel der Sonnen- und Mondfinsternisse, der Neu- und Vollmonde von 1265 v. Chr. bis 2345 n. Chr., mit erläuterndem Text*. Zürich: Naturforschenden Gesellschaft in Zürich, 1937.

al-Tawrāt: al-Tafsīr al-aṣlī min Maʿālī al-Ḥākhām Saʿdiyā Ghāʾūn b. Yūsuf al-Fayyūmī. Transcribed into Arabic script by Rabbi Yomtov Chaim Ben Yakov Daknish Hacohen. Jerusalem: Project Saadia Gaon, 2015.

The International Standard Bible Encyclopaedia. 5 vols. Edited by James Orr MA DD. Grand Rapids, Michigan: Wm. B. Erdmans Publishing Co., 1946.

The Pentatecuh and Rashi's Commentary. A Linear Translation into English. Translated by Rabbi Abraham Ben Isaiah and Rabbi Benjamin Sharfman in collaboration with Dr Harry M. Orlinsky and Rabbi Morris Charner. 5 vols. Brooklyn, New York: S. S. & R. Publishing Co. Inc., 1950.

Tuckerman, Bryant. *Planetary, Lunar, and Solar Positions, AD 2 to AD 1649 At Five-day and Ten-day Intervals*. Philadelphia: The American Philosophical Society, 1964.

Vaglieri, L. Veccia. "Fadak" in *Encyclopaedia of Islam*, New Edition, 2:725–727.

Winer, Georg Benedict. *Biblisches Realwörterbuch*. 2 vols. Leipzig: Carl Hienrich, 1847.

Zammit, Martin R. *A Comparative Lexical Study of Qurʾānic* Arabic. Leiden: E. J. Brill, 2002.

Zysow, Aron. "Karrāmiya"in *Encyclopaedia Iranica*, edited by Ehsan Yarshater. London and Boston: Routledge and Kegan Paul, 1982–in progress.

Indexes

الفهارس

A

ʿAbbās b. ʿAbd al-Muṭṭalib 102
Abbasids 14, 262
ʿAbd al-Raḥmān b. ʿAwf 142
ʿAbdullāh b. Abī Ṣarḥ 146
ʿAbdullāh b. ʿĀmir 146, 154
ʿAbdullāh b. Jadʿān 296
ʿAbdullāh b. Masʿūd 110, 148, 148n152
ʿAbdullāh b. Sabaʾ 154
ʿAbdullāh b. Salām 214
ʿAbdullah b. ʿUmar 88, 110
Abū ʿAbdullāh al-Ḥāfiẓ al-Shāfiʿī 124
Abū ʿAlī al-Jubbāʾī 250
Abū ʿAmr al-Zāhid 120, 134
Abū l-Aswad al-Duʾalī 250
Abū Bakr b. Abī Quḥāfa (= ʿAtīq b. ʿUthmān) xxvi, xxviii, 12, 12n2, 74, 76, 78, 80, 82, 84, 90, 104, 108, 118, 126, 126n129, 128, 128n121, 128n123, 130n125, 134, 134n131, 138, 148, 15, 152, 154, 158, 172, 182, 182n29, 236, 254, 258, 260, 280, 282, 284, 288, 290, 292, 294, 296, 298
Abū Baraza 110, 124
Abū l-Buḥturī 132
Abū l-Daḥdāḥ 294
Abū Dharr 80, 122, 148, 154, 168, 170, 242, 290
Abū Dujāna 256
Abū Muslim al-Khurāsānī 262
Abū Ḥanīfa xxiv, xxv, 32, 56, 250
Abū l-Ḥasan al-Andalusī *see* Ibn Razīn al-Andalusī xxiii, 198, 198n65, 200.
Abū Hāshim ʿAbdullāh b. Muḥammad b. al-Ḥanafiyya 250
Abū Ḥudhayfa 12, 12n4
Abū l-Hudhayl al-ʿAllāf 30
Abū Hurayra 208
Abū Maryam 104
Abū Saʿīd al-Khudrī 176, 194, 266
Abū Saʿīd b. Abī l-Khayr 240
Abū Sufyān (Ṣakhr b. Ḥarb) 86, 256
Abū Ṭālib xxvii, 228
Abū ʿUbayda al-Jarrāḥ 12, 12n3, 282
Abū Yūsuf 250
Ādam xix, 92, 132, 190, 224, 224n137
Aḥmad b. Ḥanbal xxvin56, 4n1, 82n67, 82n68, 96, 102, 102n86, 102n89, 108n94, 120n112, 134n131, 138n141, 180, 180n28, 184n36, 210, 210n97, 212, 212n104, 222, 222n134, 224n137, 230n142, 240, 240n145, 250
ʿĀʾisha bt. Abī Bakr 82, 84, 138, 138n141, 154, 298
Akhṭab Khawārizm xxiii, 240, 242, 244, 270
Ahl al-Bayt xi, xviii, xxiii, xxiiin43, 56, 80, 124, 182, 212, 256
Āl xix
Anas b. Mālik 102, 102n86, 108, 122, 130, 178n125, 182, 234, 236, 242, 264
al-ʿAllāma al-Ḥillī i, iii, v, ix, xii, xx, xxx, 92n76, 150, 298
ʿAlī b. Abī Ṭālib (first imam) vi, ix, xi, xvin13, xviii, xx, xxin34, xxii, xxiiin43, xxivn45, xxvn54, xxvi, xxviii, xxix, 8, 12n9, 24, 50, 52, 56, 58, 62, 66, 68, 74, 80, 82, 84, 86, 88, 90, 92n76, 92n77, 100, 102, 104, 106, 108, 110, 112n108, 114, 116n111, 118, 120, 122n114, 124, 126, 128n123, 132n129, 134, 136, 138, 140, 142, 144, 148, 154, 156, 158, 160, 162, 164, 166, 168, 170, 172, 174, 176, 178, 180, 182n29, 184n36, 186, 188, 190, 192, 194, 196, 198n64, 200n70, 202, 204, 206, 208, 210, 212, 214, 216, 218, 220, 222, 224n137, 226, 228, 230, 232, 234, 236, 238, 240n145, 242, 244, 246, 248, 250, 252, 254, 256n153, 258, 260, 262, 262, 266, 268, 270, 272, 290, 284, 390, 296, 298
Alī b. Ḥusayn, Zayn al-ʿĀbidīn (fourth imam) 8, 52, 56, 92, 250
ʿAlī b. Muḥammad al-Ḥādī/al-Naqī (tenth imam) 8, 66
ʿAlī b. Mūsā al-Riḍā (eighth imam) 8, 62, 64
ʿĀmir b. Wāthila 114
ʿAmmār b. Maymūn 104
ʿAmmār b. Yāsir 124, 148, 244, 290
ʿAmr b. Ḥurayth 262
ʿAmr b. Wudd al-ʿĀmirī 120
Ark of Noah 238
al-Ashʿarī, Abū l-Ḥasan xiin6, 154, 250
Ashʿarīs 22, 24, 24n9, 38, 108n. 98, 250

al-Ash'ath b. Qays 154
'Āṣim b. Thābit 256
Asmā' bt. Umays 226
Ayman b. Umm Ayman 260

B
Banū 'Abd al-Dār 102
Banū 'Abd al-Muṭṭalib xxv, 228
Banū 'Adī b. Ka'b xxviii, 74
Banū Hāshīm xviii, xxviii, 178, 254, 260, 290
Banū Isrā'īl xi, xix
Banū Khuzayma 90
Banū Naḍīr 258
Banū Taym b. Murra xxviii, 74
Banū Ṭālib 248
Banū Umayya (= Umayyads) 14, 144, 154, 268
Barā' b. 'Āzib 192, 262
Bishr al-Ḥāfī 60
Burayda 182
Buṣr b. Arṭāt 264

C
Christians 24

D
Dāwūd al-Ẓāhirī 24

Devil *see also* Satan, Iblīṣ and Shayṭān 32, 40, 126 (devil), 280 (devil)
Dhī l-Thadyā 262
Dhū l-Fiqār 116, 122, 256
Diḥya al-Kalbī 256
Ḍirār b. Ḍamra 246

F
Fakhr al-Dīn al-Rāzī 24
al-Farazdaq 52, 52n48, 56
Fāṭima bt. Muḥammad xxi, xxviii, 50, 54, 62, 64, 78, 80, 94, 100, 104, 106, 114, 138, 180, 182, 184n36, 188, 190, 200, 204, 206, 214, 218, 222, 224n137, 234, 270, 282
Fiḍḍa 204, 246
Fujā'at al-Sulamī 130, 130n125

G
Ghaṭafān 256

H
Ḥabīb b. Mūsā al-Najjār 104, 210
Ḥafṣa bt. 'Umar b. al-Khaṭṭāb 138
al-Ḥajjāj b. Yūsuf 184n36, 262
al-Ḥakam b. Abī l-'Āṣ 148, 154
Ḥamzā b. 'Abd al-Muṭṭalib (uncle of the Prophet Muḥammad) 88, 90, 140
Hārūn the Prophet (Aaron) *see also* kohēn xxvi, xxvii, xxviin62
Hārūnic/Aaronic Station xxvi, xxviii, 82n67
Ḥasan b. 'Alī b. Abī Ṭālib
xxi, xxviii, 8, 12, 50, 88, 94, 100, 106, 114, 180, 188, 190, 204, 206, 214, 224n137, 240, 244, 272, 298
al-Ḥasan b. 'Alī al-'Askarī (eleventh imam) 8, 66, 70
Ḥashawiyya 24, 26
Hazāqīl 104, 210
Hind bt. 'Utba 86
Hishām b. 'Abd al-Malik 52
Ḥudhayfa b. al-Yamān 224, 270, 272, 290
Hülegü (Hulākū) 4n2, 262
al-Hurmuzān 148
Ḥusayn b. 'Alī b. Abī Ṭālib (third imam) xi, xxi, xxviii, 8, 18, 50, 52, 56, 88, 92n77, 94n78, 96, 98, 100n84, 106, 114, 180, 188, 190, 204, 206, 214, 224n137, 240, 244, 262, 270, 272, 276

I
Iblīs *see also* Devil, Satan and Shayṭān 10, 28, 92
Ibn 'Abbas ('Abdullāh b. 'Abbas) 76, 94, 102n86, 112, 120, 122, 124, 136, 150, 170, 178, 184, 184n36, 186, 190, 192, 196, 200, 210, 212, 214, 216, 218, 220, 248, 250, 252
Ibn Abī Laylā 104, 210
Ibn Khalawayh 240
Ibn Sa'd, Muḥammad 92, 94n78, 134n131
Ibn Shīrawayh al-Daylamī 224
Ibn Taymiyya x
Ibrahīm (Abraham) the Prophet xi, xvii, xviii, xix, xxii, 34, 122, 132, 212, 216
Ibrahīm (infant son of the Prophet Muḥammad) 50

ʿIkrima 250, 256, 258
Infallibles 22
Ismāʿīl the Prophet (Ishmael) xvii, xviii, xix,

J
Jābir b. ʿAbdullāh al-Ānṣārī 56, 80, 240, 266, 270
Jaʿfar b. Muḥammad al-Ṣādiq 8, 58, 250,
Jaʿfar al-Ṭayyār 114
Jamāl al-Dīn b. Ṭāwūs ix, x
Jibrīl; Jibrāʾīl (= Angel Gabriel) 50, 62, 70, 116, 120, 122, 170, 226, 256
Juwayriya bt. al-Ḥārith b. Abī Ḍirār 138n141, 258
Juwayriya bt. Mushīr 262

K
al-Kaʿbī 24, 14n10
Kaʿb b. Ujra 212
Karrāmiyya 26, 16n12
Khadīja xxviii, 82, 106, 296
Khālid b. Saʿīd b. al-ʿĀṣ 290
Khālid b. al-Walīd 90, 130n125, 134
al-khulafāʾ al-rāshidūn (Rightly Guided Caliphs) ix
Kināna 256
kohēn see also Hārun the Prophet xxvii
Kumayl b. Ziyād al-Nakhaʿī 134, 262

L
Labīd b. Rabīʿa xiv, xv

M
Mālik b. Anas 130n124; 127
Mālik b. Nuwayra 90, 90n74, 134
al-Maʾmūn 62, 64
Marwān b. al-Ḥakam 154
Masʿūd b. Mudhakkā 154
al-Masʿūdī 68
al-Manṣūr 14, 14n12, 58, 74
Mikāʾīl 116, 186, 270
Mītham al-Tammār 262
Miqdād 148
Muʿādh b. Jabal 122
Muʿāwiya b. Abī Sufyān xi, xii, xxiii, 4n1, 12, 12n10, 14n11, 84, 86, 88, 92, 92n76, 112, 146, 148, 154, 198, 242, 246, 262
Muʿāwiya b. Hīdat al-Qurashī 242
al-Mughīra b. Shuʿba 138
Muḥammad (The Prophet of Islam) vii, xi, xii, xiii, xv, xvii, xviii, xx, xxi, xxii, xiv, xxv, xxvi, xxvii, 2, 8, 10, 12, 16, 22, 28, 40, 46, 50, 52, 54, 56, 58, 62, 66, 70, 74, 76, 78, 80, 82, 84, 86, 88, 90n74, 92, 94, 96, 98, 100, 102, 104, 106, 108, 110, 112, 114, 116, 118, 120, 122, 124, 126, 128, 130, 132, 134, 136, 138, 148, 150, 152, 154, 156, 160, 162, 164, 168, 170, 172, 174, 176, 178, 180, 182, 184, 186, 188, 190, 192, 194, 196, 198, 200, 202, 204, 206, 208, 210, 212, 214, 216, 218, 220, 222, 224n137, 226, 228, 230, 232, 234, 236, 238, 240, 242, 244, 246, 248, 250, 252, 254, 256, 258, 260, 262, 264, 266, 268, 270, 272, 276, 280, 282, 284, 290, 292, 294, 296, 298
Muḥammad b. Abī Bakr 84, 86, 146
Muḥammad b. ʿAlī al-Bāqir (fifth imam) 8, 56, 250
Muḥammad b. ʿAlī al-Jawād/al-Taqī (tenth imam) 8, 64
Muḥammad b. ʿAlī b. Ḥasan al-Jabāʿī (?) xxix
Muḥammad b. al-Ḥanafiyya 250, 272
Muḥammad b. al-Ḥasan al-Shaybānī 250
Muḥammad b. Kaʿb al-Quraẓī 102
Muḥammad al-Mahdī (twelfth imam, the Guided One) 8, 70, 276
Muḥammad Khudābanda *see* Öljeitu
Muhanna b. Yaḥyā 96
al-Muḥaqqiq al-Ḥillī *see* Najm al-Dīn al-Ḥillī
Mujāhid 196, 206
Mūsā the Prophet (Moses) xi, xvi, xix, xxvi, xxvii, 10, 82, 102 106, 112, 120, 132 168, 196, 220, 222, 230, 234, 246
Mūsā b. Jaʿfar al-Kāẓim 8, 32, 58, 62, 72
al-Muʿtaṣim 14, 14n12
al-Mutawakkil 66, 68

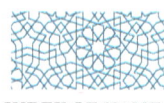

N

Najm al-Dīn al-Ḥillī = al-Muḥaqqiq al-Ḥillī ix
Naṣīr al-Dīn al-Ṭūsī ix, x, xxix, 14n12
Nūḥ xi, xix, 108, 132

O

Oath of Riḍwān 150

Ö

Öljeitu = Muḥammad Khudābanda ix, x, 4n2, 14n12

Q

al-Qāḍī al-Nuʿmān = Abū Ḥanīfa al-Nuʿmān b. Muḥammad al-Tamīmī al-Mghribī 106n94, 172n15
Qanbar 246, 262
Qays b. Saʿd 256
Qudāma b. Maẓʿūn 140
Quraysh xvii, 40, 52, 96, 146, 256, 282

R

Rabīʿat al-Raʾy 250
Radī al-Din b. Ṭāwūs ix, x, xxiii, xxiiin44, xxiv, xxix, 198n65
al-Rāfiʿī 92, 92n77
Rushayd al-Hajarī 262

S

Saadia Gaon (= Saʿd al-Fayyūmī) xxvii, xxviin62
Saʿd al-Fayyūmī *see* Saadia Gaon
Saʿd b. ʿAbdullāḥ al-Anṣārī 152
Saʿd b. ʿUbāda 290
Sadīd al-Dīn al-Ḥillī ix
Ṣafiyya bt. Ḥuyay 104, 138n141
Sahl b. Ḥunayf 256
Saʿīd b. al-ʿĀṣ 146, 154, 290
al-Shaʿbī 194
Ṣakhr b. Ḥarb *see* Abū Sufyān
Sālim (bondsman of Abū Ḥudhayfa) 12, 12n4, 142
Salmān al-Fārisī 102, 108, 148, 224n137, 290
Satan 32, 130, 150, 188
al-Sayyid al-Ḥimyarī 264, 266
Shaqīq al-Balkhī 58, 60
Shaqīq b. Salāma 240
al-Shāfiʿī, Muḥammad b. Idrīs 70, 124, 250
al-Sharīf al-Murtāḍā x, xxviii, 142n149
Shayṭān *see also* Devil, Satan and Iblīs xi, 280
Shīʿat ʿAlī xi
Shīʿat ʿUthmān xi
al-Sibṭ Ibn al-Jawzī 58, 60, 60n51, 70, 70n54, 94, 224n137, 276
al-Suddī 96
Suwayd b. Ghafla 244

T

Ṭabarī, Muḥammad b. Jarīr xxiv, xxvn54, 78n63, 106n94, 126n120, 128n121, 128n123, 130n125, 134n130, 134n131, 138n139, 172n15.
Ṭalḥa b. ʿUbayullāh al-Taymī 84, 154, 260
Ṭalḥa b. Shayba 102, 198
Twelve Imams x, xii, 8, 274, 276

U

ʿUbaydullāh b. ʿUmar 148
ʿUmar b. ʿAbd al-ʿAzīz 88
ʿUmar b. Abī Miqdām 58
ʿUmar b. al-Khaṭṭāb xxviii, 12, 12n7, 74, 76, 80, 82, 90, 110, 126, 126n120, 128, 128n123, 134, 136, 138, 138n141, 140, 148, 150, 152, 154, 172, 230, 234, 236, 252, 254, 258, 260, 280, 282, 284, 290, 292
ʿUmar b. Saʿd 18
Umayyads *see* Banū Umayya
Umm Ayman 78, 260
Umm Ḥabība bt. Abī Sufyān 84
Umm Salama 100, 102n86, 180
Usayd b. Ḥuḍayr 12
ʿUthmān b. ʿAffān 12, 12n8, 84, 84n71, 92, 92n76, 128, 142, 144, 146, 146n150, 148, 148n152, 150n158, 154, 158, 282, 286, 290
Uways al-Qaranī 260
ʿUzza 86

W

Walīd b. ʿUqba 146, 148, 154
Wāṣil b. ʿAṭāʾ250
Wāthila b. al-Asqaʿ 102n86, 180

Y

Yaʿqūb the Prophet (Jacob) xvin14, xix, xixn28, 78, 270
Yaḥyā the Prophet (John the Baptist) xix
Yaḥyā b. Aktham 64
Yaḥyā b. Ḥarthama 66
Yaḥyā b. Zakariyya 94
Yazīd b. Muʿāwiya xii, 88, 92, 94, 96
Yūshaʿ b. Nūn 102, 196
Yūsuf the Prophet (Joseph) xix, 270

Z

al-Zamakhsharī xvn13, 74, 88, 88n72
Zayd b. Abī Awfā 222
Zayd b. Arqam 264, 290
Zayd b. Ḥasan al-Ṭāʾī 154
Zayn al-ʿĀbidīn *see* ʿAlī b. al-Ḥusayn
Zubayr 84, 154, 260, 282
Zufar b. al-Hudhayl 250
al-Zuhrī 94

INDEX OF PLACES

A
al-ʿArīsh 294, 296

B
Baghdad xii, xxvii, 19, 24, 48, 60, 66, 150, 174, 192
Babel 266

E
Euphrates 266, 268
Egypt 14n12, 146, 154

F
Fadak 78, 78n63, 80, 134, 134n131, 138, 152
Fortress of Khaybar xxv, 128n123, 236

G
Gate of the Elephant 268
Gate of the Serpent 268
Ghadīr Khumm xxiv, 106, 172, 174, 176, 230, 264
Grand Mosque of Isfahan x

H
Ḥilla ix

I
Isfahan x
Istanbul xxii

K
Kaʿba xvii, 52, 60, 96, 102, 104, 122, 136
Khaybar xxv, 114, 128n, 180, 200, 236, 260, 296
Kufa 48, 62, 132, 146, 154, 260, 268

M
Mashhad xxix
Mecca xvii, xviii, xxii, xxivn47, xxv, xxvi, xxviii, 52, 56, 58, 60, 86, 88, 108, 154, 174n17, 260, 294
Medina xxii, xxivn47, xxv, xxvi, xxviii, 56, 66, 82, 84n71, 88, 96, 112, 148, 150, 154, 174n17, 186, 232, 258, 290

N
Najd 256

Q
al-Qādisiyya 58
Qom xxiv, xxix, xxx, 68

R
Rabdha 148, 154
Rayy 18

S
Saqīfa 126n120, 128, 152, 152n162, 282
Saragossa xxiii, 198n65

T
Tabūk xxvi, 82, 106, 296
Tihāma 256

U
Uḥud 90, 108, 150, 256

W
Wāqiṣa 58

Z
Zabāla 60

B
Bukhārī xxiii, 100, 150, 184, 212

E
Encyclopaedia Judaica xxvii, xxvii,
Exodus (one of the books of the Torah) xxvii

G
Gospel 132

H
Ḥāfiẓ Abu Nuʿaym al-Iṣfahānī xxi, xxii, 136, 172, 176, 192, 194, 196, 200, 202, 206, 208, 210, 212, 214, 216, 218, 220, 226
al-Hidāya (The Guide) 74

I
Ibn al-Maghāzilī xxiii, 170, 178, 190, 196, 206, 210
Ibn Māja xxiii, 100
International Standard Bible Encyclopaedia xxvii

J
al-Jamʿ bayn al-Ṣiḥāḥ al-Sitta (The Ḥadīths Common to the Six Authentic Collections) xxiii, 100, 198, 200

M
Minhāj al-karāma ix, x
Minhāj al-sunnat al-nabawiyya x
Muslim xxiii, 100, 184, 212
al-Muwaṭṭaʾ xxiii, 100

O
Oxford English Dictionary (OED) xiii

R
Rabīʿ al-abrār 88

S
Ṣaḥīḥ al-Nasāʾī 100
Ṣaḥīḥ al-Tirmidhī xxiii, 100, 276
Sharḥ al-Wajīz 92
Sunan Abī Dāwūd 100, 276

T
al-Ṭabaqāt 92
Tafsīr al-Thaʿalbī xii, 168, 172, 174, 182, 184, 186, 192, 200, 202, 204, 208, 210, 214, 218
Torah (= Tawrāt) xxvi, xxvii, xxvii, 132

INDEX OF BATTLES AND TREATIES

B

Battle of al-ʿAqaba 204
Battle of Badr (= Day of Badr) 122, 150, 254, 294, 296
Battle of the Banū Muṣṭaliq 258
Battle of the Banū Naḍīr 258
Battle of the Camel 154
Battle of the Dhī Qār 260
Battle of the Ditch [*khandaq*] (= Battle of the Confederates, Day of Khandaq) 112, 256
Battle of Ḥunayn 120, 154
Battle of Khaybar (= Day of Khaybar) 114, 200, 260, 296
Battle of Mu'ta 296
Battle of Narhrawān 262
Battle of Ṣiffīn 154, 248
Battle of al-Silsila 258
Battle of Tabūk, Tabūk campaign, expedition to Tabūk xxvi, 82, 106, 296
Battle of Ṭā'if 118
Battle of Uḥud 150, 256

T

Treaty of Ḥudaybiya 296

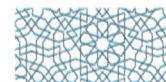

www.ingramcontent.com/pod-product-compliance
Lightning Source LLC
Chambersburg PA
CBHW061745290426
43661CB00139B/1469/J
* 9 7 8 1 8 3 8 4 9 9 6 6 2 *